S0-BSJ-193

ADMIRAL HAROLD R. STARK

Admiral Harold R. Stark
Photo courtesy of United States Naval Institute

Admiral Harold R. Stark:
Architect of Victory, 1939–1945

by B. MITCHELL SIMPSON, III

University of South Carolina Press

Studies in Maritime History
William N. Still, Jr., Editor

Stoddert's War: *Naval Operations During the*
Quasi-War with France, 1798–1801
by Michael A. Palmer
The British Navy and the American Revolution
by John A. Tilley
Iron Afloat:
The Story of the Confederate Armorclads
by William N. Still, Jr.
Confederate Shipbuilding
by William N. Still, Jr.
A Maritime History of the United States:
The Role of America's Seas and Waterways
by K. Jack Bauer

Classics in Maritime History
William N. Still, Jr., Editor

What Finer Tradition:
Memoirs of Thomas O. Selfridge, Jr.,
Rear Admiral, U.S.N.
by Thomas O. Selfridge, Jr.
Confederate Navy Chief: *Stephen R. Mallory*
by Joseph T. Durkin
A Year on a Monitor and the Destruction
of Fort Sumter
by Alvah Folsom Hunter
Edited and with an Introduction
by Craig L. Symonds

Copyright © University of South Carolina 1989

Published in Columbia, South Carolina, by the
University of South Carolina Press

FIRST EDITION

Manufactured in the United States of America

Library of Congress Cataloging-in-Publication Data

Simpson, B. Mitchell (Benjamin Mitchell), 1932–
    Admiral Harold R. Stark : architect of victory, 1939–1945 / by B.
Mitchell Simpson III. — 1st ed.
        p.   cm. — (Studies in maritime history)
    Bibliography: p.
    Includes index.
    ISBN 0-87249-596-5
    1. Stark, Harold R. (Harold Raynsford), 1880–1972. 2. World War,
1939–1945—Naval operations, American. 3. Admirals—United States-
-Biography. 4. United States. Navy—Biography. I. Title.
II. Series.
D773.S56 1989
940.54′5973′0924—dc19
    [B]   88-27292
                                                                CIP

CONTENTS

PREFACE

The only time I met Harold R. Stark was on a cold, drizzly day in November 1967. I was in Washington, D.C., doing research for my doctoral dissertation on his consultations with General de Gaulle in 1942 and 1943. I telephoned and asked if I could speak with him and he cordially invited me to his home at 4200 Glenbrook Drive. When I arrived the butler showed me to a sun porch and told me the admiral would be down in a minute.

While I was waiting, I noticed several fine watercolors on the wall, and was looking at them so intently that I did not hear Admiral Stark enter. When I realized he was there, I apologized for my distraction. He replied, "I am glad you like them. Winston painted them in 1910 and he gave them to me when I left London."

Although I knew something about his career, I had no idea that he had known Churchill that well. My curiosity was only partially satisfied during our conversation. His memory was so clear on details that it was obvious he had reviewed his own copies of many documents I had seen in the official archives. He was proud of the way he had handled General de Gaulle, but his pride was tempered by genuine modesty at having simply performed his duty.

Towards the end of this pleasant conversation he received a telephone call from a friend. I heard him say, "We are doing well for teenagers." He paused. "You know, teen 85 and 90." He chuckled. After he hung up, he turned to me and said, "That was Tommy. You know, Tommy Hart. They're on their way to Florida." (Admiral Thomas C. Hart, was formerly commander in chief, U.S. Asiatic Fleet, and later a U.S. Senator from Connecticut.)

When we had finished, he insisted on seeing me to the door and stepping outside into the bone-chilling drizzle, despite my caution that he not take cold. He stood there until I drove away.

A few years later, when I was on the faculty at the Naval War College, I started my research for his biography. The president of the college told me that I had picked a very poor subject, because "Stark failed to warn the fleet that the Japanese were going to attack Pearl Harbor." Besides displaying his ignorance, in that one comment the college president unwittingly crystalized Stark's undeserved reputation in the navy.

In this biography I have simply set forth the record of Stark's tenure as Chief of Naval Operations and as Commander, U.S. Naval Forces, Europe. Before he became Chief of Naval Operations (CNO) in 1939, he was known as a particularly competent and skillful officer and commander. As CNO, Stark literally worked day and night to prepare the navy for war. He planned the building program that produced the two-ocean navy that fought World War II. He laid the foundation for the naval and military side of the Grand Alliance with Great Britain. When the time came, he quietly stepped down as CNO so that Admiral Ernest J. King could replace him. While in London, Stark symbolized the American commitment to the war. He planned and supervised naval preparations for the invasion of Europe, without which the Allies could never have crossed the English Channel to the continent of Europe.

After the war he returned home, rich in honors from the British, to face an intensive and grueling congressional inquiry into the Japanese attack on Pearl Harbor. Although the defense of the Hawaiian Islands was an army responsibility, the navy hierarchy refused to assist Stark in preparing for his testimony. Stark's performance during that trying period showed the true measure of the man. He flatly refused to blame anyone or even to point a finger at anyone. He stated the facts as he recalled them. Despite scathing public censure by Admiral King and Secretary of the Navy James Forrestal in their endorsements of the Navy Court of Inquiry report into the attack on Pearl Harbor, Stark was untouched by rancor or bitterness. In 1949, after King finally admitted he had been wrong in his endorsement, Secretary of the Navy John L. Sullivan awarded Stark a Distinguished Service Medal (his third) for his service in London during the war.

Stark was a modest man, a rarity at the upper levels of a military organization. He valued friendship and integrity more than honors and position, and was eminently successful in his own life. When he died in 1972 in his 92nd year, he was at peace with himself and his fellowmen.

The research and writing of this book have extended over many years and I have received assistance, suggestions, and candid comments from many people. First and foremost, I express my appreciation to David W. Richmond, who as a lieutenant (junior grade) first served with Stark in London. In the ensuing 30 years, Richmond became Stark's attorney, confidant, and trusted friend. He introduced me to the Stark family and provided me with a unique insight into the naval preparations for Overlord and the congressional Pearl Harbor hearings. The Stark family was most gracious and accommodating. I am grateful to the admiral's daughters, Mary Semans and Katharine (Kewpie) Gillespie; to his nephew, Edward B. Mulligan; and to his grandson, Edward W. Semans, Jr. As part of Stark's official family, Vice Admiral Charles Wellborn, Jr. was most helpful with his candor, insight, and recollections.

Over a period of nearly 20 years I have followed the trail of Stark's long career in his personal and official papers, both of which are deposited in the Operational Archives Branch of the Naval Historical Center at the Washington Navy Yard. During that time I have enjoyed nothing less than outstanding assistance and cooperation from Dr. Dean Allard and his extremely competent staff. I am grateful to all of them.

The chapters dealing with Stark's tenure as CNO were written as part of a research project under the auspices of the Center for Advanced Research at the Naval War College. The late Captain Hugh G. Nott provided support and intelligent criticism. I am grateful to him and to his then assistant, Lieutenant Colonel Gerald Keller, USMC.

Two of Stark's successors as CNO, Admiral Arleigh Burke and Admiral Robert B. Carney, were extremely helpful with their observations and comments on the demands of that office.

I am indebted to many scholars, naval officers, and friends of Admiral Stark for their assistance. In addition to former Secretary of the Navy, the late Honorable John L. Sullivan, they include Charles F.

Adams, Vice Admiral Bernard L. Austin, Hanson W. Baldwin, Barry Bingham, Sr., Martin Blumenson, Brigadier General Charles Bolte, Capt. George A. Brewster, Donald F. Carpenter, Barbara Krick Cooper, Richard von Doenhoff, Vice Admiral George C. Dyer, Rear Admiral Henry E. Eccles, Rear Admiral Ernest M. Eller, Louis A. Gebhard, Rear Admiral John D. Hayes, Adolf A. Hoehling, Robert W. Love, Mark M. Lowenthal, Russell M. Millar, Captain W. E. Moring, Mrs. Chester Nimitz, E. B. Potter, William A. Reitzel, Ann H. Sargent (Mrs. Willis Sargent), Vice Admiral William R. Smedberg, III, Paul Stillwell, Gilchrist B. Stockton, Jr., John Toland, Rear Admiral Kemp Tolley, Captain A. Craig Veasey, and the Honorable James E. Webb.

The kindest thing anyone can do for an author is to read his manuscript. I am grateful to many people for reading parts or all of this manuscript in its many evolutionary stages. Their comments and suggestions have been invaluable. They are Dr. Dean Allard, Hanson W. Baldwin, Captain Howard Browne, Vice Admiral Walter S. DeLany, John Hattendorf, Vice Admiral Edwin B. Hooper, Robert M. Laske, John T. Mason, Edward B. Mulligan, Captain Hugh G. Nott, William Reitzel, David W. Richmond, Edward W. Semans, Jr., Vice Admiral William R. Smedberg, III, Frank Uhlig, Jr., Vice Admiral Charles Wellborn, Jr., Gerald Wheeler, and Rear Admiral Joseph M. Worthington.

At times, secondary sources and congressional documents were elusive. The Naval War College Library staff was most helpful in ferreting out various items to satisfy my needs. I am grateful to Earl R. Schwass, Ann Hardy, Katharine Ashook, Doris Baginski, and Mary-ann Varoutsos for their help. In addition to an excellent library, the Naval War College also houses the Naval Historical Collection, which contains a wide variety of primary source materials. Anthony S. Nicolosi and Evelyn Cherpak helped me utilize this rich resource.

The Honorable Averell Harriman told me, "The British thought the world of Admiral Stark." His many friends in the United Kingdom ranged from the King and Queen to ordinary people. Those whom I was able to reach confirmed Harriman's comment. Among Stark's many British friends, I owe a special debt of gratitude to Her Majesty Queen Elizabeth the Queen Mother for her good wishes and encouragement in this undertaking. The late Admiral of the Fleet the Earl Mountbatten of Burma kindly sent me copies of various letters from his personal files. Our correspondence was cut short by his tragic death at the hands of terrorists. Royal Navy officers, British civil servants, and scholars who either knew Stark or knew of his contributions to the Allied effort were extremely kind and helpful. They are Patrick Beesly, Vice Admiral Sir Ronald Brockman, Sir John Coville, Vice Admiral Sir Norman Denning, John Ehrman, Admiral of the Fleet the Lord Fraser of North Cape, Norman Gibbs, Martin Gilbert, Admiral Sir Guy Grantham, Sir John Lang, Bryan Ranft, Captain S. W. Roskill, and Vice Admiral Brian B. Schofield.

In 1978 I advertised for information about Stark and I wrote to all of his then living shipmates, as ascertained from the Naval Register and the Naval Academy Alumni Directory. They testified generally and freely as to his service reputation. I am grateful to the following officers for their help:

From the 1909 Cruise of the Great White Fleet; Rear Admiral Harry Hansen.

From USS West Virginia, 1924; Captain Gordon W. Daisley, Captain Frederick A. Edwards, Melville Bell Grosvenor, Lieutenant Colonel Terrence R. Harp, Robert D. Hicks, Rear Admiral Karl W. Hensel, Captain Kenneth M. McLaren, Captain Hubert E. Paddock, Rear Admiral A. H. Richards, Captain Emmet E. Sprung, and Rear Admiral Frederick S. Withington.

From USS Nitro, 1924; Captain Myron A. Baber.

From Dahlgren Proving Grounds, 1926–1927; Rear Admiral Boynton L. Braun, Vice Admiral Glenn B. Davis, Rear Admiral Edwin G. Fullinwider, and Captain James B. Glennon.

From USS West Virginia, 1934; W. Larned Blatchford, Rear Admiral Welford C. Blinn, Captain Frank H. Brumby, Jr., Captain Wilson M. Coleman, Rear Admiral John F. Greenslade, Captain W. E. Moring, Captain R. D. Shepard, Rear Admiral Raymond D. Tarbuck, and Rear Admiral Magruder H. Tuttle.

From the Bureau of Ordnance, 1934–1937; Vice Admiral Harold D. Baker, Rear Admiral Sherman F. Burroughs, Jr., Vice Admiral Ralph W. Christie, Rear Admiral William Granat, Rear Admiral Raymond W. Holsinger, Real Admiral William K. Mendenhall, Captain E. C. Rook, Vice Admiral Rufus E. Rose, Vice Admiral Lorenzo S. Sabin, Jr., Rear Admiral Malcolm F. Schoeffel, and Rear Admiral A. E. Uehlinger.

From Staff, Commander, Destroyer Squadrons, Battle Fleet 1929 and the Cruiser Battle Force staff, 1938; Rear Admiral Horace W. Butterfield, Rear Admiral Edward F. Jones, and Captain Edward E. Roth.

From the Office of the Chief of Naval Operations, 1939–1942; Rear Admiral George H. Bahm, Rear Admiral R. W. Berry, Rear Admiral J. W. Boulware, Rear Admiral Clarence Broussard, Rear Admiral H. H. Caldwell, Captain John F. Crowe, Rear Admiral Frank W. Dodge, Captain A. D. Douglas, Rear Admiral William M. Downes, Captain John S. Fahy, Rear Admiral James M. Fernald, Rear Admiral Frederick R. Furth, Captain E. S. L. Goodwin, Rear Admiral William K. Headden, Admiral James J. Holloway, Jr., Vice Admiral

Thomas B. Inglis, Rear Admiral John M. Kennaday, Rear Admiral Dashiell L. Madeira, Rear Admiral Robert E. Melling, Rear Admiral Robert W. Morse, Captain Henry Mullins, Jr., Captain William Outerson, Rear Admiral A. M. Patterson, Rear Admiral O. D. Waters, Jr., Rear Admiral H. Weeks, Captain Williams C. Wickham, Captain John A. Winfry.

Cindy Edwards Sanfilippo patiently typed the entire manuscript.

Finally, I owe a special debt of gratitude to my wife, Wilma, who not only put up with me being around the house for more than three years while I was writing, but who also tolerated my eccentricities, and to my children, Fiona and Isla, who understood only that I could not be disturbed. Without their support I could never have written this book.

B. Mitchell Simpson, III
Newport, Rhode Island

ADMIRAL HAROLD R. STARK

1

CHIEF OF NAVAL OPERATIONS

There was intense speculation in the Navy in early 1939 as to who would receive President Franklin D. Roosevelt's nomination to succeed Admiral William D. Leahy as Chief of Naval Operations (CNO). Roosevelt embarked in the cruiser USS *Houston* to observe the conclusion of Fleet Problem XX, a major fleet exercise. His presence in the Caribbean meant that he could also observe the principal officers and meet with them before making his final decision. He gave no hint as to who would succeed Leahy.

Shortly after Roosevelt returned to Washington, D.C., the announcement was made. Rear Admiral Harold R. Stark would be the next Chief of Naval Operations. Stark was flabbergasted at the news, as he neither sought nor expected the post.

The only drawback to appointing Stark to Chief of Naval Operations in 1939 was his relatively junior status among the other flag officers in the navy. There were 50 admirals senior to him, he was a rear admiral, and he had not had any of the senior fleet commands, such as the U.S. Fleet or the Battle Force, one of its components. Stark's selection over so many of his seniors failed to produce any serious discontent or even a flurry of hasty retirements by disgruntled or disappointed admirals, primarily because he was known and liked throughout the naval service. Whatever reservations others may have had, they were not voiced.

Despite his age and infirmity in January 1939, Secretary of the Navy Claude A. Swanson consulted with Admiral William D. Leahy, the Chief of Naval Operations, and Rear Admiral James O. Richardson, Chief of the Bureau of Navigation (which dealt with personnel), about the new slate for the flag officer assignments. Swanson gave

1

Roosevelt five possible combinations, but both men felt that only two merited serious consideration. One combination had Richardson as CNO, the other had Stark.

Sometime later, Roosevelt decided on the best slate with Stark as CNO and Richardson in command of the Battle Force, which would involve promotions to full admiral for both men. At the same time, Roosevelt decided on several other assignments and he followed Swanson's suggestion to keep his thoughts to himself until the completion of the annual fleet exercises in early March. Then Charles A. Edison, the Assistant Secretary of the Navy acting in Swanson's absence due to illness, sent a handwritten letter to Roosevelt recommending Stark as CNO and adding that Swanson approved.[1]

Roosevelt and Stark had known each other since the summer of 1914, when Lieutenant Stark was ordered to take the destroyer USS *Patterson* to Campobello, Nova Scotia, to transport Assistant Secretary of the Navy Franklin D. Roosevelt to his summer home. The tall, athletically built, patrician Roosevelt was a year younger than the slender lieutenant in command of the destroyer. Roosevelt had been a yachtsman since early boyhood and knew the waters through which *Patterson* was passing. In a dangerous stretch of channel, Roosevelt asked Stark if he could take the conn; after all, he explained, he was familiar with the waters. His august presence on the bridge did not dismay Stark, who replied, "No, sir. This ship is my command, and I doubt your authority to relieve me." Then, with a show of bravado, Stark increased speed to 28 knots and successfully conned the ship to a safe anchorage. The smooth, disciplined operation of the ship impressed Roosevelt.[2]

When he learned of his appointment as CNO, Stark wrote to Roosevelt. He referred to their cruise in *Patterson*, saying that it would be a joy to sail with him again, although this time Roosevelt was in command. He signed it with his nickname, "Betty." Roosevelt's response was informal and cordial. He remarked that they both "talk the same language". He concluded, "My only objection is that if we get into a war, you will be a desk Admiral—I cannot have you in two places at once!"[3]

Stark acquired his incongruous nickname "Betty" shortly after he entered the Naval Academy in 1899. Fourth year men, or plebes, were subjected to physical and verbal hazing to toughen them for the arduous life at sea. An upperclassman incorrectly recalled that New

Hampshire's General John Stark, a distant relative of Midshipman Harold Stark, reportedly said to his troops before the Revolutionary battle of Bennington, "We will win today or Betty Stark will be a widow tonight." He not only misquoted the general, but he also misnamed the general's lady. Actually, General Stark is reputed to have said, "Tonight the American flag floats from yonder hill or Molly Stark sleeps a widow."[4]

This historically minded upperclassman began, and soon others continued, to require Stark to come to the "brace" or strict attention and repeat the inaccurate quotation of the general. Thereafter, to the end of his life, Stark was known to his friends as Betty.

When President Roosevelt appointed him, Stark was well qualified to relieve Admiral William D. Leahy as Chief of Naval Operations. Since his graduation from the Naval Academy in 1903, Stark's career was marked by a steady growth and development of his technical seagoing skills. Between 1909 and 1934, he commanded seven U.S. Navy ships. By 1939, he had an established reputation as a first-rate seagoing sailor. He was an excellent shiphandler. As a captain in the early 1930s he served as naval aide to then Secretary of the Navy, Charles F. Adams. In Washington he developed an intuitive feel for the subtle and important organizational and political problems involved in running the navy. As Chief of the Bureau of Ordinance from 1934 to 1937 he established his political reputation as a skillful and competent administrator in the Navy Department, and as a diplomatic, and more important, an effective navy representative before Congress.

He trusted his subordinates and he let them get on with their jobs. He refused to breathe down their necks and supervise them in the performance of the details of their duties. Because he was sincerely interested in them as individuals, he earned their admiration and affection.

When he became Chief of Naval Operations, Stark took with him the qualities of modesty, kindness, consideration for others, and a great capacity for hard work and long hours on the job. These personal characteristics endeared him to his subordinates. When coupled with tact, diplomacy, and political sensitivity, they made him a particularly effective advocate before Congress and in the White House. He was a gentleman in the very best sense of the word. Ironically, it was these same characteristics that led many officers to see him as mild and lacking fire, and thus as being unable or unwilling to stand up to the President when it was necessary. In later years, these characteristics caused his service reputation to suffer, many would say unjustly, as a result of the complex and dramatic events preceding America's entry into World War II.

Roosevelt took a personal interest in almost every aspect of the navy. At times this interest created more problems for the Navy Department than it was probably worth. But the navy had a sympathetic President who drew on his own experience during World War I as Assistant Secretary of the Navy. Roosevelt knew the flag officers personally and he was well aware of their individual strengths and limitations. He personally approved the assignment of each admiral.

Stark's relationship with Roosevelt remained cordial and intimate until Roosevelt's death in 1945. At times Stark stated frank opinions to Roosevelt, who for his part refused to be stampeded into decisions and actions contrary to his better judgment, regardless of their effect on the navy. Stark's appointment as Chief of Naval Operations was a happy one for Roosevelt. It was based essentially on Stark's own service reputation and his accomplishments since his graduation from the Naval Academy in 1903. Roosevelt was undoubtedly pleased with the turn of events that permitted him to appoint an old and trusted friend to head what he thought of as *his* navy, expecially since the retiring CNO and the Secretary of the Navy had recommended Stark in the first place.

Departmental organization in 1939 made it easy for Roosevelt to think of the navy as *his* navy. The Chief of Naval Operations dealt directly with him on strategic matters and there was plenty of opportunity for the commander in chief to immerse himself in as much detail as he desired. The Secretary of the Navy had a cabinet seat and dealt largely with political matters; the Under Secretary was concerned with the shore establishment. Both men had very small staffs and, like the President, they relied heavily on the CNO and the Bureau Chiefs for technical and professional naval advice. This simple structure no longer exists. The Department of Defense has been inserted between the President and his uniformed service chiefs. The Secretary of the Navy occupies a subcabinet position and his office is filled with an Under Secretary and numerous assistant secretaries and their deputies. The effect has been to remove the Chief of Naval

Operations even more from the President and to superimpose several views on the advice he renders. The close, cordial working relationship between Roosevelt and Stark clearly belongs to another era.

Stark relieved Leahy and became Chief of Naval Operations on 1 August 1939. By then it was clear among responsible government officials in Washington, and particularly in the Navy Department, that war in Europe was inevitable.

Despite the imminence of war in Europe, Stark at first did not see American involvement in that war as a likelihood. After all, the Royal Navy was not only a potent force in the Atlantic but, when combined with the French Navy, it could confine German and Italian forces to the European continent by dominating the North Atlantic and Mediterranean sealanes. The development of airpower might require a somewhat more distant strategic blockade, but it would, nevertheless, keep the Axis forces on the continent. The French Army was generally regarded as a force capable of checking any westward movement by the German Army. Its size and obvious military potential, provided it was properly led, justified this reasonable conclusion, which was held by informed professional observers. No one, including Stark, had the least inkling of how the events of the coming year would replace this sanguine view with deep gloom and profound anxiety.

With the United States as beneficiary of Anglo-French protection in the Atlantic, Stark sensed a greater danger of U.S. involvement in war in the Pacific than in the Atlantic. The army was stressing the Atlantic and Stark felt that more thought should be given to the Pacific.[5] The Japanese were already deeply committed to what seemed to be an interminable war in China. American interests in Asia were exposed and vulnerable. For the next year Stark wrestled with the problem of correctly weighing the relative dangers to the United States in the Pacific and in the Atlantic.

In the days of waning peace, Roosevelt shared Stark's apprehension about possible Japanese action in the Far East, particularly after Hitler and Stalin came to terms on 23 August. Then it was clear that Stalin would not interfere with Hitler's designs in Europe, but it was not at all clear what Japan might do. Roosevelt told Stark that he had had in the back of his head for some time the idea of making some naval movement in the Pacific to keep the Japanese guessing in the event war broke out in Europe. Roosevelt proposed sending, at some unexpected time, a detachment consisting of a carrier, a division of heavy cruisers, and eight destroyers northward to the vicinity of Rat Island at the tail of the Aleutians.

After arrival there, Roosevelt thought the ships could transmit a large volume of garbled, meaningless radio transmissions followed by complete silence. Then in a day or so at another location they would repeat the transmissions and follow them again with silence. Meanwhile, the main body of the fleet would leave port and rendezvous with the detachment before proceeding to Pearl Harbor.

Roosevelt told Stark he thought that an occasional move of this sort "will get the Japs jittery, make them sit up and take notice, keep them guessing and be a good political strategem."[6] Roosevelt wanted to confuse and perplex the Japanese sufficiently so they would keep their fleet in home waters rather than deploy it to the south to threaten European colonial possessions there.

Stark told Admiral Claude C. Bloch, commander in chief of the U.S. Fleet, of Roosevelt's idea. As fleet commander, Bloch was the senior seagoing flag officer in the navy. His abilities, competence, and service-wide reputation, as well as his seniority, had made him an obvious candidate for Chief of Naval Operations in 1939. Stark had known him for many years, respected him greatly, and had worked directly under him in 1926 and 1927 while serving as Inspector of Ordnance. Although Stark was technically senior to him now, he always treated Bloch with becoming deference.

Bloch threw cold water on Roosevelt's idea. He thought the radio activity and silence would be devoid of results and he feared that the Japanese might be prompted "to take steps which will be very unacceptable to us." He warned Stark that Japan "is already so deeply committed and their struggle is so desperate, that if they become 'jittery' they may take steps toward sending troops to the mandated islands for the purpose of fortifying them. It is not inconceivable that if they take this threat seriously, they may even seize Guam." He told Stark that if the United States were really determined to stop Japan's expansion to the south, the entire fleet ought to be sent to the Philippines. Such a move would impose tremendous logistical problems, leave the trans-Pacific lines of communication undefended, and perhaps even render them undefendable. Although he did not say so, it was clear that he thought the best place for the fleet would be in Hawaii, where it could remain concentrated on Japan's flank and could be best supported from the continental United States. Bloch gave Stark a piece of advice, which he followed in the coming two years: "Always have sufficient force mobilized in the Pacific and either in close support or concentrated so that any possible enemy will be confronted by an equality or superiority of forces."[7] After Roosevelt ordered the fleet to remain in Hawaii in May 1940, Stark steadfastly opposed all attempts by the White House and the State Department to send fleet detachments to the Far East.

The ringing of Stark's private, direct telephone to the White House awakened him at 0330 on Friday, 1 September 1939 at his quarters on Observatory Hill in Washington, D.C. Roosevelt calmly told him that Germany had just invaded Poland. Roosevelt said that Ambassador William C. Bullitt in Paris had telephoned him a few minutes earlier with the news. Stark and Roosevelt both expected war and now that it had actually come it seemed that everything, and nothing, had changed. Neither man could see what the next six years would bring, but each knew that grave dangers lay ahead for the United States.

At first, Stark saw a more immediate threat in the Pacific. Even in the late winter of 1939–1940, his opinion that trouble for the United States in the Far East was more likely than in Europe had not changed substantially. He continually reminded Admiral Thomas C. Hart, commander in chief of the Asiatic Fleet, to bear in mind that events in Asia might be far more important to the United States than trouble in Europe. He worried that something could break "and break quickly without warning" in the Far East. He said as much to Admiral James O. Richardson, the new commander in chief of the U.S. Fleet, which was then based on the west coast.[8] Stark admitted that he could not predict what was going to happen. Still, he felt the situation in the Far East was "fraught with grave possibilities." He told Richardson that both the fleet and the Navy Department "should be ready, so far as we can for emergencies . . . which might come like a bolt out of the blue."[9]

Hart and units of the Asiatic Fleet were in China to protect American interests there. The international settlement in Shanghai was clearly threatened by Japan, whose objective was to end European and American presence and influence in China in favor of Japanese interests. Japanese forces had deliberately attacked the Yangtze River gunboat USS *Panay* in 1937, although apparently without authorization. At that time the Japanese were quick to make amends, and the incident passed without further event. However, a similar incident could prove to be more serious. The politicomilitary problem in China for the United States after September 1939 was to provide the correct mix of firmness and flexibility and the proper deployment of naval forces to prevent serious incidents and to discourage, if not prevent, Japanese intrusion into American interests. It was a difficult and dangerous game, requiring the utmost skill and judgment.

In the 1930s Japan considered China its private preserve. Almost immediately after Hitler attacked Poland in 1939, the Japanese seized the opportunity to increase pressure on the British and French concessions in China, particularly in Shanghai. Stark told Roosevelt that the time was ripe to send to Hawaii and permanently base there a detachment of 8 light cruisers, 18 destroyers, 1 aircraft carrier, 24 patrol planes, and the bulk, if not all, of the submarine force then based on the west coast. Roosevelt agreed and gave Stark permission to send what became known as the Hawaiian Detachment.

Stark thought that sending a detachment to Hawaii would be worthwhile from a "strategic, psychological standpoint." And he had another reason in mind. He was convinced that it would point up the limited capacity of the Pearl Harbor base to support even a moderate-sized force and would result in needed improvements. He told Bloch, "I am out to plug every hole I can as soon as I can."[10] Basing a detachment at Pearl Harbor, a forward area, would underline the necessity for effective training and preparation for combat operations, including logistic support facilities. Clearly, the fleet and the detachment were not ready for war, but they would be, given the opportunity to perfect or at least to improve their readiness.

The actual dispatch of this detachment to Hawaii presented some practical complications. First, Bloch had already planned a fleet problem that included the ships in this detachment. He wanted to retain them for a short while until the exercises could be completed. Then, the matter had to be discussed with the State Department because of the intended effect on Japan. During these discussions, it was suggested that a number of cruisers be sent to the Asiatic Fleet, which was then based in China. Both Stark and Bloch opposed this suggestion. In their opinion, separation of the cruisers from the main fleet would only weaken it. Moreover, both men thought that in the Far East the cruisers would be extremely vulnerable to the powerful

Imperial Japanese Navy and they were unwilling to risk loss of the ships in the event of hostilities, regardless of any possible short-term gains. Stark succeeded in killing this proposal. By the end of September 1939, he was able to order the detachment to Hawaii.[11]

Roosevelt's first public reaction to the war in Europe was to establish on 5 September 1939 a neutrality patrol in the Atlantic to keep the European war out of the western hemisphere. He proposed to accomplish this by reporting and tracking belligerent aircraft, surface ships, and submarines. He and Stark worked out the details in advance and Stark issued the requisite orders the day before Roosevelt made his announcement.[12] The patrol was a sign that the United States would defend itself if the need ever arose. It also signified hemispheric solidarity. Within a month, representatives of the American republics, at the suggestion of the United States, met at Panama and produced the Declaration of Panama on 3 October 1939. It established a hemispheric safety zone in both oceans around the continental and insular possessions of the Americas from Cape Horn to the Canadian border. Within that zone, belligerents were to refrain from hostile acts and naval patrols were authorized to insure that there were no violations of hemispheric waters. As a matter of historical record, both sides ignored this declaration, but it did serve one very useful purpose. It gave color of authority to Roosevelt's neutrality patrol. In actual practice, German ships were tracked and their positions reported in plain language, thus giving the Royal Navy a decided advantage and putting the Germans at a great disadvantage.[13]

As far as the upper levels of government were concerned, Roosevelt's proclamation was not a bolt from the blue. Stark and other top officials of the State, War, Navy, and Treasury departments had been meeting since late August to discuss and to prepare the necessary neutrality proclamations for Roosevelt to issue when the expected European war broke out. These documents were ready for Roosevelt's signature when the shooting started. Of equal, if not greater importance, the highest civilian and military officials were aware of what would be involved when these proclamations went into effect. The problem lay in translating their awareness into action. It was no easy task.

The neutrality patrol was the first wartime or war-related task the navy was called upon to perform in World War II. The patrol was required immediately upon the outbreak of war in Europe. Aside from the fact that the bulk of the fleet was in the Pacific in September 1939, the navy at that time was a peacetime operation. Habits, procedures, even states of mind appropriate to more happy circumstances, both in the forces afloat in the Atlantic and in the shore establishment, had to be modified and in some cases changed abruptly. The officers and men who manned ships of the neutrality patrol had a lot to learn in a short time. By the end of October, navy patrol aircraft had flown 600,000 miles and surface ships had steamed 120,000 miles on their Atlantic patrol duties.[14]

The problems involved were no surprise to Stark or to the Navy Department. The bulk of the U.S. Fleet was then based on the west coast. The Atlantic Squadron had been established only in January 1939 and the ships assigned to it were a relatively small portion of the total naval strength available. This squadron included four old battleships, four heavy cruisers, a destroyer squadron, and one aircraft carrier in addition to the airplanes earmarked for another carrier not yet in commission.[15] It was hardly adequate to the gigantic task of patrolling a broad strip of the western Atlantic from Nova Scotia to South America. Air bases were urgently needed for patrol aircraft and Stark arranged with officials of Pan American Airways to sublet their facilities at Trinidad. This lease was completed in the late afternoon of 24 August 1939, a full week before war broke out. He continued negotiations for similar facilities at Bermuda and St. Lucia.[16]

Ten days before Hitler struck Poland, Stark summoned his principal assistants to his office. He told them bluntly that if war broke out in Europe, there was only one safe basis on which the navy could work. It was that sooner or later the United States would become involved in the war and that the only safe assumption was that it would be sooner.[17] This assumption underlay his own subsequent strenuous efforts to prepare the navy for war. These efforts were concentrated in three main areas: (1) recruiting sufficient numbers of officers and men to man the fleet; (2) building new ships and recommissioning old ones in order to expand the size of the fleet; and (3) strategic planning, which involved the revision of existing war plans and preparation of new ones as circumstances changed. American strategic planning prior to the Japanese attack on Pearl Harbor was largely under Stark's direction and it led to the wartime alliance with Great Britain.

Stark had been concerned about manning the ships of the fleet for some time. From his own experience as a commanding officer of a battleship and later as a rear admiral in command of cruisers, he was aware of the continual movement in men, which he thought excessive.

This movement was in part a result of normal rotation of officers and men, as well as a result of a shortage of qualified men, who, once they became trained were transferred to other ships where an even greater need existed. After his appointment as Chief of Naval Operations was announced, but before he assumed those duties, Stark got in touch with the personnel officers throughout the navy to discuss their problems and to determine how he could help them in his new job. He felt strongly that the Navy Department existed for the sole purpose of helping the fleet in any way it could. He told the personnel officers that if he did nothing else as CNO he hoped to get the fleet manned.[18]

At the time Stark became Chief of Naval Operations, the navy was limited to 116,000 men. Within one month, after Stark assumed his duties, he convinced Roosevelt to expand this limit to 125,000 men for the navy and 20,000 for the Marine Corps. But Stark wanted even more men—136,000 for the navy and 27,000 Marines right away. In November Roosevelt authorized 170,000 men for the navy and 28,000 for the marines. By the end of his first year as CNO, Stark had talked the President into authorizing 191,000 for the navy and 43,000 men for the Marine Corps. Initially, Roosevelt wanted to expand the navy by only 6,000 men and the Marine Corps by 1,000 men.[19]

Stark's struggle to obtain what he thought was an adequate number of men for the navy was one of the less glamorous, but extremely important tasks he performed in preparing the navy for war. It was one of his earliest objectives and he put more time and effort into this struggle with the White House and the Congress than on anything else. He literally worked on the personnel problem almost night and day from the time he entered office. He continually reminded Roosevelt of what he saw as the needs of the navy. Roosevelt saw Stark's position, understood it, and disagreed with it for his own reasons. Stark was as persistent in his efforts, and his unceasing efforts paid off. On one occasion Stark specifically asked Roosevelt for permission to go before Congress and state the needs of the navy as he saw them. Roosevelt was apparently somewhat worn down at that time and told Stark, "Go ahead. I won't veto anything they agree to." Stark went up to Capital Hill and obtained the authorization he wanted.[20]

Roosevelt was a friendly commander in chief to the navy. He took great interest in the small details of naval administration and in many instances his personal intervention resulted in important gains for the navy. The price he extracted was to require Stark to immerse him in details. For example, one day late in 1939 he and Stark discussed at length the construction of naval facilities in the Philippines. After consideration, discussion, and even argument, Stark won Roosevelt's approval for improvement of the submarine battery charging facilities at Cavite and overhaul of a floating drydock at Olongapo, among other things. The total cost was $280,000, which came from emergency funds Roosevelt had at his disposal.[21]

In the fall of 1939 Roosevelt told Stark he wanted naval air bases built in the Caribbean to help protect coastwise shipping against submarines. Stark raised the matter with Rear Admiral Ben Moreell, Chief of the Bureau of Yards and Docks, who would have to build the bases. Moreell asked, "What are we going to do for money?" He pointed out that by law all new naval shore construction had to be specifically authorized by Congress. Moreell noted that there was a way to get around this obstacle. In view of the "limited national emergency" that Roosevelt had declared, the Secretary of the Navy would be justified in starting construction at once and charging expenditures to a dummy account to be met later by a deficiency appropriation by Congress. In the meantime, Roosevelt would have to authorize this rather extraordinary procedure by a written memorandum.

When Stark presented Roosevelt with this proposal, the President became angrier than Stark had ever seen him. Pounding his desk, he asked, "Who wants something on a piece of paper?" Stark mentioned no names, saying it was a "general feeling." Roosevelt curtly dismissed Stark. He said irately, "Well, you go back and find out which one of those bureau chiefs wants something on a piece of paper, and I will give him something on a piece of paper, but it will not be what he expects."

Moreell then pointed out to Stark that if the Secretary of the Navy wanted to accept responsibility for proceeding contrary to law, the bureau chiefs would have to follow his order. Unfortunately, both the Secretary and the Assistant Secretary of the Navy were out of town. In their absence, Stark was Acting Secretary. After a moment's thought, he gave the necessary orders in his capacity as Acting Secretary to start construction at Roosevelt Roads, Puerto Rico. Stark was in an extremely precarious position until Congress made the necessary appropriation, which passed despite a strong attack against it.[22]

The process of strategic planning that eventually culminated in the decision to defeat Germany first and in the Anglo-American alliance—Grand Alliance in Churchill's words—started in 1938 at the time of the Munich Conference, a full year before Stark became Chief of Naval Operations. At that time, Roosevelt sent Captain Royal K. Ingersoll to London to talk with Admiralty officials. The navy and army planners realized that Germany, in addition to Japan, might threaten the interests of the United States. Until that time the basic American war plan contemplated the possibility of war only with Japan. This was the famous ORANGE plan. The Joint Army-Navy Board, consisting of the Secretaries of the War and the Navy and the respective service chiefs, directed the Joint Planning Committee (the army and navy war plans officers) to devise what became known as the Rainbow series of five plans. All were based on the common assumption of war in both the Atlantic and the Pacific. However, each Rainbow plan had a different set of specific assumptions in regard to the participation of various possible allies, areas to be protected, and whether offensive or defensive action would take place in the Atlantic or in the Pacific theater.

Rainbow 1 recognized the long-range potential danger of an Allied defeat or compromise peace, which would remove the French and British shields. It was a worst-case plan and although its basic assumptions did not seem to be particularly likely in early 1940, they were possibilities that could not prudently be ignored. Indeed, the possibility of having to fight a coalition—war in both the Atlantic and the Pacific—was the rationale underlying the justification for the naval expansion program.

In February 1940, Stark reassured Admiral Thomas C. Hart, commander in chief of the Asiatic Fleet, that the war plans he read several months before were still in effect and had not been modified.[23] Stark thought a war plan should be modified only after careful thought and evaluation of the effect of the proposed change, or when war, emergency, or otherwise compelling circumstances required a change. The Joint Army-Navy Board and especially its Joint Planning Committee were continually studying developments with an eye towards necessary revisions. Rainbow 1 would not be amended until April 1940. Even then the modifications were of such minor character that President Roosevelt's approval was not considered necessary.[24]

Although war plans such as Rainbow 1 served a very definite purpose, not the least being to exercise the analytical skills of the planners, they pertained only to hostilities—a shooting war. The war plans then in force did not, however, apply to the employment of naval forces in a period of growing tension, which might or might not culminate in the outbreak of war. Stark sorely felt the need for what he called "Tension Plans" in addition to war plans. After all, he pointed out to Hart, "As so frequently exemplified in recent years, armed forces may be employed in varying degrees, without being followed by an actual outbreak of war. Even when hostilities do break out, they may or may not be accompanied by a formally declared war, and the extent of hostilities may be restricted or may be unlimited."[25]

This was an excellent description of how the U.S. Navy was in fact employed in the remaining time before the Japanese attack on Pearl Harbor. During this period, the United States had a real need for Tension Plans—reasoned, thought-out concepts for the employment of naval forces in order to achieve specific objectives in a situation not involving the outbreak of war. Tension Plans were needed in the immediate future to avoid improvisation in the actual employment of naval forces, before the United States would become involved in the war. Unfortunately, Stark's apprehension was realized: the employment of U.S. naval forces before Pearl Harbor was characterized more by haphazard improvisation than by sound planning. The best that can be said was that policy was unarticulated and at times uncoordinated. Certainly Roosevelt made no more policy decisions than were absolutely necessary, and, arguably, even fewer.

Before war plans or tension plans could be devised and written, fundamental policy decisions would have to be made on such basic questions as what objectives the United States sought and how far the United States would be willing to go to achieve them. Ultimately, the President would have to make these decisions, but for a variety of complex reasons, he was either unwilling or unable to make them. Stark was faced with a lack of guidance from above, but still had an obligation to provide guidance to his fleet commanders—Hart with the Asiatic Fleet and Richardson with the U.S. Fleet. Hart understood Stark's awkward position and coped with it well. The great distance between Washington and the Far East may have made Hart feel isolated, but it also strengthened his hand to act in accordance with his own judgment. Richardson lacked whatever advantage distance may have given Hart and he quite properly complained to Stark about the inadequacy of war plans. He also chafed at what he did not know and could not understand.

Stark recognized that Tension Plans required planning machinery. The Joint Board provided coordination, but there was no planning machinery that regularly brought in the State Department. The Liaison Committee consisted of the senior representatives of the State, War, and Navy departments and provided a means for frequent consultation among these departments. Still, things were not planned in advance and often the navy and the army did not receive advance information of State Department action, which might well have affected what they would do.[26]

The absence of adequate planning machinery meant that there could be no planned, coordinated action. It was up to naval commanders in the frontline, to use Hart's phrase, to support national policy in a manner that would not result in war. Hart would have to continue to use "firm adroitness" to maintain the delicate balance between the pitfalls of the appearance of weakness, which could encourage Japanese action, and the avoidance of provocation. Stark was certain that the American people would support firm action so long as it did not become jingoistic and that "if in the face of such a firm but restrained attitude, Japan would step on our toes . . . our country will realize that Japan herself has provoked the action." (Of course, this is exactly what happened in 1941.) Stark promised to keep Hart informed in advance whenever possible of "actions contemplated by the State Department" so that he might deploy his forces to the best advantage. It was a poor substitute for planning, but it was the best Stark could offer at the time.[27]

Strategic plans and the fundamental national policy they were based upon developed as the war in Europe took a surprising and disastrous turn for the Allies in the spring and summer of 1940. Meanwhile, the time was ripe to provide material assistance to Britain and France and to start building up the navy. It was a strenuous 27 months of unremitting effort between Hitler's attack on Poland and Japan's attack on Pearl Harbor. The first year of full American involvement in the war, 1942, was bad enough for the United States. It would have been far worse had it not been for these earlier efforts.

2

DOLLARS CANNOT BUY YESTERDAY

During the last few months of 1939 and well into 1940, while the Anglo-French land and sea forces stood firm, there was no immediate or even foreseeable danger of the projection of Axis power to the western hemisphere. But there were plenty of signs that the dictators threatened what remained of the world order. Hitler took only a month to conquer Poland. Meanwhile, Stalin occupied the eastern portion of Poland and the three Baltic republics of Estonia, Latvia, and Lithuania. At the end of November 1939, the Soviet Union invaded Finland. To the surprise and admiration of the Western world, the Finns fought well and for the most part they successfully held the Russians at bay, even though they could not win in the end. By March 1940, this little war was over. Stalemate continued on the western front. The British and French Armies in France still faced the *Wehrmacht*, which so far had not moved westward. Belgium remained conspicuously neutral.

The War and Navy Departments, with the concurrence of the President, pursued the dual objectives of making war matériel available to the Allies and of building up American forces. The cash-and-carry amendment to the Neutrality Act facilitated the purchase of war materiel in the United States. Buyers then had to transport it themselves. Stark clearly saw that a shipbuilding program was the first step to prudent rearmament now that war had broken out in Europe. At this time Stark was more worried about conditions in the Far East than he was about what might happen in Europe.[1]

For at least two years, the navy had been acutely aware of deteriorating political conditions in Europe. In September 1938, four months after the enactment of the Second Vinson Bill, which authorized a 20

16

percent expansion of the navy, the prime ministers of Great Britain and France committed the ultimate act of appeasement at Munich. Hitler was deprived of his trumped up casus belli and he was given a free hand in Czechoslovakia. Admiral William D. Leahy, then Chief of Naval Operations, and the naval planners did not see this agreement as a means of avoiding war, but simply of postponing it. Alive to the increased dangers of war, the navy began to study the size of an increase in shipbuilding to provide the necessary minimum number of ships required for national security. Studies conducted first under Leahy's direction and those a year later under Stark's direction reached the same conclusions: a 25 percent increase in the navy would barely maintain the overall 5:5:3 ratio with Great Britain and Japan that had been established by treaty.[2] Navy planners recognized the distinct possibilities of having to fight in both the Atlantic and in the Pacific, and also having to fight against a coalition of Germany and Italy in the Atlantic.

Carl Vinson of Georgia, Chairman of the House Naval Affairs Committee, shared this view. Throughout his long career, Vinson consistently favored a strong navy. He was the prime mover throughout the 1930s for naval expansion. In 1939, shortly after war broke out in Europe, he and Stark discussed at some length a two-ocean navy. On 26 September of that year Vinson telephoned Stark to discuss his own plans for an increase in the navy. Stark had to resolve two different considerations; one was technical and the other was political. The technical consideration had to do with the size of the increase necessary to maintain parity with Germany and Italy in the Atlantic and a 4:3 or, more optimistically, a 5:3 ratio with Japan in the Pacific. The political consideration involved a determination of the size increase that the House of Representatives would approve. Stark and Vinson independently concluded that Stark should ask Congress for a 25 percent increase in the navy, and Roosevelt approved of that figure.[3]

The needed increase in fleet size was determined first by the number of battleships in both the Atlantic and Pacific that could provide, at the minimum, parity of battleline strength at any time in an area of operations. With the battleline determined, it would then be possible to calculate the numbers of other types of ships—aircraft carriers, cruisers, destroyers, and submarines—needed for support and to carry out other necessary operations in both oceans. Obviously, the size of the U.S. Navy would be affected by the size of the navies of potential enemies as well as upon the type of operations desired.[4]

Stark and Vinson worked closely throughout Stark's tenure as Chief of Naval Operations. Although their relationship was a cordial one, based on mutual respect and trust, it was in the main professional rather than personal. There was greater cooperation between them in the preparation of the two 1940 naval expansion acts that provided much of the fleet with which the navy fought World War II. By mid-September 1939, Vinson and Representative Melvin Maas, the ranking Republican member of the House Naval Affairs Committee, were demanding various studies and reports on an expansion of the navy as quickly as the Navy Department could prepare them. Fortunately, the navy staff had anticipated some of their requests.[5]

Vinson went to Stark's office on 27 September to discuss the expansion of the navy with Stark and his principal assistants, Rear Admiral Robert L. Ghormley, Assistant Chief of Naval Operations, Captain Russell S. Crenshaw, Director of the War Plans Division, and his assistant, Captain Charles M. "Savvy" Cooke. In anticipation of this meeting, Stark asked Crenshaw and Cooke what types and numbers of ships they felt were necessary to combat Germany and Italy on a basis of parity in the Atlantic and Japan in the Pacific on a basis of 5 to 3 superiority. They recommended a 10-year building program to correct existing deficiencies. It would more than double the size of the U.S. Navy.[6]

Regrettably, Vinson's response to these recommendations has not been preserved. Even without Vinson's comments, it was obvious to Stark that a program of such magnitude was neither politically nor financially feasible at that time. Stark and Vinson had a good idea of how much of an increase both the White House and Congress would support. They had no intention of exceeding it. They rejected as impractical these recommendations, which were based on strictly military considerations, regardless of whatever intrinsic merits they might have had. Instead, they agreed at that time to limit their proposal to a 25 percent increase.

On Capitol Hill, Vinson was a skillful politician who knew Congress, especially the House of Representatives, and was a shrewd judge of what the House would accept. He had to weigh and balance many political considerations, including the ardent American desire to stay out of war, a general reluctance to increase public expenditures and add to the tax burden of the American people, isolationist and pacifist sentiment, a lack of public awareness of the dangers of war, and suspicion of President Roosevelt's true intentions. In addition, it was the constitutional duty of Congress to provide and to maintain a navy as part of the federal government's duty to provide for the common defense. With support from the White House, Vinson's task in Congress was made easier and he could garner support among loyal Roosevelt Democrats.

Not only was a 25 percent increase deemed feasible in political terms at the White House, in the Navy Department, and in Congress, but construction facilities in private and navy shipyards were more than sufficient to start work as soon as the necessary authorizations and appropriations were made. Starting on 1 July 1940, American shipyards had the building capacity to lay down 2 battleships each year (construction time exceeded 4 years) and to complete 5 aircraft carriers, 10 heavy cruisers, 8 light cruisers, 10 destroyer leaders, 80 destroyers, 45 submarines, and 36 auxiliaries.[7] Needless to say, this capacity greatly exceeded a 25 percent increase in the navy.

Once the size of the proposed expansion had been agreed upon, working out the details was not as simple as it might seem. The size of the navy, expressed in total tonnage, had been limited by the Washington and London treaties of 1922 and 1930. The United States was allowed 1,262,068 tons of naval ships in various categories.

The 1922 Washington treaty dealt only with capital ships. The 1930 London treaty extended quantitative limitations to all categories of combatant ships. As a matter of deliberate public policy in the ensuing years, the United States failed to maintain its navy at treaty limits while the other nations built to prescribed limits. In 1934, under the Vinson-Trammell Act, the United States commenced a naval construction program designed to reach treaty limits and thus preserve the 5:5:3 ratio established with Great Britain and Japan. At the end of 1934, Japan gave the required two-year notice and the 1922 treaty, with its quantitative limitations, expired on 31 December 1936. Moreover, Japan refused to become a party to the 1936 London treaty, which limited battleships to 35,000 tons, cruisers to 10,000 tons, and destroyers to 3,000 tons, in addition to requiring an exchange of information regarding building programs. The Japanese defection from the Washington treaty system sounded the death knell for both the qualitative and quantitative limitations on naval armaments.

In 1938, after the treaties expired, the Second Vinson Bill authorized a 20 percent increase in the navy (bringing the total tonnage to 1,557,480 tons). Thus, the expansion that Stark and Vinson were planning used this total tonnage (1,557,480) as the base. This was the starting point for the 1940 naval expansion bills.

Although the bureau chiefs were still reviewing the proposed bill, Stark discussed it with Secretary of the Navy Charles A. Edison. Then the two men went to the White House where they went over the bill with Roosevelt. They brought the President up to date on the latest studies in the navy and on Vinson's request for prompt action. The President approved Stark's proposal. The navy estimated the ultimate cost to be 4 billion dollars.

Vinson was the appropriate person to announce the proposed 25 percent increase in the navy. As a member of Congress, he would introduce the bill and as Chairman of the House Naval Affairs Committee, he could almost guarantee that it would be reported out favorably. He made it clear that he had worked closely with the Navy Department in its preparation and that he had conferred at length with Stark. It was also obvious that the bill had the President's support.

The New York Times headlined the proposal as a $1,300,000,000 bill for 95 new ships—3 aircraft carriers, 8 cruisers, 52 destroyers, and 32 submarines. In addition to 400,000 tons of combatant ships, the bill provided for 200,000 tons of auxiliaries and 3,000 airplanes.[8] The statement to the press was released under Vinson's name, but Stark drafted it and the President approved it. The press release emphasized that this increase would be sufficient to protect the United States from any one hostile power, but not from a possible coalition. The significance of this qualification was apparently lost at the time, but Stark would repeatedly emphasize it during the hearings held later on in January 1940.

The proposed program could be completed in three or four years. By 1944, it would give the navy a fighting strength of 15 battleships, 59 cruisers, 11 aircraft carriers, 173 destroyers, 37 submarines, 6,000 airplanes, and 36 dirigibles. No battleships were included because 8 were then under construction. Of those 8, 6 were of 35,000 tons each and two were of 45,000 tons. Both Stark and Vinson were convinced that those capital ships were sufficient to meet the navy's needs in the foreseeable future.

Vinson emphasized that this proposal did not provide for a two-ocean navy, but that it would be sufficient for the defense of the country and would help keep the United States out of war. In the clearest and most concise terms, reminiscent of the president's own style, Vinson said, "We want no hysteria. We seek no war. We covet not one inch of foreign soil, but we are determined to keep war away from our shores. We must have an adequate fleet—now."[9]

The bill as proposed contained several significant and far-reaching provisions, some of which would cause considerable adverse comment in the hearings yet to come. The President would be authorized to use his discretion in distributing the increase of 400,000 tons among carriers, cruisers, destroyers, and submarines, and thus would be given a free hand in determining how many and what kind of ships would be built, so long as the aggregate tonnage of the ships constructed did not exceed 400,000 tons.

In addition, the bill would give the President authority to construct replacements for all navy combatant ships when they reached certain ages specified by law. This replacement authority would apply not only to the ships included in the 25 percent expansion, but it would also apply to those already in service, recently built, and being built. Moreover, the President would be given a free hand in determining the size, armament, and design of the replacement "as he may consider best suited for the purpose of national defense."

The effect of these sections would be a virtual delegation to the President of congressional responsibility and prerogatives to provide and maintain a navy, except in the very broadest sense of establishing the ultimate size in total tonnage of the navy. It was also a naval planners' dream come true. For this reason, Stark enthusiastically supported it. If it were to be enacted into law, the navy would be able to establish the size, composition, and design of ships within the very broadest limits. It is not surprising that these sections did not survive when the bill went to the House Naval Affairs Committee.

Combatant ships were not the only ones provided for in the bill. An increase in the number of fighting ships would also require an increase in the number of auxiliary ships to support them. The bill provided for an increase of 200,000 tons for auxiliaries. The auxiliaries included tenders or mother ships for destroyers, submarines, and seaplanes; light minelayers; seaplane carriers and oilers; a repair ship; a transport; and a hospital ship. Another section specified the point at which an underage ship would become overage: battleships would become overage 26 years after completion, aircraft carriers and cruisers 20 years after, other combatant surface craft 16 years after, and submarines 13 years after completion.

In the interests of economy and efficiency, the requirement that alternate ships of any given type be constructed in government and private shipyards would be repealed. The Secretary of the Navy would be able to build ships as quickly and as efficiently as possible without worrying too much about who was going to get the orders. In furtherance of this objective, he would be given specific authority to negotiate directly with contractors and to let contracts without competitive bidding if he determined the price to be "fair and reasonable." The Budget Director, Harold D. Smith, objected to Roosevelt about this provision, because "such a contract is wide open to criticism and the burden of proof would be on the contracting officer responsible. A government contract must not only be right; it must look right."[10] In addition, the Secretary of the Navy would be authorized to advance sums up to 30 percent of the contract price to contractors to enable them to commence work.

There was no particular public reaction when Vinson made his announcement. That came along with congressional reaction in January 1940 when the 79th Congress convened for its third session and Stark was the bill's leading advocate.

The hearings held before the respective House and Senate Naval Affairs Committee from January to May 1940 provided an excellent illustration of the respective duties, responsibilities, and prerogatives of the Congress and the President, as represented by navy officials, to establish naval policy. Under the Constitution, one of the enumerated powers of Congress is to provide and maintain a navy, and the President is commander in chief of the army and the navy. Cooperation based on trust and respect between these two branches of government is indispensable to the formulation of a rational, consistent naval policy. Because navies cannot be improvised, this cooperation is necessary to produce a sustained naval policy. Stark and Vinson personified it in the formulation and enactment of the two naval expansion bills of 1940.

Stark was the star witness before Vinson's committee.[11] In his opening statement, Stark sought to justify the necessity for the proposed expansion by reviewing the course of naval arms limitation and how circumstances had changed drastically since the Washington treaty was signed in 1922. He pointed out how the Naval Arms Limitation Treaty set the upper limits of the British, American, and Japanese navies and based them on a ratio of 5:5:3 respectively. This treaty was part of a "system of interdependent provisions concurrently agreed upon," including the nonfortification provision and the Four Power and Nine Power Pacts, which dealt with political matters. No member of the committee questioned Stark about the expiration of qualitative limitations. Japan had given timely notice that it would no longer adhere to the treaty. Vinson was aware of how the United States, along with Great Britain and France, availed themselves of an escape clause in the Second London Treaty of 1936. Fortunately, this collateral issue was not raised and unnecessary confusion in the committee hearings was avoided.

Stark pointed out that by 1938 both Great Britain and Japan were building naval ships substantially in excess of the limits prescribed at Washington in 1922 for capital ships and at London in 1930 for noncapital ships. In 1938, the Second Vinson Bill authorized the increase of the navy by 20 percent above the limits of the Washington treaty. It "was designed solely to defend ourselves against any single power." Stark went on to add that although the 1938 expansion was not conceived to be adequate to defend the United States against a coalition of powers, "More recently it has become evident that we must consider such a possibility."[12]

This perception of a possible coalition of enemies was the rock upon which Stark, Vinson, and Roosevelt based the 1940 naval expansion bills. Stark's perception was based in turn on his own observations and it was shared by many, if not most, naval officers. It was also without benefit of consultation with the State Department.[13] In early 1940 leading naval officers still considered Japan to be the major naval rival, and thus a potential threat to the United States. Hitler's invasion of Poland and Mussolini's obvious Axis sympathies, however, raised the distinct possibility of a hostile German-Italian coalition in the Atlantic. Moreover, the Russian attack on Finland then underway, following soon after Stalin's annexation of the Baltic states and eastern Poland, raised the additional possibility of Soviet participation in the German-Italian coalition. Even though such an eventuality should have been, and may well have been, obvious even to the casual observer of international affairs, the American public and particularly Congress were reluctant to admit it and then to act accordingly. To add to the problem, 1940 was a presidential election year, and the most popular guessing game until July was whether Roosevelt would run for a third term. These reasons made it imperative for Stark to proceed with caution.

After mentioning the possibility of a hostile coalition, Stark told the committee, "In the world of today it seems only a fair and moderate statement to say that the best interests of our Nation will be served by keeping our forces sufficiently strong to be an effective deterrent against foreign aggression." He thought a 25 percent expansion in the navy was required. He based his recommendation upon five considerations; (1) the positive protection of the continental United States and its possessions; (2) joint action with the other American republics in preventing any hemispheric invasion or Axis penetration; (3) sufficient naval strength to maintain and defend American commerce; (4) insurance of the uninterrupted flow of vital strategic raw materials; and (5) the immense influence of adequate naval power upon preserving peace and neutrality.[14]

Stark did not discuss the details of the proposed expansion program, at least not at first. They would come out later in the hearings. He did note that the bill did not provide for additional battleships, because the present construction program of laying down two keels each year was sufficient, and that a provision had been made for auxiliaries, those ships less glamorous than combatants, but indispensable for fleet operations. Significantly, he made a point of remarking on the proposed increase in the authorized number of naval aircraft because of the increased requirements of carriers and cruisers and the need for patrol aircraft to protect coastal shipping.

In summary, Stark said, "Navies cannot be improvised. For the most part wars are fought and won or lost with the navies as they exist on the outbreak of hostilities." He observed that in 1917 when the

United States entered World War I the great need was for destroyers, which for the most part were completed only after the war was over. He concluded that "our voice in world affairs will be heeded in almost exact proportion to our relative strength on the sea . . . while preparedness will not guarantee keeping us out of war, lack of it not only invites war but utter disaster."[15]

Immediately following his initial statement, Stark and Vinson engaged in a colloquy to set forth for the record the then present and projected sized of the navy under existing legislation and under the proposed 25 percent increase. Stark made it abundantly clear that the proposed increase of 25 percent was a modest one. In light of the difference in world conditions between 1922 and 1940, to say it was modest was indeed an understatement.[16]

Under the 1938 act, the navy was authorized 1,557,480 tons of underage combatant ships. The distribution among the various types of ships consisted of 18 battleships (660,000 tons), 8 aircraft carriers (175,000 tons), 46 cruisers (412,524 tons), 147 destroyers (228,000 tons), and 58 submarines (81,956 tons), for a total of 227 ships and 1,557,480 tons. The proposed 25 percent expansion provided for an increase of 400,000 tons in new or underage ships. The increase would apply only to the construction of aircraft carriers, cruisers, destroyers, and submarines, but not battleships. If Congress approved the 25 percent expansion, the total authorized underage combatant ship tonnage of the U.S. Navy would be just under two million tons.[17]

Expression of the size of the navy in terms of tonnage was awkward and led to confusion. But it was also a handy means by which to measure the size of the U.S. Navy relative to that of the other principal navies, notably the Royal Navy and the Imperial Japanese Navy. One of the strongest and most compelling arguments Stark made in support of the 25 percent expansion bill was that it would reestablish the 5:5:3 ratio in tonnage for the United States relative to the British and Japanese navies.

There was nothing particularly magic about the ratio. It had been agreed upon first at Washington in 1922 and reaffirmed at London in 1930. The 5:3 ratio with Japan was dependent upon the forbearance of the United States to fortify her possessions west of Hawaii (notably Guam and the Philippines) along with a similar pledge by Japan in the same area. Stark did not refer to the nonfortification condition, because Congress had recently refused to appropriate funds to fortify

Guam even though all treaty restrictions had expired. Instead, Stark addressed himself to the sufficiency of the 5:3 ratio, saying, "It is not a very comfortable ratio. If it were larger, we would welcome it, but it is a reasonable ratio."[18]

In light of changing circumstances during the interwar years there was little, if any, serious examination given to the appropriateness of this ratio. The ratios had a life of their own and no purpose would have been served by challenging them so long as the U.S. Navy had not achieved its prescribed size relative to the Japanese and British navies, expressed in terms of the ratios. However, the ratios themselves were significant in that they sanctified parity between the British and the American navies and the superiority of both over the Japanese navy. This fact was not lost on the Japanese and it explains at least part of the rationale for Japanese naval expansion, which in turn induced an American response and thus contributed to an arms race.[19]

Also, the ratios placed at a decided disadvantage the opponents of naval expansion—usually pacifists, isolationists, church groups, some liberals, and those who wanted to spend the money on something else or who did not want to spend it at all. They were placed in the position of logically having to argue that maintaining a navy to the upper limits permitted by the ratios established in 1922 was not necessary for the security of the United States. Needless to say, few, if any, opponents of naval expansion directly attacked the ratios.

Although Stark did not ask for battleships in this bill, he emphasized that they were the backbone of the fleet. These ships were constructed to stand up to and fight the heaviest and most powerful ships an enemy could put to sea. The fleet, built around battleships, included cruisers, destroyers, carriers, and submarines. The role of cruisers and destroyers was to scout, escort, and attack. Even so, carriers were not slighted. As Stark pointed out, the development of shore-based aviation required naval activities to be conducted at sea at greater distances than ever before. The effect of the extension of power projected from the land onto the sea was that naval operations would be spread out over a larger sea area than ever before. There was a corresponding increase in the need for shipboard aircraft, based on battleships, cruisers, and carriers.[20] The dramatic tactical importance of aircraft, especially carrier aircraft, was demonstrated in 1942 at the battles of Midway and the Coral Sea. If Stark, Vinson, and the naval leadership could not have foreseen specific future developments, at least they can be given credit for reasonable foresight.

Stark told the committee that of eight battleships currently authorized and under construction, six were replacements for overage battleships and two were authorized by the 1938 expansion act.[21] The appropriation bill before the House at that time called for two more battleships: one to be a replacement for USS *Arizona*, which would become overage in 1942, and a second battleship, which would be the third and final one authorized by the act of 1938. Thus, in addition to the eight battleships already under construction, two more were anticipated, making a total of ten, all of which would be completed by 1944.[22] Stark explained that the reason so many battleships were planned and under construction was that none were laid down between 1922 and 1937. This large program was the price of block obsolescense. The shipbuilding industry was working to capacity on battleships and at that time could not embark on the construction of more beyond the ten already contemplated.

The qualitative limitations on battleship sizes were increased from 35,000 to 45,000 tons by 30 June 1938 when the United States, Great Britain, and France concluded a protocol to the London treaty of 1936 after Japan refused to divulge information about her building program.[23] The first six battleships laid down, comprising the *North Carolina* and *South Dakota* classes, were all 35,000 tons. The next four were the *Iowa* class ships and they were 45,000 ton battleships. Those ships were built in response to well-founded suspicions that Japan was already building battleships in excess of 35,000 tons. The larger ships would be necessary as a counter to the larger Japanese ships. Stark was "entirely satisfied" with the *Iowa* class, which he described as "splendid ships."[24]

A great deal of public interest was sparked by the prospect of even larger battleships, perhaps as large as 62,000 tons. Stark talked about battleships possibly as large as 50,000 tons. He felt that considering speed, armament, armor, and size, the *Iowa* class at 45,000 tons represented the best balance of all relevant factors.[25] The navy's General Board (an advisory body to the Secretary of the Navy) studied the matter and recommended against ships larger than 45,000 tons.[26]

The issue was only partly which ship would be ideally better—a 45,000 ton or a 60,000 ton battleship. Any one ship, no matter what its size, could be only in one place at one time. Thus, other factors being equal, two smaller ships would obviously be more advantageous than one larger ship. Stark illustrated this point by referring to the *Graf Spee* incident in which three smaller British ships brought the larger German pocket battleship to bay. To Vinson it showed the potential danger of "putting all your eggs in one basket."[27]

A more important factor was that plans were ready and construction could start in the near future on the *Iowa* class battleships. In view of the outbreak of war in Europe and the Japanese buildings program, details of which were still obscure, time was of the essence. It was important that battleship construction proceed as expeditiously as possible.

Vinson saw the need for immediate construction, but he was also concerned with economy. In an exchange with Stark he asked why the navy could not proceed to construct four ships of the *Iowa* class from the same set of plans. Not only were the plans themselves expensive—they cost about $1,500,000 for a set—but the resulting economies of constructing four identical ships would be great. Stark agreed that considerable savings could be had that way, but he was hesitant to recommend construction of four identical ships because military considerations might dictate changes in the third and fourth ships of that class. Vinson deferred to Stark's professional judgment on this point, expressing confidence that Stark would give serious thought to any future modifications in the plans. As it turned out, only minor modifications were made in the final ships of this class.

Press coverage of the hearings was generally thorough and extensive. *The New York Times* devoted front page and inside space to Stark's proposals. Not surprisingly, the headlines emphasized Stark's warning of the possibility of a hostile coalition that might "beat" the navy; the upper limit of 52,000 tons for battleships; the anticipated superiority of new cruisers; and the navy's consideration of the possibility of allied defeat. Hanson Baldwin wrote a detailed informative column for the 14 January 1940 edition, which was headlined "Big Defense Problem is in Lap of Congress. After Several Years of Increasing Outlays the Nation Now Confronts Questions Raised by War."[28]

Three consecutive days of testifying were enough to make Stark exclaim in private, "My God, I have been up there three days straight and it looks like a couple of more."[29] Besides presenting with Vinson a carefully orchestrated case for expansion, Stark was also required to submit to questions from other members of the committee, some of whom had little knowledge or understanding of naval affairs.

Despite the inevitable irritations and the seemingly obligatory aggravations of testifying at length, Stark was generally pleased with his reception by the committee. Before and after the hearings various members told him that they were generally in favor of naval expansion. In addition to Vinson, other members were infused with a spirit of cooperation. For example, Melvin Maas, the ranking Republician member, privately assured Stark that he would not press him for classified material, saying, "any question that is embarrassing or confidential don't bother to say it is. . . . Just give me an evasive answer."[30]

Despite generally pleasant and amicable relations with the members of the Naval Affairs Committee and especially with its chairman, Stark was not confident about the chances of passage of the naval expansion bill. He knew that although many members were leaning towards it and that opposition was neither particularly well organized nor strong, the presidential election year with the third-term issue, could mean that a naval expansion bill might be lost. Even so, he could take comfort in the knowledge that Roosevelt was following the progress of the hearings with keen interest and that the President thought that Stark's presentation of the case for naval expansion was "very good."[31]

Roosevelt refused to permit Stark to ask for more than a 25 percent increase in the navy. This refusal put him in a difficult position before the committee. Stark was fully aware that a 5:3 superiority might be adequate to oppose one power, but it would be inadequate against a coalition. But Roosevelt, anticipating an economy drive in Congress, would not agree to a greater increase. In 1938, Admiral William D. Leahy, then Chief of Naval Operations, had requested a 20 percent increase in the navy above the limits established in 1922. He argued at that time that this increase would reestablish the 5:3 ratio with Japan and that ratio would be sufficient to defend the United States against any single power. In 1940, Stark emphasized that instead of the possibility of having to face a single hostile power, the United States must face the possibility of facing a coalition. The committee wanted to know why a 5:3 superiority, sufficient only to face a single power in 1938, would also be sufficient to face a coalition in 1940.[32]

Stark could not very well say the 1938 request was excessive or that the 1940 request was insufficient for national defense. As a service chief he was subordinate to the President and thus it would not be politic to say that Roosevelt would approve a 25 pecent increase but no more. Such an admission in an election year could very well give Roosevelt's political opponents—both Republicans and Democrats opposed to a third term—a convenient political issue. Instead, Stark took the middle course, the only one open to him. He admitted that with the size of the navy he proposed "We would be driven back and it would be a critical situation. . . . The answer to your question is that the job probably could not be completely done."[33]

Stark's questioners on this point, representatives Melvin Maas of Minnesota and James W. Mott of Oregon, were by no means hostile. Both men stated openly that they were not only in favor of a 25 percent expansion, but they wanted an even larger navy. Mott correctly pointed out that in order to defend against a coalition, a larger navy would be needed.[34] In response to this line of questioning and to the statements by Maas and Mott, Stark replied it was necessary to strike a reasonable balance and to be aware of its limitations. Mott asked whether the request for expansion "is as large as the country at the present time can afford." Stark avoided this pitfall by replying, "That is an answer. You can make the answer to that perhaps better than I can."[35]

Although his extemporaneous replies did not particularly hurt the chances of committee approval of the bill, they nevertheless did not address the very real question raised by Mott. Another approach was needed. At the conclusion of the third day of the hearings, Stark returned to his office, where he prepared a statement to give to the committee the next day.[36]

The next morning, as soon as the committee met, Vinson introduced Stark's statement by asking him to tell the committee just why the 25 percent increase had been requested and what the navy could do with it. Stark would be permitted to reply, uninterrupted by questions and other diversions.

Stark opened his second statement by saying that European events in 1938, culminating in the Munich agreement, increased the navy's estimates of what was required to defend the country. The outbreak of war in Europe in September 1939 merely confirmed the previous estimates. He bluntly pointed out, "We must face the possibility of an Allied defeat and then measure the strength of the powers which might combine for action against the Americas. If our navy is weaker than the combined strength of potential enemies, then our navy is too small. If it is too small viewed from that angle, there is just one answer: An increase is necessary."[37]

A determination of the extent of the increase could be made from two directions—one theoretical and the other practical. Stark pointed out that theoretically "to insure victory we should be superior to the combined strength of our potential enemies and should, for example, have a 5:3 superiority available in the Pacific and a 4:3 superiority available for the Atlantic."[38] On the other hand, the practical side of the determination of the increase involved three major considerations—cost, time, and expansion of building facilities. Cost included not only industrial costs but also federal spending levels and taxes. The time factor involved the lead times for ship construction and the urgency of its completion. The expansion of building facilities, in both private and navy shipyards and various inducements to private industry to tool up and expand were other factors naval planners had considered.

As a result of weighing both the theoretical and practical factors involved, the navy determined a practical and quickly available capacity for ship construction: a 400,000 ton expansion, approximately 25 percent above the authorized levels. Admittedly this figure was a compromise and it was based on many imponderables. This increase would be superimposed on the utilization of unexpended tonnage that had already been authorized, including a small amount remaining under the 1938 act and replacement authorized under the 1934 act. By proceeding to contract for both the increase and the unexpended tonnage, economies of scale and other efficiencies could be obtained.

Stark stressed the moderation of the proposed 25 percent increase and he made it plain that it would not be enough to guarantee against every contingency. Even reestablishment of the 5:3 ratio in the Pacific would not be sufficient "to defend our home waters, the Monroe Doctrine, our possessions and our trade routes against a coalition that had been mentioned in the committee as consisting of Japan, Russia, Germany, and Italy." If the United States were to be attacked by such a coalition, "something would have to be abandoned." Despite this rather grim estimate, Stark was confident that "the fleet . . . including its vital air arm, should be able to prevent any permanent establishment by the enemy on our coast, in Hawaii or at the Panama Canal."[39]

He reminded the committee that world conditions could change dramatically and that such changes, for better or for worse, could require a change in naval policy. Stark concluded, "We cannot foresee the future but for the moment at least the possibility of an effective or determined attack against us in the Atlantic while the European nations are actually at grips appears remote. The morrow might have a different picture."[40] Indeed, the fall of France was just six months away and the summer of 1940 brought grave doubts and great anxiety to Stark and Roosevelt about the survival of Britain and the Royal Navy's continued opposition to Germany.

Stark explained to the committee that the navy would utilize the increase to build 3 aircraft carriers (72,000 tons), 8 cruisers (192,000 tons), 52 destroyers (60,000 tons), and 32 submarines (45,000 tons), for a total of 95 ships and 369,000 tons. The remaining 31,000 tons would be held in reserve to be applied among the various types of ships as design improvements and military consideration might dictate.[41]

Congress was in an economy mood and Vinson had to trim his sails accordingly. Ten days after the hearing began, Vinson introduced a substitute measure. It provided for little more than half of the originally proposed expansion. The reductions were made by eliminating the 52 destroyers and by significantly reducing the number of cruisers and submarines. Only the provision for aircraft carriers remained intact. The total cost reduction was estimated to be more than one third of the original cost. It was the single biggest reduction in the economy drive then underway in Congress. Nevertheless, further cuts were in store for the bill. The following week the Vinson committee reduced the cruiser and submarine categories by another $200 million.[42] On 31 January 1940 the House Naval Affairs Committee unanimously approved amendments that authorized an expansion of the navy of only 11 percent.

The reductions were more apparent than real. Nominally, Stark's proposed 25 percent expansion had been cut by more than half and it was now a two-year instead of a five-year program. What Vinson's committee did, however, was to authorize the first two years of the building program Stark had proposed. The committee made it clear that if international conditions continued to deteriorate, the navy would be more than welcome to return to ask for more. The committee expressly left the door open for additional authorizations.[43] Meanwhile, there were sufficient authorizations to utilize the existing navy and private shipyard facilities to capacity. In any event, the nation would not be committed to an enormously expensive five-year program, but only to a two-year program, which was expensive enough.

As finally reported out of committee, the 1940 Naval Expansion Bill provided for

- 167,000 combatant tons for 21 ships at an estimated cost of $372,750,000.
- 75,000 auxiliary tons for 22 ships at an estimated cost of $183,300,000.
- 1,011 airplanes at an estimated cost of $99,152,270.

The total estimated cost of the program was $654,902,750.[44]

The fairly extensive construction program already in progress by January 1940 further explains why the reduction of the proposed 1940 shipbuilding program from 25 to 11 percent expansion was more apparent than real. Both private and navy shipyards were building near to capacity. Stark assured the committee that the proposed expansion program plus new construction already authorized and replacements could be taken care of "if we get the money."[45] Even without the 11 percent expansion that the House Naval Affairs Committee ultimately recommended, the United States was committed to an extensive and very expensive program. Unfortunately, the program already authorized would not return the United States to the position of relative strength of five to three over Japan; a new program would be necessary. The outbreak of war in Europe and perceived Japanese intentions to expand in Asia were grim facts that had to be faced. In its report, the House committee bluntly stated, "Failure to readjust opinion—and actions—to meet changing conditions is an enexcusable form of stubborness which approaches stupidity. In other words, we must abandon all 1939 ideas which did not meet 1940 conditions."[46] On the House floor, Vinson noted that "today the language of Europe is force" and he urged that the United States be ready to meet force with force.[47]

In presenting the bill to the House, Vinson stated that because Congress would be in session every year, a two-year program would be sufficient, at least for the moment. He pointed out that the 11 percent increase in the navy would not provide parity with Great Britain nor would it provide a five to three ratio with Japan. But it was an orderly step in that direction. The bill was a bare minimum below which it would be dangerous to go. At the very least, it would permit the navy to increase step by step with the rest of the world's navies. After a relatively short debate, the House approved the 11 percent expansion bill by a vote of 305 to 37 on 12 March 1940.

The naval expansion bill was than sent to the Senate. Senator David I. Walsh of Massachusetts scheduled hearings before the Senate Naval Affairs Committee to begin in mid-April. During the month between the bill's passage by the House and the start of the Senate hearings, Vinson and Walsh agreed that instead of an 11 percent increase, the bill should provide for a 25 percent increase as it was originally drafted. Vinson sensed that Congress was no longer in an economy mood as it had been in January and that the House would support the increase. Walsh felt the Senate would go along.[48] The import of their willingness to support a 25 percent increase was that the larger program would extend over five years and the shipbuilders could plan accordingly. Efficiency and economy would thus be encouraged. There would be no increase in the number of ships built over the next two years, because the 11 percent program would utilize all existing public and private shipbuilding capacity.

It is not clear just when Vinson or Walsh told Stark of their intention to support the 25 percent expansion program. Stark knew of it on 10 April when he discussed the matter with Captain Daniel J. Callaghan, the president's naval aide, and later that day with the bureau chiefs. Stark had an appointment with Roosevelt the next morning. Vinson telephoned him before he left for the White House and they discussed the best way for Stark to convince Roosevelt to support a 25 percent increase: Stark would stress the economies of scale that would be achieved by laying down the ships in blocks rather than one or two at a time. Vinson asked Stark to call him back and let him know what happened. Before he saw the president, Stark telephoned Senator Walsh to let him know what was going on.

Stark's meeting with Roosevelt that morning was eminently successful. The President favored the increase and, more important, he approved Stark's request for more than $27 million to start the program. This additional appropriation would be necessary regardless of whether the total program was for two years with an 11 percent expansion or for five years with a 25 percent expansion. Stark informed Vinson and Walsh by telephone of the President's response. Walsh said he had an appointment with the President the next day and at his suggestion Vinson and Stark were also invited to the White House.[49]

Something happened within the ensuing 24 hours to change Roosevelt's mind. After wavering, he told Stark, Vinson, and Walsh that he favored only an 11 percent increase, rather than the 25 percent increase he had approved the day before. Probably after giving his approval to Stark, budgetary considerations convinced him to change his mind.

The Senate hearing opened on 15 April and continued into early May. Again Stark was the lead witness. In his opening remarks, he regretted the decision of the House to approve only the first two years of the original five-year naval expansion program. However, the bill as approved was acceptable. The justification for the bill was essentially the same that he presented to Vinson's committee: the 5:5:3 ratio was designed to provide security for the signatories of the 1922 Washington treaty. Other countries, notably Japan, had embarked on construction programs that had upset the naval balance. Therefore, the United States must build at least to treaty levels as a matter of prudence in view of the uncertainties and unforeseen events that lay ahead. He denied any expectation of American involvement in the current war.[50] There was no serious opposition in the committee, which reported the bill favorably in mid-May.

The Senate hearings were enlivened by the testimony of Rear Admiral Joseph K. Taussig, who was called as a witness because of his knowledge of Far Eastern affairs. Taussig emphasized that he spoke only for himself. He spoke frankly and bluntly on a very delicate topic, saying what was on the minds of many naval officers and possibly the President as well: Japan was a threat to American interests in the Far East. He added, "I cannot see how we can escape being forced into eventual war by the present trend of events." Such a war would have to be fought with the French, British, and Dutch as allies because of "our lack of impregnable bases in Guam and the Philippines. It would also be a naval war." Preparedness in the form of a big navy was necessary to deter Japanese aggressions. Simply put, Taussig's point was that war in the Far East would be inevitable unless the United States had a large navy as a deterrent to Japan. Newspaper reports of his testimony subordinated this important qualification to his more dramatic statement about the inevitability of war. It was news. *The New York Times* carried the story on page one.[51]

Official reaction in Washington came swiftly. Taussig made his statement in the morning. In the early afternoon, Secretary of State Cordell Hull telephoned Stark. He was highly annoyed at this unnecessary complication, as he saw it, in his dealing with Japan. He pointed out that Taussig's statement would not get appropriations. Rather, it would give the "demagogues and jingoes over in Japan a chance to raise the devil generally and we get nothing out of it except to scare a lot of people here against the whole government." He told Stark he would carry his protest to Roosevelt.[52]

It was clear that the Navy Department would have to issue a statement pointing out that Taussig spoke only for himself and not for the navy and reiterating official policy that naval preparedness measures were directed against no one particular country. They were dictated by prudence to maintain American strength relative to that of other nations. Stark had a draft of a statement ready when Roosevelt telephoned him later in the day, apparently after having talked with Hull. Roosevelt was understandably angry. This was not the first time Roosevelt and Taussig had tangled. In 1918 when Roosevelt was Assistant Secretary of the Navy he and Taussig had locked horns over a personnel matter. Taussig felt Roosevelt was undermining discipline, hence hurting morale. The result was a lasting and mutual enmity.[53]

Roosevelt wanted to relieve Taussig forthwith from his post as Commandant, Fifth Naval District in Norfolk, Virginia and send him home to await orders rather than convene a court-martial, which would only give Taussig an opportunity to repeat what he had said. Roosevelt was "a little tired of Joe anyway, because he has been saying a lot of loose things all around for the last two or three years." Roosevelt wanted to see Taussig "bounced for making a damn fool of himself." He told Stark, "Free speech is all right, but if a fellow makes an ass of himself. . . . In free speech he is not part of the government any longer." Although Taussig's statement annoyed him, Stark realized it would be unwise to relieve him. But first, he had to do his best to soothe the irate president. He admitted, "Your judgment is probably better than mine" and he urged Roosevelt "to ponder it just a little bit." Stark was concerned that if Taussig were to be relieved simply for stating his opinion, it would adversely reflect on the navy and on Roosevelt. He talked Roosevelt into letting him sleep on it. Once the matter had been put off, even over night, no official action was taken against Taussig.[54]

The next morning Taussig telephoned Stark from Norfolk. Stark was icy while the somewhat abashed Taussig tried to explain, saying he had been quoted out of context. Stark told him that his bald statement has already been transmitted to Japan. Taussig was anxious that Stark should understand and pass on to Roosevelt that he was not "talking about the immediate future." Taussig made it clear that he did not ask to testify at the hearings, but that he did so at the request of Senator Walsh. Stark said he would make this point perfectly plain to the President, which he did later that morning in a joint telephone call with Assistant Secretary of the Navy, Lewis Compton.[55] By then Roosevelt had calmed down.

The Tokyo press reaction was comparatively mild. *The New York Times* editorialized at length under the headline "Let's Keep Our Sanity." The gist was that Taussig's view of the inevitability of war did not represent American public opinion.[56] The most extreme reaction came from Senator Bennett Clark of Missouri who felt Taussig's statement might well be the subject of a court-martial since public rebukes by Hull and Stark were insufficient.[57]

By mid-May Stark was optimistic about the chances for eventual passage of the 11 percent expansion bill. Walsh assured him there would be no trouble in the Senate. Certainly, that committee had been friendly and well disposed towards the bill and this attitude was reflected in their favorable report of 14 May. Still, Stark refused to count any proverbial chickens until after the committee's action and the Senate vote. He was particularly pleased with these developments since he thought the fight would be lost when it started in January. He made the effort anyway because he thought the record should be clear that an attempt had been made. His hard work and perseverence paid off on 3 June when after only three minutes of debate, the Senate unanimously passed the bill. Roosevelt signed the 11 Percent Naval Expansion Bill into law on 15 June 1940.[58]

Meanwhile, a new crisis arose. France collapsed and Hitler became master of Europe.

3

SHIFTING, PROBABLE WARS

The collapse of France produced two immediate results in Washington. First, Congress eagerly accepted Stark's breathtaking proposal for a 70 percent increase in the navy and, thereby, authorized a genuine two-ocean navy. Second, the army and navy had to reassess their estimates of the future course of the war in Europe and what it meant for the United States. Stark and Army Chief of Staff General George C. Marshall were clearly alarmed at the sudden appearance of a new and possibly imminent danger to the western hemisphere. Meanwhile, President Roosevelt refused to be distracted from his concern over what the Japanese might do in the Far East as a result of the dire straits of Great Britain and the defeat of France and the Netherlands. In early May he ordered the U.S. Fleet to remain in Hawaii.

With France out of the war, the French fleet could no longer be counted on to oppose Germany. The change in the naval balance in the Atlantic was not good for the United States. Its effect was also felt in the Pacific. This change presented Stark with the insuperable problem of how to divide an inadequate number of ships between the Pacific and the Atlantic to meet growing and increasingly serious threats in both oceans. He decided, as he put it, "to go whole hog." He drafted a second naval expansion bill to provide a good sized fleet for both oceans. He could hardly come to any other conclusion.[1]

Stark consulted with his legal officers on the draft of the two-ocean navy bill on Friday, 14 June, the day before the President signed the 11 percent naval expansion bill. It was a busy weekend. He spent Saturday morning testifying before Congress in favor of deficiency appropriations. Then, over the weekend Stark enlisted Vinson's sup-

39

port and prepared his own statement. Vinson introduced the two-ocean navy bill on Monday. Stark testified on Tuesday, 18 June. He recommended a breathtaking 70 percent increase over the authorized limits of the bill Roosevelt signed only three days before. He recommended an increase of 200 ships, aggregating 1,250,000 tons for warships and 100,000 tons for auxiliaries. The breakdown for warships was: battleships, 385,000 tons; aircraft carriers, 125,000 tons; cruisers, 420,000 tons; destroyers, 250,000 tons; submarines, 70,000 tons. An appropriation bill would have to follow. This program was designed to give the navy complete freedom of action against any opposition in either ocean while carrying on effective defensive operations in the other ocean. The estimated cost was $4 billion.

Beyond saying that world conditions necessitated a dramatic increase in the size of the navy, Stark said nothing more in justification. There was little need to. The newspapers that morning carried banner headlines proclaiming the French request for an armistice. The Allied catastrophe in Europe was sufficient reason to authorize a two-ocean navy. The committee was more interested in whether Stark had asked for enough than they were in why it was needed.

Stark emphasized that all tonnage authorized by the bill just approved and replacement tonnage under the 1934 Vinson-Trammell Act would be laid down as soon as Congress appropriated the money and completed action on a bill authorizing the navy to negotiate contracts without competitive bidding and to advance 30 percent of the contract price for plant expansion in private shipyards. Roosevelt signed this appropriation bill into law on 1 July and less than two hours later the navy let contracts to construct 45 ships at a cost of $550 million.[2]

The only other witness Vinson called before the committee to approve the two-ocean navy bill was Rear Admiral Samuel M. Robinson, Chief of the Bureau of Ships. He added that since all building-ways were in use or would be shortly under the 11 percent expansion program, it would be necessary to increase building facilities at both public and private yards. As Stark drafted it, the bill originally authorized $50 million for this purpose. The committee increased it threefold to $150 million.[3]

The committee was generous with aircraft. The 11 percent naval expansion bill, as finally enacted, authorized 4,500 naval aircraft. The aviation expansion bill approved by Congress one day later on 15

June, authorized 10,000. The committee increased the number to 15,000 after their report had been made by amending the bill on the floor of the House of Representatives, a highly unusual procedure.

The Two-Ocean Navy Bill had two other significant features. The first was a provision authorizing the President to vary upwards or downwards by 30 percent the authorized tonnages for each category of ship so long as the total increase in tonnage did not exceed 1,325,000 tons. This device would help to speed up construction by allowing the navy to build more or less of one type of ship as military and naval considerations might dictate without having to refer the matter to Congress.

The second was an amendment Vinson offered. Its purpose was to prevent destroyers from being sold (already there was much public talk about selling them to Britain) without the consent of Congress and to give Congress a voice in the disposition of the Navy after the war.[4] Stark disagreed with Vinson and he objected to this provision before the Senate Naval Affairs Committee on 3 July. He felt other provisions of law were adequate. The committee agreed with him and deleted Vinson's amendment. Stark was referring to the recent act of 28 June 1940 to expedite national defense. Section 14 prohibited the disposition of military or naval material without certification by the Chief of Naval Operations and the Chief of Staff of the Army that "such material is not essential to the defense of the United States."[5] This provision caused great difficulty in August 1940 when Stark was asked to certify that 50 old destroyers were no longer essential to the defense of the United States.

The House Naval Affairs Committee reported the two-ocean navy bill out on Wednesday and the full house approved it on Saturday, 22 June. One week from conception to passage was quite a record.

The Senate acted almost as swiftly. The two-ocean navy bill was referred to Walsh's committee on Monday, 1 July. Stark testified at secret hearings two days later. The committee reported the bill out on 8 July and the Senate passed it on 10 July. It was sent to the President for signature on 13 July. The Democratic Convention intervened and Roosevelt signed it into law on 19 July, 1940, after he had been nominated for a third term.

With the two-ocean navy bill Congress authorized the navy with which the United States fought World War II. World conditions dictated the creation of a two-ocean navy. Congress willingly followed Stark's recommendation by approving a 70 percent increase in the navy. Stark expected the increase in ships to include 7 battleships, 7 aircraft carriers, 29 cruisers, 115 destroyers, 43 submarines, and 20 auxiliaries. He did not give this breakdown to Congress because the precise numbers and design characteristics would have to be worked out. But with authority to vary each category of ship by 30 percent, the navy was free to design and build ships as the exingencies of naval warfare might require. In addition to authorizing the superb two-ocean navy that fought World War II, Congress, on Stark's recommendation, also laid the foundation for the supremacy of the United States at sea.

Stark was thankful that the events of June 1940 woke up Congress with a bang. He confided to Hart, "What I would give now had I been able to get them in the June Mood six months previous [to] when I first attempted it."[6]

The stunning German success in May and June 1940 surprised and shocked Stark as much as anyone else in Washington. It was completely unexpected. The course of the first six months of the war led Stark to see it in terms reminiscent of the First World War: a stalemate on the western front; the impracticality of an Allied offensive in the Balkans without winning over or defeating Italy; German attacks on British shipping by submarines, air, and mines; and German dependence on external sources of supply, notably oil (most of which came from Rumania). On 1 March Stark sent Roosevelt a rough draft of his estimate of the foreign situation as "light weekend reading." He thought their financial situation might become serious enough to incline the Allies to seek peace. "I wonder sometimes if a quick face saving peace might not be jumped at by both belligerents," he told Roosevelt. It was not an "enthusiastic war" and Stark was concerned over the possibility of a compromise peace.[7] Events shortly proved him wrong.

After the swift enactment of the two-ocean navy bill in June 1940, the greatest concern of Stark and General George C. Marshall, Army Chief of Staff, was a determination of policy under radically changed conditions. Only the President, as commander in chief of the Army and Navy and as head of government, could make the policy, and even then he did not have a completely free hand. He required congressional and public support or at least an absence of strong opposition. Roosevelt instinctively knew he could not afford to lose public support on the transcendently important issues of war and peace. To complicate matters, presidential election years were always bad for the presentation of new policy initiatives. Moreover, in the course of Roosevelt's campaign for an unprecedented third term he would all but promise to keep the United States out of war.

Stark was well aware of the practical difficulties in determining policy in the summer of 1940. It involved ascertaining the goals or objectives the United States sought: Was the paramount American interest to stay out of the war? Or, were there other interests that implied other objectives? If so, what were they? Ever since the end of World War I naval planners had seen Japan as the major potential military and naval threat to American interests. Thus, they considered a Pacific war in defense of those interests to be the most likely. The events of 1940 did not reduce the likelihood of such a war, but instead raised the ugly question as to whether the German threat overshadowed the Japanese threat. This question required a reexamination of the priority of American interests in the light of an extremely fluid situation in which catastrophe had already overtaken one potential ally and clearly threatened to engulf another.

Finally, once it was clear who was in the war and on what side, and once a priority of American interests and objectives had been established, policy would have to determine the courses of action and specific steps necessary to achieve its objectives.

Stark knew that policy is not made in a vacuum. Major decisions may be debated, considered, reviewed, studied, and mulled over before they are actually made; sometimes decisions are the result of consensus, and sometimes a result of clear and specific determination. The decisions facing Stark and Marshall, and ultimately Roosevelt, had to be made in relation to the real world. They had to take into account the course of events and they had to be based on a reasonable degree of certainty. Events in Europe in the spring and early summer of 1940 were moving at such a rapid rate that it was difficult, if not impossible, to determine their ultimate outcome. At that time the bedrock of fact upon which policy decisions should be made did not exist. The result was a lack of policy and hence a lack of direction for the army and the navy until after the presidential election in November 1940.

One thing was certain. In the spring and summer of 1940, the United States was not prepared to fight a major war, and Stark knew it. He also knew that the U.S. Navy was unable at that time to thwart the Imperial Japanese Navy. American, British, and Dutch possessions in the Far East were vulnerable. Throughout 1940 Stark knew that each day brought the country closer to war, but that each day gave another opportunity to prepare for it. Stark recognized the utility of time, the rarest of all commodities. Preparation for war was an obsession with him in the remaining year and a half before the United States formally went to war. He was not sure how much time remained to prepare for war, but he knew that much had to be done. He became impatient over the delays and impediments to his efforts.[8]

One result of the Nazi conquest of Western Europe in the spring and early summer of 1940 was the start of a process in the War and Navy Departments that took into account what was happening in Europe and what appeared likely to happen in Asia. In the course of this process national defense policy came under the most searching scrutiny. Relevant assumptions were identified, challenged, and reexamined. Policy objectives were analyzed. The state of the American Armed Forces was appraised and found wanting. As a result, Stark and Marshall obtained presidential and congressional support and authorization to strengthen the Army and the Navy.

This process involved almost a continuous assessment and evaluation of the course of events and a constant revision of basic strategic plans. For a while it was chaotic because its end product—national defense policy—depended on the resolution of three issues,

1. Where would Hitler stop or be stopped—the Atlantic coast, North Africa, the Suez, or South America?
2. What was the fate of Britain? Did Britain have the resolve and the ability to stay the course and if Britain left the war, what would happen to the Royal Navy?
3. What were Japanese intentions in Asia? Would Japan seize the opportunity to move into Southeast Asia? If so, how? How could Japan be stopped or at least be inhibited?

In the summer of 1940, Stark lived with these unresolved issues and he understood both why their resolution was necessary and why it was not immediately available. Hitler and Japan, not the Allies or the United States, had the initiative. Still, he worried about their outcome. He saw the relationship of events in Europe to possible ones in Asia and how both could seriously affect the United States. His primary concern and responsibility was for the navy and he realized that policy guidance would have to come from the President, either directly or indirectly. The President sought to retain as much flexibility as possible, a prudent course in a rapidly changing situation, but he gave little help to Stark and Marshall.

Germany, joined by Italy in June, seemed to be able to threaten the western hemisphere, and Hitler was not to be trusted. The shock of the collapse of France, her possible defection to the German cause, and the dire straits in which Britain found herself in the summer of 1940 raised grave doubts about the continued belligerency of Great Britain, and possibly the Empire as well. To make matters worse, Japan, already deeply involved in a war in China, was casting expansionist eyes on French Indochina and the Netherlands East Indies. With Hitler occupying western Europe, the French and the Dutch were in no position to offer more than strong diplomatic resistance to Japanese encroachment. It was doubtful that the Vichy regime presiding over a truncated France would offer even that much resistance. The British had more than their hands full in the North Atlantic and in the Mediterranean. They were in no position to deploy to the Far East a fleet sufficient to challenge the Imperial Japanese Navy. The Japanese entry into French Indochina on 22 September followed five days later on 27 September by the conclusion of the Tripartite Pact among Germany, Italy, and Japan raised an expanded war in Asia from a possibility to a probability.

Unlike several senior officers, who were badly shaken at the unexpected turn of events, Stark maintained his inner equilibrium and remained unflappable, however disturbing the news from Europe became.[9] The gloom in Washington continued for several months until it was clear that Britain intended to and could hold out, at least for a while.

At a lengthy meeting at the White House on 22 May, Stark and Marshall discussed with Roosevelt the possibility of a German victory over both Britain and France. If it happened, South America would be vulnerable to Nazi supported revolution and even to actual German intervention. They sought to avoid involvement with Japan and to concentrate on the paramount U.S. interest in the security of the western hemisphere.[10]

Two days later Stark ordered the Navy's War Plans Division to prepare, in conjunction with the Army War Plans Division, a plan for the emergency occupation of European possessions in the western hemisphere. It was ready in four days. It recognized that in any proposed peace terms Germany "may demand the cession of some or all" of British, French, and Dutch possessions in the western hemisphere. In that case, the United States should assert sovereignty over these possessions rather than protective custody, the planners recommended.[11] It would preclude their cession to Germany under any circumstances.

This plan was nothing less than a recommendation for an outright preemptive seizure of the sovereign territory of other nations. Its justification was national defense, although technically the United States was not at war with Germany. Even though Congress was by no means officially in favor of supporting such drastic action before the fact, it did pass a Joint Resolution on 17 and 18 June opposing the transfer of European possessions in the western hemisphere to another power.[12] The main reason the plan was not executed was that it would give Japan an excuse to do the same thing in the Pacific, which is precisely what Washington sought to prevent.

In addition to the possible threat of external German aggression against the western hemisphere, Nazi inspired revolution was thought to be more likely. Stark conferred with his staff about what action might be required in the event of a German *Putsch* in Argentina. Roosevelt interrupted this meeting with a telephone call to Stark. He told Stark to prepare with Marshall a plan to support the Brazilian Government in any revolt instigated by the Axis powers. Captain Alan G. Kirk, the U.S. Naval Attache in London, had received information from the Admiralty that an expedition of 6,000 men was on its way to Brazil, where it would be assisted by Axis sympathizers ashore and by Axis merchant ships already in Brazilian ports.[13]

Working feverishly over the weekend, the planners had a draft plan ready by Monday, 27 May. Operation "Pot of Gold" provided for troop movements of 100,000 men to northeast Brazil. Unfortunately the U.S. Army lacked the men to execute the plan, and naval forces then in the Atlantic were also insufficient to protect the sea lanes to the area. Additional naval forces would be required if the move were opposed by the German or Italian navies. Thus, it would be necessary to move a detachment of the fleet from the Pacific to the Atlantic. In view of the deterrent role of the fleet in the Pacific, careful consideration of the effect of such a move was necessary. Moreover, the planners realized the political implications of the dispatch of American military forces to Latin America without any widely publicized invitation. They called to Stark's attention the possibility that an intervention of that kind could lead to further difficulties in other Latin American countries.[14] Indeed, the cure they proposed might well be worse than the ailment.

There was more bad news from London. American Ambassador Joseph P. Kennedy cabled the State Department on 27 May that there was a "distinct possibility" of the fall of the Churchill government, then less than three weeks old. The western front was collapsing and it looked as though the French might sue for peace with Germany. If that happened, Churchill and his government would undoubtedly fight on if they remained in office. But it was possible that Churchill would be replaced by someone who would seek a settlement with Germany.[15]

Events continued in their own inexorable way. The next day King Leopold of Belgium surrendered himself and his country to the Germans, and the evacuation of the British Expeditionary Force from Dunkerque began. Meanwhile, Roosevelt abruptly summoned Stark to the White House on 28 May to discuss the possible evacuation of American citizens from Europe.[16]

Urgency was the spirit of the day. The Army-Navy Joint Board approved a plan to meet the possibility of the neutralization or destruction of both the French and British fleets. In that situation Germany would have a free hand in the Atlantic. The service secretaries sent it to the President.[17] Plans to speed up mobilization were already in progress. On 13 June Roosevelt requested authority from Congress to call into active service portions of the national guard "to maintain our position of neutrality and to safeguard the national defense." Roosevelt stated the case for urgency and the necessity for immediate action: "The one most obvious lesson of the present war in Europe is the value of the factor of speed. There is definite danger in waiting to order the complete equipping and training of armies after a war begins."[18]

Italy ended the suspense about her intentions and attacked France on 10 June, the day after the French government moved from Paris to Tours. Roosevelt rose to the occasion at the University of Virginia where he minced no words about the threat to the United States. "Military and naval victory for the gods of force and hate would endanger the institutions of democracy in the western world, and that equally, therefore, the whole of our sympathies lies with those nations that are giving their life blood in combat against those forces. On this tenth day of June 1940 the hand that held the dagger has struck it into the back of its neighbor." He promised that America would pursue two simultaneous and obvious courses; aiding the Allies and a speeding up American mobilization.[19]

Roosevelt's speech was not empty rhetoric; it was a statement of what was already in progress. He had already requested $1 billion from Congress for national defense and on 4 June he directed Stark and Marshall "to scrape the bottom of the barrel" to provide private firms with guns and ammunition for immediate sale to the British.[20] Ambassador Kennedy underlined the gravity of the situation on 12 June when he reported, "England's only remaining defense is courage . . . not arms." He predicted a German invasion of Britain by August and a German-Italo move against South America if Britain fell.[21]

This sudden and disastrous turn of events presented the United States with an extraordinary strategic problem. Stark was perplexed and worried. The Germans, having conquered northern Europe and France, would undoubtedly turn the full fury of their air and sea forces, and quite possibly their land forces as well, against the British Isles. Could Britain hold out? Would the British people and Parliament support the Churchill government? The United States was still unprepared to face a major challenge in either the Pacific or in the Atlantic. The fall of Britain would mean the collapse of the first line of defense for the United States. Would material aid from the United States be sufficient to help Britain hold out? Would the active intervention of the still unprepared U.S. Armed Forces turn the tide and help to stem the Nazi flood? The army was certainly not ready to engage in major operations outside the United States. The navy was in better condition. It had 595 ships in commission and a significant building program had already been approved by Congress.[22]

Roosevelt had to weigh the possible effects of American intervention in the Euorpean war with ill-prepared armed forces against the dangers of remaining at least nominally neutral and risking British departure from the war. He could not avoid making some decision, and when he did, Stark and Marshall would have the policy guidance they needed. Whatever decision Roosevelt would make, the navy was by far the most powerful and combat-ready military instrument of the United States. This fact enhanced Stark's position in the councils of government.

In late June, Stark, Marshall, Under Secretary of State Sumner Welles, and their staffs conducted almost continuous discussions in and among their departments on the shape of foreign and defense policies and on the more pressing decisions that had to be made almost at once in the light of a rapidly changing strategic environment. These problems and conditions were not unexpected; they had been the subject of study and thought by the army and navy planners for at least two years. Only the precise, specific circumstances eluded them. In June 1940 they labored to ascertain which assumptions would prove to be valid. At root they were trying to determine where the German Army would stop and who would be in the war when it did. A consensus was reached and Roosevelt approved it on 24 June.

Defense of the western hemisphere had first priority. This concept underlay decisions relating to strategic planning, defense preparations, and aid and assistance to Britain. It was based on a realization of where America's primary interests lay and their paramount nature. National interests in the Pacific were important, but they were clearly subordinate to the defense of the western hemisphere. The logical corollary was that the United States would concentrate on a strategic defensive in the Pacific, even if Japan forced hostilities. Aid to Britain would be conditioned upon continued effective British resistance to Germany and Italy to prevent the Axis from gaining access to the western hemisphere.[23]

With a strategic defensive contemplated for the Pacific and with the main emphasis on hemispheric defense, Stark felt that at least a portion of the U.S. Fleet then concentrated in Hawaii should be deployed to the Atlantic where Hitler presented the most dangerous threat. Supported by Under Secretary of State Sumner Welles, Stark urged Roosevelt on 18 June to transfer a major part of the fleet from the Pacific to the Atlantic.[24] He reminded Roosevelt that the main threat to the United States was in the Atlantic and the continued belligerency of both the French and British fleets was not at all assured. This perception argued for a transfer of the fleet to the Atlantic. In regard to the Pacific, he agreed (at least for the record) that the fleet was a major deterrent to Japanese expansion into the

Netherlands East Indies and that it would remain only "so long as other manifestations of government policy do not let it appear that the location of the fleet is a bluff." Withdrawal of a portion of the fleet could be counterbalanced, however, by "maintaining pressure on Japan by the restriction of exports to Japan."[25]

The President took the matter under advisement. Roosevelt called Stark to the White House where again they discussed the deployment of the fleet. Roosevelt decided that it would remain in the Pacific. Its reassignment to the Atlantic, he felt, would be an unnecessary sign of weakness to Japan. Roosevelt still subscribed to the largely unprovable but plausible theory of the deterrent effect of the fleet on Japan and he could not see any adequate substitute for it at that time. He did, however, keep an open mind on the matter. It was agreed that if the French Fleet fell into German hands, then there would be no alternative to transferring a major portion of the U.S. Fleet to the Atlantic in view of the paramount American interests there. In other words, the President did not feel that the situation in the Atlantic was critical enough to justify a demonstration of weakness in the Pacific where American interests were agreed to be secondary.

In retrospect Roosevelt's decision not to transfer major fleet units to the Atlantic seems to have been correct. Nevertheless, Stark challenged Roosevelt's decision and made his case for transfer as strong as he could. The intimacy and trust between the two men and Stark's own character permitted him to do it. It is doubtful if any other naval officer could have obtained as complete a hearing. Once the decision was final, however, Stark loyally supported it, even though he disagreed with it.

The question of material aid to Britain was more difficult. Stark and Marshall agreed that all aid short of war should be given to Britain in the interest of national security, at least as long as it appeared that the British would be able to hold out against the German onslaught. They strongly opposed the release of new equipment urgently required by the army and navy for their own rearmament. Drawing a fine distinction, Stark and Marshall agreed with Roosevelt that material that could be spared should be turned over to the British because they felt it would help "Great Britain to resist until the first of the year" (January 1941).[26]

The risks were high in giving material aid to Britain that could be put to good use at home. They were justified, however, because the survival of Britain as a belligerent was necessary to the security of the United States. Roosevelt, along with Stark and Marshall, knew what the risks were at the end of June 1940 and willingly accepted them.

The momentum of the German military machine seemed irresistible. At the end of June Stark saw the European situation as critical. He thought it was all but hopeless as far as Britain was concerned.[27] The awful possibility that the Royal Navy would no longer oppose German expansion in the North Atlantic and European waters or in the Mediterranean, loomed large. Stark was worried that the shield the Royal Navy had provided since the early 19th century might be removed. Then, the United States and the western hemipshere would be exposed to the full force of an aggressive expansionist European power.

When France withdrew from the war, her fleet no longer opposed Hitler and many feared a benevolent French neutrality towards Germany at best, and surrender of the fleet at the worst. Even though France fell to Hitler, many French Navy ships remained in ports beyond the limits of metropolitan France. The British made repeated pleas and had extensive parleys with the local French naval commanders in Alexandria and Mers el-Kebir to join the British Fleet and continue the war against Germany, or at least proceed to British or West Indian ports. Satisfactory arrangements were made at Alexandria, but when the British efforts at Mers el-Kebir had come to naught, in early June the Royal Navy opened fire on its erstwhile ally in an attempt to neutralize the French Fleet or at least to prevent that part of it from falling into enemy hands. Regardless of the justification or necessity for this attack, it left a bitter feeling among Frenchmen and a sickening feeling among the British.[28]

The Mers el-Kebir incident was a relatively minor event, yet it underscored what could happen when an ally sought an armistice with the enemy. As a professional naval officer, Stark could sympathize with both the French in their excruciating dilemma of conflicting loyalties and with the British in their desperation. In those grim days of late June and early July 1940 it took little imagination to conceive of the U.S. Navy finding itself in a position similar to that of the Royal Navy at Mers el-Kebir, and of the Royal Navy in a position similar to the French Navy, if Britain sued for peace. This was only one of the possible nightmares that threatened to become a frightening reality. The dimensions of this possible, if not probable, strategic situation with its attendant perils were clear to Stark and to the navy planners.

Despite the grave concern and even outright pessimism in official Washington over the chances of British survival in the war, the fact still remained that only Britain stood between Hitler and the western hemisphere. Hence, all material aid to Britain was not only in the general interest of the United States, but, more specifically, when the British used it they would be surrogate defenders of the country. The transfer of 50 overage U.S. Navy destroyers to the Royal Navy in exchange for 99-year leases for bases on British territory in the New World dramatized American material and political support for Britain in the late summer of 1940. It almost brought Stark to the point of resignation.

The British desperately needed the ships to augment their forces escorting convoys across the Atlantic. The idea of lending, selling, or giving these ships to Britain was not new. The idea received a great deal of publicity in the late spring and early summer of 1940,[29] and was bruited about in the press at about the same time Stark was pleading with the House and Senate appropriations committee for supplemental funds to refit these ships and make them ready for duty with the U.S. Navy. Stark argued that because of the real and potential seaborne threats to the United States, these destroyers were necessary to the defense of the country. The chief naval lesson of World War I was clear: destroyers were absolutely necessary to insure the safe arrival at their destinations of trans-Atlantic convoys. Since Stark was responsible for preparing the U.S. Navy for the future, he did not look with favor upon suggestions to transfer destroyers to another navy, even the Royal Navy, especially because it was not at all clear that the British could or would continue to fight.

Secretary of the Navy Frank Knox was an enthusiastic and uncritical supporter of the transfer. Stark held a more objective view. Finally, on 16 August, Stark was formally brought into the discussions when Knox directed him to arrange for the transfer of 50 old destroyers to the British in exchange for 99-year leases for the bases. Statutory authorization for the proposed transfer required Stark, as Chief of

Naval Operations, to certify that the destroyers were no longer necessary for the defense of the United States. He bluntly pointed out to Knox that such a transfer was impossible. Not only would it be impossible to find a board of three officers to make such a determination, but "obviously on the face of it" the British would not be so anxious to get the destroyers if they were obsolete and useless. He told Roosevelt as much. The President cannily agreed that Stark could not make a certification "independent of other considerations."[30]

However, Stark did see a trade as the one way by which the ships could be transferred. Such a trade would be an exchange of the ships for sovereignty, not leases, over the islands of Trinidad, St. Lucia, Jamaica, the Bahamas, British Guiana, Bermuda, and part of Newfoundland. When Knox told Stark the exchange would involve leases, he did not specify the anticipated terms of the leases. Stark saw several major problems with leases. The chief one was that "a lease made today may be invalidated tomorrow." He did not think the Churchill government would renege, but he feared that a successor government, perhaps one dedicated to appeasing and placating Hitler, might attempt to abrogate the leases. He advised Knox that if public opinion were to support a ship-for-bases deal, it would have to be a "good horse trade."

Stark was not as concerned with how the American public would regard the trade as he was with possible congressional reaction. He had an established reputation on Capitol Hill for honest, frank, and open dealing with Congress. As a result, relations between Congress and the Navy Department were excellent. Having already obtained funds to refit and operate the 50 destroyers on the grounds that they were necessary for national defense, Stark simply could not certify them as useless and obsolete, no matter how much his failure to do so might embarrass the President. He threatened to resign rather than make the certification. He told Knox that his feelings on the matter were so strong that he thought he ought to be relieved if he jeopardized the navy's goodwill before Congress.[31] He was profoundly troubled by the statutory requirement of certification before the ships could be transferred, because it put him in the extremely awkward position of having to approve or disapprove a presidential decision.

Stark discussed the legal problems involved with the Justice Department. He observed how simple it would be if the President in his capacity as commander in chief of the Navy would order the ships transferred without any certification. The Justice Department was already considering that possibility. The Attorney General, Robert H. Jackson, produced a legal opinion that removed Stark from the dilemma: Stark could properly certify that the 50 destroyers were not essential to defense of the United States if the prospective bases would be of greater value for the same purpose. Jackson's opinion solved the legal problem, and provided straightforward justification to Congress for the transfer. Obviously, if the transfer would result in a net gain for the naval defense of the country, it was in the national interest. In this manner Stark would not compromise his position before Congress and he could issue the certification in good faith in accordance with the President's wishes.

Hitler's triumph in Europe and the threat it posed required giving priority to the defense of the western hemisphere. In the spring of 1940 the U.S. Fleet was based on the west coast; the naval forces in the Atlantic were only a small portion of the available American naval strength. It would have been relatively simple to transfer a significant portion of the fleet from the Pacific to the Atlantic. However, the U.S. Fleet, with its imposing battleline, was the most powerful instrument Roosevelt had at his disposal to deter Japanese moves against American, British, and Dutch possessions in the Far East. Ultimately, the size of the fleet that remained in the Pacific was determined on the basis of an evaluation of the danger and immediacy of the respective threats both in the Pacific and in the Atlantic. At first it was simply a question of how long the fleet would remain in Hawaii, away from its home ports on the west coast.

But there was more. This issue brought Stark into conflict with Roosevelt and it sorely vexed Admiral James O. Richardson, the fleet commander. Stark was caught in the middle between his fleet commander and his commander in chief. The result was that the fleet remained in Hawaii, contrary to Stark's advice, and Roosevelt lost confidence in Richardson, who was relieved by Admiral Husband E. Kimmel nearly a year before the normal end of his tour of duty.

The U.S. Fleet left its west coast bases on 2 April to conduct the annual fleet training exercise. At its conclusion the fleet was scheduled to return to its home ports where many officers and enlisted men were due to be rotated in accordance with normal peacetime procedures. Many of the ships were scheduled for routine repairs and shipyard overhauls. The fleet was scheduled to remain in the Hawaiian area until 9 May before leaving for the west coast, where it was scheduled to arrive around 17 May.

On 29 April Roosevelt met with Stark, Assistant Secretary of the Navy Lewis Compton, and Real Admiral Chester W. Nimitz, Chief of the Bureau of Navigation (later Personnel) in the White House. Among other things, they discussed a proposed dispatch to Richardson. Shortly after Stark returned to his office, Roosevelt telephoned and either approved or dictated the final text of the dispatch to Richardson. He specifically directed Stark to send it.[32] It read:

IN VIEW OF THE POSSIBILITY OF ITALY BECOMING AN ACTIVE BELLIGERENT IN MAY, YOU MAY RECEIVE INSTRUCTIONS TO REMAIN IN HAWAIIAN WATERS WITH THE SHIPS OF THE FLEET THEN IN COMPANY WITH YOU X CHANGES IN SCHEDULED MOVEMENTS INDIVIDUAL UNITS PRIOR 9 MAY NOT CONTEMPLATED X UTMOST SECRECY IS DESIRED FOR THE PRESENT[33]

He directed Richardson to acknowledge its receipt.

A major change in the operating schedule of the fleet would involve enormous problems of logistics, supply, and further training, The fleet's bases were on the west coast and the Navy's infrastructure at that time was geared to support it there, not in Hawaii. Not the least of the problems that would arise from keeping the fleet in Hawaii was the effect on the morale of the officers and men, whose families were on the west coast.

Stark was acutely aware of the problems Richardson would face if the fleet remained in Hawaii for any appreciable time. In the White House discussions, Stark vigorously pointed out to the President the problems involved, but with little success. Stark made it a rule to keep his subordinates informed to the greatest possible extent and he insisted upon maximum advance notice to Richardson. The most Stark could give him at that time, however, was a promise of "something confirmatory one way or the other" a few days before his scheduled sailing date of 9 May.[34] It was cold comfort to Richardson.

Richardson was told on Saturday, 4 May, that "it looks probable but not final" that the fleet would be ordered to remain in Hawaiian waters for "a short time" after 9 May. Officially, the fleet was still scheduled to leave Hawaiian waters for the west coast the following Thursday, 9 May. Two days before the fleet was due to sail, Roosevelt telephoned Stark and told him to delay its departure for about two weeks.[35] Stark sent this news to Richardson by dispatch. This message also concocted a cover story for the delay. Richardson was directed to issue a press release that he had requested permission to remain in Hawaii in order "to accomplish some things." Understandably this subterfuge irritated Richardson, not only because it was amateurish, but also because he thought it made him out to be a "nitwit."[36] As transparent as this explanation for keeping the fleet in Hawaii may have been, it was probably the best that could have been devised at that time.

At the White House Stark bluntly told Roosevelt he thought the fleet should return to its west coast bases, where it could be put into a higher state of readiness than was possible in Hawaii. With its combat potential enhanced, the fleet would be a more effective deterrent against the Japanese.[37] Even if the main fleet returned to the west coast, the Hawaiian detachment consisting of light cruisers, an aircraft carrier, destroyers, and submarines, would remain in Hawaii for the deterrent effect it would have on Japan. Stark favored keeping the detachment there, but not the entire fleet.[38] Roosevelt overruled him. Nevertheless, Stark delayed for one week before transmitting Roosevelt's order to Richardson, even though he was aware of Richardson's need for maximim advance notice. He hoped that Roosevelt would relent and change his mind. The President did not and the fleet remained in Hawaii.

To both Stark and Richardson the decision to hold the fleet in Hawaii was irritating, frustrating, and awkward. Indeed, it was nothing less than a haphazard improvisation by Roosevelt. Richardson disliked the unscheduled interruption in his fleet's schedule, particularly since the fleet could be placed in a higher state of readiness by returning to its home ports. Keeping the fleet in Hawaii made no sense to Richardson. Also, he had little tolerance for anyone or anything that interfered with the efficient operation of the fleet.

Roosevelt had another perspective. He was unsure how far the blitzkreig in early May 1940 would carry the Germans into Europe and he was even more uncertain of the effect European events would have on Japanese action in the Far East. The Dutch, British, and French were not in a position to offer substantial resistance to the Japanese, who could upset the political and military balance in east Asia with little difficulty. By keeping the fleet in Hawaii Roosevelt did as much as he felt he could to maintain stability in the Pacific. An expansion of hostilities there in 1940 could have involved the United States in a Pacific war when an even greater threat loomed in the Atlantic, especially if Germany should triumph over France and Britain.

Stark was caught in the middle between Richardson and Roosevelt. He was well aware of the great strategic problems the President faced. He sympathized with Roosevelt out of personal and official loyalty. He was also acutely aware of the operational and logistic problems that Richardson faced, and, as Chief of Naval Operations, he was responsible for their solution.[39] Stark was obliged by practice and common sense to keep Richardson and the other fleet commanders informed of the reasons underlying his decisions. Yet in this instance he could hardly tell Richardson that the President was engaging in haphazard improvisation, which was obvious to Richardson anyway. Instead, he wrote to Richardson on 7 May, telling him that the reason the fleet was being retained in Hawaii was because of doubt as to the intentions of Italy.[40] He wrote again on 22 May, "When we sent our dispatch it looked as if Italy were coming in almost immediately and that a serious situation might develop in the East Indies, and that there was a possibility of our being involved."[41] The fleet in Hawaii was to be used as a deterrent against Japan.

The German blitzkrieg produced in Stark a mixture of caution and apprehension about the deployment of the fleet in the Pacific. Stark agreed with Richardson that any move west would mean hostilities with Japan. Both men realized that an involvement in the Far East would reduce American capability to defend the western hemisphere. Both men saw that American interests in the Far East were important, but were subordinate to those in the western hemisphere. Stark advised Richardson to keep constantly in mind the possibility of "a complete collapse of the Allies, including the loss of their fleets." Such a development would clearly leave the United States isolated. It would be the worst of all strategic possibilities. In such an event, suspected German penetration in Argentina, Uruguay and Brazil might pose a serious threat to the hemisphere. Stark wondered, "*If* Germany should win—then what????"[42]

Richardson was aware of the deteriorating world situation and of the real and potential dangers facing the United States. But his main concern and primary responsibility was the fleet. Richardson was generally dissatisfied with the lack of policy guidance he received from Stark. He thought he could resolve doubts and clear up ambiguities if he talked directly with Roosevelt.[43] Stark welcomed such a meeting. It would be a good way to impress upon Roosevelt the needs of the fleet and also to impress upon Richardson the magnitude of the problems Stark and Roosevelt faced. However, more than two months passed before Richardson got to Washington.

Finally, Richardson could wait no longer to plan the fleet schedule and deployments for the coming months. To do so intelligently he had to know why the fleet was in Hawaii and how long it would be there. Bluntly, he asked Stark if the fleet was in Hawaii "primarily to influence the actions of other nations" or if it was there "as a stepping off place for belligerent activity?" He minced no words in outlining the implications of an affirmative response to either question.[44]

Stark's reply was conciliatory, frank, and informative. He understood Richardson's position and he assured him that "I know exactly what you are up against and . . . that here in the Department we are up against the same thing." The fleet was in Hawaii because of "the deterrent effect which it is thought your presence may have on the Japs going to the East Indies." He reminded Richardson of his previous reference to the Italian connection. "The connection is that with Italy in . . . the Japs might feel just that much freer to take independent action. We believe that the Germans and the Italians have told the Japs that as far as they are concerned she, Japan, has a free hand in the Dutch East Indies."[45]

As Stark saw it, developments in the Far East would probably follow the course of the war in Europe. If things were indefinite in Europe, they were even more so in Asia. He did not know what the United States would do if the Japanese moved into the Netherlands East Indies and he was sure "there is nobody on God's green earth who can tell you." Stark felt that American interests in Asia were important, but the security of the western hemisphere was paramount. For this reason the United States should avoid involvement in Asia. If the United States did not intend to become involved in the Far East, "we must not breathe it to a soul, as by doing so we would completely nullify the reason for the fleet's presence in the Hawaiian area." He reminded Richardson, "Just remember that the Japs don't know what we are going to do and so long as they don't know they may hesitate or be deterred. Those thoughts I have kept very secret here."[46]

Stark had no idea how long the fleet would be in Hawaii. He repeatedly asked the President this question, but was unable to get an answer. It is doubtful Roosevelt knew how long he intended to keep the fleet in Hawaii. Stark promised to let Richardson know as soon as a decision would be made. He was well aware of the advantages of returning the fleet to the west coast and he forcefully argued his reasons to Roosevelt. The best he was able to obtain was a compromise: permission to return individual ships to the west coast for repairs, overhaul, and replenishment.

Although Stark disclaimed any intention of keeping the fleet in Hawaii to develop it as a peacetime operating base, such development would naturally follow from retention of the fleet there. He pointed out to Richardson that remaining in Hawaii would, among other things, help solve logistic problems, provide training under wartime conditions, familiarize commanders with the general area, improve liaison with the army for the defense of Hawaii, and solve joint army-navy communications problems. Within the following year these indirect and incidental benefits became considerable.[47]

The consensus in Washington was that in Hawaii the fleet was then performing its most valuable service by keeping the Japanese checkmated.[48] Still, Stark was not completely convinced of the deterrent value of the fleet in Hawaii as compared with other and, in his view, more pressing reasons for its return to the west coast or even the transfer of a major portion of it to the Atlantic. Retaining the fleet in Hawaii was not easily accomplished. The problems attendant upon its retention there were peculiarly navy problems, to be dealt with by the naval establishment.

Richardson visited Washington in July. His extensive meetings with Roosevelt, Stark, and others seemed to go smoothly. When another visit was mentioned a few months later, however, Richardson was decidedly not eager to go. He informed Stark that he would go if directed.

The second trip to Washington, in October 1940, was anything but easy and pleasant. Richardson went by air, which involved extended flying time at high altitudes in an unpressurized cabin. He and an aide left California by air and flew straight to Washington, arriving at seven o'clock in the morning. When he arrived at the Navy Department he was exhausted. Nevertheless, he plunged into a round of conferences and meetings with Stark, Knox, and others in the Navy Department.[49]

The next day Richardson lunched with Roosevelt at the White House. At this meeting he deliberately put his admiral's stars on the line. He thought Roosevelt could be shocked either into changing his policies or providing adequate implementation of them. He succeeded in shocking Roosevelt, but that was all. His comments ranged over a number of matters and they were generally disagreeable to the President. He deliberately said, "Mr. President, I feel I must tell you that the senior officers of the navy do not have the trust and confidence in the civilian leadership of this country that is essential for the successful prosecution of a war in the Pacific."[50]

Richardson was aware of the risk he was taking and he attributed his subsequent early relief to this expression of his opinions to his commander in chief. Roosevelt may very well have felt that a fleet commander who disagreed with his policies so strongly and to such an extent could no longer serve. In addition to being at odds with Roosevelt over a number of matters of fundamental importance, Richardson also gave Roosevelt the decided impression that he was a tired old man, lacking confidence and opposed to doing anything at variance with normal routine. Both Roosevelt and Stark knew the navy was not ready for war. Roosevelt may have interpreted Richardson's insistence on returning the fleet to the west coast as evidence of an unacceptable peacetime frame of mind and thus Richardson ought to be relieved. Stark did not share this impression.

Stark had known Richardson since their midshipman days at the Naval Academy and had served under him in USS *Porter* in 1909. He knew that Richardson was not a tired old man, regardless of any impression he may have given Roosevelt. He had full confidence in Richardson's abilities and he understood and sympathized with Richardson's views. He defended him to the President and attempted to talk Roosevelt out of relieving him. Roosevelt remained adamant, and orders for Richardson's relief were finally issued. The most Stark was able to do for him was to delay the relief so that he might remain as fleet commander for one complete year.

Once it was clear that Roosevelt could not be dissuaded from relieving Richardson, Stark had to consider who would be the best replacement. As navy gossip at that time had it, Stark and Roosevelt were discussing the various possible officers to command the Pacific and Atlantic fleets. (The Patrol Force Atlantic was upgraded on 1 February 1941 to the status of a fleet.) Roosevelt wanted the "two toughest sons-of-bitches" to whip both fleets into combat readiness as soon as possible. He told Stark to go back to the Navy Department and consult with other officers on nominations. Stark told Roosevelt there was no need to consult with anyone on the matter. He was sure there would be general agreement that Ernest J. King and Husband E. Kimmell fit Roosevelt's criteria. Roosevelt told Stark to have the orders written for King and Kimmel to command the fleets. Stark asked if he had a preference as to which officer got which fleet. Roosevelt had none.[51] Because King was already commanding the Patrol Force in the Atlantic and Kimmel had a cruiser command at Pearl Harbor, the sensible thing was to give King the Atlantic Fleet and Kimmel the Pacific Fleet.

By late summer 1940 there had been a lot of bad news and very little good news. The best news of all to Stark was that the worst possibilities had not come to pass. True, Hitler had triumphed in the west. He had even stood on the coast at Calais and gazed across at the cliffs of Dover. But Britain had withstood the initial fury of the German offensive. Great Britain, now alone in Europe, braced herself for the air and submarine offensive to come, and for the possibility of an invasion, the first in nearly nine hundred years. Stark noticed that the war had reached a certain degree of stability. Roosevelt was nominated for a third term and American attention turned to the lively and vigorous political campaign, waged against the background of wars in Europe and China.

Stark was grateful for the additional time in which to continue preparing for war. He was determined to make the most of every day of peace that remained.

4

GERMANY FIRST

Shortly after France fell, Tokyo took advantage of British distress in Europe. Responding to Japanese pressure, the British in July 1940 agreed to close the Burma Road for three months. The Burma Road at that time was the principal route by which war material and other supplies could reach China. The Japanese venture in China had bogged down into an apparently inconclusive campaign and Tokyo understandably desired to make things as difficult as possible for Chiang Kai-shek and his Nationalist army. America opposed Japanese expansion in Asia and encouraged Chinese resistance.

Churchill told Roosevelt on 4 October that the British intended to reopen the Burma Road at the expiration of the three-month period on 17 October. At the same time he suggested sending a squadron of naval ships, "the bigger the better," to visit Singapore. Never one to let an opportunity pass, Churchill noted that such a visit would be an ideal opportunity for a "technical" discussion of military and naval matters between British and American officials. The Dutch might even be invited, he suggested.[1]

Churchill's suggestion fell on deaf ears in Washington. Stark opposed it because he felt it was necessary to keep the fleet concentrated in Hawaii, thus maintaining as credible a deterrent as the less than optimum logistic conditions there would permit. Marshall opposed it because he thought that the proposed visit would be provocative and that particular time was as "unfavorable a moment as you could choose."[2] Both Stark and Marshall clearly saw the perils of becoming any more deeply involved in the Far East, an area of secondary importance. Germany was still the most dangerous threat.

Stark's and Marshall's unequivocal opposition to sending a naval detachment to Singapore had little effect on Roosevelt's concern with the possible adverse Japanese reaction to the reopening of the Burma Road. If the Japanese took drastic action (what precisely would constitute drastic action was not specified), Roosevelt was in favor of forcibly shutting off all Japanese trade with South America by establishing two patrol lines in the Pacific: one from Hawaii to the Philippines and a backup line from Samoa to the Netherlands East Indies. In early October, he discussed this course of action with Secretary of the Navy Frank Knox and directed him to discuss it at length with Stark and the commander of the U.S. Fleet, Admiral James O. Richardson, who was then in Washington for consultation with the Navy Department.

Knox called both men into his office late in the afternoon of 10 October. It was not a particularly intimate meeting. When Stark and Richardson received Knox's summons, they were closeted with their respective war plans officers, who accompanied them to the secretary's office. Knox proceeded to relate the gist of what the President had just told him, specifically Roosevelt's proposal to establish the two patrol lines.[3]

When Knox finished, two questions were raised: Did the President intend to stop Japanese ships on the high seas? Because that would be an act of war, did the President intend to ask Congress for a declaration of war? Roosevelt had said nothing to Knox on these two points and all that Knox knew was what the President had told him.

It was clear to Stark that this proposal was simply another one of Roosevelt's spontaneous ideas. It certainly was not the result of mature and considered thought. Stark understood very well how impulsive the President could be. He was familiar with Roosevelt's improvisations, some of which were brilliant and others of which had to be throttled. Stark's immediate task was to kill the idea. He decided the best way was to let Richardson and then others comment freely. They did.

Richardson exploded. He stated flatly that the fleet was neither prepared to put such a plan into effect, nor for the war that would certainly follow. He added gratuitously that he had seen the same thing tried in war games and "it didn't work." He was not alone in his vocal disapproval. Other officers commented on the obvious flaws in the proposal: The President's idea of patrol lines would entail an unwarranted dispersal of ships, thereby subjecting them to unnecessary risk of loss. Knox was informed that it would be easier to control the course of Japanese trade by patrolling the relatively few ports involved, which Roosevelt should have known.

Somewhat suprised at this generally negative reaction, Knox was displeased. Finally, he told Stark and Richardson, "I am not a strategist; if you don't like the President's plan, draw up one of your own to accomplish the purpose."

Stark and Richardson did. The plan they devised was no more than a drill or planning exercise to convince Roosevelt the navy was doing something. Roosevelt's proposal died a natural and well deserved death after the Burma Road was reopened and the Japanese reacted mildly.

Stark had no doubt that Roosevelt would defeat his Republican challenger, Wendell L. Willkie, until recently a Democrat, and be elected to a third term on November 5. He listened to the election returns on the radio until 2230 and then went to bed confident Roosevelt had won. The next day he wrote to Roosevelt at Hyde Park to congratulate him.[4] As an intimate of the President and as a key member of the Roosevelt team, he felt the American people had chosen wisely.

If Willkie had won, there would have been nearly a three-month interregnum during which time a lame duck president would have found it difficult if not impossible to make fundamental decisions binding on his successor. With the election over, continuity in the White House and in the executive branch was assured. More important, Roosevelt, as a re-elected president, could address at once the pressing problems that had been deferred for months pending the outcome of events in Europe and Asia and the American election.

The most immediate need, as Stark saw it, was for a statement of national defense policy that would cover such fundamentals as national interests and political-military objectives and how they might be best obtained. This policy statement did not have to be made public, but it was necessary for the guidance of the army and navy planners. Washington's attention and America's limited military and naval capability should not be distracted by Japanese aggression in the

Pacific while Germany still posed a greater threat to the United States in the Atlantic. At the very worst Japan could seize the Philippines and oust the British, Dutch, and Americans from the Far East.

As Stark and others saw it, Germany could mount a serious threat to the western hemisphere. It was necessary to rivet attention to the Atlantic where the main threat lay and to take whatever steps were necessary and within the power of the U.S. Government to maintain a major defensive effort there. Roosevelt's latest ill-considered plan for naval action in the Pacific was an excellent example of the dangers of becoming entranced with the important, but still secondary, Japanese threat.

Lack of an appropriate and adequate policy upon which war plans or other directives could be based was still causing Stark as much difficulty with his immediate subordinate, Richardson, as it was with Roosevelt. Richardson needed a directive from Washington attuned to the existing naval and political realities in the Pacific in order to operate the U.S. Fleet in a responsible and sensible manner in case of war. In October 1940, Richardson had no such directive.

In the event of war, Richardson would be required to execute the ORANGE Plan, which was fatally flawed. That plan envisioned establishment of a U.S. Joint Asiatic Force in the Marshall-Caroline Islands in strengths superior to the Japanese navy. This force would proceed to the western Pacific for offensive operations against the Japanese. The ORANGE Plan was simply not feasible; that is, American naval strength was insufficient to achieve the stated objective. In addition, the U.S. Army and Marine Corps would not be able to support the westward advance. There were several other flaws in it: The proposed capture and subsequent development of advanced bases were impractical, and the time element was disproportionate to the tasks to be completed. Finally, Richardson told Stark he knew of no flag officer "who wholeheartedly endorses the ORANGE Plan."5

Richardson felt that Stark was having difficulty convincing Roosevelt of the navy's position. However, both Stark's difficulty and his subsequent achievement were much greater than simply urging a parochial view upon Roosevelt. Indeed, Stark's principal accomplishment in the fall of 1940 was to recommend a policy to the President and to obtain his tacit consent. Richardson's comments, while not entirely welcome to Stark, strengthened his hand in dealing with the President.

About that time Stark was immersed in his own personal analysis of the strategic position of the United States in the circumstances at that time. This estimate of the international situation helped Stark clear his own mind. He spent three hours in deep discussion one day in late October with the new Director of the War Plans Division, Captain Richmond Kelly Turner (soon to be elevated to rear admiral), who had been on the job less than one week. Then he withdrew to the quiet of his home and composed the rough draft of what later became known as the Plan Dog Memorandum.[6]

Starting one morning and working continuously and alone until two o'clock the next morning, he produced a rough draft. He confronted his own staff and Rear Admiral Walton R. Sexton, an old friend who was then President of the General Board, with the memorandum on Saturday, 26 October. During the ensuing week, Stark met four times with the same group of officers for periods lasting from two to three hours. They met all day Saturday, 2 November. The result was the first draft, dated 4 November of the Plan Dog Memorandum. It was not a staff paper. Stark was its sole author. He used his associates as a sounding board and as critics.

Stark saw that the moment was ripe for confronting the President with an agreed army-navy recommendation for a major policy decision. He sent this first draft to General George C. Marshall, Army Chief of Staff, for his review and concurrence before he sent it to Secretary of the Navy, Frank Knox. Marshall approved.

Stark continued to polish the memorandum before formally submitting it to Knox on 12 November. Knox sent it to Roosevelt the same day.[7] knowing Roosevelt as he did, Stark did not expect a formal, explicit presidential decision, but he hoped for tacit approval or at the very least an absence of specific disapproval. In this instance, army-navy concurrence put maximum pressure on Roosevelt, if not to accept it, at the very least not to reject it. In that case, Stark and Marshall could then assume the President's concurrence and proceed accordingly until Roosevelt told them otherwise.

Although Stark did not expect an immediate decision, he hoped the memorandum would clarify matters so that "those in authority" would be fully aware of the implications of any particular policy.[8]

Such an awareness would be something new indeed in view of the rather haphazard policy decisions, if that is what they could be called, that had been made or had occurred in the previous few months.

The document is remarkable in several respects.[9] Its language and the exposition of Stark's analysis and reasoning are clear, concise, and lucid. Unlike many later defense documents, it was written in precise, standard English, which contributed to the precision of Stark's thoughts, and it was written without the assistance of civilian political scientists and analysts. It is a masterful example of strategic analysis. In only 26 pages, Stark elucidated the relationship between the war then in progress in Europe with the dangers in Asia and precisely how both would affect the United States. He presented four possible courses of action, discussed each in turn and then made his recommendation.

The Plan Dog Memorandum has been correctly described as one of the most important, if not the most important strategic document of World War II.[10] The influence of this amazing document and its acceptance by the army planners was due in large measure to its incisive analysis, close reasoning, clear language, and general intellectual merits. It was also the right statement at the right time.

Stark made it abundantly clear that until he received an authoritative answer concerining ultimate military objectives, he would be unable to "determine the scale and the nature of the effort the navy may be called upon to exert in the Far East, the Pacific and the Atlantic." The main purpose of this memorandum was to elicit such an answer from the President. Stark did not seek just any answer. He knew what he wanted and he proceeded to state his case so that answer would logically follow.

The irreducible military objective was security of the United States, which was directly related to that of other parts of the western hemisphere. Thus, a threat to the hemisphere would also be a threat to the United States. The collapse of Great Britain or the destruction or surrender of the Royal Navy would "free European military power for possible encroachment in this hemisphere." For this reason, Britain's continuing to fight was fundamental to the security of the United States. Therefore, since Germany posed the greatest threat to Britain, Germany likewise presented the greatest danger to the security of the United States.

This reasoning underlay the memorandum's opening (and frequently quoted) statement, "if Britain wins decisively against Germany, we could win everywhere; but . . . if she loses the problem confronting us would be very great; and while we might not *lose everywhere*, we might, possibly, not win *anywhere*" (emphasis in original). When Stark used the term "win" he meant elimination of the threat, potential or real, to the United States, that is, the ultimate collapse of Nazi Germany. He was not thinking of a limited war.

Stark wanted to start staff talks at once with the British. Such talks would have to be secret, not only for reasons of general discretion, but also because the United States was technically neutral and Roosevelt had just been reelected after virtually promising the American people that the United States would not become involved in the war. Informed observers knew this promise was only so much wishful thinking. Domestic political realities and the necessity to have public opinion behind him would make Roosevelt in 1941 even more cautious and indirect than he normally would have been. Thus, if Stark's memorandum were to be approved or at least not disapproved by the President, it would have to present the case in such a manner that staff talks would be the most reasonable and logical conclusion.

Stark discussed various possibilities as to how and where the United States might become involved in the war. He believed that it was entirely possible for Britain to lose the war, and for the Empire to be disrupted, if the United States did not render active military assistance. He thought the British were overoptimistic about their chances for ultimate success. In the event of a British collapse, he feared Axis penetration in South America, "the only important area of the world not now under the control of strong military powers."

In appraising the possibility of Japanese aggression in the Far East against British and Dutch possessions, Stark saw the potential threat of the Soviet Union as a counter to Japanese ambition, which required the Japanese to maintain significant military forces in Manchuria. Until Hitler attacked the Soviet Union in June 1941, this assumption of a Soviet counterweight to Japan remained valid.

At this point, Stark reviewed the current American strategy for a war against Japan, which was based on the ORANGE Plan. Its underlying assumption was that neither Japan nor the United States would have allies. Skillfully using some of the arguments Richardson had already advanced, Stark showed how such a war would require "several years, and the absorption of the full military, naval, and economic energy of the American people." Stark pointed out the greatest defect of the ORANGE Plan: "Once started the abandonment of the offensive required by the plan to meet a threat in the Atlantic would involve abandoning the objective of the war, and also a great loss of prestige." This was another way of warning against undue involvement in a theater of secondary importance by pointing to the difficulties of shifting a major war effort from the Pacific to the Atlantic.

If the ORANGE Plan were to be adopted, it would require movement of strong navy and army forces to the Far East. It would mean accepting danger in the Atlantic and probably a specific limitation of material assistance to Britain. The naval forces remaining in the Atlantic would obviously mean a reduction, however necessary, of American forces in the Pacific. He doubted that British and Dutch forces alone would be able to hold the Malay barrier against the Japanese. American public opinion might require a stronger effort. The result could very well be that the limited offensive contemplated in the ORANGE Plan would turn into an unlimited effort and "little force would remain for eventualities in the Atlantic and for the support of the British Isles."

Turning his consideration to the Atlantic, Stark was optimistic that so long as a serious commitment in the Pacific was avoided, the purely American problem of hemispheric defense "is not so difficult so long as the British are able to maintain their present naval activity." If Britain were to fail, the United States would be alone and at war with the world. As Stark put it, "We would be thrown back upon our haunches." This was the clinching argument. Stark had reached the point where he could buttress and elaborate on his conviction that American security required the survival of Britain, which in turn required an Atlantic strategy and a recognition of the secondary importance of the Japanese threat in the Pacific.

If the United States were to enter the war as an ally of Britain and then not be at war with Japan, he continued, the British would ask for extensive naval assistance: protection of shipping from Cape Sable to Cape Horn, patrol and surveillance, escort and minesweeping. Perhaps even occupation of the Azores and Cape Verde Islands would be necessary. Naval assistance, no matter how extensive, would not assure final victory over Germany, which meant the destruction of the

German Reich. A land offensive would be necessary on the European continent. However, the British alone lacked sufficient manpower for such a major undertaking. United States air and land forces would be required to participate in the invasion of Europe. The navy would be required to transport the ground forces, food, fuel, ammunition, and all other materials necessary to support and to conduct military operations on the European continent.

Therefore, Stark concluded, the requirements of a major effort in the Atlantic would mean that the United States would be able to do little more in the Pacific "than remain on a strict defensive."

Although Stark put it delicately and tactfully, it is clear that he was asking Roosevelt to come to grips with the strategic problems facing the United States, to accept his analysis of them and to concur in his recommendation. The events of the previous six months had changed the world scene dramatically. War in the Pacific may have been more likely, but the more serious threat was Germany. Stark required an authoritative answer to the question: What is the United State's military objective? Only then could he and his staff determine the scale and the nature of the naval effort to be expended in the Far East, the Pacific, and the Atlantic. With this object in mind, Stark set forth four possible courses of action:

(A) A principal military effort could be directed towards hemispheric defense. This would mean that American influence on the outcome of the European war would be small.

(B) The United States could direct a full offensive against Japan, with the British and Dutch as allies, and maintain a strict defensive in the Atlantic. This course assumed that the British would be able to hold their own indefinitely in the Atlantic. If they were to fail, the United States would be required to reorient its efforts from the Pacific to the Atlantic.

(C) A major effort to assist the British in Europe and the British, Chinese, and Dutch in the Far East could be mounted. Fighting major wars on two fronts would be risky enough, but if one effort should fail, disaster could easily follow elsewhere.

(D) The United States could eventually develop a strong offensive in the Atlantic as an ally of Britain and maintain a defensive in the Pacific.

Stark came directly to the point, "I believe that the continued existence of the British Empire, combined with building up a strong protection in our home areas, will do most to ensure the status quo in the Western Hemisphere, and to promote our principal interests." He favored alternative D as the course of action "likely to be most fruitful for the United States." (In the phonetic, military alphabet "Dog" stands for "D." Thus this document became known as the Plan Dog Memorandum.) A necessary corollary was avoiding war with Japan and endeavoring to prevent war between Japan and the British Empire and the Netherlands East Indies.

Stark's concluding recommendation was that "as a preliminary to possible entry of the United States into the conflict" the army and navy undertake "secret staff talks on technical matters" with the British in London, the Canadians in Washington, and the British and Dutch in Batavia and Singapore. The purpose of these talks would be "to reach agreement and lay down plans for promoting unity of allied effort" in the event the United States entered the war under any of the four alternative conditions Stark had discussed.

Stark was eager to get staff talks with the British underway for two other compelling reasons. First, he was convinced of the necessity of collaboration with the British in advance of the certain American entry into the war in order to ensure an Atlantic-oriented strategy. Second, the navy's current war plan, Rainbow 3, a revised version of the old ORANGE Plan, contemplated that the major United States effort would be in the Pacific against Japan. It was based on the assumption that Great Britain would protect the western hemisphere against any Axis naval aggression. To Stark, this assumption was not warranted and hence it was a fatal flaw in the plan. To make matters worse, the army had not accepted Rainbow 3.

Since Roosevelt had just been reelected after virtually promising that the United States would not become involved in the war, he could not very well authorize public collaboration or even exploratory staff talks on technical military matters with the British. Stark realized this, but he also hoped for some definite sign of presidential consent or approbation of his Plan Dog Memorandum.

The details of what transpired in the first few weeks following Roosevelt's receipt of the Plan Dog Memorandum will probably never be known, chiefly because Roosevelt deliberately avoided direct discussions with Stark on this matter. The President's reaction and comments, if any, were conveyed to Stark by means of an intermediary, if at all.

In the meantime, Stark directed Hart to lay with the British and the Dutch "a framework for a future plan of cooperation, should we be forced into war."[11] He suggested that Hart explore with the Dutch such areas as command relationships, general objectives, and a general plan of cooperative action, including the approximate naval and military deployment. This was a significant assumption of initiative, because the Plan Dog Memorandum Stark submitted to the President that same day contained a specific recommendation for talks with the Dutch in Batavia. Obviously, Stark was confident of Roosevelt's approval, otherwise he certainly would not have authorized Hart to consult with the Dutch.

Talks with the British were an entirely different matter. Rear Admiral Robert L. Ghormley had been in London since August for "purely personal and unofficial conversations" with the Admiralty. Stark was aware that the British were anxious to hold staff talks, but in mid-November 1940, he was still not prepared to start them without some kind of presidential authorization or acquiescence.

Still not having received any word from Roosevelt about the Plan Dog Memorandum, Stark wrote Ghormley on 16 November that he intended to ask Roosevelt's permission to show the memorandum to the British Naval Attache, Captain Arthur W. Clarke, which he obtained in a few days. Stark was correct in seeking Roosevelt's permission to disclose to Clarke a document that contained specific policy recommendations. However, Clarke had already read a preliminary draft of the Plan Dog Memorandum on 29 October.[12] There is no direct evidence that Stark specifically authorized this disclosure, but it is inconceivable that any of Stark's subordinates would have done so on their own initiative. Plan Dog was not the only confidence extended to Clarke. He read Rainbow 3 on 25 October with Stark's personal permission.[13]

Stark's motives and the specific reasons for these disclosures can only be inferred. He knew the British wanted staff talks, and he did, too. Quite possibly Stark felt that by taking Clarke into his confidence and making sure the British knew the current thinking in the Navy Department, the momentum for staff talks could not only be maintained but possibly increased. He may well have sought to bring indirect pressure on Roosevelt through the British to induce him to accept Plan Dog. In bureaucratic politics, a lateral ploy of this sort frequently can be most effective in bringing pressure to bear on a superior.

Stark also sent Ghormley a copy for his own information. He cautioned Ghormley that Plan Dog was strictly unofficial and that neither the President nor the State Department sponsored it. He specifically warned Ghormley that under no circumstances should the British be given a copy or know that one was in London. Stark wanted the British to know something about Plan Dog by way of Clarke, but he did not want them to know too much about it. Thus, the Admiralty's appetite would be whetted and the Cabinet would have a good idea of the trend of thinking in Washington, but there would be no possibly embarrassing document circulating beyond the very limited circle in Washington.

Just how Stark received Roosevelt's response to the Plan Dog Memorandum is also not clear. Stark's diary does not record a visit to the White House until 16 January 1941. Stark could have gone there on Sunday, 17 November; sometimes the President would telephone him at his office on Sundays when Stark was catching up on his paperwork. Or, the matter might have been discussed over the telephone on the private line that connected Stark's office and his home with the White House. However, because of the sensitive nature of Plan Dog, it was probably not discussed over the telephone.

Most likely Roosevelt used an intermediary, such as Knox or Captain Daniel J. Callaghan, Roosevelt's naval aide. Callaghan was privy to what was going on in the White House and at the top levels in the Navy Department. He undoubtedly knew of the Plan Dog Memorandum and Roosevelt trusted him. The use of an intermediary, whether Callaghan or someone else, is entirely consistent with Roosevelt's general penchant for deviousness and with the arm's length treatment he gave the Plan Dog Memorandum. Roosevelt's comments on Plan Dog were not recorded. He filed the original without even initialing it or otherwise indicating he had read it. One thing is clear: He did not disapprove it.

No matter how much Roosevelt tried to disassociate himself with Plan Dog, there never has been any substantial doubt that he approved of staff talks with the British.[14] Indeed at a cabinet meeting on 29 November, in response to a question by Knox, Roosevelt stated that he would have no objection if the British sent some naval officers to work on joint plans with their American counterparts.[15] Stark spoke to Knox before the cabinet meeting and he may have prompted Knox to ask this question. There can be little doubt that after the cabinet meeting, Knox relayed the President's response to Stark. Somehow the British learned of Roosevelt's approval of staff talks almost at once. Lord Lothian cabled the Foreign Office on 29 November, the same day as the cabinet meeting, "The President has now agreed to staff talks in Washington."[16]

Acting on his own initiative, Stark, with the agreement of Knox and Stimson and with Roosevelt's tacit consent but without their specific knowledge, directed Ghormley on 2 December to invite the First Sea Lord, Admiral Sir Dudley Pound, to attend a staff conference in Washington in early January 1941 and to discuss certain agenda items. Stark acted without the express permission of either Roosevelt or Knox.[17] One knowledgeable observer claimed that Stark had Knox's "agreement" to issue the invitation and Stark denied he had Knox's "permission." Both are probably correct, because of the necessity of convening the staff talks without involving Roosevelt. Political necessity is the most reasonable and the best explanation of the overly fine distinction between "agreement" and "permission."[18]

At first, Stark did not tell Roosevelt he issued the invitation to the British for staff talks. He waited for a few weeks. In 1946 Stark said he thought he had told Roosevelt in January 1941.[19] At any rate, Stark knew Roosevelt well enough to know that he favored staff talks, but did not want to approve them outright. This was enough for Stark to take the initiative and get them started.

The sudden death of Lord Lothian on 11 December delayed the start of the staff talks. Churchill appointed his Foreign Secretary, Viscount Halifax, to succeed Lothian and included him in the War Cabinet, a significant step, which emphasized the importance to the British of their American connection. Finally, the British delegation to the staff talks accompanied Lord and Lady Halifax, Ghormley, and his U.S. army counterpart, Brigadier General Raymond E. Lee, on the voyage to the United States on board the battleship HMS *King George V*. If the mode of transportation were not sufficiently dramatic, Churchill himself accompanied the party to Scapa Flow where they boarded the battleship and sailed for Annapolis on 16 January 1941.

Stark was greatly relieved on 16 January 1941 to hear Roosevelt make some fairly definite statements of policy, all of which were in general accord with the Plan Dog Memorandum. The United States would be on the defensive in the Pacific, with the fleet based at Hawaii. Hart would have to use his discretion as to how long the Asiatic Fleet would remain in the Philippines and he could use his discretion in withdrawing to Singapore or to the east. The navy should consider the possibility of bombing Japanese cities. In the Atlantic, Roosevelt continued, the navy should be prepared to convoy shipping to Britain and to maintain an offshore patrol from Maine to the Virginia Capes. Every effort should be made to continue aid to Britain. Roosevelt clearly recognized that the security of the United States depended upon the survival of Great Britain.[20]

If at this meeting the President did not ringingly affirm Plan Dog and all that it entailed, his thinking was by no means inconsistent with it. Even if Stark might not have had assurance of Roosevelt's thinking prior to this meeting, it was crystal clear to him afterwards that the forthcoming conversations with the British could proceed on the basis of Plan Dog.

Roosevelt's third inauguration on Monday, 20 January 1941, provided a pleasant interlude in the quickening pace of strategic and logistics preparation for war. The event was unique in American history. Never before and quite possibly never again would any one person take the oath of office as President three consecutive times. Following the ceremony at the capitol, Stark lunched at the White House before reviewing the inaugural parade that afternoon from the presidential stand.[21]

Late in the afternoon of 21 January, Roosevelt telephoned Stark, who immediately went to the White House, a short distance away across Constitution Avenue from the old Navy Department buildings. They discussed the forthcoming staff talks with the British, including the Joint Planning Committee's report. Stark told Roosevelt that the British staff representatives were en route on board HMS *King George V*, along with Lord Halifax. Roosevelt then invited Stark to accompany him to Annapolis the following Saturday to meet the arrival of the British battleship and her distinguished passengers.

A little while later, Knox delivered to Roosevelt various documents prepared for the staff talks. The President read and approved them with only a few minor changes, such as substitution of the word "associates" for "allies" and "be compelled to go to war" for "decide to go to war."[22] Even though he approved of the staff talks, Roosevelt, nevertheless, insisted upon punctiliously maintaining in all respects the position of the United States that the talks were between military officers, that they were to be on technical military subjects not involving political questions, that they were contingent upon future United States involvement in the war, and that the results were subject to review and confirmation by higher authority.

The trip to Annapolis to meet Halifax and the British delegation on the afternoon of 24 January was another pleasant respite for both Stark and Roosevelt, who were freed from the pressures and routines of their offices for a short while. Stark made arrangements for the President in his wheelchair to board the British battleship. Unfortunately, foul weather produced a choppy bay and Roosevelt had to greet Lord and Lady Halifax on shore. Nevertheless, the fact that the President went to meet a new ambassador on his arrival in this country was significant. Politics aside, the Americans were immensely interested in all aspects of *King George V*, whose commanding officer, Captain Patterson, offered to embark a party of United States naval officers for the trip down the Chesapeake. Stark immediately accepted. The next day, 22 Americans were on board "to pick up all the information they could" on everything from communications to oil combustion.[23]

The first plenary session of the ABC (American-British-Canadian) staff conversations convened in the Navy Department on the afternoon of 29 January 1941. Following the procedure approved by the President, Stark and Marshall received the British and American representatives. Reading his prepared statement, Stark stated that the purpose of the conversations was "to determine the best methods" by which the British and American Armed Forces could defeat Germany and her allies "should the United States be compelled to resort to war." He made it clear that the American people wished to remain out of war, but they were willing to provide material and economic aid to Britain. "Therefore, no specific commitments can now be made except as to technical methods of cooperation." Any military plans must be "contingent upon future political action of both nations." He then summarized the strategic policy of the United States, notably, concentration on the Atlantic while opposing Japanese expansion in the Pacific. Both the United States and the British Commonwealth should endeavor to restrain Japan from entering the war or from attacking the Dutch in the Far East. However, if Japan should enter the war, United States operations in the Pacific would be conducted "so as to facilitate the exertion of its principal military effort in the Atlantic or navally in the Mediterranean." Stark felt that any differences in views could be reconciled. He concluded with an admonition for secrecy in the conduct of the meetings.[24]

The British delegation responded to Stark's opening statement by affirming that a decision must be sought first in the European theater. After the defeat of Germany and Italy, Japan could then be dealt with. Stark and Marshall then withdrew and the two delegations got down to work.

As host and as the American instigator in brining about the talks, Stark entertained both delegations at a dinner at his quarters the following Sunday. Aside from the opening sessions and this dinner party, Stark had no further direct contact with the British representatives. However, he met frequently with Turner and other American representatives. He was well aware of the progress of the talks and of the problems that arose in their course. He advised and guided the United States Navy delegates and he was instrumental in resolving the one impasse that threatened to interrupt the talks.

The most serious disagreement between the two delegations concerned the Far East. In a nutshell, the British urged the United States to base in the Far East a substantial portion of the U.S. Fleet then based in Hawaii. They offered Singapore as the most convenient base. Stark rejected this proposal for the same reasons he consistently opposed such a deployment whenever Roosevelt broached the subject. His reasons were complex, but in essence he and his staff felt strongly that dividing the fleet would only weaken it in the face of a strong Japanese navy. Stark was also convinced that maintaining a concentrated fleet on the Japanese flank would serve as the best inhibition to Japanese expansion that the United States could provide. There was also an unstated undercurrent of feeling in the navy and elsewhere in Washington that it would not be wise to become too closely involved in the protection of British colonial interests. Even so, the main objective was still to restrain Japan, which Stark and Roosevelt thought could be accomplished best, if at all, by retaining the fleet in Hawaii.

The Americans had no intention of reenforcing the U.S. Asiatic Fleet. The British thought they should. In the event of war with Japan, the Americans had virtually written off the Far East, including Singapore. The British were aghast. At the plenary meeting on Monday, 10 February, Turner asked the British to draw up a strategy appreciation, incorporating their views on this point.[25]

When Churchill heard of this disagreement, he was furious that the British naval delegation had allowed the secondary issue of the Far East and fleet deployment to Singapore to cloud the talks. He vented his displeasure to the First Sea Lord, Admiral Sir Dudley Pound. He wanted to avoid either challenging or offending the Americans, because once they were in the war, events would impose a logic of their own. Hence, it would be unwise to press them unduly at that time.[26] The Americans naturally did not know of Churchill's stinging rebuke to Pound.

The matter became more complicated and threatened to become serious when on 17 February the British somewhat naively told the American delegates that two days before Halifax had left a copy of the British strategy appreciation with Hull at the State Department. By informing Hull of the substance of the matters under discussion, the British transgressed upon the explicit division of political and military affairs that was the basis for U.S. participation in the talks. In addition, the U.S. delegation felt that the British were improperly attempting to influence the outcome of the talks by indirect means.

The next morning Stark and Ghormley went to the White House, where they discussed with Roosevelt the status of the talks. As a result of these discussions, the American delegation sent a lengthy recapitulation and justification of their position to the British along with a letter stating that the talks were recessed until a satisfactory answer was received.[27] With that taken care of, Stark went home to bed with an obstinate case of the flu.

Under pressure from Churchill on the First Sea Lord not to press unduly their views on Singapore, and confronted with American firmness, the British delegation had only one choice. Promising cooperation, they agreed to maintain the division between military and political matters and, thus, not to supply the State Department with military papers. The Americans were satisfied. The delegates proceeded with the business at hand and the final report was drafted on 27 March and formally approved on 29 March.

Titled ABC-1 Staff Agreement, the report was nearly 60 pages long, including five annexes on various specific topics. It also included a short addendum, titled ABC-2, on air policy, a compromise that settled a stand-up fight that erupted at what everyone thought would be the last session. The American and British air representatives did not receive the special consideration they sought, thanks largely to Richmond Kelly Turner's heated insistence. A quick conference with Stark produced the workable compromise solution: an air annex to the final report, which satisfied everyone.[28]

The importance of ABC-1 cannot be overemphasized. Stark succeeded in his attempts to establish the defeat of Germany as the primary Anglo-American military and naval objective, coupled with a strategic defense in the Pacific "in the event the United States is compelled to resort to war." The groundwork was laid, first, for the defense of the western hemisphere and, second, for providing every possible assistance to Great Britain. These were the immediate results of Stark's endeavors.

ABC-1 provided the highest degree of strategic preparation before the United States entered the war. It was the foundation of subsequent allied strategy in World War II. By establishing even on a contingency basis the fundamental military objectives of the United States and Great Britain, it provided a unity of concept shared by Washington and London that Germany must be defeated first and that a holding action or strategic defense would be undertaken in the Pacific. This basic strategic concept was the essence of Plan Dog, which Stark submitted to Roosevelt the previous November in his successful bid to bring the talks to fruition.

In addition to providing agreement and understanding on substantive strategic concepts, ABC-1 also established military and naval missions in Washington and London as a means of exchanging views and preparing plans. Thus the basis was laid for the subsequent creation of the Combined Chiefs of Staff, which during World War II coordinated the Anglo-American war effort. Without this machinery the coming coalition war could not have been planned and executed with the same degree of cooperation, efficiency, and amity. ABC-1 was strategic preparation of the highest order.[29]

ABC-1 was a personal success for Stark. It was his show, he arranged and guided the talks. The report was based on his memorandum, which crystallized strategic thinking in Washington and which Roosevelt obliquely approved. Stark was the moving force behind the convening of the talks and his advice to and guidance of the navy delegates, always with Roosevelt's backing and support, provided the necessary compromises and resolution of difficulties, which might have seriously interrupted the good work at hand. Marshall also played an important role. Because the navy rather than the army would be affected first and most directly, Marshall gave Stark his full support.[30] This army-navy cooperation contributed greatly to the success of the staff talks.

The ABC-1 Staff Agreement was, however, only one of three events occurring in the spring of 1941 that tied the United States more firmly, but still with the official trappings of neutrality, to the British cause. The other two were the Lend-Lease Act and the Base Lease Agreement. These three events came about separately in Washington and in London and by mere coincidence they all came to fruition in March 1941.

Of these three events, Stark was most intimately concerned with the staff talks. As Chief of Naval Operations he testified in favor of the Lend-Lease bill and he had a hand in the selection of Rear Admiral John W. Greenslade to head a board to inspect and to select base sites. In the Lend-Lease Act, Congress legislated the availability of enormous quantities of material goods for the British. The Base Lease Agreement, concluded in London on 27 March, implemented the destroyers-for-bases agreement of September 1940 by spelling out the conditions that would govern the leases for the eight bases. The way was clear for the United States to begin construction of additional bases in the western hemisphere.[31] Much to Stark's satisfaction, by the spring of 1941 the United States was all but formally allied with Great Britain.

Although implementation of ABC-1 was contingent upon entry of the United States into the war, the report of the staff talks was not simply filed away for future use along with the war plan derived from it. Stark spent three hours with Roosevelt on 2 April discussing national security affairs. Stark read to the President an official letter he proposed to send to the three fleet commanders. Roosevelt's approval of the text of this letter was necessary because it contained an accurate statement of strategic thinking at the highest levels. Stark specifically restricted disclosure of its contents to the fleet commanders and their immediate subordinates.[32]

In it Stark reported the completion of the staff talks and he forwarded a copy of the report, ABC-1. He said Roosevelt would approve it "at an appropriate time," which was understood to be when the United States went to war.[33] The Rainbow 5 war plan, based on ABC-1, was then in preparation and would be forwarded as soon as it was completed. In fact, Stark approved it and sent it to the fleet commanders one month later. Stark altered the fleet commanders to the essential features of the forthcoming Rainbow 5 plan so they could speedily issue new operating plans following its receipt or promptly modify existing ones if war came before they received it.

To prevent any misunderstanding, Stark specifically stated that for the navy the import of the Germany-first strategy, embodied in the ABC-1 agreement, meant that the United States would withdraw forces from the Pacific Fleet to reenforce the Atlantic Fleet; and the British, if they found it necessary, would transfer naval forces to the Far East to keep the Japanese north of the Malay barrier. The Asiatic Fleet would not be reenforced, but it would be supported by tactical offensive operations by the Pacific Fleet, even though the overall Pacific strategy would be defensive.

In the Pacific, Stark saw difficulties arising from the uncertainty over Japanese intentions. He felt that the concentration of the U.S. Fleet in Hawaii had had a stabilizing effect on the Far East, which was one reason he was dead set against a major deployment to Singapore as the British suggested. So long as the war did not go too badly for the British in Europe, he thought, the Japanese would be cautious in pressing their demands in Indo-China. All of which made the effect on the Japanese of the transfer of units of the Pacific Fleet to the Atlantic a matter of guesswork. Shipping losses in the Atlantic were three times greater than replacements. Thus, a transfer of some U.S. Navy ships to the Atlantic was necessary (especially since Roosevelt had recently directed Stark to be prepared to convoy in the Atlantic, which Stark did not mention in this letter). Because of the dangers in both oceans, the best that could be done was to avoid even a hint of transfer until the last possible moment. It was abundantly clear to Stark that events in the Pacific and in the Atlantic were intimately related. Actions taken in one theater were bound to have an effect in the other. He insisted on flexibility in planning, both in Washington and in the fleets.

Stark was convinced that war was inevitable. He saw public opinion was slowly coming to this realization. War with Germany and Italy—possibly a form of undeclared war—could well be upon the United States by June 1941. Even though there was a distinct possibility that Japan might remain out of the war, the United States could not act on it under those circumstances. He urged the fleet commanders to spend as much time as possible in training and preparation for the duties their respective fleets would be called upon to perform under the current operating plans. He concluded, "The time has arrived, I believe, to perfect the techniques and the methods that will be required by the special operations which you envisage immediately after the entry of the United States in war."[34]

By May the basic war plan Rainbow 5 was completed. Knox approved it on 5 May and Stimson followed suit on 2 June. A few days later, Roosevelt received both Rainbow 5 and ABC-1, reviewed them, and returned them. He indicated he would approve them in the event of war.[35] Stark sent Rainbow 5 to the fleet commanders for their guidance in preparing their operating plans. Rainbow 5 (or WPL 46 as it was technically designated) was the plan which would be executed when Japan attacked the United States on 7 December 1941.

Technically it was still a peacetime navy, but the period of grace was rapidly running out.

5

QUASI-WAR IN THE ATLANTIC

For Stark, 1941 was a year of anxiety, activity, and continued preparation for the war most army and navy officers saw was all but inevitable. Public opinion was still divided between the hawks, who clearly saw the dangers posed by Germany and Japan, and a conglomeration of others, including isolationists, pacifists, and many wishful thinkers. When Congress approved the Lend-Lease Act in March, the British were assured that the United States would be a source of material support. The next problem was to transport the goods across the Atlantic. Because American matériel was sent to Britain in American ships, convoys were finally formed in 1941 to guarantee their safe arrival.

In September the inevitable incident occurred: a German submarine fired two torpedoes at USS *Greer*, both of which missed their target. Then on 11 September, President Roosevelt issued his famous shoot-on-sight order. This date is as good as any to mark the start of the undeclared war in the Atlantic. From then until December there was sufficient provocation on both sides to justify a declaration of war. Both Germany and the United States had their own, very different reasons to refrain from performing that formality.

Stark favored a firm but passive strategy in the Pacific, yet he urged positive naval action in the Atlantic, because he saw Germany as the primary threat to the United States. As early as the middle of December 1940 he was convinced that the U.S. Navy should engage in convoy operations in the Atlantic. In January 1941, Roosevelt gave Stark oral approval to begin planning for convoys. On 1 February the U.S. Fleet was reorganized with the establishment of the Atlantic Fleet on an equal basis with the Pacific and Asiatic Fleets. Although

83

the Atlantic Fleet was considerably smaller than the Pacific Fleet, Stark intended it to be the first one to fight, with his hand-picked candidate, Vice Admiral Ernest J. King as its commander (King was soon promoted to full admiral). At the same time Husband E. Kimmel relieved James O. Richardson as commander of the Pacific Fleet.

Stark received alarming news on 24 March from the American naval attache in London, who reported Britain's condition as extremely critical. Britain needed battleships, carriers, and cruisers, he said, but lacked the men to man them. Stark concluded that the United States must give "full help" to the British, who might not last out the year without it.[1] This gloomy projection reinforced Stark's conviction that the Japanese must not be provoked and that the great danger to the United States in the Atlantic might well become even greater.

Stark was worried about the principal dangers facing Great Britain: the German threat to the sealanes linking Britain to the rest of the world and the deleterious effects of bombing on production and morale. The war was going badly for the British; Rommel had seized Libya and was threatening Egypt. Hitler's Balkan campaign had been successful. Greece and Crete had fallen. Stark was convinced that the survival of Britain was necessary for the security of the United States, and he was willing to do whatever had to be done to ensure British survival, even at the risk of war with Germany.

The obvious thing to do, Stark thought, was to transfer three battleships, one aircraft carrier, four cruisers, and two squadrons of destroyers from the Pacific to the newly formed Atlantic Fleet. With these additional ships, King would be able to convoy merchant ships carrying lend-lease and other needed material at least part of the way across the Atlantic. Stark went to Roosevelt, who approved the transfer on 2 April without consulting Secretary of State Cordell Hull. But he changed his mind before it could be effected. The reason was obvious. Japan had concluded a neutrality pact with the Soviet Union on 13 April, thus securing her northern flank. It was clear that Japan could turn her attention to the south. Hull felt it would not be prudent to do anything that the Japanese might construe as a sign of weakness, particularly since his negotiations with Japan at that time were at a delicate stage. A greater threat in the Atlantic was eclipsed by a more immediate problem in the Pacific.

Convoying would require more ships than King had at his disposal in the Atlantic. It was, therefore, dependent upon the transfer of a significant force from the Pacific. When that transfer was postponed, convoying was not feasible. Both Stark and Roosevelt were aware of this fact.

Despite a lack of ships, King was ready to start the convoys with the forces at his dispoal once Roosevelt gave his approval. In late April, Roosevelt summoned King to Hyde Park and told him to extend the patrols instead of instituting convoys. Stark was highly disappointed. At Roosevelt's direction, he prepared Western Hemisphere Defense Plan No. 2, which provided for extended patrols and broadcasting in plain language the positions of German and Italian submarines found to the west of Longitude 26° West. It had no teeth in it, he complained to Kimmel.[2]

Roosevelt's reluctance to institute the convoys is understandable. Technically, the United States was at peace. So far no American ships had been sunk by German surface raiders or submarines. Convoys would certainly be a provocation to Hitler and Hull feared that if war broke out between Germany and the United States, Japan might well join the issue in the Far East. In addition, Roosevelt had received reports that public opinion might not support convoying. These reports, coupled with the recent and narrow defeat in the Senate of the Tobey anti-convoy resolution, which would have prohibited convoying lend-lease goods to Britain, counseled caution. Roosevelt simply moved ahead only one step, instead of the several steps Stark, Knox, and Secretary of War Henry L. Stimson were urging.

Stark's eagerness to institute convoys was only one manifestation of his general hawkish attitude, which was derived from his conviction that unless the United States did more at once to aid Britain, the British position might be irretrievably lost. He felt that the United States should go to war to insure British survival. He doubted the British capability to hold on to the eastern Mediterranean, which was precarious at best now that Rommel was battering at the gates of Egypt. Stark wanted to involve the United States more deeply in the Atlantic war and convoying was the best way to do it. If the United States went to war with Germany, many of the problems currently vexing him would be resolved. The exigencies of prosecuting a war would govern the assignment of ships to the Atlantic and Pacific

Fleets and determine their deployment. No effort would be spared in building, manning, and equipping new ships and those already in the fleet. But more important by far, the United States could render full aggressive assistance to the beleaguered British.

Even though the issue of patrolling instead of convoying appeared to have been settled, at least for the moment, Knox and Stimson continued to press Roosevelt for the transfer of additional ships from the Pacific to the Atlantic. Stark told Kimmel to be prepared to transfer three battleships, one carrier, four cruisers, and two squadrons of destroyers at any time. In addition, he warned Kimmel, there would be more transfers because King had been given an enormous job with a "force utterly inadequate to do it on any efficient scale."3 However, Roosevelt was continuing to accede to Hull's request to defer action that could appear to the Japanese as weakening the American position. The matter was discussed at great length at a White House meeting on 6 May. Hull repeated his plea for more time. This time Stark favored transferring only the battleships. Stimson thought he "switched around and trimmed."4 Roosevelt finally consented to the transfer on 13 May, and it was soon completed.

By early May, Hitler was master of the Balkans. His future intentions became a matter of intense interest and speculation in Washington and in London. In mid-May, it was clear that the French government at Vichy intended to continue collaborating with Hitler. Unimpeded passage of German troops through unoccupied France and into Spain could seriously threaten Gibraltar, and with it the British position in the Mediterranean. French collaboration with Hitler also posed a definite threat to the western hemisphere. If Hitler could base troops and aircraft at Dakar and other places in west Africa, he could threaten the New World. The security of the Atlantic islands became a matter of immediate concern to Washington. Long-range German bombers and patrol aircraft based on the Azores could seriously threaten the sealanes of communication between the United States and Great Britain. Finally, at the end of May, the German battleship *Bismarck* broke out into the Atlantic. In the course of a brief but dramatic voyage, the *Bismarck* sank the British battlecruiser *Hood* before being caught and sunk herself.

In a late afternoon meeting at the White House on 22 May, an alarmed Roosevelt directed Stark and Marshall to prepare plans for the occupation of the Azores by 25,000 troops within 30 days. This order made painfully clear what they already knew: the United States was not ready for a major military operation. For one thing, the navy lacked enough ships to transport the troops. Over the past year, Stark had repeatedly sought permission to take over a considerable number of merchant ships. Now he obtained this authority and was delighted with the cooperation of the Coast Guard, which provided 100 officers and 1,800 sailors. This was the one bright spot in planning the Azores operation.[5]

Roosevelt called Stark to the White House on 11 June and told him that American troops would relieve the British troops then in Iceland, because the British troops were needed elsewhere. The ABC-1 agreement, concluded at the end of March, specified the American relief of the British garrison sometime after September 1941. Roosevelt simply advanced the timetable. Under the circumstances, it was the most modest step he could take.

Both Stark and Marshall opposed the idea. Stark did not want to disrupt the badly needed training and organization of the growing Atlantic amphibious forces by assigning marines to a remote island. As Roosevelt explained it, the marines would be the first American troops in Iceland, but they would be replaced by army troops when available. Since the Selective Service Act forbade the stationing of draftees outside of American territory, the army troops would have to be regulars. Marshall was dead set against the idea of assigning some of his all too few regular troops to garrison duty in Iceland. Roosevelt gave the order and the marines went.

While they were en route to Iceland, Hitler invaded the Soviet Union. The immediate effect of the Nazi involvement in the east was to lessen the pressure on the west. Britain now had an ally on the continent of Europe, which engaged the *Wehrmacht* with its own armed forces, trading territory and distance for time. The Russian winter soon became an important ally.

Stark saw an opportunity. This was the moment, he thought, to seize the psychological initiative and start escorting convoys. Knox agreed. With his permission, Stark went immediately to Roosevelt and urged that the U.S. Navy start escort operations at once and that Roosevelt make a public announcement to that effect. Stark told Roosevelt that he expected such a declaration, followed by American action, "would almost certainly involve us in war." Stark felt that every day America delayed in getting into war would be "dangerous and much more delay might be fatal to Britain's survival." Stark reminded Roosevelt that for months he had been asking for permission to start escort operations. In addition to purely naval considerations, Stark was also worried about the slow pace of war preparations on the homefront. He bluntly told Roosevelt, "Only a war psychology (can) speed up things the way they should be speeded up. Strive as we might, it just isn't in the nature of things to get the results in peace that we could (get) were we at war."[6]

Despite Stark's strong and passionate plea and despite the obvious opportunity that Hitler presented him, Roosevelt temporized with good reason. He was in a difficult position. The marines had landed in Iceland on 7 July. No provision had been made to protect the sealanes between the United States and that distant island, even though Stark and the War Plans Division had been in frequent and close consultations with the British Joint Staff Mission in Washington about escorting convoys. Roosevelt had not given the necessary authorization.

The problem lay in the Senate. On 30 June, while the marines were on their way to Iceland, Senator Burton K. Wheeler of Montana demanded that the Senate Naval Affairs Committee investigate charges that U.S. Navy ships were escorting convoys and that they had engaged units of the German Navy. Knox categorically denied that engagements had occurred between German and American ships while the American ships were carrying out patrol missions. Both Knox and Stark were summoned before the Senate Naval Affairs Committee for a closed meeting on 11 July to explain precisely what was going on in the Atlantic.

Roosevelt had to tread warily. Domestic political constraints required him to soft pedal activities in the Atlantic, but military necessity required him to ensure the support and protection of the U.S. Marines who had just reached Iceland. Stark was equally aware of the delicate balance that had to be struck between these compelling political and military considerations.

Stark, working with the British Joint Staff Mission in Washington and through his representative working with the Admiralty in London, took the April patrolling plan one step further. The intrusion of Axis vessels and aircraft within the western hemisphere was a "potential threat" and shipping between Iceland and the United States as well as shipping carrying lend-lease cargoes to Britain would be protected. In June, Stark directed Ghormley to inform the Admiralty that although the U.S. Government did not intend at that moment to execute such a plan, the Chief of Naval Operations was preparing one so the "navy would be ready for effective action under all eventualities."[7] Stark was technically correct, but he had climbed out on a very high limb.

A substitute plan, Hemisphere Defense Plan No. 4, was issued on 11 July (but did not become effective until 26 July), some five hours after Stark and Knox completed testifying before the Senate Naval Affairs Committee. It provided for the escort of convoys between U.S. ports and Iceland. It also included a provision for the inclusion of other than U.S. or Icelandic flag vessels in the convoys, but this provision was held in abeyance when the plan was executed. The plan had been worked out on 9 July in a meeting at the White House with Stark, Roosevelt, King, and the Navy's Director of War Plans, Rear Admiral Turner, in attendance.

Even though ships of other than American or Icelandic origin could not be invited formally to join the convoys, Stark was able to arrange the operating schedules of the American ships so that at least one would depart the Halifax area at the same time as British or Canadian ships. In the same manner, American ships proceeding westward would depart 26° West Longitude at similar intervals. As Stark told King on 12 July, U.S. or Icelandic flag vessels might be accompanied both east- and westbound by British convoys. The practical result, if the British followed the scheme, would be that the United States would escort all convoys in both directions. In this way Stark was able to manipulate the movement of ships to accomplish his purpose indirectly, which for reasons of sound practical politics he was unable to do directly. Further arrangements for the escort of convoys were made at the Atlantic Conference in August 1941.

Stark told his associates of Roosevelt's "stiffening" attitude. He was convinced "the rest will happen" when the convoys start. Meanwhile, he insisted to them and to the British Admiralty Delegation that "the whole thing must be kept as quiet as possible." To this end, he urged that arrangements be made orally whenever possible.[8]

Stark kept Roosevelt well informed of what was going on. Roosevelt asked that American instructions omit any reference to British convoys but he specifically wanted the British and Canadian authorities to know details of the movements of the American convoys so they could join if they wished. Stark had already anticipated his request and had so directed King.[9]

The defense plan Roosevelt authorized specified that encounters with Axis vessels or aircraft were to be "viewed as actuated by a possibly unfriendly intent." This innocuous circumlocution replaced a more forthright statement, which stated that such encounters were "potential threats . . . to be attacked and captured." Notwithstanding the toned-down substitution, Roosevelt still felt that the presence of German raiders or submarines near the lines of communications constituted a "threat of attack" and therefore it "should be dealt with by action looking to the elimination of such a 'threat of attack.' "10 Apparently, Roosevelt wanted the navy to shoot on sight any German ships approaching the convoy routes, but did not say so expressly until after the *Greer* incident in early September. One can only sympathize with a commanding officer trying to ascertain, from a directive based on Roosevelt's memorandum, whether he had authority to open fire. Happily, Stark told King to make it clear to the Atlantic Fleet that it need not avoid belligerent action any longer. With this authority King ordered the destruction of "hostile forces which threaten such shipping."11 No incidents occurred at that time because Hitler ordered his commanders to avoid scrupulously any engagements with the U.S. Navy. To this extent, Hitler failed to cooperate with Stark in providing an incident that would involve the United States more deeply in the battle of the Atlantic.

The middle of July saw a resolution of the important and nettlesome problem of protecting the sea routes to Iceland, thus insuring the means for adequate support of the marines and later the army troops stationed there. The backing and filling, the ambiguities of policy, the clever manipulations of operating schedules, the public pronouncements, and secret naval actions were all symptomatic of the political and strategic environment in which Stark had to work. He was loyal to Roosevelt, whose difficult position he clearly saw, too much so his critics have said. He was also loyal to the navy and to his subordinates. He conscientiously strove to impress upon Roosevelt the military and naval exigencies of the current situation. He constantly pressed Roosevelt for policy decisions and guidance. All too frequently he received the reply, "Betty, please don't ask me that." Then Roosevelt would tell a joke and sometimes not too gently brush aside Stark's insistent, pointed questions.12

No wonder Stark lamented that "policy seems to be something never fixed, always fluid and changing."[13] He was frustrated and he confided as much to his close associates and to the fleet commanders. He was philosophic about it to the extent that he refused to worry unduly about things he could not change. On several occasions he even went so far as to offer to resign and let someone else shoulder the burdens of the Chief of Naval Operations' office.[14] But each time he was asked to remain.

The highlight of the summer of 1941 was the Atlantic conference, when Roosevelt and Churchill met for the first time as leaders of what soon would become the Grand Alliance. The chief purpose of the meeting was to bring together these two men and their chief military and naval advisors for personal meetings. The preparations for the conference and the departures of the principals from Washington and London were carried out in the utmost secrecy.

On Wednesday, 30 July, Roosevelt summoned Stark and Marshall to the White House. He told them they would be leaving on the following Sunday for a conference. Although this was the first that Marshall had heard of the meeting, Roosevelt had mentioned it to Stark in April before King's visit to Hyde Park. While King was there, Roosevelt told him of his desire to meet with Churchill somewhere, sometime. King produced various charts and they discussed routes and means of transportation.[15]

Stark, accompanied by Turner and Commander Forrest P. Sherman of the War Plans Division, went by train from Washington to New York. At the 79th Street landing they took a navy boat out to a destroyer leader. About an hour later, Marshall and his party came aboard and the ship got underway. Stark thoroughly enjoyed the trip down the river, around the Battery, up the East River, and through the Hell Gate to the Whitestone Landing where King was waiting in USS *Augusta*, along with USS *Tuscaloosa* and three ships of Destroyer Division 17. After Stark and Marshall transferred to the *Augusta* and the others to the *Tuscaloosa*, all ships got underway and proceeded to Smithtown Bay on the north shore of Long Island where they anchored for the night.[16]

The beautiful summer weather, absence from the heat of Washington and the pressure of his office, and just being on a ship again were a tonic to Stark. He thoroughly enjoyed his brief sailor's idyll.

Later that evening, the president's yacht, *Potomac,* and her escort joined. All ships anchored for the night. At six o'clock Tuesday morning, Roosevelt came on board *Augusta,* "smiling and cheerful as usual." He even brought aboard his scottie, Fala.[17]

It was a pleasant, relaxed voyage from Martha's Vineyard to Argentia, where they arrived Thursday morning. Roosevelt spent the day fishing. Rest and relaxation were in order and a little formal business was conducted that day or the next. Stark, Turner, and Sherman boarded a navy patrol plane based at Argentia on Friday and flew over the city of St. John's and St. Mary's Bay.

Saturday morning HMS *Prince of Wales* stood into the harbor and anchored. Following an exchange of boarding calls, Churchill came on board *Augusta.* Churchill, Roosevelt, and their respective staffs spent the remainder of Saturday and Sunday in informal meetings.

Sunday morning Roosevelt and Churchill assembled with their principal military leaders and the crew of HMS *Prince of Wales* on that ship's fantail for divine services. Given the setting and the circumstances, it was a truly impressive ceremony. Churchill was host at lunch following the services, seating Roosevelt on his right and Stark on his left.

There was no agenda for the staff conference on Monday morning, which was presided over by the First Sea Lord, Admiral Sir Dudley Pound. The main purpose of the Atlantic conference was achieved when Roosevelt, Churchill, and their respective army, navy, and air force chiefs met and talked informally for an extended period. Cooperation would be easier on a basis of acquaintance, if not friendship, than between total strangers.

A second benefit was achieved when Stark and Pound made final arrangements for the escort of convoys, particularly when vessels flying flags other than American or Icelandic would be permitted to join the American convoys.[18] The U.S. Navy would escort convoys eastward to a specified mid-ocean point where the Royal Navy would take over for the remainder of the voyage. At that time, the American ships would take over escorting another convoy west. These arrangements released a significant number of British destroyers, which were badly needed elsewhere.

Although Anglo-American cooperation was exensive, in midsummer 1941 there was still a question as to whether the U.S. Navy battleships would assume antisurface raider duties in the western

Atlantic to the extent that the British could withdraw their battleships to be refitted and subsequently deployed to the Far East. The day before he left Washington for the Atlantic conference, Stark informed Ghormley that the U.S. battleships would not assume anti-raider duties to that extent until the United States assumed protection of all convoys with American or Icelandic flagships.[19] Finally, on 25 August, Stark was satisfied that these two conditions had been met. As he put it, "I think at last we have something definite—maybe."[20] He informed both King and Ghormley that Atlantic Fleet forces were "to destroy surface raiders which attacked shipping along the sealanes between North America and Iceland or which approached these lanes sufficiently closely to threaten such shipping."[21] Stark expanded this authority on 3 September to include "hostile forces," which presumably meant that submarines as well as surface raiders were subject to attack if they approached the sealanes to Iceland.[22] The greatest threat was from submarines, not surface raiders.

The import of these orders was that without a known or recorded German attack on any U.S. ships in the North Atlantic, Stark authorized the Atlantic Fleet by early September 1941 to destroy Axis ships threatening American or Icelandic flag vessels. Stark issued these orders with Knox's enthusiastic approval. Given Stark's conviction that all assistance must be given to Britain, even at the risk of war with Germany, he needed little encouragement to interpret his authority to the broadest extent possible. Roosevelt's elliptical directive to Stark in July not only showed that the President was serious about protecting convoys, but it also allowed Stark to work towards full American involvement in the battle of the Atlantic. Stark issued secret orders on 26 July and expanded them on 3 September. All that was required was an incident to justify broadening the rules of engagement to permit U.S. Navy ships to open fire on sighting German and Italian surface ships and submarines.[23]

On 4 September the long awaited incident occurred. The USS *Greer* was proceeding independently into Reykjavik when she was notified by British forces, consisting of a patrol aircraft and a destroyer, that a German submarine was in the vicinity. *Greer* located the submarine by sonar and trailed the contact for nearly three and a half hours before the Germans fired two torpedoes, both of which fortunately missed their target. Because no U.S. or Icelandic merchant vessels were threatened, the rules of engagement then in force permitted *Greer* only to trail and patrol the contact. When fired upon, *Greer* was then authorized to drop depth charges in self defense, which she did.

Roosevelt denounced the German attack as "piracy—morally and legally." He met with Stark, King, and Ingersoll the following day. At that time, he decided to proclaim the Atlantic Ocean west of 26° West Longitude as dangerous for Axis submarines and surface raiders. A few days later, Roosevelt told the nation that freedom of the seas was at stake. He announced that the navy had been ordered to open fire on Axis warships whenever sighted in the western Atlantic.[24]

In a series of dispatches to King, Stark eliminated the trail and patrol task that had been in effect for the Atlantic Fleet since April. Stark directed the Atlantic Fleet to protect shipping flying the U.S. and foreign flags (other than German and Italian) "as circumstances may require" and to destroy Axis "naval, land, and air forces encountered."[25] The dramatic part of the order was the shoot-on-sight provision, but the more important part related to the escort of convoys. With Roosevelt's authorization, Stark removed the final barriers to escorting all convoys from the Western Hemisphere to the mid-Atlantic where the Royal Navy took over. In this way, all merchant ships flying U.S. or other flags would be escorted. Indeed, King could escort convoys in which there were no American ships. The first eastbound convoy escorted under this new arrangement sailed from Halifax on 16 September and was turned over in mid-Atlantic to British escorts without incident on 25 September.[26]

For all practical purposes, the United States at that time was in a naval war in the Atlantic. The Atlantic Fleet was steaming under wartime conditions and was conducting combat operations by escorting convoys. The most surprising thing about this undeclared war was that six weeks elapsed before the next incident occurred. Towards the end of October, the USS *Kearney* was torpedoed while on escort duty. The first American sailors to die in World War II perished in this attack. Shortly aterwards, the tanker USS *Salinas* was also torpedoed. Fortunately, both ships were able to return safely to port. At the end of October, USS *Reuben James* was also torpedoed, but this time the ship was sunk, with a great loss of life, including that of her commanding officer, Lieutenant Commander Heywood L. "Tex" Edwards. These incidents aroused little public or congressional indignation.

Even as late as the end of September, Roosevelt was undecided as to whether he ought to risk the ire of the isolationists, still a powerful domestic force, by asking Congress to amend the Neutrality Act. Under then current law, American merchant ships were forbidden to enter the war zone around the British Isles. Hull asked Stark what would be the advantages and disadvantages of eliminating these war zones. Stark's response was "highly refreshing to the President."[27]

In summarizing the strategic situation in the Atlantic, Stark said that the chief advantage would be to permit American merchant ships manned by American crews to enter British ports, since aid to insure British survival was clearly in the American national interest. He was aware of the increased probability of attacks on and losses of American shipping and he accepted the risk. Germany was still the number one enemy. Stark reiterated his long held belief that "Germany cannot be defeated unless the United States is wholeheartedly in the war and makes a strong military and naval effort wherever strategy dictates."

The basic question was how and under what circumstances the United States would enter the war. He said, "A Declaration of war by the United States against Germany, unless Germany had previously declared war against the United States, might bring Japan into the war as an active belligerent." Clearly, a war with both Japan and Germany would be a disadvantage because the United States would be engaged on two fronts. It was something that the country might have to accept, but every effort should be made to avoid it. A strong stand against Japanese aggression was the best way to avoid a war in the Pacific.

Stark pointed out, "It would be very desirable to enter the war under circumstances in which Germany were the aggressor and in which case Japan might then be able to remain neutral." Nevertheless, he urged positive action, "The United States should enter the war against Germany as soon as possible, even if hostilities with Japan must be accepted." For the past two years Stark had assumed that the United States would not let Great Britain fall and "ultimately in order to prevent this, we would have to enter the war . . . I have long felt and have often stated that the sooner we get in the better."

In a postscript he added, "I do not believe Germany will declare war on us until she is good and ready; and that it will be a cold-blooded decision on Hitler's part if and when he thinks it will pay, and not until then. . . . When he is ready, he will strike and not before."[28] Hitler refused the challenge.

Stark was right in thinking that Hitler would not declare war on the United States until he was ready to do so, but he did not foresee in early October 1941 that war with Germany would come in the wake of the Japanese attack on Pearl Harbor and be almost an anticlimax. At that time, there were plenty of signs of serious trouble in the Pacific, but the imminence of war was unseen and the plans for the Pearl Harbor attack were unknown to the United States. The next two months brought a Pacific rather than an Atlantic crisis, which engulfed Stark and tarnished his reputation.

6

A VERY GLARING PHRASE

The shooting war in the Atlantic was only part of the global strategic problem the United States faced in 1941 with thinly stretched, inadequate resources. The other major part of the problem was in Asia. The United States and Japan were pursuing irreconcilable courses and the likelihood of war increased as the year wore on.

Like many naval officers of his generation, Stark had long seen Japan as the most likely enemy in any future war. Hitler's sudden and dramatic success in Europe presented the United States with a far more dangerous threat in the Atlantic than Japan did in the Pacific; nevertheless, Stark was alive to the danger posed by Japan.

Stationing the fleet in Hawaii was intended to have a deterrent effect on Japan, but moving the fleet 3,000 miles closer to a possible enemy also exposed it to an increased chance of attack by the Imperial Japanese Navy. In the late summer and autumn of 1940 and into 1941, Stark was increasingly concerned about the growing possibility of Japanese military action in the Pacific. He was particularly concerned about the safety of the fleet.

In November, 1940, when the British successfully mounted an air attack on the Italian fleet in the well-defended port of Taranto, Stark's concern for the safety of the fleet turned to anxiety. The British inflicted most of the damage to the Italian ships by airborne torpedoes dropped from a height of only 30 feet. This unambiguous lesson was not lost on Stark.

He was distinctly worried about the possibility of an attack on Hawaii from overseas. Obviously, the most profitable target of such an attack would be the fleet. Its safety was paramount, but there was little that Stark could do directly to safeguard it. He did alert the fleet commander, Admiral James O. Richardson, to the possibilities and dangers of an air attack and kept him abreast of developments.[1] He directed Richardson to work closely with Rear Admiral Claude C. Bloch, commandant of the local (Fourteenth) naval district and a former fleet commander, and with the army.

Under a long-standing army-navy agreement, the army was primarily responsible for the defense of naval bases. The army's responsibility extended to providing anti-aircraft guns on land, fighter aircraft to defend Hawaii and an aircraft warning system. Specifically, the army was responsible for the "defense of all permanent naval bases" and the "defense against aerial attack of all military and naval facilities ashore within a harbor area."[2]

For this reason, Stark insisted that Secretary of the Navy Frank Knox approach the Secretary of War, Henry L. Stimson, about preparations the army should make to provide an adequate defense for Pearl Harbor. Detection of approaching enemy ships and their engagement was primarily a naval function. But once attacking aircraft were airborne, it was the army's duty to engage them. To do so the army needed, but did not have, an effective warning net and enough aircraft to intercept attacking airplanes. On 24 January 1941 Knox pointed out to Stimson the inadequacy of anti-aircraft defense on Oahu. He urged Stimson to establish a warning net, to rush more pursuit aircraft to Hawaii, and to improve anti-aircraft defenses. Prompted by Stark, Knox made suggestions for local joint plans to coordinate the repulse of surprise air attacks. Stimson accepted them with alacrity. He was in "complete concurrence as to the importance of this matter and the urgency of making every possible preparation to meet such a hostile effort." He assured Knox that "the Hawaiian Department is the best equipped of all our overseas departments and continues to hold a high priority for the completion of its projected defenses because of the importance of giving full protection to the Fleet."[3]

Stark continued to press Army Chief of Staff General George C. Marshall to build up the defenses of Oahu and he helped the army when he could. He even provided an aircraft carrier to ferry army fighter airplanes to Hawaii.[4]

Admiral Husband E. Kimmel relieved Richardson as Pacific Fleet Commander on 1 February 1941. Before Kimmel assumed command of the fleet, Stark wrote to him. He told Kimmel precisely what was on his mind.

In my humble opinion, we may wake up any day with some of our ships bombed, or what not, and find ourselves in another undeclared war, the ramifications of which call for our strongest and sanest imagination and plans.

I have told the Gang here for months past that in my opinion we were heading straight for this war, and that we could not do anything else and personally I do not see how we can avoid either having it thrust upon us or our deliberately going in, many months longer. And of course it may be a matter of weeks or of days.[5]

Kimmel, too, was concerned about the possibility of a surprise attack on Pearl Harbor by aircraft, submarines, or both. He reported to Stark that he was taking immediate steps to minimize the damage inflicted by any attack and to make an attacking force pay dearly.[6] This positive attitude pleased Stark, who felt he had a fleet commander who would cheerfully cooperate with him.

Subordinate commanders in Hawaii were also concerned with the possibility of a surprise Japanese attack on Pearl Harbor. Rear Admiral Patrick N. Bellinger, commander of the Naval Base Defense Air Forces, and his army counterpart Major General F. L. Martin, collaborated at the end of March 1941 on a joint plan of what the army and navy would do if there were a sudden attack on Oahu or on the fleet in the Hawaiian area. They recognized that the most likely and dangerous form of attack would be by air.

Within days following the Martin-Bellinger joint plan, their superiors, Bloch and Lieutenant General Walter C. Short, approved a joint defense plan for Hawaii that assumed a surprise Japanese attack. When this plan was reviewed in Washington, Stark found it so good that he considered it a model of defense planning. He sent copies to all naval district commandants.[7] At about the same time, Stark warned the district commandants that weekends and holidays were favorite times for German or Japanese attacks. He directed them to set proper watches and to take appropriate precautions at those times. "What will happen is anyone's guess," he said.[8]

A few weeks later, he warned Kimmel to be prepared to send a considerable detachment to the Atlantic. Stark anticipated reenforcing the Atlantic fleet by three battleships, one carrier, four cruisers, and two squadrons of destroyers. Patrolling in the Atlantic and the possibility of convoying necessitated the transfer, which was made in May.[9]

Meanwhile, on 3 April, Stark informed all three fleet commanders of the ABC-1 agreement, which would govern future planning. Stark sent to them on 26 May a completed Rainbow 5 war plan based on ABC-1 with instructions to prepare their own fleet operating plans in accordance with it. Within two months, Kimmel's staff completed the Pacific Fleet's operating plan. It arrived in Washington just as Stark was leaving for the Roosevelt-Churchill meeting in Argentia. Stark formally approved the plan on 9 September. The final document for the defense of Pearl Harbor was Kimmel's directive of 14 October to the Pacific Fleet. In it he emphasized that a declaration of war might be preceded by a surprise attack on ships in Pearl Harbor. He specified various suitable measures for self-defense of the fleet.

Taken together these plans satisfied Washington in general and Stark in particular that adequate arrangements had been made both for the defense of the fleet and the base at Pearl Harbor. Kimmel allayed any anxiety Stark may have had about army-navy liaison in Hawaii by reporting on 4 June that he found it "very satisfactory."[10]

One day in early 1941, the President asked Stark and Marshall, "What can we do today that tomorrow we will not be sorry that we failed to do?" Stark suggested that the army bring home the wives and children of their officers and men who were stationed in the Far East. Roosevelt was aghast that they were still there, and they were brought home soon afterwards. Stark's purpose was not to embarrass Marshall, but to ease the pressure on Admiral Thomas C. Hart, commander in chief of the U.S. Asiatic Fleet, who had sent the navy families home several months before in the summer of 1940 as a precautionary measure in a deteriorating situation. The navy men and their families rightly saw no reason why they should be separated while the army families were not. Naturally, Hart's order had produced a great deal of grumbling.[11]

In 1941, the United States discovered the high cost of the lack of military and naval strength, something the army and navy had known for years. With the military and naval balance favoring Japan, prudence dictated improving defenses in the Pacific, husbanding American forces and taking as few risks as possible. For these reasons, Stark consistently opposed any provocation of Japan, lest war in the Pacific detract from the pursuit of the primary American interests in the Atlantic.

He also opposed the deployment of a substantial portion of the fleet from Hawaii to the Far East, not only because the Japanese might find it provocative, but also because he felt strongly that dividing the fleet in a period of increasing tension would be an unnecessary risk compared with any possible gain. For the same reason, he also opposed the imposition of commercial restrictions, such as an oil embargo, in addition to limited restrictions on the export of metal to Japan.

In early February 1941, the British and the State Department got into a jitter, according to Stark, over a report that the Japanese would attack Borneo or Singapore on 10 February.[12] Roosevelt summoned Hull, Stimson, Marshall, Knox, and Stark to the White House on 4 February for a two-hour conference on the Far Eastern situation. Stark discounted the report on its merits. He felt that Japanese forces in the area were insufficient to undertake such an ambitious operation as an amphibious landing in southern Indochina or in Borneo. He was convinced that the Japanese were not seeking, at least at that time, war with Great Britain, the Netherlands, and the United States at the same time. Rather, he thought they would try to pick off one country's assets at a time.[13]

When Hull proposed sending additional ships to the Far East, Stark opposed it. It was a lively discussion. Stark argued his position with more vehemence and with stronger language than usual. To his surprise, Stimson supported him. Stark carried the day when Roosevelt agreed that no more ships should be sent to the Far East.[14] Roosevelt was willing to risk one or two ships, but not the five or six Hull wanted to send. Stark heaved a sigh of relief.

To make sure the President had his argument in writing, the next day Stark sent him a memorandum of his estimate of the situation in Indochina.[15] Stark's oral argument and his written memorandum seemed to have killed the proposal. At least he thought so. Within a week, however, he was back in the White House arguing his point again.

Roosevelt was toying with the idea of sending a force of four cruisers, a carrier, and a squadron of destroyers on a cruise to Manila and back to Hawaii. Stark found this proposed cruise far less objectionable than the proposal of the week before that had Singapore as a destination. Still, he opposed it because the force involved would be too small to be an effective deterrent to Japan; because dividing the fleet would weaken it and thus remove a potential threat to Japan's flank; and because the United States' main interests were in the Atlantic, which meant wisdom precluded undue risk or involvement in the Pacific. This time Stark was not optimistic about his chances of squelching the proposed deployment.

The State Department won the next round. At the White House two weeks later, Roosevelt told Stark to send four cruisers and squadron of destroyers southwest from Hawaii. The first port would be Samoa. Roosevelt was undecided as to whether to send this detachment to the Philippines and possibly to other Far Eastern ports. The only thing clear was Roosevelt's immense enjoyment at deploying navy ships. Stark had lost his struggle to keep the fleet concentrated in Hawaii. After accepting the President's decision gracefully, he then proceeded to impress upon Roosevelt the importance of keeping the detachment on the Japanese flank rather than placing it at risk in the South China Sea.

In early March Roosevelt decided to send the detachment, which had reached Samoa by that time, on to Australia and New Zealand. They would not visit the Philippines or any other Far Eastern ports. Instead, they would go to Sydney, Brisbane, and Auckland.[16] Stark won at least part of his struggle. The ships would remain on the Japanese flank.

Roosevelt was delighted with the "practice cruise" to Australia and New Zealand. He told Stark to send them out again as soon as they returned. "Betty, I just want to keep them popping up here and there and keep the Japs guessing," he explained.[17]

The last thing Stark needed was another "practice cruise" in the Pacific that would divide the fleet again and might provoke the Japanese to some form of response. If the fleet were to be divided, it should be because part of it was being transferred to the Atlantic. He clearly saw the influence of the State Department in Roosevelt's idea. He not only disagreed with it, but under the circumstances, he thought it was childish.

Rather than attempt to change Roosevelt's mind, Stark went along with the idea. He agreed to another cruise so long as it remained on the Japanese flank. He suggested a northern cruise this time, possibly in the general direction of the Kamchatka peninsula. Stark knew the Japanese would be alarmed at the movement of a striking force the size Roosevelt contemplated sending. He hoped the State Department would be sufficiently alarmed to drop the whole idea. He was not disappointed. Ten days later on 12 April at a meeting in the White House, Hull, in Stark's presence, asked Roosevelt, "Please, Mr. President, don't let him do it." Roosevelt killed the idea.[18]

When Kimmel visited Washington in early June, he brought with him a letter to Stark in which he complained about the uncertainty of policy in a rapidly changing situation and the lack of information as to what forces would be available to him.[19] Stark was concerned not only about the merits of this complaint but also because it showed Kimmel's tendency to hesitate in the face of known and unknowable factors. Kimmel enjoyed Stark's confidence and he had an enviable record as a naval officer. He was Stark's candidate to succeed Richardson and his appointment was applauded throughout the navy. But his insistence upon certainty in the fluid but deteriorating situation in 1941, however justified it may have been, was a clear indication of a degree of inflexibility, of a lack of sensitivity and of an inability to accommodate to rapidly changing conditions that most everyone firmly believed would eventually lead to war. Unfortunately, there was no well known or clearly defined foreign policy upon which the navy could base its plans. In Washington, Stark accepted what he could not change, while in Hawaii, Kimmel complained that conditions were not ideal. Hart was in a far more difficult position, yet he retained a positive and realistic attitude.

Stark was properly concerned with Kimmel's point of view and with his frame of mind. While Kimmel was in Washington, Stark assembled his principal assistants for a full discussion with him of the matters raised in his letter. When Kimmel left, Stark felt he knew as much as anyone in the Navy Department about national and navy policy. In view of the circumstances, Kimmel had been educated in uncertainty.

As the summer of 1941 progressed, Stark became more deeply involved in the conduct of American relations with Japan. Not only did he maintain close contacts with Hull and the State Department, but he was also a personal friend of the Japanese Ambassador, Admiral Kichisaburo Nomura. Many navy officers knew and liked him; they felt Nomura could be trusted. Somewhat out of his depth in conducting delicate negotations on behalf of a government bent on a militant policy, Nomura held a moderate view and he sincerely desired a settlement on more reasonable terms than did his government.

Stark told Hart and Kimmel at the end of July in an informal but informative letter that Nomura talked with Stark for two hours before going to the State Department. Nomura's sincerity that he wanted to avoid war impressed Stark. It was very plain talk. Stark did not mince words in pointing out the shallowness of the reasons Nomura gave in defense of Japanese policies. Stark thought that for the time being the Japanese would consolidate their position in Indochina and await world reaction. He expected early Japanese action against the Burma Road from their Indochinese bases. He reported this conversation to Roosevelt and made arrangements for Nomura to see the President the next day. It would be wishful thinking to expect things to get better, but he wanted Hart and Kimmel to know that Washington was struggling for something better.[20]

Stark constantly urged moderation in dealing with Japanese ambitions, lest American attention to the primary German threat he diverted. He opposed an oil embargo against Japan, because he felt that the Japanese would go to war if their oil supply were cut off. He thought the war would not necessarily be with the United States, but with a power from whom Japan could take oil. The day after Nomura met with Roosevelt at the White House, Stark and Roosevelt had a long telephone conversation in which Stark again opposed any embargo. Nevertheless, the following day Roosevelt issued an executive order freezing Japanese assets in the United States and establishing an embargo of all trade between Japan and the United States. Stark told Kimmel, King, and Hart of the impending embargo before Roosevelt issued his executive order.[21]

Although Stark opposed the embargo, it was not lightly or recklessly imposed. Washington had learned by means of breaking Japanese codes that the Japanese government was bent on expansion in Asia. This policy had broad support in all of the principal Japanese political and military groups. Stark passed this information along with a warning about Japanese designs on Indochina to the fleet commanders on 3 July, noting, "This policy probably involves war in the near future."[22]

In the summer of 1941 Stark perceived that the Japanese were in one of their "indecisive periods." He still did not give up hope of continued peace in the Pacific, but he wished that "the thread by which it continues to hang were not so slender."[23] At the end of September, he told Kimmel and Hart about the decision to escort convoys and the order to shoot on sight in the Atlantic, writing, "We are all but, if not actually, in it." Turning to conditions in the Pacific, he reported that Hull had not given up hope of a satisfactory diplomatic solution. He thought chances of a settlement were very slight, even though Admiral Nomura was working hard on his home government. Hull had informed him that conversations with the Japanese were almost at an impasse. Stark sent Kimmel and Hart a one-page memorandum from Marshall setting forth just what the army was doing to reenforce the Philippines. He reassured Kimmel that Washington did not intend to reduce the Pacific fleet any further by transfers of ships to the Atlantic.[24]

Stark's pessimism grew after Nomura came to see him in late September. Nomura had the reputation among the top navy officers as an honest, reliable man who could be trusted. In describing the interview to Kimmel, Stark said he had helped Nomura before, but he was unsure if he could do so again. Conversations without results could not last forever. It looked as if they might fall through this time, in which case the situation could only grow more tense. In any event, Stark promised to keep Kimmel informed "if there is anything of moment."[25]

Time for diplomatic negotiations was indeed running out. In a conference held on 2 September, the Japanese army representatives urged the immediate rupture of relations with the United States. However, Japanese Prime Minister Prince Konoye, supported by the Emperor, obtained an additional period of grace in which to pursue diplomatic negotiations. The agreement reached at this conference specified that if by early October no reasonable hope remained of Japan obtaining her demands by diplomacy, "we will immediately make up our minds for war" with the United States, Great Britain, and the Netherlands.[26] No hint of this decision was gleaned from intercepted Japanese diplomatic messages and it was not known in Washington until after the Japanese surrender in 1945. But Washington did know the element of time had become crucial to the Japanese foreign office. Stark was convinced that the Japanese were stalling for time and "waiting until the situation in Europe becomes more stabilized.[27]

Time for Konoye's diplomacy finally ran out in October. General Hideki Tojo replaced him as prime minister. Stark informed the fleet commanders by secret dispatch of the grave situation caused by the fall of the Konoye cabinet. He specified, "Since the United States and

Britain are held responsible by Japan for her present desperate situation, there is also a possibility that Japan may attack these two powers." He specifically directed "due precautions including such preparatory deployments as will not disclose strategic intentions nor constitute provocative actions against Japan."[28]

In October the prevailing opinion in the Navy Department favored a fairly severe crisis, but Stark remained skeptical. At that time he saw war with Japan only as a possibility, requiring the navy to be on guard. When he returned to his office from a meeting at the White House, he softened the wording of the dispatch drafted by his staff. Still, he felt it prudent to be on guard until a trend developed. He diverted all United States merchant shipping in the Pacific to the south to remove it from the danger zone in the event of war with Japan. These routing instructions remained in effect until war finally broke out in December.

During the week in which the Konoye cabinet fell and the USS *Kearney* was torpedoed in the North Atlantic, Kimmel issued his instructions to the Pacific Fleet about the security of the Pearl Harbor Naval Base. He flatly stated that a declaration of war "may be preceded by a surprise attack on Pearl Harbor." One week later, Stark ordered that all army-navy transports between Honolulu and Manila be escorted both ways.[29] Although unknown to American officials, the countdown to Pearl Harbor had begun.

Kimmel informed Stark on 22 October of his force dispositions purusant to Stark's dispatch informing him of the change in the Japanese government. In approving of them, Stark worried about the next development in the rapidly deteriorating relations with Japan. On 7 November he told Kimmel, "The big question is what next? . . . Things seem to be moving steadily towards a crisis in the Pacific. Just when it will break no one can tell . . . it continually gets 'worser and worser' . . . . A month may see, literally, most anything. Two irreconcilable policies cannot on on forever—particularly if one party cannot live with the set up. It doesn't look good."[30] He was sadly prophetic. He put it more bluntly to Hart, "Events are moving rapidly towards a real showdown, both in the Atlantic and in the Pacific. . . . Whether the country knows it or not, *we are at war*" (emphasis in original).[31]

In November, the Japanese sent a professional diplomat, Saburo Kurusu, to Washington to assist Nomura. Stark did not think Kurusu would be able to accomplish much. The Japanese press stated that a solution could be had only if the United States conceded every point of difference. Stark could not see how such divergent views could be resolved. He told Kimmel, "The next few days hold much for us." He was not optimistic about the outcome.[32]

In a nutshell, the United States was willing to resume trade with Japan and to come to a political agreement, provided that Japan evacuated Indochina and settled with China. Both the United States and Japan insisted the other act first. Although this is an over-simplification, it nevertheless illustrates the intractability of the two positions. Diplomacy had just about run its course.

The Japanese made one last attempt at negotiations. Tokyo set the deadline at 25 November and later extended it for a few days. First, they presented Plan A, which dealt with trade in China, Japanese troops in China, and Japanese membership in the Tripartite Pact. Intercepted diplomatic messages gave Washington advance notice of what Nomura would propose. Hull rejected Plan A on 15 November. Meanwhile, Ambassador Saburo Kurusu arrived to help Nomura present Plan B, which they submitted on 20 November. American officials were also busy drafting a counterproposal; Hull asked for Stark's comments.[33] Both Roosevelt and Hull were pessimistic about the outcome of negotiations.[34]

A day or two after Kurusu arrived, Nomura sent a young Japanese lieutenant to see Stark's flag lieutenant, Lieutenant Commander William R. Smedberg, III. The lieutenant told Smedberg that Nomura wanted to see Stark in secret. Stark agreed and Smedberg made the arrangements. The following Sunday afternoon, 23 November, Smedberg, in civilian clothes, drove his own Plymouth out Massachusetts Avenue. When he saw an elderly, rotund Japanese gentleman walking in the same direction, Smedberg offered him a lift. He then drove Nomura farther out Massachusetts Avenue to Stark's quarters at the Naval Observatory. The Japanese and American admirals were alone in Stark's study for over two hours.

Nomura spoke frankly. He told Stark that the military-dominated Japanese government intended to go to war if the United States did not relax economic and trade sanctions. Nomura said that the Japanese army, and particularly Tojo, the new prime minister, had no concept of the military and naval potential of the United States. Nomura did, and he feared the worst if the United States and Japan went to war. Afterwards, Smedberg drove Nomura back down Massachusetts Avenue and let him out a good way from the Japanese embassy.[35]

The day after this unusual meeting, 24 November, Stark warned Kimmel, Hart, King, and others in a secret dispatch: "chance of favorable outcome of negotiations with Japan very doubtful. This situation coupled with statement of Japanese government and movements of their naval and military forces indicates in our opinion that a surprise aggressive movement in any direction, including attack on Philippines or Guam is a possibility."[36]

Two days after Stark met with Nomura, he, Marshall, and the other members of the War Council met with Roosevelt at the White House. He and Marshall pleaded with Roosevelt for more time in which to rush military equipment and men to the Philippines. They favored military action only if Japan threatened British, Dutch, or American territory. Later they sent Roosevelt a written memorandum that embodied their plea.[37]

Apparently their arguments swayed Roosevelt, who favored a modus vivendi counterproposal providing essentially for a three-month truce. Stark and Marshall were elated and greatly relieved at the prospect.[38]

Stark told Kimmel what happened at this meeting with Roosevelt. Both the President and Hull confirmed the gravity of the situation and neither would be surprised at a Japanese surprise attack somewhere. Some officials thought the Japanese might attack the Philippines, but Stark did not give it the weight others did. He admitted that an attack on the Philippines would be the most embarrassing thing the Japanese could do, but thought that Japanese advances into Thailand, Indochina, and the Burma Road area were more likely. It was clear, however, that the Japanese were about to strike at British and Dutch possessions in the Far East. What could the United States do to prevent it? Congress would hardly pass a war resolution to protect European colonies in Asia, even though their loss would seriously affect the allied war effort. It was a painful dilemma. Stark admitted to Kimmel, "I won't go into the pros and cons of what the United States may do. I will be damned if I know. I wish I did. The only thing I do know is that we may do most anything and that's the only thing I know to be prepared for; or that we may do nothing—I think it is more likely to be 'anything'."[39]

By his dispatch of 24 November and the amplifying letter he sent the next day to Kimmel, Stark conveyed the possibility of "a surprise aggressive movement in any direction," and the necessity of being prepared for anything.[40] The level of tension had gone up still another notch.

Hull went back to the State Department on 25 November and had second thoughts. He later said he decided "to kick the whole thing over." With Roosevelt's permission he reverted to his original hard-line position. Hull met with Kurusu and Nomura on 26 November and instead of the modus vivendi counterproposal, he handed them the "Ten Point Note." It simply restated the American position.[41] Neither Stark nor Marshall knew at the time what Hull had done.

The next morning, 27 November, they found out. The army-navy code breakers deciphered the dispatches Nomura and Kurusu sent to Tokyo about Hull's Ten Point Note. Stark was aghast. Instead of the modus vivendi, which held the most reasonable promise of a truce or at least a postponement of hostilities for a while until reenforcements could reach the Philippines, Hull had sent a note that would be clearly unacceptable to Tokyo. Further negotiations were highly unlikely.

Meanwhile, the Japansese had loaded somewhere between 30 and 50 transports in Shanghai. This expedition then proceeded south and great guessing games as to its destination began. The fleet commanders obviously had to be told of this ominous movement and the imminent rupture of negotiations. What to tell them and how to say it to convey correctly the gravity of the situation were uppermost in the minds of Stark and his principal advisors.

For two days, there were serious and at a times heated discussions in Stark's office about what information to send and how to word it. King, the Atlantic Fleet Commander, was in Washington at the time and he, too, joined the discussions. He saw Stark three times on 26 November and he saw Roosevelt the next afternoon. The third meeting with Stark was lengthy and included Ingersoll and Turner. They discussed at length the contents and wording of a dispatch to Kimmel, Hart, and others.

On the morning of Thanksgiving day, 27 November, Stark met with Knox and Stimson. He telephoned Hull, who confirmed that negotiations with Japan had ceased and that it was now up to the army and navy. Stark again consulted with Rear Admirals Ingersoll and Turner. Meanwhile, Turner had drafted a dispatch.

Stark read it, and at first demurred, thinking it was too strong. Turner vehemently disagreed. He said they were in agreement that war was inevitable, but they did not know how soon or when it would come. He thought the time had come to tell the fleet commanders unequivocally that war was imminent. "We must warn them," he said. The conversation was hot and heavy with Turner's outspoken forcefulness. Each facet, word, and implication in that dispatch was carefully and critically examined to make sure that it accurately conveyed the situation as Washington perceived it. Then Stark released it.[42]

The first words were ominous and unambiguous: "This dispatch is to be considered a war warning." The words "war warning" had never been used before in any dispatches to Kimmel and to the other fleet commanders, but their use had been carefully weighed and considered. They were put at the beginning to accentuate the extreme gravity of the situation. No other dispatch had carried such portentous words. The Japanese had the initiative. Washington did not know where they would strike, only that they would strike somewhere. Stark warned the Pacific and Asiatic Fleet commanders and gave them as much information as was available in Washington without confusing them with ambiguities and qualifications. With the information then available to him, he could not have been more explicit.

> This dispatch is to be considered a war warning. Negotiations with Japan looking toward stabilization of conditions in the Pacific have ceased and an aggressive move by Japan is expected within the next few days.
> The number and equipment of Japanese troops and the organization of naval task forces indicate an amphibious expedition against either the Philippines, Thai, or Kra Peninsula or possibly Borneo.

Following this general information, Hart and Kimmel received specific orders:

> Execute an appropriate defense deployment preparatory to carrying out the tasks assigned in War Plan 46 (Rainbow 5). Inform District and army authorities. A similar warning is being sent by War Department.

SPENAVO (Special Naval Observer London, Rear Admiral Ghormley) inform British. Continental districts, Guam, Samoa directed to take appropriate measures against sabotage.[43]

Although the indications were that the Japanese destination might be the Philippines, Thai, or Kra Peninsula, or even Borneo, Washington did not rule out other objectives. Three days earlier Stark had warned against a "surprise aggressive movement in any direction." He intended this first dispatch to be read in connection with the war warning dispatch of 27 November in which he provided the latest intelligence about Japanese movements. The situation was so grave that he thought all American forces in the Pacific should be prepared for the worst.

The day after the dispatch was sent, Stark met twice more with King. The second time followed a meeting at the White House. They discussed the gravity of the situation in the Pacific and the warning sent to the fleet.[44]

Washington remained in doubt as to the ultimate destination of the Japanese expedition, which had been at sea for several days. On 30 November, Stark directed Hart to patrol by air the line from Manila to Camranh Bay for three days in order to ascertain just where the Japanese were heading. Kimmel received a copy of this dispatch.[45]

Three days later on 3 December, Stark sent another dispatch to Hart, Kimmel, and the naval district commandants in Manila and Honolulu. He informed them that Japanese diplomatic and consular posts at Hong Kong, Singapore, Batavia, Manila, Washington, and London had been ordered to destroy their codes. Stark thought this urgent order by the Japanese to demolish their codes, ciphers, and secret documents to be "one of the most telling items of information we had received, and our dispatch . . . was one of the most important dispatches we ever sent."[46] War was obviously near.

Guam was particularly vulnerable. As a precaution to avoid capture by the Japanese in the event they seized the island, the Navy Department on 4 December directed the naval station on Guam to destroy "all secret and confidential publications and other classified matter." The only exception was the minimum necessary for current purposes. The Asiatic and Pacific Fleet Commanders received a copy of this dispatch.[47] It was another indication that war was imminent.

Unknown to the U.S. government and the Japanese diplomats, a major carrier task force had departed Sasebo in late November. Travelling by a northern route to avoid detection, this force was approaching its position to launch the attack on Pearl Harbor. Japanese communications deception was so good that navy officials in Washington thought the ships in question were in home waters. However, the intelligence officer on Kimmel's staff told Kimmel that the Japanese carriers had been lost, that is, he was uncertain of their location.[48] This information was not relayed to the Navy Department in Washington.

The final step in the diplomatic charade was the formal Japanese reply to Hull's ten point message of 26 November. During the night of 6–7 December, the Japanese Foreign Office transmitted the official reply. It was a long dispatch, consisting of 14 coded parts. The first 13 parts were intercepted and decoded by American intelligence officers in Washington. Roosevelt was informed of these messages. Later that evening, after Stark returned from the National Theater, he and Roosevelt discussed them on the private telephone line from Stark's quarters to the White House. There was no new information or any clue whatsoever of the impending attack. When decoded, the 14th part stated simply, "it is impossible to reach an agreement through further negotiations." This conclusion was substantially what Stark said in the war warning message of 27 November—"Negotiations with Japan have ceased."[49]

During the forenoon of Sunday, 7 December, additional information was received that Kurusu and Nomura had been instructed to present the 14 parts of the Japanese reply to Hull at precisely 1:00 P.M. that afternoon. Stark was in his office that morning preparing for a meeting with Roosevelt at 3:00 P.M. that same afternoon when Marshall telephoned him to ask if he had seen the latest message. After Stark said he had, Marshall asked what he thought about sending the information concerning the time of presentation to the various commanders in the Pacific. Stark's first reaction was that so much information had been sent to them that he hesitated to send more for fear of confusing them. He hung up.

A moment later he called Marshall back saying there might be some significance in the time of presentation to Hull. One P.M. on a Sunday was an unusual hour for a formal diplomatic call. Stark offered to send the dispatch by navy communications. But when Marshall assured him that the army communications were rapid and reliable, he asked Marshall to include instructions to inform the navy command at Pearl Harbor.[50] The time of presentation of the note was highly significant. One P.M. Washington time was 7:30 A.M. Hawaii time—30 minutes before the moment scheduled for the attack no one expected. Unfortunately, there was a delay in the army's transmission and Marshall's dispatch was not delivered until after the air attack. Stark did not use the telephone to call Kimmel because it was not secure for secret information and because he had nothing to tell Kimmel other than the time the two Japanese ambassadors had asked for an appointment.

The air raid on Pearl Harbor damaged but did not destroy the Pacific Fleet. The battleships suffered the most, but fortunately the carriers were at sea and they escaped unscathed. There was no substantial damage to drydocks and other shore facilities or to the fuel dumps. Pearl Harbor was still serviceable as the Pacific Fleet's forward operating base.

In the relatively small and closely knit navy of that time, everyone knew men serving on board the ships and staffs of the Pacific Fleet, and nearly everyone had served on one or more of the stricken ships. The USS *West Virginia,* Stark's old ship, which he had commanded and of which he was so proud, sank at her moorings, with her commanding officer, Captain Mervyn S. Bennion, mortally wounded on the bridge. Bennion and Stark had served together at the Naval Powder Factory in 1929. As painful as the air raid was for all naval officers, by far its greatest effect was the shock it gave to the nation. Public outrage galvanized the United States into action. There was no longer any doubt that Japan, Germany, and to a lesser extent Italy, were the enemy and must be destroyed. The irresistible needs of waging a total, unlimited war subordinated all other concerns, especially personal ones, to the demands of ultimate victory. No one was more aware of this fact than Stark.

7

PEARL HARBOR TO ARCADIA

As Japanese bombs and torpedoes fell on Pearl Harbor on Sunday, 7 December 1941, the fog of war descended on Washington. Stark was talking with Secretary of the Navy Frank Knox when the brief dispatch arrived from Hawaii at 1:50 P.M. It simply said, "Air raid Pearl Harbor. This is no drill."[1] Knox telephoned Roosevelt at once with the news.

A few minutes later Stark learned that the damage was heavy. He telephoned Roosevelt with this information and asked for authority to execute War Plan 46, the navy's version of Rainbow 5. Roosevelt gave him the authority and the U.S. Navy officially went to war. Less than forty minutes had elapsed.

Roosevelt summoned his war cabinet to meet at the White House within the hour. When Knox, Stark, Secretary of War Henry L. Stimson, and Army Chief of Staff General George C. Marshall met with Roosevelt they knew little more than that Japan had commenced hostilities and that there had been extensive damage and great loss of life at Pearl Harbor. The exact extent of the damage would remain unknown for at least a few more hours. The whereabouts and destination of the Japanese carriers that launched the attacking aircraft were also unknown. No one in the Navy Department was surprised the Japanese had struck, but they were appalled that the first blow was at Pearl Harbor.

Stark made several telephone calls to Rear Admiral Claude C. Bloch, commandant of the naval district in Hawaii, for additional details. Finally, at 7:00 P.M. Washington time, more than five hours after the initial report, Bloch provided the details. He told Stark that the battleship *Nevada* had been hit and set on fire; *Oklahoma* and

114

Arizona had been hit and had capsized; *California* and *West Virginia* were burning, but were still afloat. The USS *Maryland* was all right. Bloch reported tht two U.S. Navy task forces were at sea and that a submarine, later identified as Japanese, had been sunk, in the harbor. There were unverified reports of parachute troops landings.

Stark asked if army or navy planes were in the air when the Japanese struck. Bloch told him some patrol planes were out, but he was not sure what sector they were patrolling. Stark wanted to know, "Did our patrol planes get them before they hit us?"

"No," Bloch said, "The first word we had was that a destroyer was torpedoed by a sub and ten minutes later the Japs came in a flock and that is what did the damage." Stark asked if the submarine were German, but it had not yet been identified.

Reminding Bloch that he had prophesied a morning raid, Stark told him to tell Kimmel, "I will be asking him that I want to know how far out they (patrol aircraft) were and in what sectors."

Bloch ended the conversation with, "The answers will be sad—very unsatisfactory. They caught us flat footed. That is my judgment. We had patrols out, but the first thing we saw were those planes coming in."

The following day, details of the extent of the damage became more clear. Then Washington received reports of another attack by thirty planes. Forty-five minutes before Roosevelt was scheduled to address a joint session of Congress on Monday, 8 December, Stark's Assistant Chief of Naval Operations, Rear Admiral Royal E. Ingersoll, telephoned Bloch again for the latest information. Bloch assured him there had been no further attacks on Pearl Harbor, adding, "We have had more false reports during the night than you could shake a stick at."[2]

At midday Stark joined Marshall, members of the cabinet, the Supreme Court, and both Houses of Congress at the capitol to hear President Roosevelt denounce the Japanese attack. He asked Congress to recognize the existence of a state of war between the United States and Japan. Congress quickly approved a war resolution with only one negative vote, cast by Representative Jeannette Rankin of Montana. The United States was now legally at war with Japan. Three days later Hitler gratuitously declared war on the United States, thus making official the unofficial naval war that had been waged in the Atlantic since the previous September.

Stark was faced with the immediate necessity of dealing with the aftermath of the attack on Pearl Harbor: assessing the damage, providing salvage and repair equipment, deploying the Pacific Fleet and the Asiatic Fleet. The Pacific islands of Wake, Midway, Samoa, Johnston, and Palmyra were in grave danger. It was necessary to keep open the sealanes to Australia and the Southwest Pacific. Wartime procedures and operations from the simplest to the most complex had to be implemented. One of the simplest procedures was to ban the wearing of civilian clothes by on-duty military officers in Washington, D.C. According to one officer, on the morning of 8 December there was an overpowering odor of mothballs from uniforms hastily retrieved from closets.[3]

A pressing problem confronting the navy at that time was command of the Pacific Fleet. It was imperative to have the right man in command of the fleet. Acting on his own initiative, but with Roosevelt's express permission, Knox left for Pearl Harbor on 9 December. The purpose of his trip was ostensibly to assess at firsthand the damage at Pearl Harbor, but he really wanted to assess the Pacific Fleet's commander, Admiral Husband E. Kimmel. Knox returned to Washington on Sunday, 14 December.

Within an hour of his return he informed Stark and other officers in the Navy Department of the extent of the damage at Pearl Harbor. At a meeting lasting until midnight Knox described it in detail in words and with photographs: six ships lost, two of them battleships; 91 officers and 2,638 enlisted men killed; nearly 650 wounded. After reporting to the President the next day, Knox released this information to the press. There was more to come.[4]

Knox went to Hawaii because he felt it was imperative to clear up what he saw as a nasty situation.[5] He decided that Kimmel should be relieved and he advised Roosevelt to that effect. Kimmel was summarily removed from command on 17 December and ordered home. His successor was Rear Admiral Chester W. Nimitz. Nimitz was in Washington and it would take him a few days to arrive at Pearl Harbor. Meanwhile, command of the Pacific Fleet temporarily devolved on Vice Admiral William S. Pye. Although Knox had lost confidence in Kimmel, Stark had not. He felt that Kimmel could be useful in some other capacity, even if it were necessary to relieve him of command of the Pacific Fleet. Both Roosevelt and Knox turned a deaf ear to Stark's intercession for Kimmel.

Knox had in mind one other major shift of command. He felt that King ought to become Commander in Chief, U.S. Fleet (COMINCH). In that capacity he would be in command of all the navy's operational forces. Roosevelt agreed on 16 December and the appointment was announced a few days later. Neither Roosevelt nor Knox consulted Stark in this decision, but Stark knew King and approved of the appointment.

Stark had great confidence in King's abilities and had rescued King from oblivion on the General Board in 1940 by assigning him to command of the Atlantic Squadron. As a result, King was promoted from rear admiral to full admiral. Moreover, in 1941 King was a confidant of Stark. Frequently the two men had lunch in Stark's office while they discussed various naval matters, and in the days immediately following the attack on Pearl Harbor, King was almost a constant visitor in Stark's office. The cordial relationship that existed betwen them when King commanded the Atlantic Fleet continued when King became COMINCH.

When Roosevelt appointed King to command the U.S. Fleet, he also issued an executive order separating the functions of Commander in Chief, U.S. Fleet (COMINCH) from those of the Chief of Naval Operations. Arising out of wartime necessity, this executive order clarified the functions and specified the authorities of COMINCH and CNO. King was vested with supreme command of the operating fleets and the naval coastal commands. To this extent the functions of the Chief of Naval Operations were reduced. Henceforth Stark was to concern himself with the professional administration of the Navy Department, with long-range war planning, and with the provision of men and material.[6] Ever since the creation of the post of CNO during World War I the authority of the CNO over the several navy bureaus had been vague and ill-defined. At one stroke Roosevelt produced a radical and beneficial change in naval administration.

The COMINCH's headquarters would be in Washington where he would be able to command naval forces in both the Pacific and the Atlantic, thus establishing a second four star command in Washington. King said he was content to remain subordinate to Stark, because he thought it logical and sensible.[7] But when he relieved Stark at the end of March 1942, the positions of COMINCH and CNO were merged. Then there was no doubt whatsoever as to who was in command of the navy, both afloat and ashore.

For the three months prior to March 1942, the navy got along under the dual direction of Stark and King. This awkward arrangement worked as well as could be expected, simply because both Stark and King were determined that it should. Regardless of what Stark and King may have intended, resentment was inevitable. Some of Stark's closest associates felt King was doing all he could to eclipse Stark and assume the functions of CNO. However, this arrangement was convenient and useful because it left Stark in Washington to work with the various bureaus of the navy and to work with Roosevelt, Churchill, and the British chiefs of staff at the Arcadia conference.

When Churchill heard of the Japanese attack on Pearl Harbor his first thought was to proceed to Washington to coordinate war strategy with Roosevelt.[8] Following an exchange of telegrams, Roosevelt agreed and within a week of American entry into the war Churchill, accompanied by the British chiefs of staff, embarked in the new battleship, HMS *Duke of York* bound for the United States. The British were apprehensive lest the Japanese attack deflect American attention from Europe to the Pacific.

While Churchill and his party were at sea, Stark felt it necessary to make changes in the disposition of the U.S. naval forces in the Pacific. Instead of the offensive operations contemplated in Rainbow 5 (the capture or neutralization of the Marshall and Caroline islands), the sudden turn of events required a more defensive posture than had been previously projected. A thrust by United States' naval forces through the central Pacific was not possible at that time. Stark informed the British naval staff in Washington on 16 December that the primary duties of the Pacific Fleet were essentially to protect the sealanes of communication from the United States to the Southwest Pacific and to prevent the expansion of Japanese military power to the Western Hemisphere.[9]

This summit meeting between Roosevelt and Churchill was known as Arcadia. It presented difficulties for Stark. By the Executive Order of 16 December Roosevelt assigned operational control of the U.S. Navy to the COMINCH and he assigned the CNO responsibility for "preparation of war plans from the long range point of view."[10] King did not formally assume his new duties until 30 December, a week after Arcadia convened. But he was in Washington and was privy to the preparations the Americans made for this conference.

While at sea Churchill cabled a proposed agenda to Roosevelt. When he received it, Roosevelt called Stark, Marshall, Knox, King, Secretary of War Henry L. Stimson, and Chester W. Nimitz, the new commander of the Pacific Fleet, to the White House on Sunday, 21 December to explain the scope and purpose of the forthcoming conference with the British. At that time Roosevelt asked them to attend as his advisors. After Stark and Marshall had an opportunity to examine Churchill's proposed agenda, they met again at the White House with Roosevelt and the Secretaries of War and the Navy.

Stark and Marshall told Roosevelt that the primary strategic objective should be the defeat of Germany and her allies. Initially it would be necessary to maintain the strategic defensive, but local offensives could be conducted in appropriate theaters. Ultimately they envisaged an all-out offensive against Germany and her allies first and then an offensive against Japan.

On the eve of the Arcadia conference Roosevelt and his civilian and military advisors were agreed on the overall strategy for the conduct of the war and on the necessity for a high command to implement it. All that remained was to reach a similar concurrence of views with Churchill and the British delegation, who would arrive the following afternoon.

HMS *Duke of York* steamed into Hampton Roads late in the afternoon of 22 December. Churchill and his party then flew to Washington and Roosevelt met them at the airport. Churchill stayed in the White House where he and Roosevelt enjoyed an intimacy that was both amiable and productive. The two men began at once a series of informal conversations at all hours. The first wartime summit formally convened late the following afternoon. It was devoted to a discussion of the general world political and military situation. Roosevelt spoke first and outlined his views on conditions in the southwest Pacific and in northwest Africa. Then Churchill took the floor. He noted the "ferment in the French minds" over the entry of the United States into the war and the German reverses in Russia. He thought the British Eighth Army might well push the Axis forces in Libya back into Tunisia. In which case the situation would be "pregnant." He thought that at that moment the French people at home or in North Africa would no longer accede to German demands.[11] Then the British and the Americans must act. This perception formed the genesis of the great Anglo-American interest in North Africa at the Arcadia conference. It also led to advance planning for unilateral British action in North Africa, known as Operation Gymnast, or possible Anglo-American action there, Operation Super-Gymnast. In fact, it would be nearly ten months before Allied armed forces entered North Africa and then it was primarily an American operation. Nevertheless, the seed had been planted at the highest Anglo-American levels.

Roosevelt said categorically that since the United States was now at war he could see no further necessity for transferring American ships to the British. Before the President could go too far, Stark pointed out that because of the lack of sufficient numbers of trained men such a transfer might be necessary to get the ships to sea and operating against the Axis. The matter was hastily disposed of by directing Stark and the First Sea Lord, Admiral of the Fleet Sir Dudley Pound, to resolve it by pooling their resources.[12]

That evening, while Roosevelt and Churchill, with presidential assistant Harry Hopkins, discussed the military subjects raised by their respective chiefs of staff, the American and British delegations, including the secretaries and under secretaries of the Navy and War, dined at the Carlton Hotel. After dinner, the large gathering broke up into smaller groups and chatted over the problems facing them. The relaxed informality of this meeting enhanced the spirit of cooperation and harmony that pervaded this and subsequent meetings.[13]

The next day was Christmas Eve. Early that morning Stark conferred with his associates before meeting with the British Chiefs of Staff at the Federal Reserve Building. This was the first meeting of the British and American military and naval staffs without the overwhelming presence of Churchill and Roosevelt. No civilians were present.

Stark presided. The first meeting of the British and American military and naval staffs was devoted to discussing various matters that Roosevelt and Churchill had brought up the previous evening at the White House. To the great relief of the British, Stark opened the meeting by stating the general concensus that the British Isles were the "fortress which must be protected at all costs."[14]

The three hour meeting covered a wide range of topics. The most pressing naval problem in the Atlantic was the German submarine threat. Stark promised that the U.S. Navy would continue its collaboration with the Royal Navy. Now that the United States was officially at war there would be no inhibitions on what the navy could do. Churchill had mentioned the possibility of the Royal Navy getting additional American destroyers. Stark pointed out, "We just don't have any destroyers to spare and in fact have far fewer than we require for our own needs."[15] The construction program for destroyers was the farthest behind, primarily because the 1940 shipbuilding program had eliminated destroyers as a matter of economy.

Although the Chiefs of Staff were concerned with the possibilities of offensive action in the Atlantic as required by the Germany-first strategy, they were also greatly concerned about the course of the war in the Pacific. They agreed that a strategic defensive in the Pacific was appropriate, given the great momentum of the Japanese advance. Nevertheless, Field Marshal Sir John Dill thought the British defenders of Singapore would be able to hold Johore State. Unfortunately, future events did not bear out his optimism. Stark enumerated the Anglo-American aims in the Pacific: protection of the Burma Road in order to assist the Chinese, aid to the Netherlands East Indies, holding Singapore and the Philippines, and using Australia as a base. Neither he nor anyone else, other than Dill, ventured an opinion as to whether Singapore and the Philippines could hold out. If they had any doubts, they were held and expressed privately.

Stark asked if bases in China could be used for air attacks on the Japanese home islands. Lt. General Henry H. Arnold opposed bombing Japan until the Army Air Forces were strong enough to work substantial damage. He feared that sporadic or token attacks would only serve to solidify Japanese morale. Yet in April 1942 James H. Doolittle and his B-25's took off from the deck of USS *Hornet* for a daring raid on Tokyo. It was a signal example of what seapower could do.

A proposal for the occupation of French Morocco came up when Stark raised the question of relative priorities for Anglo-American overseas expeditions in the Atlantic area. Operation Gymnast called for the British to occupy French Morocco, but only if French authorities invited them. It still was not clear if Roosevelt and Churchill intended to pursue the matter with Marshal Pétain's government at Vichy. From a strictly military standpoint an allied occupation of Morocco would be necessary if German troops entered Spain.

This interest at the Arcadia conference in an occupation of French North Africa arose from an aggressive, confident state of mind, born both of determination and of optimism that the Allies would somehow triumph in their death struggle with the Axis. Although Stark's role as a dominant force in the navy was clearly waning, he articulated and organized a consensus for an Atlantic strategy, first in the upper levels of the War and Navy Departments and then with the British. Arcadia made official what Stark had started.

If Stark deserves the credit for the strategic concept and its adoption, Marshall rightly should be credited with proposing and piloting the conference through to acceptance of the principle of unity of command. This principle ranked in importance with the strategic concept Stark articulated because its adoption provided the means to implement the basic allied strategy. Speaking solely for himself at the chiefs of staff meeting on Christmas Day, Marshall said the most important consideration facing them was the question of unity of command by which one man would be in command of the entire theater—air, ground and ships. He felt that a unified command would solve nine-tenths of their troubles.[16]

Stark mustered support among the Americans for the concept of unified command. It was clear that since Marshall had proposed a unified command, Stimson favored it. However, King was at best lukewarm, if not actually opposed to the idea.[17] He had no desire whatever to lose operational control over any portion of what he saw as his navy. Stark did not want to argue against King in public. He did speak to Knox, however, and enlisted his support for the idea of unity of command. With Knox as a strong and vocal supporter of it, Stark outflanked King and insured that the U.S. Navy supported Marshall, despite the qualms and reservations of its COMINCH. King agreed to support this important principle at a meeting in Stark's office on 27 December.[18]

Conditions in the Far East required an early decision both on the principle of unity of command and on the designation of an allied commander for that area. Within three days Churchill agreed to this principle, and the British Gen. Sir Archibald P. Wavell became the allied commander in the Far East.[19] Wavell's command was soon overwhelmed by the Japanese tidal wave that engulfed the Far East in late 1941 and early 1942. Nevertheless, the principle itself was not compromised. It was applied again in 1944 in the European theater with Dwight D. Eisenhower as Supreme Allied Commander. There it contributed significantly to the planning and successful execution of the cross-channel operation of 1944 and ultimately to the liberation of western Europe. It is safe to say that without a unified command to execute the basic Allied strategy, the course of World War II could have been very different.

Subsequent plenary sessions, which included the President, Prime Minister, and their civilian and military advisors, dealt with immediate and practical matters, such as approval of a directive to General Wavell, the first allied theater commander, and the American expedition to Northern Ireland. They discussed at length the details of various military operations, including the much talked about occupation of Northwest Africa. Roosevelt saw that military and naval action would depend upon political plenary sessions. It was problematical, he said, what would happen in France and in Northwest Africa. But plans must be prepared for whatever situation might arise.[20]

The convoy with the American expedition to relieve the British garrison in Northern Ireland was scheduled to sail on 15 January 1942. Churchill attached tremendous importance to the 15 January convoy, because of the effect it would have on raising morale when the British people learned that American troops were arriving in the British Isles.[21]

Besides dealing with immediate problems for the conduct of the war the conference also produced an eminently sensible and practical command structure. This absolute necessity to the Allied war effort implemented the principle of unified command, but only after a discussion that "kicked up a hell of a row."[22] The British thought no special body should be formed, because the necessity for consultations with home governments "would tend to clog the machine." Instead they proposed that the Supreme Commander telegraph the respective American and British chiefs of staff in London and in Washington. London would then telegraph the British representatives in Washington, where the problem would be considered and a recommendation made to the President and Prime Minister.[23]

Roosevelt asked King for his advice. King felt that because rapid decisions would be necessary, existing machinery should be used. He felt that the Prime Minister should appoint a deputy who would act with the President on recommendations made by a military body consisting of American, British, Dutch, Australian, and New Zealand representatives. Marshall disagreed. He felt that the complicated issue of machinery should not be introduced into the business of setting up a unified command. King retorted that the establishment of machinery was an indispensable part of the establishment of unity of command. Marshall backed off and accepted the British proposals. Stark and King then agreed to them. Acting as the de facto chairman of the American chiefs of staff, Stark said he would submit these proposals to the President at once.[24]

The next day Roosevelt sent a draft for the American and British chiefs of staff to discuss. Roosevelt thoroughly disagreed with what they had submitted and made his own proposals. The chiefs of staff accepted some of Roosevelt's proposals, but not all. They felt that whatever procedure was adopted, it ought to be expeditious, and this was the basis of their objection.[25]

The immediate question of a directive to Wavell was resolved with appropriate dispatch. However, the broader question of a unified command structure above the theater level was put aside for a few days. Nearly two weeks later the British chiefs of staff raised the subject again; this time under the heading of post-Arcadia collaboration. It was discussed in some detail at the chiefs of staff meeting on 13 January, the day before the conference adjourned.[26]

The outcome of the deliberations at Arcadia was the creation of the Combined Chiefs of Staff. Field Marshal Sir John Dill was the British representative. He and the American chiefs of staff, at first Stark, King, Marshall, and Arnold, met at least once or twice each week. They acted as an executive committee for the direction of the Anglo-American war effort. More specifically, their collective function was to "recommend the broad program of requirements based on strategic considerations," to establish policy governing the distribution of available weapons of war, and to settle the broad issues of the priority of overseas military movement.[27] The body enjoyed an unprecedented success.

The Arcadia conference was the first of a series of wartime summit conferences that included Roosevelt, Churchill, and their respective military advisors. It was a decided success in a number of ways, and for this reason it was enormously important. First, the basic Allied strategy of defeating Germany first received official sanction, to the great relief of the British. They feared that since the United States had been attacked in the Pacific, the major American war effort might be devoted to that theater. Roosevelt, Stark, and Marshall clearly recognized that Germany was the most dangerous foe the United States faced. They adhered to the strategic concept expressed in the Plan Dog Memorandum of November 1940, affirmed at the ABC-1 talks and implemented in the Rainbow 5 war plan. The success of the conference in this respect can be attributed to the extensive preliminary negotiations of the preceding year or so, especially the ABC-1 talks.[28]

Second, unity of command was established in the Far East, primarily as a result of Marshall's insistence, but with Stark's support, which insured a solid army-navy front. A logical outgrowth of the principle of unified command was the Combined Chiefs of Staff, which provided the most extensive and successful allied cooperation in any war. With the basic strategy clearly defined and accepted, and the command structure established, Roosevelt, Churchill, and the chiefs of staff could then address the many pressing and immediate questions relating to the prosecution of the war.

Finally, the close, personal and, on the whole, harmonious relationships established among the British and American chiefs of staff, insured that the Allies would remain allied in practice as well as in rhetoric. Generally speaking, these men knew, liked and, more importantly, trusted one another. There were serious differences of opinion, but they were aired, discussed, and resolved.

The success of the Arcadia conference cannot be attributed solely to any one individual. All the major participants must properly be awarded their share of the credit. Stark participated fully in the deliberations as the senior American service chief. To his great credit, he scrupulously avoided infringing on King's responsibilities and functions as COMINCH, ill-defined as they were. Instead, he limited his formal participation to matters relating to long-range planning and he maintained harmonious relations with King.

Stark was particularly adept at making personal relationships work. Nowhere was this skill more apparent than in his dealings with Marshall, King, and the British. He was the organizer and mentor of the ABC-1 talks with the British in early 1941. At Arcadia he and the other chiefs of staff understandably played secondary roles to those of Roosevelt and Churchill. Nevertheless, Stark was the senior service chief and was clearly in charge of the Joint Chiefs of Staff meetings as long as he was CNO.[29] Acting in this capacity he ran interference with the White House through Harry Hopkins when it was necessary. At other times he quietly and unobtrusively mustered support and minimized opposition.

After the Arcadia conference adjourned, Stark could once more devote his full attention to the navy. It was time for the navy to set its house in order at the highest levels. The division of functions between COMINCH and CNO bothered Stark. Not only did he recognize it was not the best arrangement, he also felt King was the best candidate for a wartime CNO. Three years before when both he and King were with their respective commands at Guantanamo Bay Naval Base and the announcement was made that Stark would become CNO, King was disappointed that he had not been chosen. When he offered his congratulations, Stark replied, "Rey, you are the man that should have had the job." Stark was not only being polite and modest, he was speaking from conviction.[30]

By February 1942 the time had come to act on that conviction. Stark wrote to Roosevelt on 9 February 1942, suggesting that King be appointed CNO, thus merging that position with COMINCH. He also suggested that he be sent to London to head the naval command there, because of his experience in negotiating with the British and his prior duty there with Admiral William Sims during World War I.[31] He made these suggestions privately to Roosevelt, who respected his wishes for discretion. The pressure of the war prevented Roosevelt from acting on them for nearly a month.

8

A MEETING WITH THE PRESIDENT

The sun shone brightly a few minutes before nine on Saturday morning, 7 March 1942. Admiral Harold R. Stark walked up 17th Street from his office in the Navy Department building on Constitution Avenue. At 61, he was in good physical condition, standing a shade over 5 feet 8 inches in height and weighing a trim 162 pounds. His 35-inch waist was a bit more generous than he would have liked, but it was not bad for a man of his age. He had a thick crop of white hair, piercing blue eyes, and wore rimless glasses. His appearance was not unlike that of a kindly bishop. As a seasoned leader of men, he seldom became angry. Rather, he would either simply remove the object of his wrath or move around it. On those rare occasions when he did become angry, he kept it under such tight control that even his closest associates were hard put to notice it.

He had made the short trip many times since he became Chief of Naval Operations two and a half years before. Sometimes his appointments with the President were scheduled. But many times, especially on weekends, his private White House telephone would ring and he would hear the familiar patrician voice say, "I have a few things I'd like to talk over with you." As he walked on this winter morning, Stark tried to sort out his feelings about the forthcoming meeting with the President. He hoped that this one would not be the exception to their many other meetings which had been pleasant, even if they had disagreed about one thing or another.

In early March 1942 the war was going badly for the United States. Stark knew that the intimacy he enjoyed with his commander in chief would be a casualty of the war. He expected that this would be his last private meeting with Roosevelt as Chief of Naval Operations. He was

127

doubly sorry because never at any previous meeting had he felt as he did this morning. After a smooth rise to the top of his profession, he was about to take a step down. His resignation as Chief of Naval Operations was imminent, and his successor was to be Admiral Ernest J. King.

Stark knew that King was a fighter and was particularly well suited for a wartime command. In 1940 King was a rear admiral, serving on the General Board, an advisory body to the Secretary of the Navy. It was made up of admirals who were usually serving their final tour of duty before retirement. At that time the United States was not officially in the war, but in the Atlantic the Navy was engaged in the neutrality patrol and all signs indicated that war with Germany could break out there at almost any time. Roosevelt approved Stark's assignment of King to command the Atlantic Squadron. When the squadron was upgraded to the status of a fleet in early 1941, Stark urged Roosevelt to appoint King its commander, with the rank of a four-star admiral.

King's conduct of the undeclared naval war against Hitler in the summer and autumn of 1941 showed Roosevelt that he was a fighter. Shortly after the Japanese attack on Pearl Harbor, Roosevelt summoned King to Washington to tell him that he would be the new Commander in Chief of the U.S. Fleet. As COMINCH, King had operational command of all naval forces in both the Atlantic and the Pacific. Although the Executive Order issued by Roosevelt distinguished, separated, and delineated Stark's duties as CNO and King's duties as COMINCH, the arrangement was unwieldly and worked only because both King and Stark were determined that it should work. It was doubly awkward because King had established his headquarters in Washington.

No organization can function well with two heads. One of the two top commanders had to go. By resigning as CNO, Stark eased the situation and ended an awkward arrangement that could have hampered the country's naval efforts during the first year of the war. He was willing to retire to accomplish this, even though the thought of sitting out the war his long professional career had trained him to fight and for which he had labored so hard to prepare the navy went against his sense of duty.

Stark entered the White House through a side entrance, and he was shown to the President's office at once. This morning Roosevelt was all business. The two men were alone in Roosevelt's office for more than two hours. Roosevelt accepted Stark's offer to resign so that the posts of CNO and COMINCH could be combined under King. Loyalty to his old friend notwithstanding, the President knew that the merger would strengthen the navy's wartime organization. He softened the blow by telling Stark that he would not be put out to pasture but would be given a sensitive job, one that required a senior officer with the confidence of the President and access to the highest levels of the government. It was tailor-made for Stark. As a former CNO, Stark would have the requisite seniority, and he retained the confidence and friendship of both the President and Secretary of the Navy Frank Knox, who next to Roosevelt was Stark's closest official friend in Washington.

The job Roosevelt had in mind was Commander, U.S. Naval Forces in Europe, with headquarters in London. With Knox's hearty approval, Roosevelt resurrected the long dormant command Admiral William S. Sims held in 1917. It was a happy decision for Stark personally and, more importantly, for the success of the Anglo-American naval war against Hitler. It was also made with American interests in mind. Knox fully intended for Stark to become one of the most influential men in London, which would be extremely useful to the United States.[1]

Stark was the architect of Anglo-American cooperation and of the strategy to defeat Germany first. By sending him to London, Roosevelt wanted to show the British that the United States was committed to defeating Germany first. It would also be a fitting exchange for Field Marshall Sir John Dill, whom the British had sent to Washington as their representative on the Combined Chiefs of Staff. Dill thought Stark could perform much useful service in London, although he regretted losing personal touch with him.

The President wanted a personal representative at the highest levels in London to inform him outside of official channels of what the British were thinking. It was not that Roosevelt distrusted or suspected British motives. He wanted to keep up on British thinking so he could anticipate their proposals and have a little time to think before having to act. He did not want to be committed in advance to any specific course of action. He did not necessarily want freedom to improvise, although he dearly loved to do so. Roosevelt simply did not want the British to be able to foreclose any options for him. In early 1942 Great Britain was the senior partner in the Grand Alliance, but Roosevelt knew that as the war progressed the United States, by virtue of its enormous human and industrial reserves, would succeed to the senior position.

Even though there was general agreement on a Germany first strategy, it was clear at Arcadia that there would be disagreement on the best way to pursue that goal. In the coming months, these differences came into the open and they were frankly and sometimes heatedly discussed. They were not based on obstinacy, but rather on differing viewpoints and interests, particularly in the Mediterranean, where American and British interests were quite divergent.

Stark's personality made him the ideal choice for a naval diplomatic mission of the highest importance. He was well prepared for the quasi-diplomatic position of the kind Roosevelt had in mind. He had been on the staff of Admiral William S. Sims in London during World War I, and since then, had obtained experience both in the intricacies of dealing with allies and in commanding large naval forces. Largely on his own initiative in early 1941, Stark arranged secret staff talks with the British while the United States was still technically at peace. The talks arrived at tentative arrangements committing the army and the navy to the Germany first strategy, which was later confirmed by Roosevelt and Churchill and their military and naval staffs at the Arcadia conference in Washington in December 1941 and January 1942. Stark thus had good relations with the senior British army and navy officers, who not only liked him, but trusted and respected him as well. As a man of stature and recognized importance at home, Stark's presence in London would both flatter and placate the British.

In addition, Stark was wholeheartedly a Roosevelt man. He was intensely loyal and the President knew he would speak his mind freely and frankly both in London and in his reports back to Washington. The bond between the two men was one of admiration and mutual affection. Roosevelt knew he could trust Stark and he had confidence in Stark's discretion and initiative. He also knew Stark was particularly attuned to the subtleties of high-level politics. Not only was Stark eminently suited for this diplomatic staff command, but Stark knew his talents lay in that direction more than as a wartime Chief of Naval Operations.

Roosevelt felt that Stark's departure from Washington would be taken as a demotion for the results of the surprise Japanese attack on the fleet at Pearl Harbor. He thought that the recently released Roberts Commission report, which blamed the army and navy field commanders at Pearl Harbor and left official Washington untarnished, would mitigate some of the blame. Although by long-standing arrangement, the army was responsible for the defense of Pearl Harbor, its Chief of Staff, General George C. Marshall, remained in office after the disaster (and would for the duration of the war) and received a promotion as well. Nevertheless, Stark's sense of duty to his country and the navy, his desire to make a contribution to the war effort, and his loyalty to the President justified in his own mind the appointment of King and his own reassignment. He willingly accepted the possibility of damage to his professional reputation because he felt it would help to prosecute the war.

Roosevelt and Stark knew well that the demands of war took precedence over any purely personal preference. When Roosevelt regretfully accepted his resignation, he told Stark that he was reactivating for him the post Sims held in World War I, but under a slightly different name. Stark would retain his rank of admiral, with seniority over both King and Chester W. Nimitz, then commanding the Pacific Fleet. Whatever feelings Stark had about leaving the post of CNO, at least he was assured of an important wartime command. He was thankful that he could continue to serve, but he would miss the intimate association with Roosevelt and Secretary of the Navy Frank Knox. Roosevelt would miss his friend of 30 years but the conduct of war would occupy so much of his time that he would not be able to indulge in the pleasantries and informal contacts that had given him so much pleasure in the past.

It was nearly noon by the time Stark returned to his office. He asked Mrs. Hull, his secretary, to step into his office and take down his formal letter of resignation "to become effective at such time as may be directed by the Secretary of the Navy in order that I may assume new contemplated duties."[2] He sent it to the White House at once.

Then, because he was still Chief of Naval Operations, he returned to the business of running a wartime navy. That afternoon, he attended a regular meeting of the Combined Chiefs of Staff.

The news of his resignation was made public on Tuesday, 10 March. Stark had little more than a fortnight to conclude his tenure and turn the job over to Admiral King, who formally relieved him on 26 March. Stark wrote to the chairmen of the Senate and House Naval Affairs Committees, thanking them for providing the shipbuilding programs and authorizing increased numbers of officers and men in the navy. Senator David I. Walsh of Massachusetts replied that he was impressed by Stark's conscientious, candid, and cooperative manner in dealing with the Senate Committee. Representative Carl Vinson of Georgia complimented Stark on the fine job he had done in preparing the navy for war.

Vinson also proposed to Roosevelt that Stark receive the Distinguished Service Medal, the navy's highest noncombat decoration, in recognition of his service as CNO. Roosevelt enthusiastically approved Vinson's recommendation and told Knox to see to it. Knox was heartily in favor of it and the red-haired, ebullient, former Rough Rider, newspaperman, Republican, and all-round dynamo added a few plaudits of his own.

No service chief and service secretary ever worked in closer harmony than did Knox and Stark. Knox admitted that he had come to the job with little except good intentions, energy, and a desire to serve his country in a grave crisis. He was deeply grateful to Stark for being a "tower of support" and for the "scores of times" Stark saved him from serious missteps. He told Stark that in a long and busy life, he had never had "a more dependable, constructive and self-effacing associate." He lauded Stark for discharging his duties "with brilliance and single-minded devotion to the navy and to the country." He was convinced that Stark would leave "an indelible impression on the naval establishment for many years to come."[3] Knox was not a man given to perfunctory congratulations. He spoke from his heart.

In a brief, pleasant meeting Roosevelt surprised Stark by presenting him with a citation and Gold Star in lieu of a second DSM. (Stark received his first for service in World War I.) The citation referred to Stark's responsibility for "building and administering the largest peacetime navy in the history of this country." It mentioned his "exceptional qualities of leadership and his outstanding ability to effect a high state of training for war and the building of a two-ocean navy."[4] Stark was naturally pleased and gratified with this official recognition of his labors. He accepted the honor gratefully as tangible evidence of Roosevelt's and Knox' high esteem for his work, but he valued their friendship and his association with them even more.

On a far more personal plane, Stark wrote to Sims' widow in Boston with the news of his command. She was both touched and flattered that he took the time to write to her and she told him he would "start new traditions of [his] own and write another page in Anglo-American naval cooperation. . . . All of us Simses send you our truest good wishes."[5]

Stark was granted leave for the month of April, giving him time to set his personal affairs in order and to move out of the CNO's quarters at the Naval Observatory off Massachusetts Avenue. He and Mrs. Stark moved into the house they had bought a few years before at 4900 Glenbrook Road, in the Spring Valley section of Washington, beyond the National Cathedral. While Stark was in London, Mrs. Stark would be joined by their youngest daughter, Katharine ("Kewpie"), recently evacuated from Hawaii with her two little girls. Kewpie's husband, Harold Gillespie, was a civilian sent by his company to work in Hawaii.

Roosevelt sent for Stark two days before he left for London. They spent an hour and a half alone discussing the progress of the war. Roosevelt was adamant that the convoys to Russia must go through. In London, Stark could help coordinate the U.S. and Royal navies in their efforts to protect the Murmansk convoys. Roosevelt told Stark that he hoped to establish a western front in 1943, but in 1942 it might be possible only to stage large-scale raids of about 25,000 men at one or two places on the French Atlantic coast to keep the Germans guessing and possibly to force them to withdraw large numbers of men and airplanes from the Russian front. He stressed the necessity of gaining control, not simply superiority, of the air from the Netherlands to Brest.

Roosevelt gave no specific instructions, but he did ask for information about the command structure and function of the British air forces. He opposed creation of a separate U.S. Air Force, but was aware that the Army Air Force and many informed laymen were in favor of it. He wanted to have anything that Stark could send him that could be useful to combat this proposal.

Roosevelt thought holding operations were the most the Allies could do in the Middle East and in the Pacific for the present. He defined a holding operation as one with enough power to secure a position but lacking sufficient strength to take the offensive. He wanted to destroy Japanese ships and planes faster than they could be replaced and to wear down Japan with a strategy of attrition.

At this point, Stark said he assumed that the general policy still held of not only holding in the Pacific, but hitting where opportunity offered or where it could be created while still stressing winning in the Atlantic. He asked Roosevelt if the way he expressed it in the Plan Dog Memorandum still met with his approval. Stark quoted the memorandum, saying, "If we win in the Atlantic, we will win everywhere, but if we lose in the Atlantic. . . ." Roosevelt finished the quotation, "We will lose everywhere." Stark tactfully corrected him. "No, sir," he said, "the phrase is 'If we lose in the Atlantic, we might not win anywhere.'" Roosevelt agreed. "That is right," he said.

The discussion left no doubt in Stark's mind that the overall strategy was still to defeat Germany first. This knowledge would be most useful to him a few days later when he met the senior British naval officials and with Churchill.

Roosevelt expressed concern that after trying periods at sea, men must have adequate recreation and a complete break from their duties. He pointed out that in the past, transit to combat areas was not particularly hazardous. But in 1942 the possibility of submarine and air attack subjected men to danger from the moment they left port. He was alarmed at a report that in one 55-day expedition, the men involved lost an average of 15 pounds. As a result of extensive combat experience, the British knew the approximate length of time men could perform reasonably well before recreation became an absolute necessity.

The rambling conversation ended on a pleasant note. Roosevelt told Stark of the time during World War I when, as Assistant Secretary of the Navy, he visited American headquarters in London. It was 9:30 in the morning. He found only three people there: the charwoman, the communications officer, and one radio operator. Stark laughed and replied that Roosevelt certainly had not visited his office. Stark said he ran a taut ship and there was no slackness in his office ashore. Roosevelt continued, commenting unfavorably on British work habits: leisurely office hours, afternoon teas, and long weekends.[6]

Two days later Stark boarded a military flight for London via Montreal, Gander, and Prestwick. Frank Knox was at the airport to see him off. Stark thought of Knox more as a much loved older brother than as a boss; saying good-bye to him was like saying it to his family all over again. Knox's courteous gesture moved Stark greatly. As they said their good-byes, they both wished that Stark could have stayed in Washington but they realized they had to bow to circumstances that required Stark's posting to London. Stark boarded the plane. The engines turned over, warmed up, and the plane took off and headed toward Canada.[7]

9

ARRIVAL IN ENGLAND

It was an easy and pleasant flight from Washington, D.C., to Prestwick, Scotland, by way of Montreal and Gander. The longest leg was across the ocean at night. The other passengers on board were John G. Winant, the American ambassador in London, Mrs. Winant, and Lieutenant Tracy B. Kittredge, USNR. Stark and Kittredge had served together on Sims' staff in London during World War I. Afterwards Kittredge spent most of the interwar years in Europe, where he became fluent in French and German and exceedingly knowledgeable about European affairs. Although he was well into middle age, Kittredge still held his former junior rank. Soon after arriving in London, Stark received authority to promote him first to lieutenant commander and then to commander. Kittredge became indispensable to Stark in the discharge of his political and diplomatic duties. The scholarly Kittredge later became historian of the Joint Chiefs of Staff.

Stark had some very definite ideas about the relationship of his new command to the Navy Department and the Admiralty. Kittredge, having served with Stark on Sims' staff in London during World War I, was familiar with the problems that Stark was going to face. Both men saw eye to eye on what had to be done; both saw Stark as Sims's successor.

Sims thought of the London headquarters as the advance headquarters of the U.S. Navy in Europe. Stark succeeded in making COMNAVEU exactly that. As King's representative in Europe, he was a naval viceroy. King trusted him and knew that he would scrupulously insure the execution of naval policy. While King and the Navy Department were thoroughly engrossed in waging war in the Pacific,

136

Stark succeeded in translating his concepts into reality, partly by default, partly by persuasion, and partly by a commonly perceived necessity.[1] Nevertheless, it took some time for the bureaucracy to adjust; the Navy Department finally came to deal only with Stark's headquarters, which in turn coordinated all of the many and varied naval groups, at first in the United Kingdom and later on the continent of Europe.

In 1942, as in 1917, close coordination between the American headquarters and the Admiralty was necessary. The great difference between the European naval commands established in World War I and World War II was that in 1917 Sims started from scratch in the midst of a great war, while in 1942 Stark took over an existing command. Not only could he draw on previous experience, but he also had the great advantage of several months in which to organize and establish his command before great demands were placed upon it. Finally, he enjoyed with King and Knox a professional intimacy and personal frienship that obviated misconceptions and misperceptions. Despite his obvious abilities, Sims, the innovator and reformer, did not enjoy the same felicitous relationship with the Chief of Naval Operations and with the Secretary of the Navy, Josephus Daniels, who later became his nemesis.

Daniels had greeted Sims' request that he be allowed to sit as a member of the Board of the Admiralty as a case of advanced anglophilia. However, Sims did attend daily conferences at the Admiralty and officers from his staff were in close contact with their opposite numbers in Whitehall. Stark made no such request, because Admiral Sir Dudley Pound, the First Sea Lord, told the Admiralty that Stark should know everything he knew, and because Vice Admiral Sir Geoffrey Blake served as an exceptionally effective liaison between Stark and the Admiralty. This happy and successful assignment was later capped by a deep friendship and profound mutual respect.

The specific machinery Stark created, with the assistance of Kittredge and others, for the closest possible coordination between subordinate officers on his staff and those in the Admiralty, was a vast improvement over the hastily erected structure of 1917. During World War II, the London headquarters was sufficiently large to permit orderly staff procedures for coordination both with the Admiralty and with the Navy Department. Given the extent and the complexity of the naval and military operations during World War II, orderly administration was absolutely necessary to create, train, maintain, and operate combat forces.

The last leg of the journey to London, on a beautiful spring day, was again by air. Stark and the Winants were formally welcomed with full military honors, including honor guards from the Royal Navy and the U.S. Marine Corps. The First Sea Lord, Admiral Pound, was there in person to greet them. Churchill sent a representative to invite Stark and Ambassador and Mrs. Winant to visit the Prime Minister's country home at Chequers the next day and to spend the night. In the meantime, Stark went to his new office at COMNAVEU headquarters, 20 Grosvenor Square, and to the comfortable quarters provided for him at Claridge's.

Late the next afternoon Stark and the Winants drove from London to Chequers, a trip that took nearly an hour and a half. It was a lovely drive through the English countryside, most of which was like driving down a country lane. That evening Churchill was in high spirits. A movie followed dinner and then, after the ladies retired, Churchill started talking. He was in fine fettle and the men talked until after two o'clock the next morning.

Throughout this long and rambling conversation, Churchill stressed again and again his one great objective—the defeat of Hitler. He would not trade places with the Germans for one second, because he believed that at that time the Allied military situation was better than that of the Germans and that it would continue to improve. He told Stark that some of the recent bombings in Germany had left towns in a worse state than the worst the Germans had been able to do to England. Even Coventry had not been hit as hard as some of the towns the R.A.F. recently bombed. The British had plans to give Germany a bombing from the air in the months to come such as no one had ever dreamed of.

Shortly after 0200, Churchill telephoned to find out whether there had been any raids against the British sea coast or elsewhere that evening. When the answer came back "No" he was visibly disappointed. It was foggy and Churchill was sorry not only that the R.A.F. had been unable to get over Germany, but also that the Germans could not get to England. He was greatly encouraged by the considerable toll the British were extracting from recent German flights over England. Churchill was particularly pleased that R.A.F. forces were able to intercept the Germans at the coast and hit them so hard and effectively that they were not able to penetrate into the interior. He wanted the Germans to keep on coming, because he thought the British would make it so expensive for them that they would not be able to keep up the air attacks.

The wide ranging discussion touched on Russia, where Churchill predicted a "hot month" in May if the weather did not hold back the expected German offensive. They discussed the submarine menace in the Atlantic. He and Stark saw eye to eye on the Middle East and its importance to the Allied cause. Churchill was still sensitive about the loss of Singapore to the Japanese. With considerable heat and emphasis, he said he would not permit an inquiry into that British defeat because it would do no good for the country and would contribute nothing to winning the war.[2]

Stark's appointment to London meant that there would be close contact and cooperation between the two navies in London. Pound felt it was essential that Stark be as well informed as he and the other British Chiefs of Staff so that their discussion would be based on a common background. Pound offered to appoint Vice Admiral Sir Geoffrey Blake as Stark's personal liaison officer with the Admiralty. Blake was well suited for the job. He was an intimate friend of Pound. His distinguished naval career included service as naval attaché in Washington and an important sea command in the Mediterranean. Except for illness, which forced him to retire prematurely, many thought that Blake would have become First Sea Lord. Shortly after war broke out, Pound called him back to the Admiralty as Assistant Chief of Naval Staff for Foreign Operations.

Stark accepted Pound's offer and on 18 May 1942 Blake and his small staff moved into offices at Stark's headquarters. Blake's official title was Flag Officer Liaison, United States, or FOLUS for short. Stark thoughtfully provided PFC Erie Harlan, USMC, as an orderly for him. When Blake moved in, neither Pound nor Stark was quite sure just how he would fit into their respective organizations. However, within a short time Blake proved indispensable to both.

Blake's primary function was to be a personal link between Pound and Stark. His first duty was to see that information available to Pound was made available to Stark.

Pound directed that the British Hush Most Secret dispatches be sent to Blake, who then forwarded to Stark extracts that would be of interest to him, on condition that only Stark and his immediate staff (chief of staff and flag secretary) would see them. Dispatches of lower classification presented the twin problems of selection and editing to ensure that nonessential matters were eliminated and that important information got to Stark's desk. Blake did not want to and could not handle the 4,000 or so dispatches that passed daily through the War Registry (the Admiralty's communications office). He established topical categories that the head of the War Registry used as a screening device. Blake sorted the dispatches that were sent to him daily at 1000 and 1700.

The Cabinet War Room Record and the First Lord's Report were two daily reports that contained organized and rather complete information, and were sent to the War Cabinet and to the Board of Admiralty. The Cabinet War Room Record, issued each morning from the War Cabinet offices, summarized on two pages the naval, military, and home security events of the preceding twenty-four hours. Distribution was limited to a fixed number of people and was controlled by Churchill. The Prime Minister agreed to add Blake to the list. The First Lord's Report was prepared in the Admiralty for the First Lord, A. V. Alexander, and for the King. It was a summary of all naval events up to 0615 each morning. Policy limited the distribution to only 39 named individuals. An exception was made and Blake's name was added so he could obtain the report for Stark.

Blake was soon flooded with other highly classified, sensitive information. Clearly, Stark did not have the time to read all of it. Blake, therefore, prepared for Stark a daily summary in which he distilled in a well-arranged and readable manner all the salient points that Stark should know. He called this series "S.H." which stood for "Hush" because of the sensitive nature of its contents. S.H.s were always passed by hand.

The various reports and summaries Stark received filled an obvious need and their quality was impressively good. Stark received permission to send sample copies of the Cabinet War Room Record and the First Lord's Report to King in Washington. When King was in London in July 1942, Stark showed him the S.H.s that Blake prepared. King was impressed. On his return to Washington, he asked the British Admiralty Delegation if something of the same sort could be supplied to him.

Blake and his small staff provided other services for Stark and the Admiralty. They dispensed advice on who was the right person in either the Admiralty of the COMNAVEU headquarters to deal with various matters. They made the necessary arrangements for American naval officers in their contacts with the Royal Navy, and vice versa. As time went on, the influx of American navy men necessitated a clearing house for various problems. Some were easy and others difficult, but Blake and his staff handled them expeditiously and tactfully.[3]

London was Stark's forte. He genuinely liked people and they liked him in return. This important personal characteristic, his intimate knowledge of Washington politics and policies, and his contacts there, go far to explain his extraordinary success in the British capital. His first task in London was to make a series of courtesy calls. Both First Lord of the Admiralty A. V. Alexander and Pound emphasized their willingness to cooperate with him and to share whatever information was at their disposal. Alexander was deeply concerned over Churchill's apparent fixation with bombing Germany. At the conclusion of their talk, which touched on many subjects, Alexander asked Stark if he would emphasize to the Prime Minister the importance of maintaining the sea lanes of communication. Stark said he already had.[4]

The Board of Admiralty held a formal luncheon in Admiralty House to welcome Stark to London. It was a signal honor. In addition to the First Lord, the sea lords (very roughly, the British counterparts to the U.S. Navy bureau chiefs), and the ranking British naval officers in and about London, the guests included Ambassador Winant and Prime Minister Churchill. Alexander, the First Lord, explained that it was the first time such a gathering had been held at Admiralty House since the war started, which enhanced the honor to Stark and made it a happy occasion for all. Churchill told Stark he was delighted not only to welcome him, but also that it was the first time he had been to Admiralty House since he left his post as First Lord some two years before.[5]

One of the more pleasant tasks Stark undertook was renewing old acquaintanceships, including his friendship with Vice Admiral Lord Louis Mountbatten. They had met for the first time scarcely a year earlier in Washington when Stark was Chief of Naval Operations and

Mountbatten was a captain. Mountbatten later recalled that despite the disparity in age and seniority, they took to each other and became firm friends. In the spring of 1942 Mountbatten commanded Combined Operations and was responsible for the training of commandos and the planning and execution of commando raids against Hitler's Europe.

He brought Stark up to date on what the commandos were doing. At that time they were conducting two raids each month and were gradually increasing the scope and number of raids. By the end of the summer they hoped to be able to conduct raids with forces as large as a reinforced division, including the necessary air and naval support. On several occasions, planned raids got as far as the enemy coast, but they had to be called off at the last minute because of adverse weather conditions. Training of the troops was progressing well and within a few months the factor limiting the number of troops that could be landed would be the number of landing craft, not the number of trained troops available. Mountbatten requested that an American line naval officer be assigned to his staff, preferably with the rank of commander or captain. Stark thought it was a good idea and he said he would urge King to make the assignment.[6]

Stark's contacts with the Admiralty were frequent and at Pound's direction all doors were opened to him. One day at the end of May 1942, Blake took Stark and his chief of staff, Rear Admiral Alan G. Kirk, to the Admiralty's Intelligence Center. They spent over an hour in this underground, bomb-proof room where they were thoroughly briefed on the progress of the war. Stark noticed that charts and offices were jammed in everywhere in that subterranean chamber. When he remarked on it, the officer-in-charge replied, "It is just about half the size we should have built and now we are fixed so we just can't expand."[7]

When Stark talked with Alexander at the Admiralty the first topic they discussed was the vital part Russia was playing in the war against Hitler. The Soviet Union was hard pressed in 1942. German troops were deep inside Russia and there was serious doubt that Stalin would be able to hold out against Hitler. If Russia collapsed, the full weight of German arms would be turned against the west. Stalin urged Churchill and Roosevelt to open a second front to relieve the pressure on him, but the most they could do was to go forward with Operation Torch, the invasion of North Africa, which was scheduled for

November. In the meantime, it was necessary to send material aid to the Soviet Union by convoy. Alexander was particularly worried about the convoys from Britain around North Cape to the Russian ports of Archangel and Murmansk. These convoys were subject to almost unrelenting attack by German aircraft. The obvious solution was to atack the German airfields in northern Norway, but the British simply did not have the means to do so and it was up to the Russians to take the offensive. Unfortunately, the Russians were unwilling to mount such attacks or even to discuss the matter with the British.[8]

Stark thought that a direct approach to the soviet ambassador, I. M. Maisky, would cost nothing and that it might possibly do some good. It was worth trying. Maisky put Stark off for two weeks, but finally gave in and agreed to see him on June 1.

Maisky was a wily diplomat who had held his London post for ten years. He spoke excellent English and was quite cordial and willing to talk to Stark, but only to a certain point. Several times Stark tried to bring up the matter of driving the Germans out of their air bases in northern Norway or even attacking them. Each time Maisky only expressed a vague hope that something was about to be done. He tried to leave Stark with the definite impression that he knew of, but could not discuss, some plans along these lines. Stark did not take the bait. He remained skeptical. He wanted to see some tangible evidence that the Russians intended to redeem their promise to do something about the German air forces in that region, but there was none.[9] Stark's talk with Maisky did not produce any noticeable results.

Throughout 1942 and in 1943 Allied convoys continued to make the extraordinarily hazardous voyage around the North Cape to Murmansk in the Kola Inlet. In late spring and early summer of 1942, the continuous daylight provided the Luftwaffe with splendid opportunities to ravage the convoys. One convoy, PQ 17, suffered enormous losses in early July.

In Washington, King and the head of the British Admiralty Delegation, Admiral Sir Andrew B. Cummingham, known as "A.B.C.," discussed the North Russia runs with Roosevelt at the White House. King cabled Stark, "Intense concern here in regard to Murmansk-Archangel convoys which Russians continue to expect, although they do not do much to help cover them." Roosevelt wanted to know what the prospects were of getting convoys through if all practicable naval effort was made and if air support was considered indispensable. He was considering the possibility of stationing American or British air units in northern Russia. Roosevelt needed a response before deciding whether to load any more merchant ships for Murmansk.[10]

The disaster that overtook PQ 17 prompted the Admiralty to suspend these convoys, at least for the time being. Before Stark could respond to King's urgent dispatch, Pound told him that Churchill had already taken up the matter directly with Roosevelt. It was out of naval hands.[11]

Suspension of the convoys for several weeks, the loss of nearly one third of the ships in the next convoy, PQ 18, and the urgent need for surface escorts elsewhere gave a hearing to the advocates of sending merchant ships to Russia independently, instead of in convoy. Stark told Knox of the extensive discussions that took place in the Admiralty. The pessimists feared a German cruiser or the Luftwaffe "just scooting along the path of these single ships and knocking them out one by one." However, the advocates of independent steaming argued that "by judicious spacing, weighing the factors of actual distance, day and night zones, weather, geographical danger areas, [and] air reconnaissance limitations," among others, the chances of success were good. Stark felt that the importance of getting war supplies to the Soviet Union warranted a try at independent steaming. He admitted, "It is true it will be tough on the fellow who has to take to boats up there all by himself, but there is a lot of toughness in this war."[12]

Averell Harriman, as lend-lease expediter in the United Kingdom, cabled Roosevelt on 8 October that he and Stark recommended sailing five ships, singly at first, and more later if feasible. Roosevelt gave his assent the next day.[13] However, the trickle was already underway. Starting on 7 October, thirteen merchant ships (five American, seven British, and one Russian) sailed from Iceland at ten hour intervals for the north Russian ports. Any of the civilian merchant seamen who did not volunteer were segregated and held incommunicado until the completion of the voyage.[14]

Of the thirteen ships that set forth on this lonely, nerve-wracking voyage, five arrived safely at their destination; two returned to Iceland for unspecified reasons; four were either sunk or missing; one went aground off Spitzbergen and was lost; and another struck an iceberg, but was saved.

With the onset of the long arctic nights and bad winter weather, the trickle movement was discontinued and convoys were started again. Convoy QP 15, composed of twenty-nine merchant ships, left Archangel on 17 November for the westward movement to the United Kingdom and the United States. It was scattered by gales and only one ship was torpedoed. It was significant, Stark noted, that German aircraft in northern Norway did not attack the convoy.[15]

The first naval commander outside London visited by Stark after his arrival in England was Admiral Sir Percy Noble, Commander in Chief, Western Approaches. Noble's command, in Liverpool, embraced the crucial ocean area generally to the west of the British Isles, through which the convoys supplying Britain had to pass. German submarines, operating primarily from French ports on the Bay of Biscay, posed the greatest threat to the safety of the convoys.

Noble met Stark at the airport and they drove in a heavy drizzle through the dingy streets of heavily bombed Liverpool to Noble's headquarters at Derby House. Noble enjoyed an excellent reputation in the navy. At the end of 1942 he went to Washington as a member of the British Admiralty Delegation, where he became well known and well liked in American naval circles.

There was an opportunity for plain talk when Stark was shown around R.A.F. headquarters at Liverpool. Politely, but firmly, he said how he, personally, and the U.S. Navy felt about the R.A.F. failure to attack the German warships, *Tirpitz* and *Scharnhorst*. They had been almost on the British doorstep for nearly two years. In addition to the threat from submarines, one of Britain's greatest menaces and greatest worries was the ever-present threat of the two ships, which could make sorties against surface shipping. Bluntly, he told the R.A.F. officers he thought they should go after the ships and submarines. It was music to the ears of the Royal Navy officers.[16].

Then it was Stark's turn to listen, as Noble described some of the problems he experienced in cooperating with the U.S. Navy in the trans-Atlantic convoys. One problem was caused by moving westward the place in mid-ocean where the British and American naval escorts met. It prevented full efficiency on the part of the British escorts, because it unduly taxed their fuel capacity. There was a real possibility that they might run out of fuel. When Noble's destroyers had an escort job somewhere near the limit of their fuel endurance, the destroyer skippers in the early part of the voyage were loathe to take any action that would involve extra steaming or fuel consumption when it did not appear absolutely necessary. Offensive sweeps or searches for shadowing submarines were likely not to be taken. Instead, they would usually act only against immediate threats. Moreover, the mid-ocean meeting point was sometimes inaccurately signalled and destroyers missed the convoy track by considerable distances.

Noble stressed the necessity for escort commanders to report promptly all attacks and losses. In one incident, twenty-four hours elapsed between the time convoy ON-92 was attacked and word of it was received at his headquarters. There was a second attack on that convoy that might have been prevented had the first attack been reported and had long range aircraft been able to reach the scene. By the time the report was received, however, the convoy had proceeded beyond the range of the aircraft.

Shipping losses in the western Atlantic, particularly along the eastern seaboard of the United States, were alarmingly high, but, fortunately, losses in British home waters were relatively light. To Stark this meant that antisubmarine forces in British waters should be reduced and those in American waters should be strengthened. Noble agreed, but pointed out that the situation might reverse itself at any time, because the submarine had the initiative. Thus, both the British and the Americans should be prepared to shift quickly the opposing forces and the convoy routes. Delay would be costly.

Noble asked for an American naval officer to serve on his staff. Stark understood the reason to be, although not expressed, that Noble would like to have an American see at first hand the difficulties of cooperation and have him, rather than someone in the Royal Navy, make any necessary complaints to Stark. Stark promised Noble he would look into these complaints and he did so in a lengthy, detailed report to King.

Luncheons and dinners were a convenient means by which Stark and high ranking British officers could gather for more or less informal conversations and exchanges of views. On one such occasion shortly after his arrival in London, Stark gained precisely the kind of information Roosevelt was looking for when he asked Stark to be alert for ammunition to oppose a separate air force.[17]

Stark was having dinner at the United Services Club where he was joined by two British rear admirals, Roger M. Bellairs and Sir Bernard Rawlings. In the course of the conversation, Rawlings brought up the German invasion of Crete and the resulting British defeat. He then proceeded in no uncertain terms to decry the British system, which prevented the Royal Navy from having its own air force, lock, stock and barrel, as the U.S. Navy did.

There was nothing in particular unusual about a naval officer giving vent to the deeply held feelings that the naval air should be an integral part of the navy. It was a widespread belief. There was, however, an unusual aspect to this conversation. Proponents of a separate air force, particularly in the United States, usually cited the Luftwaffe as the great example to prove the efficiency of a unified air force. Not so, said the British officers. They proceeded to explain that, in their opinion, the damage done to the Royal Navy in the Mediterranean, while great, was nothing compared to what it could have been had the Germans designed, trained, and operated a separate naval air arm. The Germans came off badly in comparison with the Japanese.

The German air force, they said, was a separate entity and although it had been trained to coordinate with both the army and the navy, it operated almost exclusively with the army. The emphasis was on military operations, chiefly land objectives, and it enjoyed outstanding success in the field.

However, when it was employed against naval objectives, the British were pleasantly surprised to find the results to be much less severe than they had anticipated. Rawlings based his feelings on his extensive experience in the Mediterranean. The German air force, particularly in Crete, failed to score anything approaching the success that could have been possible. The British fleet in the Mediterranean at that time was practically destitute of air support and had little to offer in opposition to German aircraft other than shipboard anti-aircraft fire. The Germans missed the opportunity to annihilate the British Mediterranean Fleet.

The Japanese, on the other hand, succeeded where the Germans had not. There was no separate Japanese air force. The naval air arm was part of the navy and the British were decidedly impressed with the skill that the Japanese naval aircraft displayed against them. Needless to say, the loss of the *Repulse* and the *Prince of Wales* in December 1941 to Japanese air attack made a definite impression.

The Japanese showed marked ability in other engagements. Specific targets were assigned, attacks were made vigorously, and excellent results were achieved.

One of the most effective weapons against submarines was aircraft. Long range patrol aircraft could force submarines to remain submerged, which meant they had to proceed at relatively slow speeds on battery power rather than at higher speeds on the surface by using their diesel engines, which required air. Also, these aircraft could attack a surfaced submarine more quickly and with less warning than could destroyers or other surface ships. Submarines were vulnerable to air attack while in French and north German ports, and production of them could be interrupted by air attack on construction yards.

Stark was well aware of these elementary facts and he did not hesitate to reiterate them to British military and naval officials. However, the army and navy officials with whom he spoke in 1942 complained bitterly to him about the lack of cooperation they were receiving from the R.A.F. Even Air Chief Marshal Sir Philip Joubert, who headed the Coastal Command and was responsible for antisubmarine operations, was exasperated. The Germans wisely built concrete bomb-proof shelters for their submarines while in their bases. Joubert knew of this construction when it started. He told Stark that he had continuously begged and implored the R.A.F. to bomb the submarine homeports and to attack the construction during the five months it was in progress. His pleas fell on deaf ears. Finally, in early 1942, after the shelters were completed, the R.A.F. sent a squadron of forty-seven bombers to attack the newly constructed submarine pens. They reported several direct hits, but the bomb-proofing withstood the attacks. Joubert summed up his disgust to Stark by saying, "We don't even have a single separate air force over here. We have four separate air forces."[18]

At root the problem of what targets the R.A.F. should attack lay in differing concepts of how the war should be waged. The R.A.F. was wedded to the concept of bombing cities, factories, and population centers on the theory that Germany could be defeated best that way.

Royal Navy officers made no bones to Stark about their feeling towards British air policy. Admiral Sir John Tovey, commander in chief of the Home Fleet, told Stark that the R.A.F. was "fighting their own war and it never can be won by bombing Germany alone." Heatedly, he told Stark that Germany had had over two years to diversify and spread out her industries and that in April the R.A.F. dropped 4,500 tons of high explosives on Germany while at the same time the Germans dropped 6,000 tons on Malta and Malta was still functioning. Tovey was exasperated because one of his tasks was to keep open the British lifelines to the rest of the world, upon which continued British survival depended. He was getting no cooperation from the R.A.F.

Tovey frequently asked for long range aircraft to help get the conveys through to British ports. He said, "I am told that the Americans would never stand for it; that they are sending their bombers and long range reconnaissance planes to England for bombing the continent and if we started using them over the sea they would protest." Stark reported Tovey's comments to King and suggested that they be passed along to Secretary of the Navy Frank Knox and to the President.[19]

It was soon clear to Stark that Churchill was backing the R.A.F. in their refusal to lessen their attacks on Germany so they could assist the army and the navy. If he had an opening, Stark intended to talk to Churchill about it; but he felt that it would be far better for Roosevelt to broach the subject. He told King as much.[20]

The issue remained unresolved through the summer of 1942. In August British and American intelligence agreed that the Germans were producing between twenty-three and twenty-eight new submarines each month. Air Marshal Sir Arthur T. Harris of the Bomber Command told Churchill that his bombers had severely damaged all the yards building submarines. When Harris was asked how the yards could produce that many submarines if they had been severely damaged, he was unable to offer any kind of an explanation.[21]

The U.S. Army Air Force B-17s were a welcome addition to allied air power. Stark reported to Knox that the "flying fortresses" began daylight raids, whereas the R.A.F. had heretofore limited itself to night attacks. By attacking in daylight, the Americans were able to see their targets and correspondingly increase the accuracy of their attacks. Stark reported to Knox that it was an eye-opener for the British and that many in the lower echelons were asking how the Americans could come over and do in daylight what they have never been able to do. He said, "Some faces are a little red."

Not only did the flying fortresses prove their ability to hit their targets with an enviable degree of accuracy, but they were also able to knock down attacking enemy fighters. The aircraft were proving to be tough as well. A German projectile exploded inside the fusilage of one, killed the radio operator and did a considerable amount of damage, but the plane continued to operate and returned safely to its base.[22]

The closeness with which the United States and Royal Navies worked inevitably brought forth comparisons. This was particularly so when Task Force 39, comprising the new battleship USS *Washington*, the heavy cruisers USS *Wichita* and USS *Tuscaloosa*, the carrier USS *Wasp*, and Destroyer Squadron 8 arrived at Scapa Flow on April 3, 1942. Task Force 39 was sent to operate with the British Home Fleet for about three months as relief for the Royal Navy's Task Force "H," which was ordered to participate in the seizure of Diégo Suarez on the island of Madagascar to preclude a suspected Japanese move against that strategic island.[23]

Observers soon concluded that the American ships were better designed, better built and far more mechanically efficient than the British ships. Although the U.S. Navy paid more attention to adjustment, upkeep, and repair of material than the British, the Royal Navy paid far more attention to discipline, indoctrination, and especially the training of officers and men. In 1942 the U.S. Navy was just beginning to establish a training system, starting with shore-based schools and continuing on board ship and in the fleet, which would be adequate to the demands of antisubmarine warfare.

Stark, a gunnery specialist, had been Chief of the Bureau of Ordnance less than ten years before; he was delighted when Admiral Sir John Tovey, commander in chief of the Home Fleet, told him that the American ships were so far ahead of the British ships in antiaircraft high angle fire that there ws no comparison. Tovey also said that the American antiaircraft fire was better than that of the British.

Tovey ordered a surprise gunnery practice in which various ships fired in succession at airborne targets. First *Wichita* fired in turn with the British cruisers and did far better. Then *Washington* fired after the British battleship *Duke of York* and there was hardly any comparison. When it was the destroyers' turn, the first American destroyer shot down the towed sleeve on the first salvo, taking only about twenty-five feet of wire with it, a fairly close cut. Tovey was so impressed by the performance of Task Force 39 ships in this respect that he made a special trip to the Admiralty to inform their Lordships of the unfavorable showing of the British ships and to see what improvements could be made.

Tovey was also impressed by the cleanliness of the American ships and the efficiency of their engineering plants. He praised the shipshape appearance of the American ships to a British vice admiral, saying there was no comparison between the standards of the two navies. He told Stark that the *Duke of York* burned 30 percent more oil than the *Washington*, although the *Washington* displaced approximately 2,000 more tons. Stark attributed the main reason for the greater fuel economy to the fact that the *Washington* had higher steam pressure than did the *Duke of York*. The greater efficiency of higher steam pressure vindicated Stark's insistence when he was Chief of Naval Operations about installing high pressure steam engines, despite some ardent advocacy to the contrary.[24]

When Stark was at Rosyth near Edinburgh in September 1942, he called on the captain of HMS *Delhi* for his evaluation of the 5 inch 38 batteries with remote fire control, which he had authorized installed on that ship under the Lend-Lease program when he was Chief of Naval Operations. The captain was enthusiastic about the battery. He told Stark that it was years ahead of anything in the Royal Navy. It was reliable and it was a "real joy the way it knocks down targets." His comments delighted Stark, but not the two British admirals who listened in on the conversation. One reason Stark was pleased at how the battery worked in actual use on board ship was that he favored it as a useful improvement while others in the Navy Department opposed its development and installation because it was "too intricate."[25]

The design and construction of the American ships may have produced the finest antisubmarine equipment afloat, but in 1942 the crews, as a rule, did not know how to use it effectively. Rear Admiral L. H. Thebaud gave Stark a sobering picture of the inadequacy of training American ships and crews for antisubmarine warfare. The ships were fitted out with the latest equipment and were furnished with pamphlets and manuals explaining how it was to be used. But the ships and their crews were expected to train themselves.

The British had what Thebaud reported as a definite advantage in the area of training. Their ships along with the officers and men were sent to working-up bases, where they were boarded by experts who inspected, checked and analyzed the gear, the men, and the methods used. Stark visited one such British base at Tobermory on the Isle of Mull off the west coast of Scotland. With experts on board, the ships were then put through their paces to disclose any defects or unsound practices, which were corrected on the spot. He urged the adoption of this principle and the establishment of working-up bases on the east coast of the United States.[26]

On 13 May King George VI asked Stark to call at Buckingham Palace. The two men spent more than an hour alone. It was an easy meeting for them; both were sailors and their personalities were compatible. As Stark was taking his leave, the King said that in early June he would be visiting the Home Fleet at Scapa Flow, where the American task force was operating as a part of the Home Fleet. The King asked Stark to meet him there. Stark accepted immediately. Not only would he have the privilege of receiving the King on board U.S. Navy ships, but he could visit Task Force 39, and while in Scotland would also have the opportunity to visit American and British naval installations there.

At Scapa Flow Stark broke his flag in USS *Washington*, the flagship of the task force commander, Rear Admiral Robert C. "Ike" Giffen. He took full advantage of this opportunity to visit as many of the U.S. Navy ships as he could. Stark was pleased with the conditions he found on *Washington* and he thought the heavy cruiser *Wichita* "looked exceptionally well." He told their captains that the conditions of the ships and the appearance of the men were particularly to their credit since they had been at sea for a considerable period of time. Stark's inspections were rehearsals for the King's inspection.

Stark and other senior officers joined Admiral Sir John Tovey, the Home Fleet commander, on board his flagship, HMS *Duke of York* for a dinner at which the King was guest of honor. The next day Stark accompanied the King on inspection tours first of *Wichita* and then of *Washington*. When he had nearly finished his inspection of *Washington*, the King turned to Stark and said admiringly, "She is so clean."

There were twenty for lunch that day in Admiral Giffen's cabin on board *Washington*. The guests included the King, his Naval Equerry, and the British and American admirals, their chiefs of staffs, and aides. Giffen and Stark also thoughtfully included the U.S. Navy unit commanders and commanding officers of the ships present at Scapa

Flow, including two commanders and three lieutenant commanders. They were somewhat awed by the august company to which they had been admitted.

Stark proposed to Tovey that the next day when King George was due to return to the mainland that he go to Thurso on board an American destroyer. Tovey agreed and plans were made accordingly. However, when it came time for His Majesty to leave, the weather was so bad that Tovey was unwilling to risk the King's making a transfer from a small boat to a destroyer. Arrangements were made for him to go by a merchant ship instead.

The King invited Stark to ride in his private train back to London, but Stark's schedule prevented it and he had to decline the invitation. Stark told the King of the American victory over the Japanese at Midway. The King was delighted at the good news, which was a fitting climax to his visit to the U.S. Navy task force serving with the Home Fleet. Referring to the King, Stark told Knox, "He's all right."27

There were sad duties, too, that had to be performed. Ensign John Howard, USNR, and Lieutenant Commander R. B. Edwards, RN, performed the delicate and hazardous task of disarming and disassembling German sea mines so the two navies could better learn how they worked. Something went wrong with one mine and both men were killed. Stark wrote a long and sympathetic letter to Ensign Howard's parents, telling them of the importance of their son's work and how he met his untimely death. Howard's father asked if his son's commission could be transferred to him so he could perform some useful services ashore to ease the burden on regular officers and liberate them for sea duty. He and Mrs. Howard looked on Stark as a friend and hoped some day to meet him in person.28

Stark's round of calls and other official engagements was removed from the grim reality of the war then being waged in the Atlantic, in the Libyan and Egyptian deserts, and in the heart of Russia. It lacked the élan and the excitement of what are normally considered to be wartime duties, but what Stark was doing was necessary and important. It symbolized America's participation in the war, and lent a visible and tangible support to America's closest and most powerful ally. Great Britain had stood alone for over a year and had pledged the Empire and its resources to defeating Hitler. Stark's presence in London in 1942 symbolized America's presence at Britain's side. His close relationship with President Roosevelt and Secretary of the Navy Frank Knox showed the British that the United States had sent them a knowledgeable and well-connected friend.

In his first six weeks in Great Britain, Stark touched all official bases in London and established himself as a welcome, honored, and trusted representative of Britain's major ally. The Admiralty accepted him as one of their own.

10

NORTH AFRICA AND DE GAULLE

The summer of 1942 was a time for establishing a U.S. military presence in Great Britain. Stark's arrival in the spring symbolized America's devotion to the Allied cause. The arrival of General Dwight D. Eisenhower and the establishment of the European Theater of Operations in the early summer presaged a build-up of American forces, many of which saw action in North Africa before the year was out. Immediately upon Eisenhower's arrival, Stark said to him, "The only real reason for the existence of my office is to assist the United States fighting forces in Europe. You may call on me at any hour, day or night, for anything you wish. And when you do, call me 'Betty,' a nickname I've always had in the service."[1] Thus began their official relationship, which developed into a warm, personal friendship. It testified to their own good sense and to their common understanding of the overriding purposes of their commands.

Early in 1942, while Stark was still CNO, the Joint Chiefs of Staff (JCS), of which he was then a member, determined that an eventual Allied invasion of the European continent would be necessary to defeat Hitler. The location and especially the date of that invasion remained matters of debate and even acrimony among the Combined Chiefs and between Roosevelt and Churchill. The Joint Chiefs took a first step towards that invasion by preparing a plan for a build-up of U.S. Army forces in the United Kingdom. This operation was given the code name Bolero.

Bolero was planned in Washington to be implemented in London. One of the first problems Stark faced when he arrived in London was establishing command relationships. It was clear that Stark as COM-NAVEU would be the administrative commander, responsible for

155

maintaining and supporting the naval forces assigned to Bolero. However, an operational commander remained to be appointed and whatever arrangements were made would have to be consistent with JCS policy.

In the spring of 1942, shortly after they both arrived in London, Stark and Eisenhower met with Admiral Lord Louis Mountbatten, Commander of Combined Operations (the British commandos). According to Eisenhower, the army intended to man all small landing craft in the proposed cross-channel operation and he assumed the navy would man all craft over one hundred and five feet. Although this arrangement sounded reasonable to him, Stark felt he ought to check with Washington for a determination of Navy Department policy. King wired back that the navy was already overextended in manning small craft. However, Coast Guard instructors would be loaned to the army to train their boat crews.[2]

King also told Stark that the army would command all United States forces in the United Kingdom that would directly participate in Bolero. This decision was made pursuant to the principle of unity of command, which had been thoroughly discussed and adopted at the Arcadia conference in January 1942. Fortunately, Stark had been a participant in those discussions and he grasped at once the importance and significance of one commander, army or navy, exercising operational command. He had to use all of his considerable talent as the administrative commander to ensure that the navy men and their equipment were properly supported in the United Kingdom.

The amphibious forces in the United Kingdom required a naval commander under the recently established European Theater Commander. Stark urged King to send one. By mid-July a newly selected rear admiral, Andrew C. Bennett, was on his way to Great Britain to direct training and to establish bases there for the reception, organization, assembly, and maintenance of amphibious forces, all of which would be under Stark's administrative command. Eisenhower would exercise operational command.

Bennett required Base Two at Roseneath in Scotland for Operation Bolero. Although the Americans had built it, it had been turned over to the British for use by Mountbatten's forces. Stark made the necessary arrangements in London for the base's return to the U.S. Navy. In doing so, he made sure that it was taken over gradually, so as not to disrupt the British program already underway there. Even though the

British were given less than one month's notice to vacate, the transfer went smoothly, and the base reverted to American control on schedule.

In July, while Stark and Eisenhower were making the complex arrangements for Bolero, King and U.S. Army Chief of Staff General George C. Marshall arrived in London to talk to the British Chiefs of Staff and to Churchill about the conduct of the war. Specifically, they sought to obtain British agreement for a cross-channel operation in 1942.

The Americans were installed on the fourth floor of Claridges Hotel where they plunged into a round of conversations with Stark, Eisenhower, and General Carl Spaatz, who were the senior American military officers in Britain at that time. Both Eisenhower and Spaatz were eager to proceed with the cross-channel operation in 1942. Stark, on the other hand, was more cautious; one observer said he was lukewarm.[3]

The discussions during the ensuing week were intensive, thorough, and sometimes hot as King and Marshall attempted to convince their British counterparts and Churchill to support Operation Sledgehammer, a cross-channel operation scheduled for 1942. The British were equally adamant in their opposition to it, based largely on the prudent reasons that the Anglo-American forces were not yet sufficient for such an undertaking. The upshot of this series of meetings was the agreement that some offensive action ought to be taken that year. Accordingly, Operation Gymnast, which had been discussed extensively at the Arcadia conference, six months before, was revived. It called for allied landings in northwest Africa. Churchill rechristened the operation "Torch" and in time the wisdom of changing its name was proved when it became essentially an American operation, partly in deference to the fact that the Vichy French, who had much against Churchill and the British, were in control of the area.

The decision to mount an attack in 1942 on French north and west Africa instead of on the continent of Europe was made on 25 July. The amphibious operation was a compromise between the Americans, who generally favored a cross-channel assault on the continent in 1942, and the British, who objected on grounds that sufficient Allied forces were not then available for such an enormous undertaking, which could not be allowed to fail. Moreover, Stalin continually complained that the British and the Americans had not opened the second front they had promised him. Roosevelt was determined that American troops would see action in the European theater in 1942.

The week ended on a pleasant note. Friday evening Stark joined Churchill, Alexander, Pound, and Harry Hopkins, to go by boat down the Thames to the Royal Naval College at Greenwich where the Royal Navy feted King, who went by automobile. It was a black tie, stag dinner in the best British tradition. Dinner was in the famous Painted Hall and it was attended by the Lords of the Admiralty and most of the British flag officers on duty in London. Although King's anglophobic proclivities have since become well-known, they did not disturb the festive air that evening of the gathering of about one hundred men.[4]

The decision to go ahead with Operation Torch meant that Bolero would be suspended in favor of the new operation.[5] The growing naval organization in Europe would have to shift gears quickly and smoothly from building up forces to attack Europe to supporting those involved in the North African landings.

Stark knew what was behind this decision. King and Marshall brought Eisenhower and him up to date on the recent debates on war strategy. In early August, a week after the decision was made, Stark reported to King that British plans for operations in North Africa were tentative and that they had not yet been approved by the British Chiefs of Staff, although the estimated target date was barely three months away. These tentative plans assumed that the mission would be to capture French Morocco, Algeria, and Tunisia in order to open the Mediterranean. The British planners specified that the naval forces required would include a large number of ocean escorts, transports, and a covering force of warships to prevent interference by the Italian or French fleets.[6]

From the start, Stark participated in the planning on the American side. By early August the specific mission was set and the assault was scheduled for 5 November. (It actually occurred on 8 November.)[7] Ten days after Stark reported on the status of British plans, Eisenhower, who by then was the prospective commander of the entire expedition, assembled the principal naval and army officers concerned, primarily to orient the navy to what was involved and to enlist its full cooperation. With Stark in London, King had no cause to worry about cooperation, despite any misgivings he or anyone else may have had in Washington. In addition to Stark, there were several admirals and captains present, many of whom had been specifically sent to England to start planning the naval side of Operation Torch.[8] In the early stages of the planning, Eisenhower made requests directly to King for navy men and ships, but each time King insisted that Stark screen any such requests first.[9]

Within Stark's command, the first and most immediate effect of giving priority to Torch over Bolero was to focus attention on bases for training boat crews and other amphibious forces. Base Two at Roseneath in Scotland became the center of this activity and Rear Admiral Bennett established his headquarters there by the end of August. There was also a second base at Lishally near Londonderry. Surveys were made for other bases on the south coast of England, but they were not built until 1943. At that time they were used to prepare for the 1944 Normandy landings.

Under Bolero, more than 2,700 landing craft of all kinds were scheduled to go to the United Kingdom from the United States for use in storming Hitler's Fortress Europa. The higher priority given to preparations for Torch and the shortages of landing craft and both trained and prospective crews precluded sending additional landing craft to Great Britain at that time. However, the evolving plans for Torch contemplated that the U.S. Navy would provide men and equipment for bases and their defense at the French naval base at Mers el-Kebir, at nearby Oran, and at adjacent minor ports. This change in plans cut deeply into the training plan Stark anticipated at Base Two and at Lishally.

Stark and Eisenhower agreed that Bennett should head the new unit and that he would be under Eisenhower's operational control. His forces would be drawn from the naval forces already stationed in the United Kingdom. Stark and Bennett protested several raids by King on the men already assigned to them, but to no avail. The men received their orders and they left for other duties, frequently on short notice.[10]

Controversy broke out between Bennett and the British planners. At that time, Admiral Sir Andrew B. Cunningham was the British commander in chief in the Mediterranean. His plans called for Bennett's force to make a frontal assault on the port of Oran, although clearing out resistance in the port was an army responsibility. Bennett objected vehemently. His force of two ships assigned for that job would be inadequate to cope with French resistance, if there was any, and if the French did not resist, a naval assault would be unnecessary. With Stark's support, Bennett took the matter directly to Eisenhower, who let Cunningham's plan stand as written. It turned out to be a costly mistake. In the assault, the entrance of the two ships alerted the port of Oran. Both ships were lost with heavy casualties to their crews and to the landing parties embarked.[11]

As early as August 1942 there was a flood of rumors in North Africa of plans and preparations for a landing in the French African territories, near either Dakar or Casablanca, or at both places simultaneously. These rumors spread to Vichy and were broadcast on Vichy and German radio programs. Stark was told that the German Armistice Commission even demanded that Pétain recall General Noguès, the governor general of Morocco, because of his suspected sympathies for the British and the Americans.[12] These were only rumors, but there was a more serious breach of security.

A British correspondent in New York for a London newspaper sent a dispatch in September 1942 in which he said that a North African expedition was imminent. It tore to shreds what Knox saw as the last vestige of security. Even more serious was a protest from the British chiefs of staff to Eisenhower, who sent it on to the U.S. Army Chief of Staff, General Marshall. They complained that while he was in London, William C. Bullitt, an American envoy, told the Fighting French that the Americans were working on plans for operations in French Morocco. Marshall in turn informed Roosevelt, who, understandably, was greatly distressed. Roosevelt directed Knox to investigate the source of the leak. As it turned out, Bullitt was blameless, even though the men with whom he had been in contact either had learned of the plans by some means or simply had made a good guess. Despite tight security and splendid cooperation of the reporters in Britain, Stark was convinced from the German and French broadcasts that they knew something was brewing.[13]

As the day appointed for the landings in North Africa drew near, Stark's innermost thoughts were directed to that momentous event. On 20 October, Vice Admiral H. Kent Hewitt's task force departed the east coast of the United States, bound for the Moroccan coast where it would land on 8 November. A few days later, British forces left the Firth of Clyde and Milford Haven bound for the Mediterranean, where they would land at Oran and Algiers. Stark gathered from what Churchill said to him that the Prime Minister had little concept of the magnitude of effort Operation Torch would require. He noted that Churchill "has been educated a lot these last few weeks." Support of the Mediterranean part of the expedition alone required four ships to pass through the Strait of Gibraltar every day.[14]

Although his duties required his presence in England, Stark was very much with the expedition in spirit. He was in an aggressive, warlike mood, but he could not show it in the course of normal daily activities. He let off steam to Knox, saying, "Killing Germans and killing Japs is our principal business now, and until we kill enough of them there will be no 'peace on earth and good will among men.' That's sort of a h—— of a way to put it, but it's true."[15]

The most Stark could do to satisfy his yearning to be with the expedition was to go to the south coast of England to inspect naval installations and facilities. The closest he got to the front lines in 1942 was at Dover, where he climbed the conning tower, which Churchill liked to do, and looked across the channel to France. At Newhaven he saw the underground combined operating center. It was a splendidly laid out place with working and sleeping areas and a completely equipped galley. The communications and tactical display facilities were excellent. He observed that it would be possible to live there in comfort for a long time. The fervor and military smartness of the reserve naval officers undergoing training at HMS *King Alfred* (not a ship, but a commissioned building) impressed him greatly. Enthusiasm and martial spirit were not limited to these young officers. He met a man who had once retired as a vice admiral and had come back on active duty as a captain. He was told of others who had retired as full admirals and yet had returned to active duty as commanders because it was the only way they could participate in the war effort.[16]

Back in London on the eve of the landings, Stark made a brief courtesy call at the Soviet Embassy where the Russians were celebrating the twenty-fifth anniversary of the Bolshevik revolution. He went in, shook the ambassador's hand, and then retired to his quarters.

"Either we go to the enemy or the enemy will come to us. That's the real issue sea power will decide," Stark told an audience in Edinburgh less than two weeks before American and British forces landed in North Africa on 8 November 1942.[17] The modern armadas that mounted the landing in Morocco and Algeria illustrated how the Allies could use the seas for their own advantage, despite Hitler's capability to wage intense and deadly submarine war.

Stark had no direct responsibility for the conduct of Operation Torch. His task as administrative commander was to provide the indispensable support for the American naval forces then in European waters and for those which would soon arrive there. He also had the difficult and delicate task of keeping General de Gaulle and the Fighting French from creating an undue disruption over this Anglo-American military and naval expedition into what was indisputably French territory. Stark's task was complicated by a deliberate exclusion of these Frenchmen from planning the operation, participating in it and even from having official knowledge of it before it was made public.

While Eisenhower directed operations from Gibraltar and then from North America, Stark remained in London along with General Charles de Gaulle. At first de Gaulle applauded the bold Anglo-American action. Then he fumed. Like Churchill before him, Stark soon came to feel the full weight of the Cross of Lorraine, the symbol of de Gaulle's Fighting French. By November 1942, as a matter of expediency and necessity, Stark had become a de facto ambassador to General Charles de Gaulle, who in 1942 led the only French military resistance to Germany.

When France collapsed in June 1940, Charles de Gaulle was a French brigadier general who refused to accept either the capitulation of his country to Germany or the legitimacy of the French government established at Vichy under the leadership of the aged Marshal Pétain, which he viewed as little more than a Nazi satellite. De Gaulle escaped to England, where he rallied Frenchmen willing to continue the fight for the honor of France and for her restoration to the councils of the great powers.

In the course of the ensuing two years, various territories of the French Empire rallied to de Gaulle and broke their allegiance to Vichy. North and West Africa remained loyal to Marshal Pétain, but sub-Saharan French Africa joined de Gaulle's Free French, later renamed the Fighting French. Even before the Japanese attacked Pearl Harbor, President Roosevelt recognized that the defense of the territories under the control of General de Gaulle was necessary to the defense of the United States. On 11 November 1941, he authorized the extension of Lend-Lease aid to the Free French on a retransfer basis of aid extended to the British. Nevertheless, the United States maintained diplomatic relations with Vichy for a variety of reasons. The British backed de Gaulle.

De Gaulle further complicated this confused and difficult situation in December 1941 by ordering the seizure of the two small French islands of St. Pierre and Miquelon off the Canadian coast, to the complete surprise of the Canadians, Americans and British, and against British advice. The military importance of the islands was more potential than real. While St. Pierre was under the control of the French government at Vichy, there was a possibility that the radio station on the island could transmit information to German submarines; but it never did. Whatever de Gaulle's political gain may have been, his act thoroughly soured his relations with the United States.[18]

Meanwhile, the Japanese advances in the South Pacific made the Wallis Islands and New Caledonia, both of which were French territories, important staging areas for the United States. At first the United States dealt with local authorities. But because these islands had rallied to General de Gaulle and not to Vichy, it became necessary to deal directly with him. Shortly after Stark arrived in London, Admiral Ernest J. King, the Chief of Naval Operations, asked him to make arrangements with de Gaulle so that the U.S. Navy could use the Wallis Islands and New Caledonia in the South Pacific as a staging area. The local French officials insisted on de Gaulle's approval before they would accede to the American requests.

Stark had been told that de Gaulle's "ego stuck out all over him." He expected to find the general pompous and rather difficult. Instead, he was pleasantly surprised when de Gaulle turned out to be calm, easy going, and very agreeable. At the outset, Stark made it clear that he intended always to be perfectly frank with him and that cordial cooperation would be impossible without full communication, no matter how disagreeable the circumstances might be. His candor pleased de Gaulle. He, too, might have some disagreeable things to say, but they could be said pleasantly. De Gaulle was prepared to accede to the American requests, provided the territorial rights of France were preserved and any action taken was in accordance with general French constitutional and administrative practice. Stark felt that de Gaulle had gone just as far as he could go.

In order to prevent confusion, Stark convinced John G. Winant, the American ambassador in London, and the American ambassador to the governments-in-exile, Francis J. Biddle, to leave the negotiations with de Gaulle over New Caledonia in his hands. It was a military matter, he said.

Stark's next meeting with de Gaulle was stormy. When de Gaulle started to get himself worked up, Stark became even more calm; his smile was broader than usual. It took about 20 minutes for Stark's soothing manner to calm de Gaulle down. Stark bluntly told de Gaulle that he could neither admit nor countenance one or two statements the French general had made about the U.S. Army's General Patch who commanded U.S. forces in New Caledonia. De Gaulle accepted Stark's candor and by the end of their conversation they were both smiling.

These two meetings were important because they showed Stark both sides of de Gaulle's formidable personality. Stark was now forewarned. He had a clear idea of the kind of man with whom he was dealing.[19]

A few days later Anthony Eden, British Foreign Secretary, congratulated Stark on the way in which he dealt with the general. Stark had gotten along so well with de Gaulle that Eden jokingly asked if he would like to handle British relations with de Gaulle. To be sure, Stark was the only person in London who regularly got on well with de Gaulle. Stark thought the reason for his success was that at their first meeting he bluntly told de Gaulle that he might have some unpleasant things to say and that he would not hesitate to do so if it became necessary. De Gaulle appreciated plain talk.

The problem of dealing with de Gaulle was difficult from the start for many complicated political reasons. The United States had to deal with two French groups, one of which it formally recognized as the legal government of France at Vichy. The other, Fighting France, under de Gaulle, was a source of potential military aid against the Axis. Unfortunately, each group had anathematized the other. These political difficulties were compounded by de Gaulle's personality.

When the United States entered the war, de Gaulle commanded only a handful of courageous Frenchmen in the British Isles and the loyalties of others in various parts of the French Empire. The Vichy government, on the other hand, still retained control of the formidable French fleet, then in Toulon, and French North and West Africa.

The sizable French North African Army was loyal to Vichy. Therefore, it was in the interest of the United States to maintain relations with Vichy, even though it was necessary to deal with de Gaulle. Relations with Vichy became even more necessary when a cross-channel operation was postponed in 1942 in favor of the more feasible operation in North Africa. To facilitate this operation, every attempt had to be made to enlist the support of the French authorities in North Africa, or at least to avoid outright opposition. Fortunately, American efforts by and large were successful, which was justification enough for this policy.

In January 1942, when the French National Committee was formed in London under the leadership of General de Gaulle, the British recognized it as competent to represent the French citizens and French territories that rallied to the Committee. The British hoped the United States would follow suit.

Without informing Stark in advance, the State Department announced in a press release on 11 July that he and Brigadier General Charles L. Bolte had been designated to consult with the French National Committee on matters relating to the conduct of the war. This was, indeed, news to Stark. Fortunately, King was in London at the time and he gave Stark his oral okay to confirm the news release. Still, it was unclear whether Stark and Bolte were representing the navy and the army respectively, or the United States government. Washington sent no clarifying instructions. The nub of the matter was that many of the questions Stark had already discussed with the French related to the conduct of the war, but they went beyond specific questions of direct military cooperation. Stark received no general instructions or even directions to discuss specific questions. In his contacts with the French, he simply exercised his own best judgment.

Even if the Americans thought their position was ambiguous, the French did not. De Gaulle welcomed "the distinguished representatives of the United States."[20] René Pleven of the French National Committee attempted to raise the consultations to a quasi-diplomatic level. He told Lieutenant Commander Tracy B. Kittredge, a member of Stark's staff, that the French assumed Stark and Bolte to be representatives of the United States government. Pleven wanted the COMNAVEU staff to set up something like a small embassy so it would not be necessary to refer every matter to Stark and Bolte.

Kittredge demurred, saying he could envisage a simplified procedure without establishing a complicated system of diplomatic relations.[21] As it turned out, in the ensuing months, Kittredge almost single-handedly provided the staff support for Stark by attending to details, which left him free to deal with larger questions.

Secretary of State Cordell Hull approved the procedures Stark and Bolte proposed as a means of consulting with de Gaulle. All communications directly or indirectly relating to the conduct of the war would be addressed to the French National Committee or to the chief of General de Gaulle's personal military staff, as he preferred. No communications were to be addressed to the Commissioner for Foreign Affairs as such. Stark and Bolte were the only Americans authorized to consult with the French National Committee on the prosecution of the war, even to the specific exclusion of embassy personnel. Clearly, Hull did not concede governmental status to de Gaulle.[22] As long as he dealt with de Gaulle, Stark made no such concession, despite de Gaulle's best efforts to maneuver him into making it.

Frankness and cordiality generally characterized the personal meetings between Stark and de Gaulle. Their formal meeting on 3 August 1942 was no exception.[23] De Gaulle wanted to discuss many questions not of an exclusively military or naval character, since the conduct of the war necessarily involved cooperation and agreement on them. That might be so, Stark pointed out, but his instructions from the State Department limited him to political questions ancillary to the conduct of the war. He and Bolte were not authorized to discuss the post-war political organization of France. A direct exchange of intelligence between American and French services on the situation in France, the disposition of German troops and other developments, was desirable. The Americans reminded him that such matters must be discussed by British as well as American authorities. De Gaulle appreciated Stark's friendly and sympathetic attitude, the U.S. Navy's agreement to aid Fighting French forces and to train naval aviators, and the authorization of direct consultations on matters relating to the conduct of the war. The British had been and would continue to be informed only of negotiations on matters in which they were directly concerned. De Gaulle was satisfied.[24]

For a moment in the summer of 1942, a high tide of good feeling was reached, which was no mean achievement, considering the very different outlooks, positions, and objectives of the two parties. These differences would emerge in the next few months to vex de Gaulle, to try severely Roosevelt's patience, to test Stark's diplomatic skill, and to confirm the opinion of the State Department. Stark's patience, skill and, above all, his good personal relations with de Gaulle did much to ease the strain.

The Allied landings in North Africa gave rise to a host of French problems. An American general was in command. Morocco and Algeria were loyal to the Vichy government, and when Vichy broke diplomatic relations with the United States later that same day, the vestigal remains of the Third French Republic were eliminated from the active consideration of the United States. But a French problem still remained. Stark was on the front line in dealing with it.

The Allies, and particularly the Americans as the dominant partner in the invading forces, needed someone to rally the North African French, if not to active opposition to the Germans, at least not to oppose the Allied landings. The United States put General Henri Giraud forward as "Commander-in-Chief, French Army of North Africa" as a rallying point for opposition to the Axis and hopefully the leader of a new force. As an escaped prisoner of war, Giraud's anti-German credentials were unimpeachable. On the morning of the landings, Giraud appealed for French support of the Allied landings, saying there was but one passion, France, and one goal, victory. The unexpected presence in Algiers of Admiral Jean Darlan, a high ranking official of the Vichy Government, was a complicating factor, the extent of which would be apparent within the week.

Eisenhower's immediate problem was to secure the area at a minimum cost. It involved obtaining active cooperation of the local civil authorities as well as inducing the French military authorities not to resist the landings. Because de Gaulle claimed that the Vichy government lacked legitimacy, he was clearly not the man for this task. If the substantial French forces in North Africa could be added to the Allied forces, that army would constitute a major factor in future operations.

Such an army would also constitute a major political development, since it would be a large non-Gaullist force on the Allied side. A fusion of the Fighting French and North African French forces for more effective prosecution of the war would be desirable. De Gaulle was also interested in a fusion of the French forces, but for other reasons. He saw a political rival in the creation of another French force within the Allied camp.

During the ensuing weeks Stark became the buffer between de Gaulle and his Fighting French and the British and Americans. The relationship the two military men had established over the past few months was based on candor and mutual respect and it allowed Stark to exercise a restraining influence over de Gaulle. This restraint was mutually beneficial because it minimized the Gaullist nuisance to Roosevelt and Churchill and provided an outlet for de Gaulle's very real frustrations as they developed and came to a head.

Whether Stark was aware of de Gaulle's perception of a rival in Giraud and the forces he might rally is not clear. Kittredge received a visit on 8 November, the day American troops landed in North Africa, from an unidentified member of de Gaulle's staff, who asked whether the United States command would help to bring about a fusion between the Fighting French and the North African French forces. He said that if an armored corps of French troops were to be created and if de Gaulle were invited to organize, train, and command it, he would probably accept.[25]

The supposition that de Gaulle would accept a field command subordinate to a higher French authority was not preposterous in November 1942. He had stated on several occasions that he was prepared to place himself under the orders of any higher officers or of any group better qualified to bring a united French nation back into the war. He repeated his offer to Prime Minister Churchill at lunch on 8 November when Churchill informed him of the North African landings.

Later that day, de Gaulle broadcast a stirring speech to North Africa in which he exhorted Frenchmen there to rise up and help the Allies.[26] Stark called on de Gaulle the next day to tell him how much he appreciated the broadcast. De Gaulle was still enthusiastic about the landings and he confirmed to Stark what he had told Churchill: He would support any action that would contribute to bringing a united France into the war, including an agreement with General Giraud.

De Gaulle and Stark discussed the current situation in North Africa in a very friendly conversation. Unfortunately, Stark had no detailed information on the current talks in North Africa and he could offer very little by way of specific information, which was what de Gaulle wanted. Nevertheless, de Gaulle inquired about future United States policy and he discussed objectively and philosophically the future role of the French in collaborating with the Allies in the liberation of North Africa.[27]

Five days after the landings, de Gaulle and the Fighting French no longer looked forward to an immediate agreement with Giraud to unify the French forces. They knew that something was going on between the Allies and Darlan in Algiers. At nine o'clock in the morning on Friday, 13 November 1942, Darlan made a second broadcast from Algiers. In the first broadcast two days before, he had called on all French forces in North Africa to cease fighting against the Allies. In the second broadcast he stated that as French High Commissioner, he had assumed responsibility for French interests in Africa, with the approval of the American authorities. Darlan called on governors and residents to remain at their posts to ensure the administration of their territories. Stating he was acting in accordance with Marshal Pétain's wishes, Darlan concluded the broadcast with *"Vive le Maréchal."*[28]

The invading Allies, represented by General Mark Clark, had reached an agreement at least in principle with the local French officials, who held their offices by virtue of prior Vichy appointments and who would continue to remain in power. The Allies, particularly the United States, made a deal out of necessity with an odious regime headed by Admiral Darlan. Darlan was an opportunist and his loyalties ran more to himself and to the French Navy than to France or to the Allied cause. The Clark-Darlan agreement, formally concluded ten days later, created consternation and evoked strong criticism in Great Britain and the United States.[29]

Darlan and his Vichy gang were incompatible on ideological and general political grounds with the United States. René Cassin, a member of the French National Committee and legal advisor to de Gaulle, made this point abundantly clear to Kittredge, who passed it on to Stark.[30] Stark knew perfectly well that Darlan was a Vichyite and hence not exactly an ally. He was also aware of the inescapable fact, ignored by the critics in the ensuing uproar, that Darlan and company controlled North Africa. It was true the Allies had the capability of ousting them, which would have required the institution of a military government and quite possibly extensive mopping up operations. Faced with the choice of setting up a military government, or coming to terms with Darlan so he could prosecute the war against the Axis, Eisenhower chose to pursue the military objective—the expulsion of the Axis from North Africa.[31]

There has been little dispute that the alternative would have been costly in time, casualties, and equipment.[32] The criticism grew from outrage and indignation that the Americans should come to terms with the likes of Darlan and the Vichy French in North Africa. This criticism was voiced by many people, including the Fighting French, who bore no responsibility for the prosecution of the war against the Axis in North Africa.

The Fighting French did not criticize the Clark-Darlan deal because they were an irresponsible group of men who had been frustrated in an attempt to participate in civil and military arrangements in North Africa. If anything, they were certainly not irresponsible. Their opposition was based upon the fundamental grounds of political legitimacy. The Gaullist position since the 1940 armistice had been consistently that their movement represented the real France, the true France that had been betrayed by Marshal Pétain and his associates. They claimed the support of the French people, in addition to drawing on the mystique of France. The French National Committee would have nothing to do with Darlan. On 14 November they threatened to issue a communique dissociating Fighting France from the arrangements made in North Africa. Dissension among the Allies was a real possibility.

Stark wrote to de Gaulle for the record. He candidly reiterated the point that military considerations had made it necessary and inevitable for the Allies to deal with the people "found on the spot and to deal with them quickly in order to avoid all unnecessary shedding of blood. That, as I view it, is what has happened to date."[33] Shortly after receiving this letter, de Gaulle decided to delay issuing the threatened communique for twenty-four hours.

Radio broadcasts from Algiers only confirmed the worst fears of the French National Committee and General de Gaulle. Not only had they been unable to enter into any position of political power in North

Africa, but, as the Gaullists saw it, the Americans had given their support in French territory to those men who had betrayed France and continued to support the illegitimate Vichy regime.

Officially the French National Committee reacted by dispatching René Pleven to call on Stark with a formal protest against the agreements with Darlan. The Fighting French could not accept any arrangements that would in effect legitimize the Vichy regime in North Africa.[34] Pleven requested the transmission of his note of protest to the United States government. Stark forwarded it to Winant for transmittal to the State Department, if he thought it advisable.[35]

By this time de Gaulle was highly irritated and thoroughly frustrated. He wrote to Stark, saying "I understand the United States buys the treachery of traitors, if this appears profitable, but payment must not be made out of the honor of France."[36] Stark read the letter and told Kittredge to return it to de Gaulle personally. He explained that it must have been sent in error, unless it was de Gaulle's intention to render impossible further conversations with representatives of the United States Government and armed forces. Realizing he had gone too far, de Gaulle sent Colonel Gaston Palewski in full dress uniform to Stark to convey his regrets that the letter had been sent and to express appreciation that the admiral had been charitable enough to return it without comment.

Stark thought this letter was not typical of de Gaulle's usual gentlemanly demeanor. Certainly it was out of character with their usually cordial relationship. He thought members of de Gaulle's staff talked him into sending it as a result of his understandable frustration, disappointment, and even bitterness at the turn of events in North Africa. Stark was willing to let the matter drop, but events in North Africa still rankled de Gaulle.[37]

Churchill was disturbed by the deal with Darlan and he said so in a personal message to Roosevelt. Rather than attack it in principle as de Gaulle had done, he urged that "it be only a temporary expedient justifiable by the stress of battle."[38] He reminded Roosevelt of the possible serious political injury that could be done to the common cause by the perception that the Allies were ready to deal with local quislings. The Foreign Office paralleled Churchill's message with a cable in a similar vein to their embassy in Washington and asked that their views be conveyed to the State Department.[39]

President Roosevelt publicly clarified the position of the United States with a cogent explanation of the deal with Darlan. His statement was transmitted first to Churchill and then released to the press on 17 November. The political arrangements made in North Africa were only temporary and were justified by the stress of battle. No permanent arrangements should be made with Darlan and the Vichy Government should not be constituted anywhere. Future political arrangements for the French people would be made freely by them after their liberation. The Darlan agreement not only prevented bloodshed but it also allowed the time that would have been spent in mopping up operations to be spent in pursuing the Axis. He noted that French troops under General Giraud were already in action in Tunisia. Finally he called for the liberation of all political prisoners and the abrogation of Nazi-inspired Vichy legislation.[40]

One immediate effect of Roosevelt's statement was that de Gaulle canceled a press conference scheduled for Wednesday, 18 November, at which time Stark said de Gaulle would have been "rough—to put it mildly."[41] It was a successful culmination of American efforts to contain or at least limit the effects of the understandably vehement Fighting French objections to the arrangements made with Darlan. Both Winant and General Walter B. Smith, Eisenhower's chief of staff, credited Stark with successfully acting as a buffer during the period prior to Roosevelt's statement, and keeping de Gaulle from publicly criticizing the Allied command in North Africa.[42]

Stark continued his efforts to soothe de Gaulle by pointing out to him that Roosevelt's statement confirmed Stark's interpretations of events. The prime objective was still to drive the Germans and Italians out of North Africa as quickly as possible. Stark tactfully reminded Pleven, instead of de Gaulle, that Roosevelt and Churchill's intentions and their policies would shape future events in North Africa. It was fortunate, he said, that the power of final decision rested in the hands of the President and Prime Minister.[43]

Gaullist pressure on Stark continued when French Air Force General François d'Astier de la Vigerie and a trade union delegate, Léon Moranda, informed him that the resistance movement in France was solidly behind de Gaulle. They had left France on the night of 17-18 November, and reported that French public opinion was enthusiastic at the North African landings, but that disillusionment had set in when Darlan was recognized as French Commissioner in North

Africa. D'Astier impressed Stark as a clear thinking, practical officer. Stark thought he was much more suited to head the Fighting French than was de Gaulle.[44]

A second and more significant effect of Roosevelt's statement on de Gaulle was reflected in the inquiry his staff made to Stark. Would Roosevelt receive André Philip, French National Commissioner for the Interior, who was then in Ottawa? So far Roosevelt had not received Adrien Tixier, the Fighting French delegate in Washington. After talking to Winant, Stark cabled Secretary of the Navy Frank Knox about the possibility of such a visit.[45] Within six hours Knox replied that Roosevelt would see Philip the next day, which was Thursday, 19 November, or the following day.[46] Using U.S. Naval Communications facilities, which Stark had made available, de Gaulle directed Philip to go to Washington immediately and to inform Knox of the time of his arrival so arrangements could be made for an interview with Roosevelt. De Gaulle told Stark how much he appreciated the navy's prompt action.[47]

While Philip was en route from Ottawa to Washington, de Gaulle asked to see Stark. It was important, he said. But he refused to call at Stark's office. He insisted that Stark call at Carlton Gardens, the Fighting French headquarters. Canceling a number of other appointments, Stark went to de Gaulle's office late in the afternoon, only to be read a statement on a trivial matter that did not seem to warrant a personal meeting. De Gaulle simply wasted Stark's time. Stark felt the purpose of the meeting was not its substance, but rather than de Gaulle wanted to see if he would call on him in view of what had transpired in the past few days.[48] It was a somewhat unusual way to see if their prior relationship remained unaffected, but it was typical of de Gaulle.

After Roosevelt's statement, Stark perceived a rapid reversal of the attitude of the French National Committee. One of de Gaulle's staff asked unofficially if the United States would approve of their designation of General Giraud as the Fighting French High Commissioner and Commander in Chief in North Africa.[49] Stark hoped that the Fighting French were ready "to start playing ball again."[50]

This inquiry may have been a good omen. But any optimism Stark may have had was diluted by sober reflection on his relations with de Gaulle. Stark was clearly becoming exasperated with de Gaulle. His own seemingly inexhaustible supply of patience was running low. It was important that de Gaulle realize the necessity for the utmost speed of the Allied advance into Tunisia and for assuring a square deal for all Frenchmen in North Africa.

Stark wanted to tell de Gaulle some unpleasant truths, notably that upon arrival in North Africa General Giraud found himself without support and urged Eisenhower to make arrangements with Darlan, whose presence was as much a surprise to the Americans as it was to everyone else. Eisenhower dealt with Darlan out of sheer military necessity. No responsible officer would have acted otherwise. Not only could and did Darlan terminate French opposition, but he also assured French support of the Allied mission. Only Darlan could provide any hope of delivering the French fleet to the Allies, and so far he had kept it out of German hands. Once he decided to climb on board the Allied bandwagon, Darlan gained the support of the North African French by invoking the fiction that what he was doing was really the will of Marshal Pétain, who, as a prisoner of the Germans, was unable to give him support.[51] De Gaulle's influence in North Africa was zero and use of his name would only have inspired opposition. Finally, Stark felt de Gaulle should be told that political prisoners in North Africa were being released.

Stark bided his time. He felt it necessary to enlist the active cooperation of de Gaulle in the allied effort, not only for the practical reasons of military necessity, but to give him something positive to do in place of brooding about his frustrations. It would also keep him out of mischief.

Fortunately, de Gaulle soon had something positive with which to occupy himself. On 27 November, André Philip reported that Roosevelt would see de Gaulle if he came to Washington.

This was the only positive result of the meeting between Philip and Tixier with Roosevelt the day before. The two Frenchmen thoroughly exasperated the President by demanding that the administration of North Africa be turned over to the French National Committee and by failing to express the slightest gratitude for the liberation of North Africa. De Gaulle saw Roosevelt's comment as an invitation, which it was not. De Gaulle's staff told Kittredge the next day that he planned to visit Washington and that he would seek Stark's advice on the details of the trip. Plans were made for de Gaulle's imminent departure, because the President suggested that he visit Washington before 15 December, or after 8 January. The earlier period was preferable.[52]

Washington said nothing to Stark about the visit. All he knew was what the French told him. This was embarrassing enough, but to add to it, the British approved of de Gaulle's trip. Finally, Stark could wait no longer. He cabled Knox and asked if de Gaulle had been invited and if so, what arrangements were suggested. Whatever the arrangements might be, it would be up to Stark to make them.[53]

De Gaulle was delighted that Roosevelt had "invited" him to visit Washington. He asked Stark for advice on the organization and plans for his visit. His tentative plans were to arrive in Washington, D.C., between 8 and 10 December and to spend approximately a week there and then a few days in New York before returning to London. He planned to take only three or four persons with him.[54] Because he had received neither instructions nor information, Stark could only agree in principle with the general's suggestions.

Stark's uncertainty ended on 26 November with a cable from Admiral William D. Leahy, Chief of Staff to the President: No invitation had been issued to General de Gaulle to visit Washington.[55] Winant received the details by telephone. It was officially clear that de Gaulle was going to the United States on his own initiative, but in response to an expressed willingness of the President to receive him should he arrive.

Again de Gaulle urgently requested to see Stark. This time he went to Stark's office early in the morning on Thanksgiving Day. The day before, Kittredge had spoken frankly to one of de Gaulle's officers, saying that Stark felt de Gaulle's attitude recently had not exactly been one of a gentleman. Both he and Stark thought that de Gaulle wanted to apologize. When de Gaulle arrived he was in an especially good mood. Apparently he sought to mend fences with Stark before going to Washington, if not to apologize in so many words.[56]

As soon as de Gaulle left, Stark went to Westminster Abbey for a special Thanksgiving Day service. Afterwards he attended a small reception at Buckingham Palace, where he spoke with King George VI, King Haakon of Norway, and the Prime Minister. Churchill was delighted at the prospect of de Gaulle's trip to Washington. He told Stark he hoped the President would like him, at least a little, because it would help. Knowing both men personally, Churchill hoped de Gaulle would not antagonize Roosevelt.[57]

Stark and Churchill talked about a letter Darlan had recently written to Eisenhower. In it he said he was being used as a lemon and when squeezed dry he would be discarded. He acted not for personal gain, but only, he said, for the good of his country when the Germans violated the armistice. When possible he intended to lay down the burdens of office and retire to private life.[58] They were joined in this conversation by Eden, the First Sea Lord, Admiral Sir Dudley Pound, and General Sir Alan Brooke, Chief of the Imperial General Staff. Stark thought de Gaulle should see it. Brooke and Pound agreed. Churchill felt it would do no good. Stark replied that whether it did or not, it would be a good idea for de Gaulle "to get the picture" and besides it would at least acquaint him with Darlan's point of view. Afterwards, Stark doubted it would be shown to de Gaulle in London. He left open the possibility of its disclosure by the President.[59]

King Haakon of Norway engaged Stark in some spirited conversation. Apparently the king sympathized with de Gaulle's stand and voiced approval of it. What Stark said was not recorded, but he made a strong case for Allied unity. He felt he made the king "see the light of day before we finished."[60]

General Georges Catroux, the French High Commissioner in Syria, was a recent arrival in London. Although he was senior to de Gaulle, Catroux voluntarily placed himself under the latter's command. De Gaulle was unsure about including Catroux in his small party for the trip to Washington. So he sent him around to meet Stark. Stark liked him at once and thought Roosevelt would, too. Catroux, with his good sense and realistic and ethical outlook impressed Stark as much as d'Astier had. Stark enjoyed talking to him and thought Marshall would enjoy a long talk with him.[61]

Plans for de Gaulle's trip were proceeding apace in the strictest secrecy. He and his small party planned to leave England about 1 December on one of the oceanliners. Stark placed de Gaulle on twenty-four hours notice to depart.[62] When preparations were complete, Stark cabled the details to Knox and indicated that de Gaulle could arrive in the United States about 6 December.[63] When there was no reply the next day, Stark again cabled Knox and asked if the arrangements were satisfactory.[64]

Finally, Admiral William D. Leahy, Roosevelt's Chief of Staff, replied. Unforeseen developments made it necessary to postpone de Gaulle's visit until after 9 January 1943, at which time Roosevelt would reserve the necessary time to see him.[65] Exactly what the unforeseen events were was not made clear, but Roosevelt was not particularly anxious to see de Gaulle and the Joint Chiefs of Staff advised him that if he saw de Gaulle, it might seriously affect the Tunisian campaign then in progress.[66] De Gaulle accepted the postponement gracefully; indeed he could not do otherwise. Surprisingly enough, he agreed with it because he felt the British were giving him weak support.[67]

De Gaulle invited Stark to dinner at the Mayfair Hotel on 30 November. It was a quiet and congenial meal, over which they discussed sending a mission to North Africa. The French National Committee wanted to send General François d'Astier immediately to North Africa to discuss the unification of French participation in the war. When d'Astier finally went to Algiers, it was as personal representative of General de Gaulle, rather than on an exploratory mission for the French National Committee. This fine distinction seemed to satisfy everyone. More significantly, he was the first Gaullist representative to go to North Africa.

Eisenhower approved the visit because he hoped it would provide greater stability in the area. He was worried about subversive activities, a fifth column, and untrustworthy officials to the extent that he could not dismiss them from his military calculations.[68] At that time the Tunisian campaign was his primary concern and he needed a secure rear area. This campaign finally bogged down at the end of December and was suspended until spring. General d'Astier arrived in Algiers unannounced on 19 December on what turned out to be a short visit. After d'Astier had been in Algiers for only three days, Eisenhower was sufficiently alarmed about the adverse effects of his visit that he asked d'Astier to leave, on the official grounds that the basic purpose of his visit had been accomplished.

Thanks to Kittredge's tireless efforts and his own extensive contacts with de Gaulle and other Frenchmen, Stark was well-versed in the complexities of emigré-French politics. In anticipation of de Gaulle's visit to Washington, Stark planned to return home for consultations and to brief Roosevelt in advance of the meeting. On the eve of his departure from London, he had a long and fruitful conversation with de Gaulle. It was a quiet, relaxed talk during which de Gaulle eloquently elaborated on a wide range of topics. Whatever their official problems and differences may have been, Stark and de Gaulle still respected and even liked each other. Neither would stand for any nonsense and each man knew it. As a result, they got on well and when they talked, each said what was on his mind.

Stark asked de Gaulle if he had any messages or a memorandum of questions for the President. De Gaulle magnanimously said he was at Roosevelt's disposal and would furnish any information or discuss anything the President might wish. However, it would be preferable for his visit not to coincide with that of General Béthouart, a deputy of General Giraud, to avoid speculation that he was making a secret deal with Darlan under American auspices.

De Gaulle agreed with the immediate decisions and arrangements Eisenhower made for establishing his expeditionary forces with a minimum of local resistance and achieving maximum support for the Tunisian campaign then in progress. Significantly, de Gaulle was willing to permit Fighting French troops under French officers to fight under Eisenhower's command or even under Giraud. Were it not for Darlan's assumption of leadership in North Africa, de Gaulle would already have sent Fighting French forces to serve under Generals Giraud, Juin, or Barré in Tunisia.[69]

Stark immediately wrote to Eisenhower to tell him that de Gaulle for the first time went so far as to say he understood Eisenhower's intentions in dealing with Darlan. Stark also told him that de Gaulle was willing to put his troops under his or Giraud's command, but not under Darlan's.[70] A few days after this rather encouraging conversation, Stark left for Washington. He left affairs in the hands of his chief of staff, Rear Admiral Alan G. Kirk, and his exceptional staff man, Lieutenant Commander Tracy B. Kittredge.

The assassination of Admiral Darlan on Christmas Eve 1942 was one of those unexpected events that suddenly transforms a political situation. Each day that he remained in power Darlan had become more and more of a political liability for the United States. His death meant the end of an embarrassment and it provided an opportunity for de Gaulle. Although he condemned the criminal act of murder, he also felt that Darlan's death eliminated obstacles to practical cooperation of all French forces in the common war effort. For this reason, he was most anxious to discuss the unification of French forces with Roosevelt.[71]

Churchill had some second thoughts about the wisdom of de Gaulle's trip. De Gaulle was at the airport on 26 December and just about to board an airplane when he received a message from Churchill asking him to delay his trip for twenty-four hours. He immediately telephoned Churchill, who asked to see him prior to his departure.

The meeting could not take place until the next day, so the departure would have to be delayed until 28 December.[72] Churchill wanted de Gaulle to delay his trip because the elimination of Darlan meant it was possible to build a nucleus of a new, unified French organization. He thought that at least a start should be made before de Gaulle went to Washington.[73]

The White House also had not been idle. Roosevelt decided that in view of the unsettled conditions in North Africa caused by Darlan's death, de Gaulle's visit to Washington ought to be postponed for a second time.[74] Kittredge orally conveyed this message to the French staff. Four hours later they reported to him that de Gaulle received the message and that he agreed to the postponement.[75]

The next day, 27 December, de Gaulle asked Kittredge to call on him. De Gaulle agreed that it was wise to postpone his trip for the time being. He wanted to await developments in North Africa and to begin discussions with Giraud, who had just been selected to succeed Darlan. Specifically, he wanted to wait for Giraud's reply to his Christmas message in which he proposed an immediate meeting. Also, he wanted time in which to make tentative arrangements with the North African French before his arrival in Washington. He and General d'Astier were to lunch with Churchill and later they might have a communication for Washington, he told Kittredge. He asked Admiral Kirk to call on him later in the afternoon.

The meeting with Kirk was not pleasant. De Gaulle was in one of his more disagreeable moods, perhaps induced by Churchill's strong talk. He had no message for Kirk, but he expected Kirk to propose another date for his trip to Washington or for a meeting with Giraud. To make matters worse, the Fighting French representative in Washington had told de Gaulle that Roosevelt could not see him between 10 January and 31 January. This additional delay irked him. He complained of the previous postponements. He wanted to see the President immediately before he met Giraud. De Gaulle went further and complained of a pro-Vichy attitude in the State Department, which, he said, was proven by the agreements Eisenhower made with Darlan and other Vichy administrators in North Africa. De Gaulle was desperate to go to Washington to insure Roosevelt's approval of the proper kind of agreement for a union of French forces in the war.[76]

Once de Gaulle unburdened himself, he accepted the postponement of his meeting with Roosevelt and set about to make the best he could of the new situation. A few days later he delivered a stirring speech in which he called for the union of all French forces in the war and expressly approved of the military leadership of General Giraud. Despite these soft words, a bitter rivalry between the two French generals had begun. The next day Roosevelt said he hoped to see General de Gaulle "very soon." He also hoped a complete union could be achieved between leaders of all French groups and territories wishing to participate in the common effort for victory over the Axis. Neither Roosevelt nor de Gaulle had changed his mind.

At the end of January 1943, de Gaulle met Roosevelt at Casablanca. While there, de Gaulle also met reluctantly with Giraud. At first there was neither cooperation nor union between the two French factions. Instead, there was rivalry that extended to French merchant ships, where one faction recruited seamen, who in turn left their ships or refused to sail them. The shortage of shipping made it imperative that all ships sail on time. It was a knotty problem, which British and American officials approached from very different viewpoints. It reflected divergent policies and threatened to strain Anglo-American cooperation.

In early 1943 Stark kept up a steady flow of information to Washington on the current status of de Gaulle's adroit maneuvering to conclude an agreement with Giraud and then ease him out of leadership of the French forces. Finally, by the summer of 1943 de Gaulle succeeded in unifying all French forces outside of France under his leadership. When he moved his headquarters from London to Algiers, Stark's embassage came to an end.

Of all the American and British officials who dealt with de Gaulle during this period, Stark was the only one who actually got along well with him. Perhaps there was some form of inherent compatibility between the two professional military men, one a deep water sailor and the other a tank commander. Both were frank and honest with each other and they enjoyed mutual respect. This is not to say that both men were immune to anger, frustration, and irritations. The point remains that despite whatever difficulties may have existed, personal relations between the two men never became bitter. No breach was ever so serious as to be irreconcilable.

The specific problems Stark dealt with were derivatives of larger political questions, which were the specific concern of the highest levels in Washington, London, and Algiers. Despite their relatively minor importance, these problems could have grown to major proportions if they had not been handled properly.

The question of recruitment of seamen was one issue that could not be resolved in London. The ultimate solution was an agreement between de Gaulle and Giraud. But Stark did succeed in reaching a compromise, which de Gaulle repudiated in a heavy-handed manner. That this repudiation did not do any permanent damage testifies more to Stark's patience and his good personal relations with de Gaulle than it does to the diplomacy of the general.

In an incident involving a French merchant ship, Stark protected a specific American interest. His order to place an armed gangway watch on the ship was a determining factor in the sailing of the ship as scheduled. He stood firm. He refused the blandishments of various Fighting French officials to ask de Gaulle to insure the timely sailing of the ship. This firmness succeeded in frustrating Gaullist attempts to wrest control of the ship and its crew.[77]

Stark was only an interested bystander in the events leading up to the British refusal in April 1943 to provide transportation for de Gaulle for his proposed North African odyssey. The situation came to a head when the Allied staff in Algiers replied in the name of General Eisenhower and suggested a delay in de Gaulle's visit until the Tunisian campaign ended. De Gaulle took this message to be a personal reply from Eisenhower. He addressed a stinging reply to him and asked Stark to send it through the United States military communications network. Stark's tactful return to de Gaulle of this reply saved him later embarrassment and avoided what would have been a wholly unnecessary and unpleasant situation.

In each of these incidents as well as in many other minor ones, American relations were conducted with firmness, tact, and a notable absence of rancor, whatever may have been the private feelings of Stark and Kittredge. This absence of rancor in London was in direct contrast to the harsh comments of Roosevelt to Churchill about de Gaulle and the then prevailing State Department predilection against him. Although American officials in London may not have agreed with de Gaulle, they at least understood the essential elements of the Fighting French position and the Gaullist rationale.[78] The same could not be said of Washington.

The saving grace of United States relations with Fighting France was the good personal relations between Stark and de Gaulle, as well as those between Kittredge and the French staff. Without these bright spots the story might very well have been an unrelieved one of suspicions, frustrations, and recriminations. Whatever success there was could be measured more in terms of people than of policy.

11

THE SUBMARINE MENACE

The decision to invade North Africa in 1942 and later decisions for continuing offensive action in the European theater meant that the sea lanes of communication, which hitherto had simply sustained the British in their valiant efforts against Germany and which were the major means of sending needed war materials and supplies to the Soviet Union, would henceforth be utilized to mount that offensive action. The submarine was Hitler's best weapon against those lifelines. Thus, German submarines had to be destroyed wherever possible, not only in their hunting grounds, but also on the way to their hunting grounds, at their bases, and in their construction yards.

The Battle of the Atlantic took on added importance. There would still be differences at the highest naval levels in Washington and in London as to whether the major antisubmarine effort should be defensive, in the form of protection of convoys, or offensive, in striking at submarine bases and construction yards, or a combination of both. The R.A.F. and the U.S. Army Air Force still favored bombing cities and factories in accordance with the prevailing concepts of air power, rather than concentrating on the targets urged by both navies. Now that major action against the Axis in the Atlantic was assured, Stark's role as an observer and as the liaison between the two navies took on a new importance.

Stark's initial round of conferences and meetings with Admiralty officials in 1942 confirmed his long held belief that the submarine constituted the greatest menace in the Atlantic. In April 1942 he had told Rear Admiral Robert L. Ghormley, who was at that time Special Navy Observer, London, that the greatest possible effort should be devoted to protection of British sea communications by convoys with

183

ample surface escort, and by long range aircraft with fighter escorts if necessary. In addition, unremitting air attacks should be made against German submarines and surface raiders in their bases.[1]

By May 1942 the British had driven the German submarines away from home waters. They moved to the Western Atlantic, off the east coast of the United States. Stark was not surprised that next they moved into the Caribbean and the Gulf of Mexico where they sank seventy-one ships (as opposed to eight in the North Atlantic) in the month of May alone.[2] Clearly, the U.S. Navy could profit from the British experience in antisubmarine warfare. Towards the end of May, Stark sent Commander John P. Vest to Washington to bring both Knox and King up to date on the antisubmarine measures taken by the British Coastal Command. King found his comments and observations most interesting and ordered him to duty in the antisubmarine section of his headquarters. Knox was so enthused after meeting Vest that he wanted to make his own study of how the British had virtually eliminated German submarines within three hundred miles of the British Isles. He thought seriously of asking Roosevelt to let him go to England for this purpose. However, he was unable to make that trip until September 1943.

There were two ways to attack the submarine problem. The first was to increase the number of aircraft available for bombing submarine bases and for antisubmarine operations, especially in the Bay of Biscay, through which German submarines had to proceed to and from their bases on the French coast. The second way was to produce more escort ships to protect the convoys. As Secretary of the Navy, Knox was vitally concerned with the production of these valuable escort ships.

The Royal Navy constantly asked for a moderate number of long-range bombers to be used against submarines at sea or in their bases. The struggle for aircraft was both complicated and nettlesome. Air Chief Marshal Portal refused to give up airplanes made in the United States for the British lend-lease account of 1941. He wanted them for the R.A.F. King and Marshall were understandably irked, because they needed at least some of them for operations in the Pacific and the Atlantic. They took the matter directly to Roosevelt, who in turn sent a strong cable to Churchill about the necessity of resolving the allocation problem.

Roosevelt felt that any discussion with Churchill about the numbers and types of aircraft would be inappropriate at that level. Instead, he sent Rear Admiral John M. Towers, Chief of the Navy's Bureau of Aeronautics and Lieutenant General Henry "Hap" Arnold, head of the Army Air Force, to London to iron out details with the British chiefs of staff. Roosevelt also asked Churchill to send Portal back to Washington for final discussions. As King told Stark, he, Marshall, and Roosevelt were determined to break the British "stranglehold" on aircraft so "we may get on with the war."[3]

The British developed an effective technique to attack surfaced submarines from the air. Airplanes were equipped with radar which picked up the surfaced submarines. When the planes closed to about half a mile, they turned on their Leigh search lights and dropped depth charges. By the end of July 1942, the British were making fifty sorties each week and Pound had every reason to hope for good results.[4]

It did little good to produce one hundred cargo ships each month if enough escort vessels to protect them were not also built. At first Knox favored construction of relatively small ships, which could be built quickly and delivered to the fleet in a relatively short period. However, the real need was for a larger ship that could be used in the open sea in all kinds of weather. When he was Chief of Naval Operations, Stark struggled unsuccessfully to convince Roosevelt of this need, because Roosevelt favored smaller patrol craft. However, by October 1942 Knox succeeded in obtaining a decision to build 310 escort vessels in 1943. He told Stark he feared a tremendous outbreak of submarine activity in the future and he wanted these ships to be ready when it happened.[5]

Losses of merchant shipping appeared to have been stabilized by the end of the summer of 1942 and Churchill declared that the Allies were building ships faster than the Germans were sinking them. Even so, Stark was not ready to cheer. The sinkings, 83 in July and 102 in August, were still too many.[6] Submarines remained the greatest threat and the most dangerous areas were where air coverage was poorest or nonexistent. Stark saw that the limited numbers of land-based aircraft and the unavailability of escort carriers in the autumn of 1942 meant that little could be done to provide more air coverage. With the North African landings scheduled for early November, he knew the Germans could strike hard, if and where escorts were weakened, or they could go to the new hunting grounds off the African coast. Only time would tell.[7]

Fortunately the numbers of merchant ships sunk in British home waters were significantly reduced in 1943. But the depredations of German submarines in other areas clearly continued to threaten the sea lanes to Great Britain, now a staging area for the coming assault on the European continent. These marauding submarines were based in French ports and they entered the Atlantic by crossing the Bay of Biscay. As early as the summer of 1942, the British cabinet recognized the necessity for a high level committee to coordinate the British response to this threat and to enlist whatever assistance was available from America.

Churchill personally convened the Cabinet Anti-U-Boat Warfare Committee on 4 November 1942. Its members included the Ministers of Production, Labour, Aircraft Production, War Transport, and Air and the air force and navy officers most concerned. At Churchill's invitation, Stark participated in its deliberations, along with another American, Averell Harriman, who was in England as the lend-lease expediter.

With Churchill presiding, the committee met every week or two for two hours and more at a time. It was clear to the members that German submarines were the number one enemy and that the ability of the Anglo-American alliance to bring its potential strength to bear in the Atlantic depended upon defeat of that enemy. Stark noted that the discussions were full, frank, sharp, and to the point, "but with an earnest endeavor to get the other fellow's point of view, and no rancor."[8]

This body provided the means for the exchange and examination of a great deal of information and a variety of viewpoints. The seniority of its members meant that action could be taken swiftly and decisively on whatever was decided. Stark's presence as the representative of King meant that whatever the committee formulated would receive an authoritative response from the American member. Stark, however, was careful not to exceed his authority and he immediately referred doubtful cases directly to King along with his own comments and recommendations. His professional judgment and opinion, and his advice on the likelihood of Washington's reaction to various proposals aided and at times guided the Committee in its deliberations. In this way he performed a highly useful service for the British, while at the same time he obtained a comprehensive view of the British anti-submarine effort, which he promptly reported to King and Knox.

Both Washington and London agreed that the number one priority for antisubmarine forces of both countries was the protection of the North Atlantic convoys. In February 1943 heavy air raids on the bases at St. Nazaire, L'Orient, and La Pallice produced disappointing results, because of protective submarine pens. There was little disruption of submarine activities, although the towns were virtually destroyed.[9]

Stark was convinced that offensive action against the German submarines would pay handsome dividends in increased safety of the vital North Atlantic convoys. Using highly technical studies produced by his staff, he proposed an air offensive against the submarines as they crossed a broad belt of the Bay of Biscay. Since the submarines had to transit that belt, intensive and vigorous patrolling by air, would tend to keep them submerged, necessitating operation on battery power at much slower speeds. If a submarine surfaced, it would be subject to immediate attack. In brief, he proposed killing 100 submarines and seriously damaging 139 others in a four month period. Stark said "It would save innumerable cargoes by taking away from the enemy the overwhelming tactics of large concentrations of attacks on two or three convoys simultaneously. . . . It is the only program coming close to breaking the morale of the U-boat fleet."[10]

Churchill convened a special meeting of the Anti U-Boat Committee at 10 Downing Street to discuss Stark's proposal. Everyone was in favor of sinking German submarines. But because an offensive of the dimensions contemplated in Stark's proposal required an additional 160 aircraft, it produced heated debate on the source of those aircraft.

The First Lord of the Admiralty, A. V. Alexander, opened the meeting by stating that both the Admiralty and the R.A.F. Coastal Command were convinced that a Bay of Biscay offensive could be made effective "if the necessary aircraft could be made available." The Secretary of State for Air, Sir Archibald Sinclair, disagreed. He doubted that such an offensive would be effective.

Stark joined the debate, saying that an increase in the Bay of Biscay patrols would give the Allies the capability for the first time to carry out an all-out offensive against the submarines. The airpower enthusiasts who favored only bombing Germany objected. Stark fully realized the issues involved in diverting air effort to the Bay of Biscay. "But," he said, "if we don't stop this ever increasing flood of submarines, there will be no bombing of Germany or anything else."

These sharp exchanges clearly showed the wide divergence of views between the Royal Navy and the civilian and military leaders of the R.A.F. After a while, Averell Harriman, the other American member, suggested that agreement should first be reached on what was desired in regard to an offensive in the Bay of Biscay. Then it could be determined to what extent this requirement would be met from British resources and what additional aircraft were needed. When all of this was decided, the whole case could be put before the Combined Chiefs of Staff in Washington, who would have to decide whether they were willing to agree to divert aircraft from other sources.

Churchill was all in favor of a Bay of Biscay offensive, but he would not countenance slackening the air offensive against Germany under any conditions. The obvious source of the additional aircraft was the United States. Stark declined to commit the United States, saying he was not in a position to forecast what, if anything, could be spared or even to suggest any redistribution of aircraft. He simply did not have enough information at his disposal. Authoritative comment on this point would have to come from King.[11]

Churchill then drafted a letter to Roosevelt in which he clearly laid out the matter and he gave credit to Stark for the proposal, possibly because he thought that Stark's name might lend weight to it.[12] For reasons that are not entirely clear, this letter was never sent. Instead, the British cabled their Joint Staff Mission in Washington to request additional aircraft from the United States Joint Chiefs of Staff. In so doing, they used Stark's name to influence the American decision. This ploy thoroughly annoyed King, who saw it for what it was. He told Stark that he heartily welcomed his views on any and all matters, but he preferred to have them directly from Stark and not by way of the British.

King's annoyance was exacerbated by his different view of the demands of the two-ocean war. The Joint Chiefs had to consider the submarine menace everywhere in the Atlantic and they did not know when they would have to deal with similar troubles in the Pacific. In fact, King informed Stark, trouble was then brewing off the east coast of Australia and in the vicinity of Samoa, Fiji, and New Caledonia. He told Stark, "To us, it seems that the British have a 'chronic case' of what we have come to call 'localitis' and that they are now having an acute attack with regard to the Bay of Biscay. For them, their own locality is the key to what concerns them—vitally, to be sure, but there are also other localities in which vital considerations exist, or may arise at any moment."[13]

At that time King simply could not release any American aircraft from their patrols in the North Atlantic. During April and May 1943, submarines sank 85 merchant ships in the North Atlantic. Nevertheless, the Coastal Command continued the Bay of Biscay offensive with the planes at its disposal.

The numbers of merchant ships sunk by submarines reached a low point during the winter months of 1942-1943, but in March 1943 there was a sudden sharp rise that worried Knox. He confided to Stark, "We are going into the spring in pitifully weak condition" in regard to both surface ships fit for the work in the mid-Atlantic and aircraft. The destroyer escorts that Knox succeeded in ordering built were still under construction and would not be ready for duty with the fleet until July. He dreaded to think of what would happen in the interim.

Despite Knox's well-founded worry, the tide was turning slowly in favor of the Allies. Stark pointed out to him that the summary of gains and losses of merchant ships since the end of December 1941 showed that at the end of March 1943 there was a gain for the first time since the United States entered the war. It was a milestone the Americans and the British had long been hoping to reach. A few days earlier, Stark told King, "Tough as the submarine situation is I feel there is no cause for discouragement, though God knows there is none for congratulating ourselves. However, we will win this struggle before we are through with it."[14]

By the end of May, Stark had some really good news for Knox. The Admiralty reported that they estimated an average of one submarine per day had been sunk during the month, the best rate to date. As a result, Stark anticipated that the Allies would gain a million tons of shipping. It was, indeed, good news.[15]

There were numerous factors that contributed to this welcome turn of events. Chief among them was that the British and American antisubmarine organizations were starting to produce results, thanks to intensive training, perfection of tactics, and development of new weapons and techniques. Early in 1943, King and Knox convened their own antisubmarine conference, which went into the whole question of allocation of forces with admirable thoroughness. King was aware of the difficulties of implementation. To him the most important change was turning over responsibility for the North Atlantic convoys to British and Canadian forces. He told Stark it was a move toward simplification.[16]

By far the most important development in Washington in the submarine war was the establishment of the TENTH Fleet in late may 1943. King explained to Stark that it would be an anti-U-boat command, attached to, but differentiated from his headquarters. Roughly speaking, it was the U.S. Navy's equivalent to the Anti-U-Boat Warfare Committee Churchill chaired in London. King saw it as a means by which "interested parties other than the Navy" could gain a better understanding of how antisubmarine warfare is conducted.

The TENTH Fleet took over all antisubmarine activities, including organization and routing of convoys, and the allocation of antisubmarine aircraft, escort carriers and escort vessels. For the time being, King would technically be "Commander, TENTH Fleet," but his chief of staff was the brilliant and energetic Rear Admiral Francis S. "Frog" Low, a man admirably suited for the task.[17]

The submarine war news continued to be good through May and into June. Knox felt it was too good to last. He was impressed with the effectiveness of the British antisubmarine air operations from bases in Iceland and Northern Ireland. He hoped that the U.S. Navy aviators based in Newfoundland and Greenland would soon become equally skilled. Although Stark realized the news could not always be so good, he dared hope for even better news. Stark and the Admiralty could only guess at German intentions for future submarine operations. Even though the submarines had the initiative, the creation of the TENTH Fleet made it possible to ascertain quickly where they were going to operate and to attack them there. Stark told Knox that in the recent killings of submarines "the Hun lost some of his best skippers." He felt it was a favorable development, which might otherwise escape notice.[18]

The intelligence developed by the Admiralty in early June 1943 showed that despite recent Allied successes in the war against the submarines, a formidable threat remained. There were 227 German submarines then operating; another 207 were training, refitting, or training in the Baltic. Since the beginning of the war, 237 German submarines had been sunk, which came to 34 percent of all submarines in commission at the outbreak of war and those commissioned after the war's start. By June, 1943, the British had lost 28 percent of their submarines. The experience level of the German skippers at sea was slowly declining. Approximately 20 percent were on their first cruise, while another 20 percent had only one or two cruises under their belts. As a rule, captains with six or seven cruises were ordered ashore as instructors.

At that time there were about 100 German submarines at sea in the North Atlantic, with about 20 on the United States/United Kingdom route and another 20 on the United States/Gibraltar route. The remainder were assigned to the east coast of the United States and off the coasts of Brazil, West Africa, and the Cape of Good Hope. Lately in the Bay of Biscay transiting submarines traveled in both directions in fighter-escorted packs. It was the German response to the success of Allied aircraft attacks on the submarine packs. Stark expected more shifting of tactics as Allied measures and German countermeasures became effective.[19]

German submarine strength was formidable. By the middle of July sinkings of merchant ships were nearly double what they had been for the entire month of June. By the end of the month the submarines had sunk 24 ships, more than three times the number sunk in June.[20] Knox was not surprised. At his press conference he vigorously denounced overly optimistic statements that had been made in Washington and he said bluntly that submarines would be a threat until the end of the war: "I do think we have pretty well mastered the art of knocking off submarines, but we will not be able to completely banish them while the war is on. We can take a heavy toll of them wherever they go." Stark agreed. Fortunately, by the end of July the Allies were doing a little bit better than they were at the beginning of the month as far as losses of merchant ships were concerned. By early August Stark was pleased with the way the war against the submarines was going. More than 80 submarines were sunk in May, June, and July. August started well.[21] Nevertheless, "The Hun in contesting every inch of our progress in the Bay of Biscay," he told King.[22]

The importance and effectiveness in July 1943 of American air antisubmarine operations was increasing. The army had two Liberator squadrons, totaling 24 planes, and the navy had a patrol squadron operating from the United Kingdom under the Coastal Command. General Jacob L. Devers, commander of the U.S. Army troops in the United Kingdom, suggested to Stark that Major General Ira C. Eaker, Commander of the U.S. Eighth Air Force, sit on the Cabinet Anti-U-Boat Warfare Committee, because he could keep the Army Air Force staff informed of the problems involved. Besides, Devers thought Eaker would make a substantial contribution to the discussions. Stark took the matter up with Portal, who favored it, and Portal in turn promised to talk to Churchill.[23]

In August 1943 the Admiralty concluded that the air offensive in the Bay of Biscay, for the time being, at least, had sufficiently neutralized that body of water so that German submarines could no longer safely use the French ports of Brest, L'Orient, La Pallice, and Bordeaux. Instead, some began operating from the less convenient German and Norwegian ports, which necessitated longer passages from their bases to their hunting grounds. Very few newly commissioned submarines left port during the early summer, although the rate of commissionings did not decrease. The Admiralty's best estimate was that about 30 new submarines were waiting for a propitious moment to put to sea, to be added to 120 submarines, already in operation.[24] Stark agreed with the Admiralty that the Germans were unlikely to regain the initiative, although they still had the capability to work great mischief in the North Atlantic.

Vast numbers of escort vessels and aircraft were still necessary to insure safe passage of Allied shipping on the convoy routes. Successes to date could not justify any reduction in the construction and provision of antisubmarine ships and aircraft. Air Chief Marshall Sir John Slessor urged King to insure that navy antisubmarine aircraft be equipped with the new search lights. He pointedly asked Stark to take up the matter "strongly with King."[25]

The submarine situation still looked good, Stark told Knox in the early autumn. He warned against public complacency, which would be "dangerous if it entered into any of our marrow."[26]

There were still fierce encounters in the North Atlantic. A slow moving convoy, ONS 18, sailed from Milford Haven on 12 September with 27 ships and a Royal Navy escort of eight ships. Three days later ON 202, a faster moving convoy of 40 ships, sailed from Liverpool with an escort of six Canadian ships. The two convoys joined several days out. German submarines sank six merchantmen and three of the escorts, while losing five of their own number between 20 and 23 September. The sinking of the third escort, HMS *Itchen*, on 23 September was particularly tragic. She had on board the survivors of the two escorts that had been sunk three days before, HMS *Polyanthus* and HMCS *St. Croix*. There were only three survivors from all three ships.[27]

The Germans claimed that they sank 12 destroyers in this encounter and that they had probably sunk three more, along with nine merchantmen. When the cabinet Anti-U-Boat Warfare Committee met after these sinkings, Churchill wanted to report publicly the actual losses and thus show the German claim for what it was. Stark pointed out to him that the Germans might very well not know what they had accomplished and that telling them would be playing into their hands by giving them information they sought. Churchill reconsidered and dropped the matter.[28]

Stark summed up his views of the war against the submarines at a press conference in the autumn of 1943. He said, "We thought we had the Hun licked once and for all in 1918, but we didn't. It is never safe to assume your opponent out until he takes the count, and that will be when he yells 'Kamerad.' The submarine is not licked once and for all, and obviously the German scientists are hard at work, as are ours, to continue the search for new weapons. No one can see what tomorrow will bring forth in this respect."[29]

Before D-Day Anglo-American planners worried about the possibility of German surface or subsurface attacks on the vast armada that would set out from England for the Normandy coast. Stark, too, shared their apprehensions. Everything possible was done to establish a veritable wall on the surface of the Channel and in the air over it to protect the invasion forces from German submarines. The Allied efforts were enormously successful. German submarine efforts against the stream of shipping across the channel could be written off as almost complete failures.[30]

When the Allied armies broke through the German lines in early August 1944, the German submarine bases at Brest and St. Nazaire became untenable. Some of the German submarines moved south to Bordeaux and La Pallice, while the bulk of the force moved north to Norwegian bases, from which they sought a relatively easy access to the Atlantic through the North Sea. Thanks to Ultra intelligence, the

Admiralty was aware of the repositioning of the German submarines. This information was given to Stark in London, who passed it on to King in Washington.

So long as the main German submarine bases were on the Bay of Biscay, there was little division of effort between offensive and defensive antisubmarine operations. The patrol aircraft based in the south of England provided air coverage both for convoys and for attacking the submarines as they proceeded to and from their bases. When the bases moved to Norway, however, a division of effort became necessary. Stark worried that this division would detract from the primary antisubmarine objective, notably the safe arrival of convoys in English ports.

Stark made it abundantly clear to his staff that convoy safety was paramount and that all dispositions of antisubmarine forces should be made accordingly. Naturally, he wanted to kill as many submarines as possible, but he pointed out "if we don't kill a single submarine yet get in our convoys with 100% safety, we are doing our stuff."[31] When every precaution was taken to safeguard the convoys, then and only then was he in favor of using whatever means were left over to attack submarines.

With this clear statement of the first and primary mission of antisubmarine forces uppermost in their minds, Stark's staff got to work on a detailed analysis of how additional patrol aircraft might be used. In September 1944, King was contemplating sending Fleet Air Wing 15 from North Africa and he asked Stark for comments on where they might be based and how and by whom they should be operated. There was a possibility that this wing might be based on air fields in Brittany. This possibility raised a host of questions, such as provision of necessary services and logistic support.

If based in Brittany, the aircraft would be under the operational control of Rear Admiral Alan G. Kirk, who commanded U.S. Naval Forces in France, rather than under the R.A.F. Coastal Command. Stark favored the principle of unity of command, by which the U.S. Navy's Fleet Air Wing 7 operated as a unit under the overall direction of the R.A.F. Coastal Command. That principle worked well in actual practice and he saw no reason to discard it. As it turned out, Dunkeswell in the south of England, rather than Brittany, continued to be the principal base for U.S. Navy antisubmarine aircraft for the remainder of the war. The reason was that these aircraft were most effective while operating under the control of the Coastal Command. Basing them in Brittany would mean another command and divided areas of responsibility, additional complicating factors that could be easily eliminated. The common sense approach was adopted.

Stark thought the R.A.F.'s Coastal Command Anti-Submarine Plan in September 1944 implied that the Coastal Command felt that relatively few aircraft were required to provide adequate convoy coverage. This implication and the recent shift of air antisubmarine operations from the south of England to the North Sea concerned him. He felt that perhaps too much effort at that time was being placed in the North Sea, possibly at the expense of convoys approaching the British Isles around the south of Ireland. Stark told the First Sea Lord, Admiral Sir Andrew B. Cunningham of his concern, saying, "While the killing of every possible submarine is important, it is secondary to the major consideration of protecting the convoys."[32]

Cunningham reassured Stark that the timely arrival of the convoys was the first objective of the plan in question and the destruction of the submarines was secondarily important. He pointed out that the Coastal Command could move its antisubmarine squadrons more quickly than the Germans could move their submarines. Thus, they could be flown back to their bases in the south of England if the need arose. With flexibility of this sort, the Germans could be opposed with maximum force wherever they might be.[33]

By early autumn of 1944, the Germans had established submarine patrols around the northern approaches to the Northern Channel. The Coastal Command, applying the principle of flexibility Cunningham mentioned, reinforced the squadrons patrolling these areas. Although the Germans had withdrawn their submarines from St. George's Channel, at least for the moment, the routing of convoys to the south of Ireland was certain to lure more submarines to that area. For this reason, the Coastal Command favored stationing any American reinforcements in the southwest to cover this vital area.[34]

Stark, the Admiralty, and the Coastal Command had anticipated a submarine offensive for some time. In November Stark was sure it was about to break. King was so concerned that he sent twelve destroyer escorts to reinforce Admiral Sir Max Horton's hard-working, hard-pressed surface forces of the Western Approaches command.[35] Churchill was apprehensive about what the Germans might have in store for the Allies. The entire situation was thrashed out in some detail when Churchill presided at a meeting of the Cabinet Anti-U-Boat Warfare Committee at the end of October. Once he fully understood the situation, Churchill felt better. He and Cunningham told Stark how much they appreciated King's sending additional help.

The meeting turned to the progress of construction of German submarine pens in Norway. Stark interjected that with so many bombers going to the continent, certainly some could be diverted to submarine targets.[36] Churchill was amazed at the progress the Germans had made on the Norwegian submarine pens. He turned to Chief Air Marshall Portal and said, "Why in the world with all the precision bombing you talk about, have you permitted this to occur?" Portal had no direct reply. He simply restated the standard R.A.F. reasons why a day must not be lost in bombing oil plants in Germany, and so on.[37] Clearly, the advocates of strategic bombing never really understood there was another war on. Churchill directed the Admiralty and the R.A.F. to study at once the feasibility of bombing naval targets.

By early January, Cunningham for the navy and Portal for the R.A.F. agreed that the Bomber Command would initiate attacks beased on Admiralty priorities, subject to tactical and meterological conditions that might prevent the Bomber Command from adhering strictly to the priorities established. They both agreed that close personal consultation between their respective staffs was the best way to keep the navy and the air force "alive to each other's problems."[38] Cunningham provided Stark with copies of his correspondence with Portal.

As winter came on, the submarine problem became worse. The Germans developed the snorkel that allowed their submarines to use diesel engines while submerged. It was a relatively simple device: a pipe approximately 26 feet long with a tube or air intake and exhaust outlet with a float valve that kept sea water from sloshing in. When not in use, it folded back on the hull. The great advantages of the snorkel were that submarines with it could run on diesel engines and charge their batteries while submerged. The snorkel, about the size of a periscope, was difficult to see and almost impossible to pick up on radar.

German submarines equipped with snorkels were now moving close inshore to the British Isles. Use of the snorkel in late 1944 made Cunningham uncomfortable. Admiral Sir Max Horton, in command of the Western Approaches, feared the German submarines could have a great deal of success if they started operating in convoy waters with determination and guts.[39]

A dramatic sinking took place on Christmas Eve, 1944. The SS *Léopoldville,* a Belgian freighter, was ferrying troops from Southampton to Cherbourg when she was torpedoed near the French coast. Over 800 soldiers were lost.[40] The Admiralty's response was to reinforce surface forces in the area and to lay additional minefields. They gave urgent consideration to laying nets in the English Channel, in addition to a 30-mile net barrage off the Shetland Islands. In France, Rear Admiral Kirk was so concerned that he seriously considered halting the transfer of wounded men by LST from Cherbourg to England in favor of ferrying them from Calais to Dover, the shortest distance across the Channel.[41]

At this time, seven ships were torpedoed and sunk while under escort in British waters. The new threat of snorkel-equipped submarines operating close inshore around the western and northern British ports required a reversion to more defensive measures. Cunningham explained the problem to Stark and what the British were doing about it. To help in the Atlantic, the British transferred patrol aircraft from the Mediterranean to Gibraltar. It was necessary to keep the pressure on the Germans as they left and entered their Norwegian ports. For this reason, Cunningham was averse to shifting antisubmarine aircraft from their North Sea patrols to other areas. Would Stark ask King to transfer three squadrons of naval aircraft to reinforce the Coastal Command in the southwest of England?[42]

When Stark transmitted Cunningham's request to King, he was genuinely concerned at what seemed to him to be a worsening of the submarine situation. As a stop-gap measure in January 1945, King authorized Stark as Commander, TWELFTH Fleet, to retain twelve U.S. Navy subchasers that were scheduled to return home. Although small, these sturdy 100-foot craft might help solve some of the escort problems in the Channel, Stark told Cunningham.[43]

When they both were attending the Yalta Conference in February 1945, Cunningham asked King if he would confirm his offer made some months before of making more surface ships available for Atlantic operations. King said his offer was still good and suggested that Admiral Sir Max Horton deal directly with CINCLANT, who was then Admiral Jonas Ingram.[44]

German submarines continued to be a serious thorn in the sides of British and American naval officials in London until the German collapse in early May 1945. Even then, the submarines at sea that had not received the word presented a potential threat. Meanwhile, Stark continued to be concerned with the employment of convoys and a wide variety of antisubmarine measures. Among them were proposals to float wires of great length in areas known to be infested with snorkeling submarines so that the movement of the wires through the water would make the snorkels easier to see.[45] The U.S. Navy experimented with infrared light to detect submarines. Horton told Stark with great delight that from June 1944, when submarines started inshore operations, until the end of February 1945, 31 had been sunk as a result of initial detection by ASDIC, an underwater sounding device and the forerunner of sonar.[46] The U.S. Navy sent a blimp at the beginning of April to assist in the antisubmarine work.[47]

Finally, in May 1945, German submarines at sea began surrendering in accordance with orders from their home command. On 28 May 1945, the U.S. Navy and the Admiralty suspended trade convoys in the Atlantic. Ships were directed to burn navigation lights and there was no need to darken ship.[48] Only then was the sea war finally over.

12

NAVAL PREPARATIONS FOR OVERLORD

When Roosevelt and Churchill met at Casablanca in January 1943, they approved preliminary plans for the Combined Chiefs of Staff for a cross-channel operation. Its code name was Operation Overlord. The naval portion of the plan came to be called Operation Neptune. A Supreme Commander was not appointed at that time, but the British were asked to nominate a Chief of Staff to the Supreme Allied Commander (COSSAC) and to prepare the first directives.

The day after his return from Casablanca, Roosevelt briefed Stark in Washington on these developments. It was clear to Stark that the preparations for Operation Round-Up, which had been suspended only a few months before, would soon be resumed. But it was not clear to him whether the command arrangements and procedures already established would also be revived, or whether they would be modified, and if so, how.

After Stark returned to London, the War and Navy Departments in Washington made decisions and reached agreements that were fundamental to the invasion effort. Previously, the army was prepared to undertake amphibious training and the handling of the smaller landing craft. But on 8 March 1943, the army and the navy agreed that amphibious training would be a navy responsibility and that the theater commander, whoever he might be, would determine the control and assignment of amphibious units and training activities in overseas theaters. In addition, a basic logistical plan for joint army-navy operations was established. Under it, the theater commander was responsible for coordinating the logistical needs and the organization of the army and navy forces in his theater.

199

This sound and reasonable arrangement followed the best command relationships and planning procedures taught in the war colleges. For Stark, the senior naval officer in the European theater, it meant that he and his command would be responsible for all amphibious training of United States forces in the United Kingdom; he would also be responsible for meeting the logistical requirements of the United States naval forces that would participate in the cross-channel operation.

Under Stark's watchful eye, representatives from both staffs got to work immediately. The army was anxious to establish the first amphibious training center. They recommended a site in the Woolacombe-Appledore area of North Devon on the Bristol Channel, where tidal conditions closely resembled parts of the French beaches that probably would be used by United States forces in the assault. Stark sent officers to inspect the area; they found the British were using part of it and that it was suitable for the training of only one batallion team at a time. Negotiations with the Admiralty and other British officials produced additional space. When these preliminaries were completed, Stark requested that King send 106 officers and 745 enlisted men, together with landing craft.

Officers on his own staff and even some British officers advised Stark that Appledore was not suited for his purposes, because of the dangers of wind and tide, among other reasons. Disregarding the advice of some "pretty level heads" as he called them, Stark took Appledore for amphibious training. It was well that he did, because it turned out to be one of the most valuable training centers in the British Isles.[1]

Senior British and American officers met in June 1943 at the Hollywood Hotel in Largs on the Firth of Clyde to study and to anticipate the combined operation problems in Operation Overlord. They represented the U.S. Army, the Royal Navy, and the British Army. Stark was represented by his Chief of Staff, Rear Admiral George B. Wilson. Vice Admiral Lord Louis Mountbatten opened the conference. He said Churchill and the British Chiefs of Staff hoped the conference would come to definite conclusions on which the provision of equipment and future training and planning could be based.

It was a well-conceived conference. Meeting for five days, they discussed such matters as the German defensive systems, mounting of the operation, naval and air aspects of it, and assault support craft. Wilson was particularly interested in the discussion of the buildup, which would involve Stark's command extensively.[2]

It was clearly understood that U.S. Navy and Army forces arriving in the United Kingdom would already be basically trained in combined operations. It was important that they should be because facilities at Appledore and at Base Two in Scotland would be available only for refresher training, not for basic amphibious training.[3] More significantly, there was a consensus on the necessity of constructing artificial ports. These ports, later known as Mulberries, became a matter of the utmost concern of the U.S. Navy and were indispensable to the success of the 1944 Normandy landings.[4]

One of the continuing, nagging problems the Allies faced in World War II was the shortage of landing craft. Stark first faced the problem in 1942 when planning got underway in earnest for the North African landings. At that time the contemplated buildup of forces, including landing craft, to be sent to Great Britain for the proposed cross-channel attack in 1943 was necessarily postponed. In September 1942 Washington decided to allocate these landing craft to other theaters, notably the Pacific, where they were sorely needed. The result was that the American amphibious forces in Britain were reduced to a skeleton of what had been planned only a short time before.[5] The flow of landing craft almost ceased.

Further reductions were made to meet the pressing needs of the naval base at Oran, following the landings near there in early November. The sound reasons for these reductions were immediately obvious to Stark, who did all he could to meet the immediate demands of military necessity. However, he was concerned lest the skeleton organization in the United Kingdom be impaired so that when the inevitable buildup for the invasion of Europe began, it would not be able to function efficiently.

Stark was particularly concerned about Base Two at Gareloch in Scotland, which would be needed when the buildup for the cross-channel operation was resumed. He pointed out to King in 1942 that it was the only naval activity in Britain capable of receiving and maintaining landing craft; in addition, it provided limited training facilities for amphibious warfare. He bluntly told King, "The complete lack of properly equipped and efficient maintenance and repair bases for landing craft in the United Kingdom is a compelling motive for the full operation of the shops at Base Two to repair and maintain craft. The shortage of competent artificers in England and the deplorable condition of the landing craft which have been delivered to the U.K. make it highly desirable to train the British to operate U.S. machinery in a U.S. base, with the U.S. personnel already here in the U.K. It is the only way our own investment in landing craft can be protected."[6]

At first, conflicting signals came out of Washington. King told Stark in September 1942 that the few landing craft being sent to Great Britain would go to Stark's command. Other directives said they were to be turned over to the British. King finally resolved the issue by decisively putting all U.S. naval amphibious forces in the United Kingdom into a deep freeze at the end of 1942. Any landing craft sent were for the British, who would have to maintain them and obtain spare parts through lend-lease. Furthermore, Base Two was turned back to the British in early February 1943 along with the stores depot at Staines, which contained extensive stocks of spare parts. The only portions of Base Two the U.S. Navy retained were a few finger piers for berthing the six submarines of SUBRON 50 and some office space and berthing accommodations.

Meanwhile, Stark was doing all that was within his power to assure maximum cooperation with the army. He and the army officials established coordinating groups to this end. The cordiality and spirit of cooperation at the upper levels between Stark and his staff and their counterparts quickly percolated down into their respective organizations and produced results.

One of these was a joint Army-Navy agreement set up in June 1943 to insure that the needs of the services would be supplied with an economy of shipping space and a minimum of manpower. At that same time, priorities of strategic and tactical needs were established, an extremely important step. The army, navy, and army air forces standardized material as much as possible and there was a free interchange of supplies among the three services. Local procurement was used as much as possible to reduce demands upon shipping, which was always scarce. Implementation of the agreement had its snags, and other difficulties appeared from time to time, but the job was done.[7]

Stark assigned navy representatives to the staff of the European Theater Commander. In a personal letter to King, he pointed out that the navy was inadequately represented in this work. Each of the six bases planned for the United States naval forces required a commanding officer. It would be far more efficient to have a flag officer in overall command of these bases than it would be for headquarters in London to supervise and coordinate their activities. Naval forces in Europe were operating on a "personnel shoestring," he said. Preparations for the cross-channel operation required a change.

A part of the personnel problem arose from the fact that the Navy Department had used COMNAVEAU as a burying ground for officers who were not ready for retirement but who were not useful under wartime conditions. King was concerned primarily with the war in the Pacific; he thought the Royal Navy should have the full responsibility for the naval aspects of a cross-channel operation with little or no help from the U.S. Navy. He barely had the manpower and equipment necessary for the Pacific campaigns. Apparently, he considered that it was not necessary to give Stark department heads who would be capable of organizing a major operational and logistical effort. Stark's chief of staff was not fully recovered from a serious illness; the captains who headed the medical, supply, and construction departments had been passed over for assignment to the Pacific. Captain (later Commodore and Rear Admiral) Howard A. Flanigan, who headed the department concerned with merchant shipping—the convoys—was the only senior officer with extensive operational and logistical experience.

Things began to happen after Roosevelt and Churchill met in Washington in May 1943 for another summit meeting, known as Trident. On the basis of agreements reached by Roosevelt and Churchill at this meeting, the Combined Chiefs of Staff made further decisions regarding the invasion of Europe, which were the basis of Navy Department directives issued in June and July. It was apparent that Roosevelt had agreed that the U.S. Navy would have to be an active participant in the invasion, and the Royal Navy could not do it alone. King must have been a reluctant party to the agreement;

although steps were taken to implement it, there was no rush to begin the buildup operations in the United Kingdom. Even had King been disposed to help the British, nearly all of the landing craft being built in the United States were earmarked for Pacific operations.

First, King told Stark to repossess for a second time Base Two at Roseneath in Scotland, which would be used as an advanced amphibious training base. Fortunately, the base had been turned over to the British with the provision that the U.S. Navy could have it back on 60 days' notice. The admiralty had no objection, but asked to retain part of it. Stark thought the request was reasonable and King agreed to it. Next, King approved Stark's amphibious training program for Appledore, and he announced a schedule for delivery of a limited number of landing craft to the United Kingdom. This schedule was based upon decisions reached at the Trident conference.

Finally, the Navy Department made Stark's command the sole authority to determine what demands would be made on the U.S. Navy for logistic support. COMNAVEU would screen all requests from British forces, the U.S. Army, and all other forces in Europe for equipment or facilities to be supplied by the U.S. Navy for operations in or to be mounted from the United Kingdom.[8] Given the magnitude and the complexity of the proposed cross-channel operation, it was an awesome task.

In July 1943, Stark realized that Base Two could not be used to the extent he originally contemplated because it would unduly interfere with the British programs already in progress. But it was still useful enough to repossess. More importantly, better training conditions existed in the south of England. Since landing craft and their crews would have to be sent to the south coast for assembling the cross-channel assault, it made sense to base them and train them there. Also, by the summer of 1943, Allied air superiority over England made it feasible to establish and maintain bases on the English Channel, which had not been the case in 1941 and 1942. Stark ordered a survey of sites suitable for bases in and around Plymouth.[9]

The establishment of bases for the United States Navy in the United Kingdom was an extremely complex operation. Facilities were ultimately furnished to serve more than 125,000 men and over 3,000 ships and landing craft. The Navy Department had organized components for establishing various sized bases on Pacific islands as they were captured. Those components included everything from operators to housing necessary to support the number of men and ships expected at the island base. The situation was different in the United Kingdom; bases had to be squeezed into urban areas already crowded with British installations whose facilities were strained almost to the breaking point. The Navy Department had decreed that British housing, supplies, and equipment were to be used to the fullest extent possible.

By mid-1943, Stark had decided to make Flanigan the Deputy Chief of Staff for Logistics. In practice, Flanigan was made responsible for all the administrative and logistical aspects of the U.S. naval buildup for the invasion and was directly responsible to Stark. Flanigan, a member of the Naval Academy Class of 1910, was a man of extraordinary energy and ability. He retired from the navy during the 1930s and then became executive vice president of the 1939 New York World's Fair. He returned to active duty and was assigned to Admiral Ghormley's staff in London. A no-nonsense man who cut through a problem to its essentials, Flanigan had the ability to recognize an officer's capabilities without regard to rank or whether the man was regular or reserve.

At about this time, Washington began to supplant the superannuated department heads with younger, more able captains. The department heads and a few other officers were from the regular navy; most of Stark's staff, which began to increase in mid-1943 to about 500 just before the invasion, were reserve officers who brought with them expertise from civilian life in areas such as petroleum supply, housing, personnel, and civil engineering.

Flanigan started with a personal staff of three reserve officers: Lt.(j.g.) David W. Richmond (a lawyer) and Lt.(j.g.) J. Scott Charles (an engineer). He soon added Lt. Barclay G. Johnson (a civil engineer), who had been one of his assistants at the World's Fair. He established a logistics department under Captain Neil K. Dietrich, one of the newly assigned younger captains. Dietrich's department included, among others, sections for petroleum products, civil affairs, harbor control and defense, public works, and engineering. Flanigan relied for personnel management on Lt. William I. Leckie.

In mid-1943, Stark still had been given no clear idea of what to expect, either in terms of men or ships, for the training program or for the invasion. Flanigan and his people began to piece together bits of information that would give them some idea of what to expect and when. This information was carefully collected in black loose-leaf notebooks by Richmond and Leckie and was the basis for more or less sophisticated guessing about what to expect in terms of men, ships, and supplies.

This lack of solid knowledge, so essential to sound planning, was not confined to COMNAVEU. In response to Stark's request, King created a new command in July 1943 and designated a flag officer, Rear Admiral John L. Wilkes, to be in overall command of the amphibious training bases. Wilkes, as Commander, Landing Craft and Bases, Europe (COMLANCRABEU), was subordinate to Stark. When Wilkes arrived in London early in September, he had just came from Washington. His first question was, "What am I supposed to do?" The planners in Washington had given him very little information; they told him to ask Stark. A few days with Flanigan and his people enabled Wilkes to begin guessing the extent to which U.S. naval forces would be committed to the Normandy invasion and what he would be expected to do in the way of training and supporting them.

Wilkes arrived in England six months after the Advanced Amphibious Training Base at Appledore had been commissioned in March 1943. Also, Stark had established the Naval Amphibious Supply Base at Exeter to serve as a central reception point for the supplies necessary to service the amphibious bases. Spare parts depots were set up at Tidworth, Tiverton, Launceston, and Rillamills. Other Advanced Amphibious Training Bases were proposed for Plymouth, Dartmouth, Salcombe, and Falmouth.

Wilkes began the task of establishing the other bases and getting ready for the influx of men and landing craft. The Admiralty was fully cooperative, but the task was monumental. Housing was to be supplied by the British to the greatest extent possible. Old hotels, vacant houses, warehouses, and sheds were requisitioned in the towns where the bases were to be. For example, the flat above St. David's School at Fowey housed seven officers. In most places, water and electricity were wholly inadequate to service a base, which in some cases would be larger than the town. The requisitioned housing seldom had adequate bathing facilities. The 13th Construction Regiment, under Captain (later Rear Admiral) John J. Manning (CEC), was brought over from the United States and added to the Wilkes' command; the Seabees rehabilitated old housing facilities, installed showers, improved or built new water facilities. At best, however, housing was inefficient and had to be supplemented by Nissen huts in many places. The Seabees rehabilitated—a great understatement—a hospital at Southampton that had been built during Queen Victoria's reign. It became one of the primary evacuation hospitals for the wounded from Normandy.

In one of their most magnanimous acts, the Admiralty turned over the facilities of the Royal Naval College at Dartmouth to the U.S. Navy. In addition to its use as an Advanced Amphibious Training Base, it was to have facilities to repair large landing craft and ships as large as destroyers. The planners in Washington sent a repair component of the kind they were using for Pacific bases but without any power source because the power was to be supplied by the British. Washington forgot—or perhaps did not know—that British power was 220 volts, so none of the electrical tools requring 120 volts would work. London educated Washington, and generators and transformers were sent to make the tools serviceable.

Wilkes' staff, aided by Flanigan's group of planners, negotiators, and trouble-shooters, worked miracles between September and the end of 1943. In addition to the five Advanced Amphibious Training Bases, Wilkes established smaller sub-bases at Teignmouth, Calstock, Saltash, Fowey and St. Mawes. Stark opened U.S. Navy port offices at Hull, Plymouth, Southampton, London, Milford-Haven, and Leith to facilitate the unloading of merchant ships carrying the material required to supply the amphibious bases.

When Roosevelt and Churchill met with the Combined Chiefs of Staff in late summer of 1943 at the Quadrant Conference at Quebec, commitments were finally made for the landing craft to be supplied by the United States. King notified Stark of a revised schedule for delivery of landing craft to his command. The United States was committed to supplying 110 LTSs (landing ships tanks), 40 LCI(L)s (landing crafts infantry), 146 LCTs (landing craft tanks), 250 LCMs (landing crafts medium) and 470 LCVPs (landing craft vehicles personnel) for the cross-channel operation. Some of these landing craft would be sent from the Mediterranean after being released from other operations; the rest would come from the United States. The LCTs and smaller craft were deck-loaded on Liberty and other merchant ships coming from the United States. There was some consternation when Stark had to inform Washington that there were no cranes on the South Coast capable of lifting LCTs. A scheme for loading LCTs had to be devised in order to make it possible to slide them into the water from the deck of a merchant ship. Minor crises of this kind were plentiful, but were taken in stride by Stark, Flanigan, Wilkes, and their staffs with the willing cooperation of the Admiralty and the British Ministry of War Transport.[10]

By September 1943, Stark commanded a wide variety of naval forces throughout the entire British Isles and more were on the way. The increasing pace and the complexity of preparation for the cross-channel operation sometime in the following year demanded a flexible arrangement for the orderly administration of these forces and those that would be assigned in the coming months. The solution was simple. King announced creation of the TWELFTH Fleet on 9 September 1943 and designated Stark as its commander.[11]

The navy had recently adopted a system of numbered fleets, with even numbers in the Atlantic (more or less) and odd numbers in the Pacific. Fleets were subdivided into task forces, task groups, task units, and task elements; each group, unit, and element being set off by a decimal and identified by a number following the overall designation of 12. Thus, there were Task Force 122, Task Group 122.4, Task Unit 122.4.2 and so forth. In this manner it would be clear precisely to whom each subdivision reported and who commanded it. The designation of Stark as fleet commander did not materially add to his authority or to his powers, but it was a great convenience and it made for more efficient management of a complex organization. New commands could be created for new tasks and then dissolved or absorbed by other commands when those tasks were completed. Stark as fleet commander could do this himself or he could delegate authority to do it.

When the TWELFTH Fleet was created, King asked Stark to form an operational task force to direct the training for and later participation in the cross-channel operation. The commander of this task force was Rear Admiral Alan G. Kirk, who had been Stark's chief of staff in 1942. When Kirk arrived in England in early November 1943, Stark activated Task Force 122 with Kirk as its commander. He specifically directed that the COMNAVEU and CTF 122 staffs work closely together; in order to ease the burden on CTF 122 he specified that the COMNAVEU communications facilities were to serve both organizations.[12] Plymouth became the hub of U.S. Navy activity outside London. Kirk's staff worked with Stark's staff in London until 24 April

1944, when Kirk moved to Plymouth and broke his flag in the cruiser *Augusta*. Wilkes and RADM John L. Hall had already moved their headquarters there during the first week of January 1944. They were later joined by RADM Don P. Moon, who along with Hall, would be an amphibious group commander at the invasion. Moon landed the invasion forces on Utah Beach in June 1944.

As Commander, TWELFTH Fleet, Stark was Kirk's operational and administrative commander; as administrative commander, he provided the physical means and the wherewithal for the support, equipment, maintenance, and training of Task Force 122. The operational commander eventually was Admiral Sir Bertram Ramsay, the Allied Naval Commander in Chief (ANCXF) for Operation Overlord. Ramsay was under the overall command of the Supreme Allied Commander, who had yet to be appointed. But Ramsay's control did not become effective until the assault phase of the operation began in late May 1944. Until that time Stark retained ultimate operational control.

Two good reasons justified this command structure. The first was the principle voiced by Stark and continued by King: U.S. Navy ships and forces should operate in units under United States' commanders. In other words, individual men and ships would not be assigned to an allied force commanded by other than United States officers. Instead, individual units, such as SUBRON 50, commanded by a U.S. Navy officer, could be assigned to an allied force where there was unity of command in various operations. Both King and Stark understood that unity of command was necessary, but they felt that since each navy had its own methods of training, operating its ships, and maintaining itself, better results would be obtained if United States forces and ships operated in units under U.S. Navy commanders.

The second reason justifying this command structure was that it would relieve Ramsay and his staff from the myriad important logistics problems of bases preparation and build up of forces, men, and equipment by leaving them to Stark as the administrative commander. Thus Ramsay and his staff were free to focus their full attention upon the task of planning how the naval phase—Operation Neptune—of the enormously complex cross-channel assault on the European continent could be fought successfully. They were concerned with establishing objectives to be accomplished, with estimating anticipated enemy resistance and the extent of Anglo-American forces required; and with developing machinery for coordination of the diverse elements involved. Stark and Ramsay were responsible for very different, but equally important phases of Operation Neptune.

Planning for specific command relations could not be worked out until there was a Supreme Allied Commander. Following the Cairo and Tehran summit conferences, Roosevelt and Churchill agreed to appoint Eisenhower to this position. It was a happy and wise choice. The announcement was made on 6 December 1943.

The decision to invade Europe in 1944 cast a new light of importance upon Stark's command. The U.S. Navy was given the task of transporting the men, their equipment, and supplies from the advance bases in Great Britain to the far shore during the assault. This task would not be completed until adequate ports in France and Belgium were open and capable of handling upwards of 40,000 tons daily. Then the navy would be responsible for operating these ports. The invasion of Europe was the most complex military operation in the history of war.

Up until late 1943 the Navy Department in Washington devoted the great bulk of its attention to the war in the Pacific. Then it became clear that preparations for Operation Overlord involved a whole host of different problems and considerations. King asked Stark to return to Washington in late December 1943 for a series of talks with him and others in the Navy Department about preparations for Overlord, among other matters.

King's dispatch was good news to Stark. He had an extensive list of things he wanted to talk about in Washington. Clearly, the naval preparations for Overlord required the closest coordination between his headquarters and the Navy Department. Stark set about preparing for his trip by having detailed memoranda compiled on virtually every subject related to the proposed buildup. These papers documented conditions as they existed, anticipated future needs, and described the most effective way to meet those needs.

His Deputy Chief of Staff, Captain Howard A. Flanigan, was his right hand man in this project. He suggested that Stark take Lt. (j.g.) David Richmond with him to Washington. "He helped put together those black books and he knows as much about our problems as anyone," he explained.[13] Stark took his advice.

Stark and his party left Glasgow on board the *Queen Mary*. In addition to Richmond, Lt. Jerry G. Bray, his Flag Secretary, his Flag Lieutenant, and other officers, Stark also took Commander Alfred R. Stanford, USNR. An expert yachtsman, Stanford was Stark's authority on small boats. Six months later he was second in command of the artificial harbor (Mulberry) at Omaha Beach on the coast of Normandy. After the war, he wrote an exceptionally fine account of Force Mulberry.[14]

The trip to New York was helpful to Stark, who could work without interruption. He reviewed with Bray and Richmond the contents of the black books in preparation for his coming conferences in Washington. Richmond was also useful in that he and Stark's writer, Ships Clerk H. L. Ashenfelter, each carried one half of the map overlays for the invasion beaches (Omaha and Utah) in locked pouches, which were handcuffed to them. When they arrived in New York, King sent a navy plane to fly Stark to his home in Washington. Because Richmond also lived in Washington, Stark thoughtfully offered him a ride. Richmond was particularly anxious to get home; he had an infant son he had never seen.

Stark knew his way around the Navy Department; he knew most of the bureau chiefs personally. The Vice Chief of Naval Operations, Vice Admiral Frederick J. Horne, was a friend. But Stark's reputation did not extend beyond his circle of friends and acquaintances among the senior officers. The wartime expansion of the Navy Department had brought up a number of younger officers who had not been there when Stark was CNO. The officers at working level in the Navy Department, the captains and senior commanders, did not know Stark personally. By and large, many of these men thought of him as the man who headed the navy at the time of Pearl Harbor and who, a few months later, was relieved by a dynamic, fire-eating, fighting admiral and sent off to an unimportant sinecure in London. To them the main war was in the Pacific; the European war was definitely of secondary importance. Many saw Stark as a relic from the pre-war navy. Some in the Navy Department even seriously doubted his competence to superintend the naval buildup for Overlord. On a visit to Washington in October, Flanigan had sensed these feelings and he warned Stark that he and his officers had better be ready to overcome this misperception in Washington.

Richmond encountered this attitude when he called on Captain (later Rear Admiral) Don Moon, War Plans Division, with respect to some aspects of the Overlord buildup. Moon questioned him closely about Stark's competence. It was an extraordinary conversation in which a captain asked a lieutenant (junior grade) to comment on the professional performance of a four-star admiral. Specifically, Moon wanted to know if Stark were simply a figurehead and if someone else, such as Flanigan, were actually organizing and coordinating the COMNAVEU preparations for the buildup. Apparently, Moon was surprised at the excellent impression Stark and his officers were making in Washington. Richmond stated flatly and with as much truth as loyalty, "The Admiral is the man who is doing it, and he knows what he's doing. He relies heavily on Flanigan, but the Admiral is the man in charge."[15]

In a relatively short time between 21 December 1943 and 5 January 1944, Stark and his group of three or four officers stirred up quite a bit of activity. They asked any number of questions, many of which the Navy Department officers could not answer and some of which they had not addressed. It became clear that Stark would have more questions to which answers were embarrassingly not available. Two days before his departure for London in early January 1944, Stark met with Horne, the bureau chiefs, and several senior captains in Horne's office. Bray and Richmond accompanied Stark.

Horne made it clear that the Navy Department wanted one individual with whom it could deal on all requests from the United Kingdom. Stark was that man. Therefore, only COMNAVEU would send requests to Washington for personnel and material. All such requests would be addressed to the Chief of Naval Operations. They would not be sent directly to the cognizant bureaus.[16]

It was Stark's opportunity to ask questions of the Bureau Chiefs face to face and to get information about Navy Department plans and schedules for the delivery of men, equipment, and supplies. Much of what he wanted was simply not available at the moment. Some questions could not be answered but those present. He could have, but did not, take a hard line with the officers whose replies did not satisfy him. Certainly, that was King's style, but it was not Stark's. Instead, by asking the right questions in a gentlemanly way, Stark made it abundantly clear that he was very much in charge of the naval buildup in the United Kingdom and that he knew what he needed and when he needed it. When some of the Bureau Chiefs attempted to get off the hot seat by suggesting that they would discuss his questions later with his staff, he pointed to Lieutenants Bray and Richmond, indicating that they were his staff. They would receive any data or information that might be available, he said.

Admiral Horne confessed at the meeting that the Department had sometimes not given Stark the highest quality officers for his senior staff; he said the demand for them was great in the Pacific, which had first priority. Pacific operations were now at a point where some of the best officers could be spared. Stark said he would welcome any help he could get but the fact that he had only a few regular offices on his staff was not troublesome. He said the reservists he had were excellent and well suited to the tasks of a training and logistics command.[17]

The plan for Overlord provided that when the British and American armies landed in France, the only avenue of supply for them would be directly over the beaches until sufficient ports were wrested from the Germans. The plan called for the construction of artificial harbors, one to be operated by the British and the other by the Americans. These harbors required some form of piers for direct off loading from ships, which would be far easier and more efficient than transferring tanks, trucks, and bulk supplies to lighters to carry them ashore. Sea and beach conditions were complicating factors. The gradients of the most likely beaches for the assault were gentle, which meant that water deep enough for shipping was a considerable distance from shore. The normal rise and fall of the tide was 23 feet. Thus, at low tide deep water was even farther out. To make matters even worse, there was usually a three knot current running roughly parallel to the beach. Finally, the beaches were exposed to wind and sea from the north and northwest, thus necessitating construction of some sort of breakwater to insure reasonably smooth water, a basic requirement for normal harbor operations. Stark, Flanigan, and the COMNAVEU staff had to deal with this knotty problem.

The first requirement was to provide enough tugs to tow the bits and pieces of the Mulberry from England to the far shore where they would be assembled. It was the greatest towing job in history. Eventually ocean-going tugs were brought from as far away as the Far East; tugs and railroad car ferries were brought from New York harbor. This mammoth effort was commanded by Captain E. J. Moran, head of the Moran Towing Company of New York, who was brought into the Navy for that purpose. Stark dealt with the tug deficit when he was in Washington and he proposed various ways to meet it, including an extension of the time allowed to assemble the Mulberry.

The next requirement was to provide some sort of breakwater. Successful experiments and tests at the David Taylor Model Basin indicated that Liberty ships moored broadside to the wind would suffice. This proposal was discarded, and the ships were sunk in place in a line 9,000 feet long to make a partial part of the breakwater off the Normandy Coast. They were known as Gooseberries.

Next came the Phoenixes: Huge concrete caissons were constructed in England to be towed across the channel and then flooded and sunk. They made solid but makeshift piers large enough for merchant ships to moor alongside. The shallow gradient of the beach and the extensive range of the tides, about 23 feet, required long pontoons from the beach to floating pier heads a considerable distance away. For several months after D day until more permanent ports were open, all trucks, tanks, and other motor vehicles crossed these pontoons on their way into France. Finally, bombardons were to be moored on the seaward side of the Phoenixes and Gooseberries. They were enormous floating steel shells placed to bear the initial blows of an angry sea.

Insisting that his staff should be prepared for everything to go wrong, Stark felt that that was the only way to find out just what they could expect. "We just can't put too much thought on this whole problem of Mulberry," he said.[18]

In December 1943 Stark found that navy officials in Washington had little concept of the magnitude of the problems involved in constructing an artificial harbor. One of his efforts in Washington was directed towards educating them. He left Commander Stanford in Washington for a few extra days to continue the educational process. Meanwhile he told his Chief of Staff in London, Rear Admiral George B. Wilson, to start drilling and training hard. "Personnel will be green, most everything will be green (including the sea). We must view this thing from every angle and be prepared for squalls."[19]

One of the most important things Stark worked out with the Navy Department was a common understanding of his requirements for scarce amphibious craft and equipment, which were needed as urgently in the Pacific as they were in the United Kingdom for the naval buildup. Complicated arrangements and understandings were reached as to the availability, use, and ultimate reversion of pontoon causeways, pontoon drydocks, and the ugly, uncomfortable, but extremely useful LSTs. Stark was told that assignment of extra ships and craft had "torn the heart out" of certain planned operations in the Pacific.[20]

Because the United States was extended to the maximum extent for possible operations in Europe and the Mediterranean, both Stark and the Navy Department insisted that at least 95 percent of these craft be ready for combat operations on D day. The British, incidentally, planned on only 85 percent. As it turned out, Stark's command produced almost 100 percent readiness. In regard to LCVPs, the smallest of all landing craft, Stark sought a reverse of at least 50 percent because he anticipated significant losses from attrition and enemy action.

British supply and service ministries were submitting requests directly to the Navy Department. Both Stark and the Navy Department felt that COMNAVEU should screen all such requests. However, because the term "screen" might unduly offend British sensitivities, it was replaced by the phrase "adequacy of support." Indeed, the purpose of the screening was to insure "adequacy of support" of operations in the European theater.

While he was in Washington, Stark and King talked about command organization. Both men saw eye to eye on the subject. They favored the principle of unity of command, both for American forces in Europe and for those assigned to allied commands. But they also wanted to insure adequate U.S. Navy representation at all levels. This had not been the case with the organization in the Mediterranean. There Vice Admiral H. Kent Hewitt, the American naval commander, was subordinate to the Allied naval commander, Admiral Sir Andrew B. Cunningham, who had no American naval officers on his staff. Stark insisted that combined staffs (those involving both American and British officers) should include U.S. Navy officers to prevent "complete British domination and insufficient representation for us." Stark obtained "wiring diagrams" prepared by an Army-Navy committee, which corrected this fault. Since the Joint Chiefs of Staff had not yet approved them, they were unofficial. However, they were useful for planning purposes.[21]

One of the most important tasks of any commander is to insure that his command has sufficient manpower to accomplish its task. When he looked into the personnel situation, Stark found that a manpower shortage was looming in the not-too-distant future. For this reason, he told Wilson, "We've got to be darned sure we are able to support any request we make either for officers or men."[22] Ships had first call on any available men. Nevertheless, he was able to obtain commitments to flesh out his staff with adequate numbers of intelligence, supply, and civil affairs officers. The latter would be needed when Europe was liberated.

Sometime before, King had refused to order any more Seabees to the United Kingdom. These hard working construction battalions were indispensable in constructing bases and facilities, first in Great Britain and then on the continent. Stark went directly to King, who relented and ordered one additional Seabee battalion to Europe. Since there was a great demand for Seabees in the Pacific, Stark realized this extra battalion was all that he would get. He would have to make do with what he had.

All in all, Stark's trip to Washington was highly successful. He cleared up many areas of possible ambiguity, and hence future difficulty, with King. He made known his requirements and in turn he was told the extent to which Washington could or could not meet them. The toughest problem of all was planning for the Mulberry.[23]

Unlike the year before, Stark planned to return to England by ship. He embarked on the *Mauretania*. It was a pleasant, relaxing week at sea. Stark and his assistants went over papers they had collected in Washington and prepared memoranda of their interviews in the Navy Department. The ship arrived at Liverpool on 17 January 1944 in wet, murky weather. Fog prevented entry into the harbor, but Admiral Sir Max Horton sent a naval launch to the ship for Stark and his party. After dinner with Horton, they took the night train to London.[24]

On 13 February 1944, the Combined Chiefs of Staff assigned all the naval forces committed to Operation Overlord to Eisenhower and directed him to select a naval commander. Admiral Sir Bertram Ramsay received the formal designation in early March along with the responsibility for planning and executing the naval phase, Operation Neptune. Four days later, Stark directed that effective 1 April 1944, "all U.S. Naval Forces allotted to Overlord" would be placed under Ramsay's operational command.[25]

One day in February 1944, Churchill invited Stark to dinner at 10 Downing Street. It was a small, intimate gathering of ten men. The guest of honor was King George VI. Stark and Ambassador Winant held places of honor at the dinner table. Winant was seated on the King's right and Stark was on Churchill's right. The King was in fine fettle and never looked so well. It was clear to Stark that he loved a small party of service people. It was a pleasant, convivial dinner party. Stark was fond of that dining room, because its heavy beams, low ceiling, cozy atmosphere, and lack of formality made for good fellowship. When he greeted his guests, Churchill could hardly wait to show them what he called "a nice bottle of brandy." It was at least three feet high and a foot across at the base. After dinner Churchill insisted on pouring the brandy himself. His contortions in doing so greatly amused Stark, who wished he could have photographed them. When the brandy was finally poured, Churchill offered the first glass to the King, who, along with the other guests, pronounced it exceptionally fine.

The conversation ranged over many topics and Churchill's memory startled Stark. When the recent U.S. naval operations in the Marshall Islands came up, Churchill turned to Stark and reminded him that Stark had had a great deal to do with the installation of 16-inch guns on the American battleships and with the American decision to build ships as honestly as possible up to the maximum allowed by treaty. If the final product were a little over, no one could complain.

Churchill said to him, "Supposing we had asked you if we had spilled over on our battleships, say, 2,000 tons, what would you have said?" Stark replied that he would have made no objection. Stark surmised that Roosevelt had probably told Churchill about the running battle he had with Stark as Chief of the Bureau of Ordnance in 1934 over the design of the new battleships. Stark consistently favored 16-inch guns, but Roosevelt was not convinced. So Stark carried the ships on a design that could take either 14- or 16-inch guns until the point when a final decision had to be made. Stark won and the new battleships carried 16-inch guns.

Understandably Churchill was in good form that evening. The conversation turned to battles and dates and then to the American civil war. Churchill accurately described the house in Frederick,

Maryland, where Barbara Fritchie waved the flag. He then proceeded without a break to recite John Greenleaf Whittier's poem. "He recited it beautifully, very effectively and just like he talks," Stark noted. Finally, when the King got up to leave, everyone was surprised that it was after one o'clock in the morning. It had been a happy party.[26]

Stark's thorough and complete enjoyment of this dinner party stands in sharp contrast to a luncheon he had with a group of Russian officers. That gathering, too, was convivial, perhaps too much so in the Russian manner. Stark thought the Russian custom of bottoms up with vodka time and again using glasses somewhere between a cocktail and a wine glass in size was terrible. He survived by eating all the bread he could put his hands on.[27]

In preparation for the forthcoming cross-channel assault, United States naval bases were mushrooming in south and west England in late 1943 and early 1944. At the end of February, Stark spent a week inspecting them.

Fleet Air Wing 7 was based at Dunkeswell in Devon. Mud was everywhere on the base. The Seabees were just starting to tackle that tremendous problem. The quarters were untidy and generally unsatisfactory. It was a quarter of a mile from some of the quarters to the nearest head. Bathing facilities, with only cold water, were a mile away. The Seabees were expected to install additional heads and showers.

The supply depot at Exeter provided 5,000,000 cubic feet of storage space, but Stark felt the concentration of buildings there contributed considerably to danger from an air attack. He directed that sub-bases be stocked to the limit as a precaution.

At the amphibious training base at Teignmouth he recommended toughening up the men by a planned conditioning program. He also had his first ride in a jeep. It was a thrilling, wild ride across the beaches and up and over the dunes.

The usual organizational pains afflicted the base at Dartmouth. They were compounded by a lack of administrative personnel and the arrival of considerably more men and landing craft than called for by the original plans.

The base in the best condition was at Salcombe. Morale was high. Health and food were good and the men were getting on with the job. One afternoon each week was devoted to infantry training and improvement of quarters. The rather simple expedient of assigning men who appeared at Captain's Mast to duty in the gravel pit improved both roads and discipline.

The U.S. Navy and Army had a joint operations room underground in Mt. Wise at Plymouth. This impregnable chamber had eight feet of concrete in the ceiling and was under thirty feet of solid rock. Stark was duly impressed. At Plymouth, he conferred with Hall and Wilkes. The captain of Hall's flagship, USS *Ancon* (AP 66) asked Stark to inspect the ship and the crew. Stark had other things on his mind, but he finally agreed. He drew the necessary items from the Jack-o'-the-Dust and gave the ship and the crew a thorough admiral's inspection.

At Fowey, the Admiralty had requisitioned Fowey Hall for billeting naval officers. It was the lovely home of Lord and Lady Hansen. Stark made a point of introducing himself to Lady Hansen to tell her how much the navy regretted the necessity of temporarily taking over her home.

The extensive repair facilities at Falmouth were fully utilized. So far they had completely overhauled 36 of the 49 LSTs, which had been transferred from the Mediterranean. The mess hall was a decided improvement over its predecessor. The men could be served and also eat in the same building, whereas before they had been served in one building, but had to eat in another.

Stark and his two aides stayed in the Falmouth Hotel. The next morning he had difficulty in locating his razor and in his search for it he unpacked both of his bags. While he was in the bathroom, one helpful aide repacked both bags to save a few minutes. By accident, he also packed Stark's trousers. Stark was stranded temporarily in his underwear until the other aide heard his call for help and located the missing trousers. They arrived only a few minutes late for breakfast.

Appledore on the Bristol Channel coast of Devon was an important center for training army and navy men in loading and unloading a variety of amphibious craft. Stark and his aides embarked in a DUKW, an amphibious vehicle. After a long run over the sand the strange craft entered the water. It was the first time in Stark's 44-year naval career that he had ever been to sea with an army coxswain. The demonstration thoroughly delighted him.

Stark returned to London with a clearer picture of the extent of the naval buildup and with firsthand knowledge of conditions and problems. It would be invaluable as preparations for the invasion of Europe moved into the final stages.[28]

Preparations for the impending assault on Europe took more and more of Stark's time, to the detriment of his informal correspondence with Knox. Knox wrote from Washington that he missed Stark's letters. They brought him up to date on what was going on in London and on the point of view from Grosvenor Square. "Don't let your duties weigh so heavily upon you that you completely eliminate me from your list of correspondents," he told Stark.[29] Stark resumed his letters with pleasure.[30] They both eagerly looked forward to Knox's planned trip.

Then on the evening of 28 April Stark learned of Knox's sudden death. "It is difficult to take in" he wrote in his diary.[31] Knox's death was a great personal loss for Stark. He valued friendship most of all and in Knox he had had a true and sincere friend. Knox's death also had grave and unpleasant consequences for Stark's career. His successor, James V. Forrestal, was no friend.

The late winter and spring of 1944 was a time of feverish activity for the Allied forces in Great Britain. The country was an armed camp. Enormous quantities of material and large numbers of men were poised, waiting for the assault that everyone knew must come soon. While Stark tended to matters at the highest levels, Flanigan and his men ceaselessly strove to make sure that all naval preparations were in order.

With less than a month to go before the scheduled date of the assault, Captain Edward Ellsberg, U.S. Navy, an expert in salvage operations, informed Flanigan of what seemed to be a fatal flaw in their plans. The gigantic caissons called Phoenixes had been built in various places in Great Britain. They were towed to staging areas on the south coast and then flooded and partially sunk until they were needed. Plans called for the Phoenixes to be pumped out and towed across the English Channel to the far shore where they would be sunk in rows in specified locations to form a breakwater for the artificial harbor at Normandy. Ammunition, fuel, supplies, and men would flow through this harbor to the American Army ashore in France. Without the Phoenixes, the water off Omaha Beach would be too rough to permit the construction, let alone operation of the piers onto which the vehicles and supplies would be off-loaded. In other words, without the Phoenixes the flow of supplies would be restricted to a trickle. Ellsberg told Flanigan that the Royal Engineers were unable to float the Phoenixes so they could be towed from England to France.

Ellsberg recommended that U.S. Navy salvors replace the Royal Engineers immediately, in order to work on the vital problem of refloating the caissons.

Stark saw the gravity of the situation, but Churchill was adamant. The Phoenixes were built by British hands and British hands would float them, he said. That was all there was to it. Stark's problem was how to get around Churchill without endangering Anglo-American relations. The only way was to go over his head to King George VI. Within a few days the opportunity presented itself.

Senior Allied commanders, British government officials, and the King met at St. Paul's School in mid-May for a briefing on the forthcoming operation. At that briefing Stark told the King that the Royal Engineers had not a hope of floating the Phoenixes, upon which the artificial harbors depended. The King saw Stark's point, and asked Churchill to go to the south coast himself, look into the matter, and report back.

Churchill made a brief stop at Selsey Bill, looked at a few Phoenixes and departed. The next day Royal Navy salvors relieved the Royal Engineers and succeeded in floating the Phoenixes. A few days later, Stark, too, went to Selsey Bill to see how things were going. The operation remained in British hands and was successfully concluded. The Phoenixes arrived at the far shore at the appointed time and were sunk in their designated places.[32]

13

THE INVASION OF NORMANDY

The week before the Allied forces landed on the beaches at Normandy, Stark made one final trip to the south coast of England to satisfy himself that the navy was ready. In Portland and in Plymouth he talked with the amphibious commanders Hall and Kirk. He saw for himself the advanced state of naval preparations. There was little more that he could do.

When the assault was launched in the early hours of Tuesday, 6 June 1944, Stark was in London. Soon afterwards he talked with Cunningham and Ramsay at the Admiralty. It seemed to them that the Allies had a good start. Information later that day showed that General Omar Bradley faced tough German opposition and that a touch and go situation lasted for several days. Finally, after much bloody fighting, the beach-head was secure.

Three days later, on 9 June, King, Marshall, and Arnold arrived in London. They were eager to cross the channel to see for themselves the progress the British and Americans had made. On D plus 6, 12 June, an American destroyer took them from Portsmouth to the far shore where they spent the day.

Stark did not accompany them. Instead, he crossed the channel on 14 June on board HMS *Scorpion*. At Omaha Beach he and Kirk boarded a small subchaser and toured the nearly complete artificial harbor. Next, he went to Utah Beach in a PT boat, where he went ashore to inspect the navy's off-loading arrangements there and then returned to Portsmouth on board *Scorpion*.[1]

In the first 12 days after D day things appeared to be going reasonably well for the Allies. The Americans' Mulberry was in full operation and the British Mulberry was coming along nicely. All told,

222

314,514 men, 41,000 vehicles, and 116,000 tons of supplies had been landed over the American beaches.[2] Then on 18 June, the winds and seas increased, and the first northeast gale in June in 20 years hit the Normandy coast with full force.

The effect on the Mulberries was devastating. The Phoenixes were badly damaged. The pier heads sustained great damage but survived, but the runways from the beach were almost completely wrecked. The most intensive and prodigious efforts were necessary to restore the breakwaters, piers, and runways. Without them the vast flow of supplies to the army ashore would be curtailed. Without supplies, the army faced disaster.

Cunningham and Stark were appalled at the storm damage and were alarmed at what could happen if it were not set right. Both men accepted this set-back philosophically. With more truth than comfort, Cunningham told Stark, "Once in a while the elements have to tell man how puny he is."[3] After the storm passed and the extent of the damage was known, Stark went to Southampton to discuss with British, U.S. Army and U.S. Navy officers how to speed up cross-channel traffic and the repair of storm damage.[4] While repairs were underway, the flow of supplies continued unabated, some going in directly over the beaches.

Enemy action in the summer of 1944 was not confined to France. It seemed the Germans launched buzz bombs continuously over England. These unmanned jet aircraft were simply aimed at random in the general direction of London or other targets in the south of England. They were more distracting and worrisome than the previous air raids. In fact, when Stark first arrived in London in 1942 he slept through air raids by German bombers in his quarters on the top floor of his headquarters in Grosvenor Square without giving a thought to the possibility that a German bomb might come hurtling through the roof some night. At that time the greatest concession he made to the ever present threat of air attack was to maintain the mandatory blackout.

But the buzz bombs in 1944 were different. Perhaps it was because they lacked a guidance system and neither the Germans nor anyone else knew where they were going to land. Perhaps it was the unsettling noise they made. Nevertheless, they made sleep difficult, if not impossible at times. Fortunately, the V-1s failed to start fires, but the effect of the blasts was bad enough. Stark watched one come in over the COMNAVEU headquarters and hit not far away. "They made us not love the Hun any better," he said. In one 24 hour period they killed 900 people, thus bringing the total at that time to about 9,000 from that weapon alone.[5]

The bulk of Stark's time and attention was devoted to matters at the highest military and governmental levels. From that vantage point he had as clear on overall view of the progress of the war as anyone. But it was a view far distant from the concerns of the soldiers and sailors to whose lot fell the task of the actual fighting. Even at the four-star level, Stark never lost his affinity and affection for the enlisted men.

The deployment of the Allied forces onto the continent of Europe in June 1944 produced inevitable casualties. One part of Stark's extensive responsibilities for support of the U.S. Navy in Europe was the maintenance and operation of hospitals and other medical facilities. On 18 June he visited the south of England to see for himself how casualties from France were being handled, as well as to observe loading and moving of the outbound convoys. By his own reckoning he spoke to at least 200 men in the naval hospital at Netley, near Southampton. Their injuries ranged from relatively minor to particularly serious ones. In talking to them, Stark drew on his extensive fund of jokes, but the mood of the men and the atmosphere of the place were not conducive to laughter, although it would have been helpful to release tension. There was only one good laugh that day. It was produced by a parachutist who explained to Stark how he had broken his leg. He landed on a cow, fell off, and then the cow kicked him and broke his leg.

He found the spirits of the men, their bravery, their uncompromising attitude, and their cheerfulness unbelievable. When he left the hospital he felt very humble. Back in London that evening he reflected on what he had seen in the course of a very long day. He thought of the men, whom he described as a "fine looking lot of boys, whether in the hospital or on the road or at the docks, cheerful, bright and likeable." Planes were roaring overhead almost continuously through the pale evening sky. He wrote to his wife at home in Washington, "What this one man Hitler has brought on the world, though we cannot shake all responsibility for it because the ground had to be plowed for the planting of his seed! Please, God, this time, may we win the peace, not only for ourselves, but for all mankind. It is the most wonderful opportunity that statesmen have ever had. May they be equal to it."[6]

The Overlord plan did not anticipate a sudden German collapse. It provided for the liberation of Cherbourg and the Contentin peninsula, then Brest, and finally the Biscay ports. King wanted to establish a flag command in these ports, the operation of which would be to support the army. This command would come into existence when one major French port was opened. It would include that port and the artificial harbor, Mulberry A, which was under U.S. Navy control, and it would be under Stark's overall command as COMNAVEU. Admiral Sir Bertram Ramsay, the Allied naval commander for Operation Overlord, objected to what he thought was an awkward arrangement, since he was responsible to Eisenhower, the Supreme Allied Commander, for the naval phase of the invasion. Ramsay and the Admiralty solved the problem by agreeing to interpret King's directive to mean that Stark would be the administrative commander and Ramsay would exercise operational control as Eisenhower's naval deputy.[7]

Early in March 1944 Stark and his planners reached an agreement with the army on the division of army-navy responsibilities in captured ports. It was amended as conditions changed, but it remained the controlling understanding between the two services in the operation of U.S. administered ports in France and later in Belgium and Germany. Known as the Stark-Lee Agreement it was signed by Stark and Major General John C. H. Lee, Deputy Theater Commander, for the army.

Under it, the army's responsibilities were completely on shore. The navy was responsible for everything afloat, including pilotage, harbor movements, harbor nets, and ship repairs. An army port commander and a navy commandant were to act jointly to discharge their responsibility for the operation and safety of each port. But if time would not permit referring any matter to higher authority, the army port commander was authorized to make local decisions most covered by the agreement. The Stark-Lee Agreement underlay the generally smooth and successful operation of numerous ports at a time when they were absolutely essential to the support of the Allied armies.[8] The first major port, Cherbourg, fell to the Allies on 27 June, three weeks after the initial landings, and the Stark-Lee Agreement was implemented to operate the port.

Meanwhile, a pattern was set that was followed during the remaining 10 months of the European war. A week before Cherbourg fell, Stark directed Kirk and Wilkes to start planning for the closing of certain bases in the United Kingdom and the transfer of their men and equipment to the forward areas in France. As the war progressed, bases in the rear areas first in Great Britain and then in France were closed and new ones were established where they were needed nearer to the front. A new command was needed and Wilkes became Commander, U.S. Ports and Bases, France (COMNAVBAS-FRANCE). With Stark as his administrative commander, Wilkes reported directly to Eisenhower with respect to his operational responsibilities. They included supporting the buildup of the U.S. Army on the continent; developing and operating bridgeheads and major and minor ports; and defending assault and port areas against air attack and attack from the sea.[9]

Before D day, Allied planners anticipated using Brest and other ports on the Brittany peninsula as the major ports of entry. They even planned a large artificial harbor at Quiberon Bay. But the rapidly changing tactical situation changed all that. By the middle of August, Allied forces broke through the German lines, captured Paris, and sped on towards Germany. Brest was bypassed and allowed to wither on the vine. It fell to the Allies on 18 September. Four days later Flanigan visited Brest. He reported to Stark a scene of "almost complete devastation and desolation." Brest was the most completely destroyed city in France or England. It compared closely with photographs of Stalingrad, he said.[10]

The Allies captured Cherbourg within a month of the first landings in Normandy. In mid-July Stark got a first hand view of Cherbourg and the navy set-up there for clearing and operating the port. In September the Germans yielded Le Havre, which was opened in October and put to good use, along with Rouen and Cherbourg. In the early autumn Antwerp fell to the Allies, but the port could not be used until December when the Scheldt estuary was cleared of German forces and allied ships could enter the port unmolested.

The U.S. Army in France needed nearly 40,000 tons of supplies daily in September, Flanigan reported to Stark. There were very few days when the beaches and the French ports were able to off-load that amount. Thus, cargo needed at the moment in France received priority for discharge and movement. Other less important cargo had to wait. At the end of September Cherbourg could handle about 9,000 tons of real cargo daily; Rouen, about 4,000 tons at most; Utah Beach about 4,000 tons; and Omaha Beach about 10,000 tons. Even so, there was still a gap between what was needed and what could be off-loaded. Intensive efforts were underway in Cherbourg, Rouen, and Le Havre to clear debris, to repair destroyer quays, piers and dockside railroad terminals, and to restore cranes and other heavy equipment to some sort of operating conditions.[11]

Until these ports were in full operation, the Mulberries on the Normandy coast were indispensable as the main conduit to reinforce and supply the British and American armies. These artificial harbors were literally a godsend to the Allies, especially in view of the delayed opening of Cherbourg. In one day, 31 July 1944, nearly 26,000 tons of supplies were off-loaded across Omaha and Utah Beaches, which operated at 158 percent and 175 percent of their respective rated capacities. In addition to supplies, men also debarked across the beaches. Excluding the assault, the record for numbers of men disembarking had been reached on 23 June when 31,000 men went ashore. In July alone slightly more than 100,000 vehicles crossed the beaches. Both beaches continued in full operation through September. The onset of autumn and the long awaited opening of French ports reduced the efficiency and the necessity for these artificial ports. They were finally shut down in November, after 167 days of operation.[12]

Port facilities were still critical in early October. Stark made a three-day trip—his fourth since D day—to see for himself the condition of the French ports and the beaches. He left England in abysmal flying weather, which extended over the channel and into France. After conferring with Kirk and Wilkes at Cherbourg he flew on to Le Havre. Unfortunately, bad weather prevented his small plane from landing near Omaha and Utah beaches or even at Le Havre. However, he told the pilot to circle Le Havre at a low altitude so he could see for himself the condition of that port. Four or five times around the port clearly revealed its deplorable state. Le Havre was a wreck. It was also an American responsibility. Wilkes and his men had their work cut out for them.

The navy was responsible to insure the continued flow of ammunition, fuel, supplies, and men across the channel from the United Kingdom into France. General Omar Bradley's First and Third Armies needed this steady stream of support if they were to keep hammering at the Germans. At the end of October Stark attributed an improvement in the supply situation to the fact that momentarily there was comparatively little forward movement on the front line. The supply of ammunition was not too good at the time, but he expected it to improve by the end of the month when ammunition ships would be able to enter Le Havre.

The army wisely avoided additional congestion in the French ports then in operation by diverting six divisions to the United Kingdom. This meant, however, that Stark had to retain several LSTs to transport these men and their equipment across the channel. The ultimate effect was that the LSTs were not available for use in the Pacific as the Joint Chiefs had planned.

Based on his own observations and those of his staff members, Stark informed King of the state of the French ports and their tonnage capacities. Rouen was in good shape: the quays were in excellent condition, four coaster berths were already clear, and two 60-ton cranes were on the way to help clear other berths. Stark estimated that when they arrived they would be able to clear four additional coaster berths each day. Railroad connections to the main line to Paris were almost complete.

Although Le Havre was badly damaged, three berths for Liberty ships were available. Four additional berths were going to be constructed by moving five Phoenixes then off Omaha Beach into Le Havre where they would be sunk between two lines of piles. Then they would be housed over and fitted with railroad tracks. In this way the Liberty ships berthed alongside would be able to discharge their cargo directly into freight cars. Conditions in Cherbourg were steadily improving and Stark anticipated that the port would be able to handle 15,000 tons per day before long. Even though all the French ports at that time, including the Mulberries at Omaha and Utah Beaches were handling more than 32,000 tons of supplies and equipment daily, more was clearly required.[13]

Continuing on, Stark went to Supreme Headquarters Allied Expeditionary Forces (SHAEF) at Versailles. He stressed in no uncertain terms the importance of Antwerp. Fortunately, that great port had sustained relatively little damage and it held the promise of becoming the major port of entry for the Allies on the continent of Europe. While he was there he learned that Antwerp was safely in Allied hands, but enemy forces remained in the Scheldt estuary between Antwerp and the sea. It would be several weeks before they could be cleared out and the way made safe for Allied shipping. Moreover, only 5,000 Belgian stevedores were available, instead of the expected 15,000.

Eisenhower was grateful to Stark for his efforts in planning and preparing for the naval aspects of the cross-channel assault. In July 1944, he recommended Stark for the army's Distinguished Service Medal. He said, "More than 4,000 naval ships and craft and over 100,000 naval officers and men were used in the D day assault. The fact that these ships and men were available is directly attributable to the efforts of Admiral Stark. . . . Planning for the assault was complete in the smallest detail, and served to make the combined naval and ground forces of the United States an integrated unit." In conclusion, he stated flatly, "The results so far accomplished in this assault on the Fortress of Europe would have been impossible without the complete and wholehearted support on the part of the Navy." Following normal military channels, the recommendation was submitted to and favorably endorsed by King.[14]

Eisenhower presented Stark with the Distinguished Service Medal at a simple ceremony in his Paris office on 5 October 1944. There were less than a dozen people present. The citation referred to his "keen foresight and exceptional administrative ability." Stark confessed that usually "these things just don't mean much to me." But, in this instance, he said, "I took it as appreciation from the Army over here for what the Navy had done for them . . . and it was a great satisfaction. I just happen to head up the organization of a great bunch of subordinates who did the job, all the way down to and including the fellow with the blue shirt on his back. God bless them all.[15]

While in Paris, Stark sent word to General de Gaulle, now head of the Provisional French Government, that he would like to make a personal call. Word came back asking if Stark would be willing to see General Alphonse Juin, Chief of Staff of the French Army, instead. The American Embassy discovered that Stark's message had been received by subordinates and not by de Gaulle. When de Gaulle finally learned that Stark wanted to see him, he promptly set a time.

It was a very pleasant meeting. Stark was surprised to find de Gaulle warm and cordial. The general hoped that Stark would come to Paris frequently. If so, de Gaulle said he would be delighted to see Stark, regardless of the circumstances. They talked about a number of things: de Gaulle asked about the Stark family, he pointed out with pride that the table he was using had been used by Georges Clemenceau and Paul Reynaud; and he said the war would last through the winter. Stark felt that de Gaulle was genuinely glad to talk to a friend, and when Stark rose to leave, de Gaulle accompanied him to the door. It was a gesture people waiting in the anteroom noticed as significant.[16]

When he returned to the Embassy, the chargé d'affaires asked Stark if he intended to report his conversation to Secretary of State Cordell Hull. Stark said he did not, because no official matters were discussed. Finally, the diplomat confessed that he had not been able to see de Gaulle. He asked Stark to report his talk to Hull. Stark complied willingly. He wrote a long, chatty letter to Hull in which he reported his conversation and included his observations of conditions in the recently liberated French capital.[17]

The expanding navy during World War II opened the way for rapid promotion of officers, particularly those assigned to the seagoing forces. However, reserve officers, especially men assigned to shore staffs, were not always promoted as rapidly as regular officers. During 1942 and 1943 the Bureau of Naval Personnel, which handled promotions, was not particularly impressed with the importance of the COMNAVEU staff. Promotions came, but they were routine.

There were certain anomalies. For example, Tracy B. Kittredge, who was Stark's chief diplomatic advisor, arrived in London in 1942 as a lieutenant, the same rank he held while on Sims' staff in London in 1919. Kittredge, who by that time was in his late forties, was soon promoted to lieutenant commander and finally to commander near the end of the war. Other officers with similar extensive civilian experience were in equally junior naval ranks. Their duties required them to deal with army and air force officers who were far more senior and many awkward situations arose because of it.

Stark did what he could to correct the situation. He made recommendations to the Bureau of Naval Personnel, frequently in vain. In the case of Captain Howard A. Flanigan, he recommended to King and the Bureau that Flanigan be promoted to commodore. Flanigan was Stark's Deputy Chief of Staff and he was responsible for operations, establishment of training bases, shipping, port offices, and petroleum matters. In addition, he was the U.S. Navy representative on the Admiralty Anti-U-Boat Warfare Committee and the British Oil Control Board, and was an assistant to Averell Harriman.

King was sympathetic to Stark's request. But even in the summer of 1943 he was not yet ready to approve promotion to commodore for officers on staff duty. At the same time, he told Stark that he was contemplating putting Stark's command in a "fleet" status in anticipation of the build-up for the cross-channel operation and the tasks to be given to Stark's command after the assault. Clearly, Stark's "fleet" would qualify Flanigan for promotion to commodore. Finally, in March 1944, Secretary of the Navy Frank Knox recommended to Roosevelt that twelve captains on staff duty be promoted to commodore. Flanigan was one of them. It was the occasion of much satisfaction in Grosvenor Square.[18]

The continual round of conferences, meetings, and briefings superimposed on the reading and approval of a ceaseless flow of dispatches, official letters, and reports, to say nothing of a voluminous personal and official correspondence, meant that while in London Stark was always on duty and subject to pressure of his office. At first he lived in a flat on the top floor of his headquarters in Grosvenor Square. Eventually, he rented at his own expense a house in the country outside of London as a weekend refuge. Then, when he could, Stark adopted the fine British custom of leaving town on the weekend. This custom was observed at the highest British levels even during the war.

Frequently Stark would invite a small group of officers to join him at Romany in Virginia Water, Surrey. When he did, it was not for idle amusement. It was for serious work in informal surroundings. The first thing they did when they arrived was to shift out of uniform and into civilian clothes. Stark preferred a wool chief petty officer's shirt and a pair of slacks. With rank more or less suspended, he often conducted extensive brainstorming sessions. Stark made it clear that anyone with an idea was to speak up. Rank had no monopoly on brains or ideas. Whatever proposals that were made were examined carefully and thoroughly. Most officers took quite well to this approach, although some few regular officers did not.

Walking was Stark's favorite exercise and he pursued it diligently on his weekends in the country. Frequently, he walked into the local village where he greeted the inhabitants and introduced himself simply as Stark. Many had no idea who he was, other than he was the friendly American with a shock of white hair who lived on the other side of the golf course.[19]

In the course of becoming accepted by the British establishment, he made many friends. The redoubtable Astors were among the closest and best friends Stark made while he was in England. Lady Nancy Astor was a red-haired Virginian who married Viscount Waldorf Astor. Using her considerable wit, charm, and drive, she was the first woman elected to the House of Commons. She became a force to be reckoned with in British politics. Her outspoken statements and sharp tongue frequently put her on the front pages of the newspapers. Her husband was somewhat more retiring, but he was keenly interested in politics and public affairs. They were an extremely attractive couple. Stark was particularly fond of Lady Astor's ebullience and warm personality. He described Lord Astor as "one of God's noblemen."

Before the outbreak of World War II, the Astors' home at Cliveden outside London was a well known gathering place for famous and influential people. During the war, Stark found it a welcome relief from the hustle and pressure of his office. A frequent weekend visitor, he drove the short distance from London in his Chevrolet convertible. He found Cliveden restful beyond measure. There were always interesting people at table and the conversation was spirited. There was always plenty of opportunity to walk, nap, and enjoy the extraordinary loveliness of that great house and the English countryside. He never felt he was a guest, just one of the family. He felt it even more when they asked him to join them for Christmas dinner. They became lifelong friends.[20]

Stark reached the age of 64 on 12 November 1944. It was an important date. Officially it meant that he had reached the statutory retirement age and his continuance on active duty henceforth would be because of wartime necessity. Personally, it gave his friends, associates, and subordinates in London an opportunity to honor him.

One set of English friends gave a party for him at Claridge's. Another gave a small luncheon in the private dining room at the Ritz. The hotel produced a birthday cake with 64 candles. First Lord of the Admiralty, A. V. Alexander, gave him a book in the Bedford Historical Series, *Sir Richard Granville of the "Revenge."* He wrote on the fly-leaf, "To my friend Admiral Stark, U.S.N. as a souvenir of his notable birthday spent in London on November 12, 1944 and with grateful appreciation of his cooperation and many kindnesses." At another party he received another book, which pleased him very much, *Old Naval Prints, Their Artists and Engravers.*

The most notable party of all was the one prepared by the American naval officers in Great Britain. It was a surprise party and the secret was well kept. It expanded from a relatively small gathering of officers in London to include several hundred officers from all over the country. Some even made it back from France for the occasion. It took Stark completely by surprise.

As part of the ruse, Stark's aide, Lt. John Williams, told him that Admiral Glassford was having a small supper party of just three guests, one of whom was Admiral Cunningham. Williams made the arrangements in an official manner so that Stark did not connect this event with his birthday. Stark thought it was odd that Glassford's party was at the Savoy, because his quarters were adequate.

When Stark and Williams arrived at the Savoy, Stark noticed an unusual number of officers' caps in the cloakroom. Williams simply said, "Yes, I think some of the officers are having a party or dance here tonight."

Williams led him upstairs and into the reception room outside the ballroom. When Stark saw two or three hundred officers present, he said, "John, this is the youngsters' party. We have gotten into the wrong place." He started to turn away, still unaware of what was up.

Then Williams said to him quietly, "Well, you have a birthday, haven't you?"

Stark was thunderstruck. It had never crossed his mind. He was even more amazed at the secrecy in which the preparations had been made. Williams escorted him to the head table, where the First Lord, A. V. Alexander, the First Sea Lord, Admiral Cunningham, and several other high ranking officers were already present. The entire assembly stood up and sang "Happy Birthday" with gusto.

The music, the food, and the wine were an exception to wartime austerity. They were the products of ingenious and resourceful navy cumshaw. Of the speeches, Stark later told his wife, "If I could believe even half what was said, I would be so far up on a pedestal as to be unapproachable." In the course of the evening Stark was presented with a Georgian silver tray, measuring 19 by 31 inches, which had been the object of a concerted search in London. Beneath a four star admiral's flag was inscribed:

Admiral Harold Raynsford Stark
United States Navy
Presented
on the occasion of his Sixty-Fourth Birthday
by the officers who have had the
honor to serve under his Command
in the
United States Naval Forces
Europe
November 12, 1944

Thanks to his prodigious self-control Stark was able to respond with graceful and entertaining extemporaneous remarks, in which he managed to present Mrs. Stark, although she, like other navy wives, was absent.[21]

This birthday party was in a very real sense the acme of Stark's tour of duty in London. It was a coming together of the things that he valued the most. The obvious, sincere and spontaneous outpouring of good wishes on this occasion testified to the respect and honest affection American and British naval officers accorded him. The growth of the gathering from a relatively small group to one that filled the Savoy ballroom was witness to the extent to which Stark's personality and physical presence permeated his far-flung command. His officers knew their admiral and they cheerfully conspired to give him a surprise party to end all birthday parties. And they were enthusiastically joined by the high command of the Royal Navy.

Stark cherished friendships and fellowship with navy people. He never turned down honors, awards, and high position when they came his way, but he took thim in stride. He valued more the friendship and the fellowship of the many people he met in his long career. Both were there in abundance that evening.

A few days later Stark gave a small surprise party for his aide, Lieutenant John Williams, to celebrate his twenty-eighth birthday.

14

THE END OF THE WAR

Waging World War II in Europe required extensive planning and coordination. Similarly, the period immediately following the end of the actual fighting also required extensive planning to consolidate the victory and to avoid chaos. "Unconditional Surrender" meant that Hitler's Third Reich would cease to exist as a functioning government. Since the Allies intended to exercise total control over Germany, the details of the surrender terms, the administration of public affairs, the supervision of the dismantling of the German war machine, and the establishment of control machinery had to be planned carefully in advance of the time they would be needed.

Planning of this kind was right down the diplomatic and political alleys of Stark's command. Unfortunately, Stark was handicapped to a great extent throughout 1943 by the absence of any definite Navy Department policy other than insuring the defeat of the German forces. As it turned out, after the fighting was over the navy exploited technical intelligence, data, and objects pertaining to the German navy, supervised the disarmament and demobilization of the German navy, and operated the ports of Bremen and Bremerhaven to supply and support the American occupation forces in Germany.[1]

As early as May 1943, Stark asked the Navy Department to send a small group of officers qualified in civil administration to prepare for reestablishing civilian governments in the countries the Allies planned to invade. In November the Big Three, the United States, Great Britain, and the Soviet Union, agreed to create machinery to deal with problems arising in the post-hostilities period. There was some urgency about the matter, according to the optimists who thought Germany might collapse rather suddenly.[2]

The machinery created was the European Advisory Commission. Its function was to make recommendations relative to the cessation of hostilities and to recommend specific surrender terms. It was mainly concerned with German and Austrian problems. The American representative was the United States ambassador in London, John G. Winant. The Joint Chiefs of Staff in Washington agreed to appoint military advisors to assist Winant. However, King appointed Stark as naval advisor to the commission, rather than as advisor to Winant. This distinction produced little else than a flurry in official correspondence.

Stark's appointment as naval advisor was more than honorary, but it was decidedly less than full and active participation in the work of the commission. Only official representatives normally spoke at its meeting. Because the military and naval advisors were expected to remain silent, Stark attended the preliminary meetings, but was represented in the day to day work and in official meetings by Lieutenant Commander Willis Sargent, USNR. Sargent's office was in the embassy across Grosvenor Square from Stark's headquarters. He kept Stark abreast of what was going on in the commission and he drafted the reports Stark sent to Washington.[3]

Stark had complete confidence in Sargent's administrative abilities and in his judgment, but he did not abdicate his responsibilities to Sargent. He simply let Sargent act as his representative and right-hand man. He agreed to let Sargent sit on the Joint U.S. Advisors' Committee, which worked under Winant and included political and economic advisors as well as military and naval representatives. It performed the important staff function of preparing the American position on matters to be discussed by the full European Advisory Commission.[4]

The great advantage of this arrangement was that Stark's seniority and prestige as the only full admiral in Europe were loaned to the work of the commission. But Stark was freed from the details of its work. He had far more pressing tasks to tend to in superintending the myriad naval preparations for the coming assault on the European continent.

Sargent was one of three men nominated to Stark for the position of Diplomatic Deputy. The other two candidates were Phillip Jessup, a noted authority on international law and a future judge of the International Court of Justice; and a navy captain with considerable experience in politico-military affairs. Technically, Sargent was a lieutenant commander in the U.S. Naval Reserve. In civilian life, however, he was a distinguished attorney from Syracuse, New York, with a broad background and extensive experience in negotiations and government affairs. Specifically, he had been a member of the Working Security Committee in Washington, where army, navy and State Department representatives hammered out the American draft of the Nazi surrender terms. Sargent arrived in London in early February 1944 and went to work at once.

Regardless of his abilities and his background, a lieutenant commander working at the flag officer level is always at a disadvantage. Sargent was no exception to this rule. The army's representative was General Cornelius Wickersham, whose father at one time was Attorney General of the United States. Before he returned to military service in 1940, Wickersham was senior partner in a Wall Street law firm. Sargent found him aggressive and ambitious. They were not strangers, having crossed swords in Washington in 1943. When they arrived in London for duty in connection with the European Advisory Commission, Wickersham attempted to pull rank on Sargent and make Sargent his naval aide. When Sargent outlined the situation to Stark, Stark gave him clear and explicit instructions. Sargent was Stark's alter ego and not naval aide to Wickersham. Stark would determine the navy's position insofar as advice was given to Ambassador Winant. Stark told Sargent, "If serious difficulty arises with Wickersham, you come to me and we will determine the course of action." Difficulties were not long in appearing.

Wickersham thought the American draft of the surrender terms, which Sargent helped to prepare in Washington, prescribed not only the substance but also the exact wording. Sargent maintained that the framers of that document intended only to guide Winant in his negotiations with the British and the Soviets, and that Winant was not to be bound by its substance, let alone its wording. Sargent reported Wickersham's dissent as "adamantine." The result was an impasse that delayed negotiations for some time.

Almost at his wits' end, Sargent prepared a dispatch that he hoped Stark would send to King as a member of the Joint Chiefs of Staff. It described the deadlock. It asked for explicit authority for Winant to negotiate with the British and Soviet members of the European Advisory Commission, regardless of the language of the American draft, and for power to change its substance whenever Winant deemed it necessary or desirable. Any change, of course, would be reported to the Joint Chiefs. Stark sent the dispatch. There was danger that if the Joint Chiefs did not increase Winant's authority as Stark requested, Winant might have to disavow Stark's move.

Fortunately, nothing of the sort happened. At the end of April 1944, the Joint Chiefs approved Stark's request and Winant was free to negotiate. The log jam was broken and the European Advisory Commission produced American, British, and Soviet agreement on surrender terms for Nazi Germany.[5]

Even though Stark was thoroughly occupied with the immediate problems attendant upon the forthcoming cross-channel operation, he made sure that his staff was concerned with longer range planning for the post-hostilities period. In March 1944, he established a post-hostilities committee to start work on civil affairs programs for the ports, which would be occupied by naval forces. It soon became the chief planning agency for the U.S. Navy's postwar endeavors in Europe. Among other things, it made plans to seize scientists and their advanced research laboratories at the earliest possible moment.[6]

While Stark in London was working out the details of what the navy would do in Europe once hostilities ceased, King, in Washington, was concerned with establishing an adequate command structure. As soon as the assault phase of the Normandy landings was complete, he took up with Stark the creation of two commands, each to be headed by an admiral. One command was Stark's deputy for post-hostilities affairs and the other was the naval forces command on the continent. King proposed two candidates to Stark and permitted him to choose his own deputy. They were Rear Admiral Alan G. Kirk, who commanded the American naval phase of the assault, and Vice Admiral William Glassford.[7]

Although Stark had worked closely with Kirk, he much preferred Glassford as his deputy. Glassford had recent and extensive experience in the politico-military arena as head of the U.S. Military Mission to Dakar and as President Roosevelt's personal representative to the Governor of French West Africa. Three years before, in 1941, when Stark was Chief of Naval Operations, he and Admiral Thomas C. Hart, commander in chief of the Asiatic Fleet, considered Glassford as a possible relief for Hart in that difficult and politically sensitive command.

Glassford arrived in London at the end of July 1944 and went to work at once. His first task was to work out with Stark the precise nature of his duties. When this was accomplished, Stark submitted a draft directive to King for his approval. By the end of the summer of 1944, it was clear that Glassford would remain in London in a planning and advisory capacity. Given the number of Allied organizations planning for the post-hostilities period, a flag officer was required in London just for the liaison required, to say nothing of superintending the navy's side of the planning.

At first Glassford was concerned only with planning for the occupation and disarmament of Germany and Austria. Then Stark asked him to recommend policies to be followed in setting up SHAEF (Supreme Headquarters Allied Expeditionary Forces) missions to France, Belgium, the Netherlands, Denmark, and Norway; to see that all arrangements for them were made; and to follow them up to the point that the naval elements of these missions reported to their superiors on the continent. It was a difficult and demanding task, requiring close coordination with Allied and U.S. Army officials, and with the Navy Department. Although Glassford did much of the work, it was under Stark's overall direction and Stark remained responsible for it. When his task was completed in April 1945, Glassford left London and relieved Admiral H. Kent Hewitt as Commander, U.S. Naval Forces, North African Waters.[8]

As preparations progressed, the outlines of what the navy would do in Germany and how it would be done became increasingly clear. Stark's former Assistant Chief of Naval Operations in 1939 and 1940 and his immediate predecessor in London, Vice Admiral Robert L. Ghormley, arrived in London as the prospective Commander, U.S. Naval Forces, Germany. His command was designated Task Force 124, in keeping with the tidy naval fleet organization. Ghormley's specific tasks were organizing, equipping, and training naval forces assigned to Germany, as well as planning everything pertaining to the U.S. Navy's participation in the occupation of Germany. He had to be ready to move into Germany at a moment's notice when the tottering German Reich finally collapsed.

There was some difficulty in working out the precise command relationships between Ghormley and the European Theater Command. Stark favored the principle of unity of command by which one American officer commanded all United States forces in Europe.

However, he felt strongly that Ghormley should have operational and administrative control over all United States naval forces in the theater and that he should be subordinate only to the commanding general. He insisted on this point in a letter to King. The army planners disagreed. They wanted Ghormley to be subordinate to Eisenhower's staff, in a position similar to that of the various army units. Stark's insistence paid off when the army agreed that Ghormley should be able to go directly to Eisenhower, thus bypassing the theater staff.[9]

Success crowned Allied arms in France during the summer of 1944. After extensive and prolonged bitter fighting in Normandy, American and British forces broke through the German lines. The people of Paris rose against the Nazi occupiers. The City of Light was once again free on 25 August when General LeClerc led French troops into their capital and General de Gaulle established a provisional government. On 1 September, Stark sent Captain H. F. Cope to Paris as Senior Naval Officer Present and as his representative.

Meanwhile, Rear Admiral Alan G. Kirk returned to Washington after the naval phase of the Normandy invasion was concluded. After Stark chose Glassford as his deputy, King appointed Kirk commander of all U.S. Naval Forces in France. Kirk was also promoted to vice admiral. In giving Kirk this operational command, King also specified that Stark would be his administrative commander. Kirk's new command was designated Task Force 122, the same designation as his previous command at sea. Stark explained these arrangements to Eisenhower and offered to go into them in greater detail if Eisenhower or his Chief of Staff, General Walter B. Smith, wished him to.[10]

In response to Eisenhower's request, King extended Kirk's command in October to include operational control of all U.S. naval activities on the European continent. This expansion was necessary so that Kirk could support army operations in Belgium, the Netherlands, and in Germany. However, the EIGHTH Fleet in the Mediterranean was excluded.[11]

One more major amphibious operation remained in the European war. The Allies and then the retreating Germans had destroyed the bridges across the Rhine River, but it had to be crossed. The river may not have been as wide as the English Channel by a long shot, but it was a formidable barrier requiring the whole panoply and paraphernalia of extensive amphibious forces. Kirk had operational control of these forces and it was up to Stark and his command to see to it that the necessary landing craft, men, equipment, and supplies were provided. These forces were assembled along the south coast of England at Dartmouth and Portland. British ships carried the landing craft to Le Havre. Then they were trucked overland to Germany. Some of the rigs were over 70 feet long and weighed 70 tons. In March 1945, the landing craft were put to use ferrying the Third Army across the Rhine in a hail of enemy fire.[12]

A less dramatic, but also important naval task in Europe was the gathering, evaluation, and dissemination of intelligence. A COM-NAVEU Special Intelligence Unit operated with the First U.S. Army from 6 June until 20 June 1944. These men went ashore on D day to gather intelligence in connection with the occupation of ports and bases by the U.S. Navy. It was a mobile, self-contained unit with orders to travel close to the area of activity and to exploit intelligence targets wherever they might be found.[13]

As the Allied forces in the late summer and autumn of 1944 captured former German submarine bases in France and as they swept into Germany, there was a great deal of intelligence work to be done. In October, 1944, Stark concluded that the joint army-navy intelligence arrangements did not sufficiently meet the navy's needs. He felt that an independent organization was required. By early December, Secretary of the Navy James V. Forrestal approved the plan for a Navy Technical Mission in Europe. The technical mission was established to meet the needs of the various bureaus of the Navy Department. Stark was given both administrative and operational control of this new unit. Its head reported directly to him "in person," an extraordinary relationship.

The Navy Technical Mission existed for less than a year. It was a large organization of over 300 officers and 450 enlisted men and civilian technicians. During that time it compiled more than 600 formal reports on almost every conceivable naval subject and shipped huge quantities of captured documents and other material to the United States for further examination and study.[14]

The impending conclusion of the war in Europe required that considerable thought be given to the military and naval structure required to administer the occupation of Germany and support United States forces there. Modifications and other changes to the existing wartime arrangements were obviously necessary. Any changes meant that new positions would be created and that existing ones might well be eliminated. There was a clear opportunity for personal advancement.

Vice Admiral Alan G. Kirk, commander of U.S. Naval Forces in France, aspired to a position of greater importance and higher rank, notably a fourth star. He recommended in a personal letter to King that Stark's London command be phased out and that the senior naval commander be designated as Commander, U.S. Naval Forces, Continent. The clear implication was that the new command, with Kirk at its head, would supplant both Stark and his London command.

When King received Kirk's letter, he sent it to Stark for comment. King was surprised to learn that Stark knew nothing of what Kirk proposed. He rebuked Kirk, saying, "Please bear in mind that Admiral Stark is my representative in Europe for planning matters connected with the occupation of Germany. Your suggestions should have been made to him."[15]

Stark was not particularly upset at Kirk's abortive attempt to undercut him. Incidents of that sort did not disturb him. He had seen too many power plays in his long career to be concerned about this one, and it was not the first one Kirk had attempted in Europe. Late in 1943, Kirk tried to woo Stark's Deputy Chief of Staff Captain (later Commodore), Howard A. Flanigan, away from Stark to be his chief of staff. Flanigan was the kind of man who could get a job done on time and done well.

Kirk's flattery and his derogatory remarks about Stark failed to move Flanigan, who said, "I have been with Admiral Stark for some time and I have a high respect for him. He has given me a Hell of a good job with a lot of responsibility. And, I am going to carry it through for him."[16] Flanigan simply did not want to, and felt he could not, leave Stark at that time. At the same time, without consulting Stark, Kirk tried to get some of the junior officers who were involved in the planning for Normandy to leave Stark's staff and join his. He was unsuccessful. None of the officers propositioned were willing to leave Stark and Flanigan; some were also not anxious to work for Kirk. Although Stark knew of Kirk's attempted piracy of his officers, he was willing to put up with Kirk's arrogance. Stark knew what Kirk could do, whatever his shortcomings and ambitions.

Shortly after his arrival in London, Kirk telephoned Stark at his apartment and asked if he could come around. Stark replied that he was busy, but would be free in about half an hour. About 30 minutes later the doorbell rang and Lieutenant Commander Willis Sargent, USNR, with whom Stark had been conferring about post-hostilities matters, answered the door. He greeted Kirk pleasantly, but Kirk replied gruffly and with scant courtesy.

When the two admirals were alone, Stark remarked that Kirk had not been very polite to Sargent. Kirk saw no reason why he should have been polite to a lieutenant commander. Stark bluntly told him, "It would have been nice in any event, but since Sargent knows many of the United States senators by their first names and the President has called him by his first name since before he was Governor of New York, I should thank you would be serving your own purposes as well by treating him with courtesy." A few days later Kirk invited Sargent to be his guest for a round of golf.[17]

At the end of October 1944, Eisenhower's chief of staff, General Walter B. Smith, abruptly confronted Flanigan with several complaints Kirk had made. Kirk said it was not fair to send him to a command that was unworthy of his rank and to surround him with a great many restrictions on his authority. Either he told Smith or let him think that there were over 400 naval officers in France who were not under his authority. Smith also received complaints about Flanigan, which Kirk may have made as well.

Flanigan bluntly told Smith he was misinformed on all counts. Flanigan said that considering all factors, Kirk's command was worthy of his rank of vice admiral. There were no restrictions on this authority and within the limits of his command he was as dominant as Stark. All naval officers in France were under Kirk's authority, except those very few sent by the Combined Chiefs of Staff and those assigned to Eisenhower's staff.[18] Kirk's complaints had no foundation in fact. It was a transparent attempt to undercut Stark and it failed, thanks to Flanigan.

Franklin Roosevelt took the oath of office as President for the fourth time on 20 January 1945. A week later he was at sea, embarked in the cruiser *Quincy* bound for the Mediterranean. At Malta he met Churchill and the Combined Chiefs of Staff before they went on to Yalta for a meeting with Stalin.

For several days before Roosevelt and Churchill arrived, Malta was the scene of much high level activity. King, Marshall, and Arnold met the British Chiefs of Staff to discuss the final phase of the war against Germany. Stark was there, too, in his capacity as Commander, TWELFTH Fleet and because he was the senior U.S. naval officer in Europe. Stark flew to Naples to board the cruiser *Memphis*, Admiral Hewitt's flagship for the EIGHTH Fleet in the Mediterranean, for the trip to Malta. As a result of a communications failure, the military airport at Naples had not been informed of Stark's arrival. When his plane approached Naples, it was soon caught in a cone of light from three search lights, a sure sign that antiaircraft batteries were about to fire. Fortunately, the pilot calmly dropped recognition flares in the correct order for that day and the plane was cleared to land. It was a close call.

Stark had several long talks with King and he had both Generals Marshall and Walter B. Smith, as well as King on board *Memphis* for dinner. Finally, *Quincy*, with Roosevelt embarked, entered the harbor. Stark went on board with many others to call on the commander in chief, who received them on the fantail. He was surrounded by Hopkins, Stettinius, Byrnes, and other members of the United States delegation. Roosevelt, Stark observed, was bright and cheery as usual, but he was a little thin and looked very tired. It was a very pleasant, but public, meeting. It was also their last. Within three months Roosevelt was dead. When Roosevelt and the others went on to Yalta, Stark returned to London.

A few days after Stark returned to London, King George VI awarded him the G.B.E. (Honorary Knight, Grand Cross of the Military Division of the Order of the British Empire). It was Britain's formal and grateful thanks to Stark for his contributions to the Anglo-American war effort. Afterward the two men had a pleasant half hour's chat, which Stark thoroughly enjoyed.[19]

As the war in Europe entered its final phase, the extent of Stark's command expanded. Originally concentrated in the United Kingdom during the buildup for the cross-channel assault, the command expanded into France and then into Germany and Austria in the wake of the American army. Although the press of his many duties required him to spend much time in London, he liked to get out into the field, to talk with his subordinate commanders, and to see for himself what was going on, what the problems were, and what he could do to help solve them.

In April 1945 it was clear that Germany could not last much longer. The end of hostilities would bring enormous changes in Stark's far-flung command. Stark wanted to make sure that it would be ready to meet this new challenge and that it completed the tasks at hand. To satisfy himself that the adjustment would be made as smoothly as possible, Stark planned an inspection tour of France and Germany. He was particularly curious to see Germany.

With some difficulty he arranged his schedule so he could be away from his office for a week in mid-April 1945 to visit the Belgian ports, SHAEF Headquarters in France, and cities along the Rhine. But, first, he went by way of Chester, where he had been invited to speak at the graduation of the Royal Naval College. He felt it necessary to go there, because in the summer of 1943 he asked the Admiralty for the buildings and facilities of the Royal Naval College at Dartmouth to meet a desperate need for American enlisted men's housing, for landing craft, repair facilities, and for the use of Dartmouth harbor for amphibious training.[20] The Admiralty moved the college temporarily to Easton Hall near Chester, the home of the Duke of Westminster. Stark knew how he would have felt if it had been necessary to turn the Naval Academy at Annapolis over to another navy. He wanted to show the Royal Navy how much he appreciated their act and that he was sympathetic to the inevitable dislocation it caused.

Flying on to Brussels by way of a quick stop in London to read important incoming dispatches and mail at the airport, Stark arrived in the Belgian capital in time for a quiet dinner at the American embassy. Driving through the streets, he noticed an unending stream of Flying Fortresses headed east to Germany. At dinner he met the Princess de Ligne, who told him of her efforts during the German occupation in behalf of the Belgian people. At one time the organization she founded and directed was feeding 39,000 people.

When the port of Antwerp was finally opened in December 1944, it was literally a godsend to the Allies. This magnificent port escaped significant destruction and became the major port of entry for the Allies in the final six months of the European war. Stark had studied the maps of the port and he knew its tonnage capacity. However, he did not fully comprehend its extent until he saw with his own eyes and then he was staggered.

In Paris Kirk brought him up to date on U.S. naval activities in France. The next day, 13 April, Stark learned of President Roosevelt's death the day before in Warm Springs, Georgia. Like everyone else, he was shocked and saddened. Only a month before Stark and Roosevelt exchanged letters. That occasion, too, was a sad one. Stark sent a letter of condolence to Roosevelt on the death of his trusted and able assistant, General Edwin M. "Pa" Watson. Roosevelt's reply was brief, but cordial.

The morning briefing at SHAEF gave him the overall picture of military operations, which were now in their final phase. At Wiesbaden General Omar Bradley made his open Cadillac touring car available. It was the ideal way to observe conditions along the Rhine in the mild, sunny spring weather.

The destruction of Mainz across the river from Wiesbaden seemed to Stark to be total. Bridges across the Rhine were destroyed, along with the railroad centers and towns that had been the points of German resistance. At Heidelberg Stark was told how the burgermaster surrendered the town to save it from destruction. Other towns did their best to get the German soldiers out; the people knew that if they put up a fight, their town was sure to be wrecked.

In the long drive along the Rhine, the sight that impressed Stark the most was the very great number of children, from the very young to those in their teens, working in the fields or in gardens in front of their cottages. He saw one little girl of about six swinging a pick. The children were healthy-looking and ruddy, but didn't seem to him to be as rugged as the British children. There were a great number of people on the road, presumably returning to their homes. They were hauling carts of every size, laden with belongings of every kind and description.

The physical destruction of the country, the laboring children, and the homeless, ordinary people were pitiful sights. The war had finally been brought home to the Germans, Stark thought. Now they were experiencing woes similar to those they had visited upon nearly every other country of Europe. He was far more compassionate towards the Germans in 1945 than he had been in Hamburg in 1919.

Generally, the Germans he saw simply stared at him and he stared back. Sometimes there was genuine and obviously intentional hatred in their expressions, occasionally smiles, and once in a while a little child would wave. He noticed many large "Don't Fraternize" signs and he was told that so far the rule was being followed. He hoped that there would be no fraternization until the fighting was over, but realized that it would be difficult to avoid, "particularly where the children are concerned and particularly when the fighting men are relieved by new recruits who will see the misery and who, being human, will be impressed by it and will forget the terrible misery in other lands caused by the Huns."[21]

At Heidelberg, an American officer urged him to see the enormous airplane factory, which was completely underground. Stark was amazed at what he saw. The factory was vast, modern, wonderfully equipped with the finest machine tools, plenty of metal and perfectly air conditioned. When Stark visited the site, the Americans had not yet determined the source of the electricity, so they could not turn on the lights. Stark's only apprehension was that his guide, who had been there for only a day or two, might get lost in the vast maze of galleries and corridors.

Stark flew back to Wiesbaden from south Germany in an army cub, the only aircraft small enough to land in that particular area. He thoroughly enjoyed the low altitude flight.

Three weeks later the war in Europe was over.

St. Paul's Cathedral in London, that magnificent creation of Sir Christopher Wren, survived the Blitz and became a symbol of Britain's endurance and fortitude during World War II. Within one month, in the spring of 1945, St. Paul's was the scene of two important, but very different, events. First there was a memorial service for President Roosevelt; a few weeks later, there was a service of thanksgiving to celebrate the Allied victory over Germany.

Roosevelt was loved and admired by the British people from the King and Queen to ordinary people. They saw him as a stalwart friend in a time of national peril. When Stark saw Roosevelt for the last time in Malta, he told Roosevelt how the British people loved him. They discussed the possibility of a presidential visit to Great Britain, which Roosevelt hoped to make. Stark told Roosevelt he would receive a welcome as no man had ever received outside of his own country.

On the morning of the memorial service, 17 April, the great cathedral was packed to the doors and there were great crowds outside. Within, Ambassador Winant and Admiral Stark, as the senior Americans, with the King and Queen and the Prime Minister, occupied the front pews and led the mourners. Numerous bishops and other clergy, a full choir, and the Dean of the Cathedral performed their offices in the best Anglican tradition.

Seated in the pew directly behind Churchill, Stark looked at the doughty symbol of the British Empire and could only imagine his feelings that morning. He knew how close Churchill and Roosevelt had been and from thirty years of friendship with Roosevelt he knew the extent of Churchill's loss. It had been a long time since the young lieutenant and the new Assistant Secretary of the Navy met on the bridge of the *Patterson;* but then, it only seemed like yesterday.

It was a pity, he thought, that Roosevelt died when he did. Still, he had the marvelous satisfaction of knowing that Hitler had been defeated and that it was only a matter of time before Japan, too, would submit to the Allies. Stark prayed, "God grant that from the terrible ordeal we have been through and still have to go through, much good will come." He would have lost heart without that hope.[22]

The instrument of German surrender was signed in a schoolroom near Rheims in the early hours of 7 May 1945, and all hostilities were to cease at midnight the following day. Victory in Europe had been achieved at long last. The general euphoric joy and relief enveloped Stark and his headquarters at Grosvenor Square. Cheering crowds jammed the London streets and moved to Buckingham Palace where they cheered the King, the Queen, the Prime Minister, and everyone else.

Five days later a national service of thanksgiving was held in St. Paul's Cathedral. It was both a joyous and a solemn ceremony in which King George VI, Queen Elizabeth, and the Archibishop of Canterbury led the nation in thanks to "Almighty God for the Victory granted in Europe to Britain and her Allies." Stark was given a prominent place among the glittering assemblage.

The congregation assembled to music played by the R.A.F. Symphony Orchestra, which concluded with Howard Hemming's "Threnody for a Soldier Killed in Action." After the great procession of the King and Queen, Archbishop, and clergy took their places, the Dean of the Cathedral spoke the bidding,

Brethren, we are met together on this day to pour out our hearts in fervent thanksgiving to the God and Father of us all, and to dedicate ourselves afresh to the service of His Kingdom. We desire to thank him for the deliverance from the hand of our enemies; for the devotion, even to death, of those who for the five years past have stood between us and slavery; and for the hopes of a better world for all His people. I bid you, therefore, lift up your hearts that you may tell the praises of our God, and pray that His wisdom may lead us, and His spirit strengthen us, in the days that are to come.

An anthem, the lessons, and prayers were followed by the Archbishop's sermon. There were more prayers and then the congregation rose and sang the "Te Deum." Afterwards they knelt and received the final blessings from the Archbishop. A fanfare from the west gallery announced the National Anthem. The patriotic multitude sang with heart and voice, "God save the King!," filling the ancient cathedral with their joy and thanksgiving.[23]

Now that the Allies were prepared to occupy Germany and assume responsibility for civil administration in the absence of a functioning central German government, the next step was the dismantling of the enormous military machine that had brought victory to the Allied cause. Already many of the bases in the United Kingdom had been closed and their equipment moved to central locations where it could be shipped home or disposed of locally. Stark and his staff saw to that in 1944 shortly after the cross-channel assault. One of the principal administrative tasks facing Stark in the spring and early summer of 1945 was the reduction of the naval establishment within the geographic limits of his command.

Ironically, as this reduction began, the geographic limits of Stark's command expanded as other commands were dissolved or merged with his. Vice Admiral William Glassford left Stark's staff in April 1945, and went to the Mediterranean where he took command of the EIGHTH Fleet and U.S. Naval Forces, Northern African Waters. The following month the EIGHTH Fleet sailed for home and Stark's TWELFTH Fleet took administrative command of the naval forces remaining in that area. Under Stark's direction, Glassford began the task of closing the American naval bases in North Africa and the Mediterranean as rapidly as possible. The jurisdiction of the TWELFTH Fleet was expanded again to include the U.S. Naval Air unit in the Azores. In mid-summer, 1945, the TWELFTH Fleet exercised administrative control over all U.S. naval forces from Norway in the north, west to the Azores, east to Yugoslavia, and as far south as 10° North Latitude. There were even liaison offices as far east as Egypt and the Persian Gulf.[24]

The stream of United States naval forces westward across the Atlantic continued through the summer of 1945. In July the antisubmarine patrol and reconnaissance chores of Fleet Air Wing 7 were finished and these squadrons left their English bases for home, along with numerous landing craft. Officers and enlisted men went home.

Demobilization, reduction in forces, and adjustment to new conditions of post-hostilities, if not peacetime, required Stark in June 1945 to make a personal inspection of the Mediterranean additions to his far-flung command.

There were numerous command and administrative problems to be solved. Most of these were attendant upon the shift from wartime to peacetime. For one thing, Glassford needed to know if the basis upon which the Americans used Italian bases was going to be changed, and, if so, how. Although Stark did not have the answer to this and other questions, he wanted to see for himself the extent of the problems and to advise Washington accordingly.

In Rome Stark found great concern among American and British civil and military officials about the possibility of a complete withdrawal of American forces from Italy. They felt that the retention of American troops in Italy would have a stabilizing effect. At that time a possible reversion to fascism was seen as more dangerous and more likely than a triumph of the Italian Communist Party. They feared a repetition in Italy of the troubles that were then afflicting Greece if the American army left.[25]

It was the first time Stark had been in Rome since 1919 when, as Executive Officer of USS *North Dakota* he helped convey home for burial the body of the late Italian ambassador to the United States, Count di Celleri. The highlight of his visit in 1945 was a private audience with Pope Pius XII. In dress white uniforms, Stark and his party of eight officers were led through what seemed to them to be countless hallways and anterooms before they reached the papal chamber. The Pope sent word that he would like to confer with Stark alone, before meeting the others.

When he entered the Pope's receiving room, the Pope rose and greeted him in a friendly and pleasant manner. They shook hands and he bade Stark sit down in a chair alongside his desk while they talked. Their free and unrestricted talk covered the range of world problems. Stark asked some direct questions, to which he received equally direct and pointed replies.

The Pope put Stark completely at his ease; so much so that Stark, with his usual ingenuousness said, "I am going to say something to you which is perhaps completely unorthodox, but I just want to tell you I have never met a Pope before. I have had an idea of what he should be and I simply want to say to you, you look the part."[26]

The Pope's eyes sparkled and he laughed cheerfully. Stark was very glad he had not suppressed his impulse, because it obviously pleased the Pope no end. The Pope graciously thanked him for saying so. It seemed to Stark that his remark put them and their talk on a happier and even more frank basis. Later Stark said he had yet to find a man, big or small, who would not be pleased with a little sincere, simple compliment.

When Stark felt he could not take up any more of the Pope's time, he stood up to go. The Pope then asked that the other members of his party be brought in. Stark performed the introductions. The Pope shook hands and engaged each one in cordial conversation. He then presented each of the visiting Americans with several rosaries, which he blessed. As they parted he gave them his blessing. Stark left the Pope with the feeling of having been in the presence of a sincere and good Christian of broad gauge and tolerance, steeped with a desire to do what he could to help lift the burdens and troubles of the world.

Stark and his party spent the rest of the afternoon as tourists in the Eternal City. Some had never seen St. Peter's and Stark was anxious that they see it and the other notable sights, including the Villa Borghese. Stark himself particularly wanted to see once again Canova's famous marble statues. He described to Mrs. Stark how the right toe of the bronze statue of St. Peter was wearing away from being kissed several thousand times each day. He added, "None of which can be accredited to our party."

Back in Naples he embarked in the ancient cruiser *Memphis* for the second time that year. Stark and his party went first to Palermo, where he inspected the various American naval activities there, and then went on to Malta. The voyage to Malta was more for his own pleasure and convenience than it was for American naval business. Stark was again appalled at the destruction the Germans and the Italians had worked on the island. He marveled that it had held out. He was especially sorry to see that the lovely little opera house in Valletta was gone. He had heard a particularly fine opera there in 1919.

He conferred with the senior American and French naval officers in Algiers. In Oran he inspected the extensive American naval facilities—barracks, warehouses, recreational facilities, and repair shops. It had been an extremely useful supply port. In Morocco he saw the American naval installations at Port Lyautey, Rabat, and Casablanca. The night on board *Memphis* en route from Algiers to Marseilles was his last night at sea on a navy ship while on active duty. It was a beautiful moonlit night with a gentle breeze. He saw the movie on deck with the ship's company, the best company of all, he thought.

He extended his trip an extra day to give his hard-working loyal assistants the chance to see the French Riviera. He specifically brought along his faithful Chief Yeoman McConnell, and Conolly, his marine orderly, so they could visit Nice, which was set aside solely for enlisted men. The officers with him thoroughly enjoyed Cannes, which was off-limits to enlisted men. Stark stayed at the hotel reserved for general officers at Cap d'Antibes.

In southern France he saw numerous parties of German prisoners of war working in the navy yards along the roads. Some even worked in the galley at the enlisted men's mess in Marseilles. They gave no trouble to their captors and they were glad to be so employed because of the abundant food they received.

The last leg of this journey took him to Paris. At the French Admiralty his friend Admiral Lemonnier presented him with the Legion of Honor and with the Croix de Guerre in a formal military ceremony with a band and full guard of honor. Following the ceremony there was a champagne reception in his honor in the Minister's office.[27]

Stark, as the senior and highly respected United States naval officer in Europe, was the ideal choice to deliver a personal message from President Truman to the kings of Norway and Denmark. In late July he left London on what turned out to be a delightful three-day odyssey. It was his first visit to Norway and he looked forward to it. Ever since he learned knotting and splicing at the Naval Academy under a Chief Boatswain's Mate named Gustafson, he had wanted to see Norway. Now at last he had the chance.

It was a pleasant flight to Oslo, where he received full military honors at the airport. The next day he went early to the royal palace, at the request of King Haakon VI, for a private audience. At the conclusion of their talk, the King took Stark completely by surprise. He presented Stark with the Grand Cross of the Order of St. Olav, the highest decoration of the Norwegian government.

King Haakon was grateful to Stark for the many kindnesses extended to him while he was in exile in London. He saw them as help to Norway. On a more personal note, on the morning the King had left London, Stark had taped a four-leaf clover, one of several Mrs. Stark had sent to him, to a card on which he had written Good Luck. He sent the card to the King, who told him that it confirmed and rendered memorable every thought of friendship he had for Stark. The two men remained friends for life and corresponded until the King's death a few years later.

Flying on to Copenhagen, Stark had an equally pleasant time. He had never met King Christian, brother of Norway's King Haakon. Their meeting was cordial, but it lacked the personal warmth Stark found in Oslo. Stark was struck by the goodwill, which he said "just radiates from these fine people." Wherever he went he said everyone waved and smiled. At one stop, two little girls, one Norwegian and one Danish, went up to him and asked for his autograph. When he complied, the little Norwegian girl gave him a small enamel pin in the shape of the Norwegian flag. The gesture touched him greatly.

He had liked Danes ever since his first meetings with them in the Caribbean in 1904–1905. He found them the "cleanest, smilingest, happiest, healthiest, sturdiest, best dressed people I have ever seen anywhere." As pleasant as these three days had been, it was even more pleasant to find letters from home when he returned to London.[28]

Stark played no role in the Potsdam conference. His role at or near the center of events was drawing to an end. Nevertheless, Stark squeezed in another trip to Paris to meet Admiral King, who was en route to Potsdam for the conference. Then, in July, he was off to Frankfurt and Brussels before going to Antwerp to meet his new commander in chief on board USS *Augusta*. In the middle of August, he hauled down his admiral's flag for the last time and sailed for home. Still, his final fortnight in Great Britain was eventful.

He went to Plymouth on 2 August to greet President Truman once again. The President's plane was scheduled to land at St. Mawgen's, but fog forced it to divert to Harrowbeer. Hastily summoned automobiles took the President and his party to the nearest dock where boats were rushed in from the *Augusta* to take him aboard. The people of Plymouth were understandably disappointed at not being able to see the American president.[29] Stark performed his duty with his usual grace, but there was no warmth or closeness with this president as there had been with his predecessor.

Several weeks earlier, in mid-June, before official notification was sent, King told Stark that he would be relieved late in the summer. Even though he expected it, the news still came as a blow. A summons to retire comes only once in a career. The new Secretary of the Navy, James V. Forrestal, had been trying for months to ease Stark out, but Roosevelt would have none of it while the fighting in Europe continued. Roosevelt was gone, Stark was past the retirement age, and he no longer had a champion in Washington. Stark's relief and retirement would be a major step in the shift to a peacetime navy in Europe, although Japan had not yet surrendered.

Admiral H. Kent Hewitt had orders to relieve him, as soon as he finished the supplemental report on the attack on Pearl Harbor that Forrestal had asked him to prepare. Hewitt told Stark in early July that he was concentrating every minute on the report, but that he realized that he would have to start for London sometime about August 1. Stark thoughtfully sent Hewitt detailed suggestions on what clothing to bring (evening dress was not worn in London at that time) and on arrangements for his quarters.[30]

Frequently the departure of a four star admiral is the occasion for great pomp and ceremony. Stark wanted nothing of the kind. He simply wanted to be relieved and to leave London quietly for home. When he told Cunningham, the First Sea Lord, of his intentions, Cunningham said, "Nothing doing." The British government and the Admiralty would not tolerate Stark's quiet departure. They were determined to give him a proper send-off.

Originally, Stark planned on leaving about 1 August 1945. However, Cunningham asked King, who agreed, to delay Stark's departure until the middle of the month so the King, the government, and the Admiralty could say their farewells properly. They did, on Monday, 13 August.

First, King George VI invited Stark to tea at Buckingham Palace. Queen Elizabeth and the Princesses Elizabeth and Margaret joined them. Stark sincerely liked and admired the King and Queen, who were as friendly to him as they could possibly be. Stark was fond of the two princesses in a grandfatherly way. On one occasion he sent them maple sugar candy when he returned from the United States. For her eighteenth birthday, he sent Princess Elizabeth a four-leaf clover. Twice she responded with warm, friendly notes of thanks. He was a friend of the Royal Family and as his friends they wished to bid him a private farewell.

A few hours later, he boarded an admiral's barge at Westminster pier for the Royal Naval College down the Thames at Greenwich. There, in the Painted Hall, he was the honored guest of the British government and the lords of the Admiralty. He had been there on similar occasions to honor other distinguished guests. Now it was his turn. The Prime Minister, the Foreign Secretary, the First Lord of the Admiralty, the First Sea Lord, and the other lords of the Admiralty were there. The hall was filled with other officers and guests. It was a mess night in the best tradition of the Royal Navy.

After toasts to the King and to the President of the United States, Admiral of the Fleet Sir Andrew B. Cunningham, the First Sea Lord, rose to offer a toast to the guest of honor. It was a sad moment for Cunningham. He was "profoundly grateful" to Stark for his unstinting help and "wise counsel." Cunningham was convinced that Stark "must come near to possessing all of the exacting qualities laid down by his great-predecessor, Paul Jones, as the requirements of the U.S. Naval Officer." This redoubtable sea dog, with a war record equal to any man in the long history of the Royal Navy, spoke simply and from his heart. He said,

> Our Naval life is fraught with changes in our shipmates. Some pass in and out of our lives and mean little more to us than the name or date, while others become engrafted in our lives in permanent friendships. The nature of our profession, however, with its frequent changes of ships and stations brings with it many separations and farewells, which frequently cause lasting regret, and our parting with Admiral Stark is truly one of these.

The assembly rose as one man and, acknowledging Cunningham's words, drank the health of their guest.[31]

Stark addressed his response to the dignitaries present and to his brother officers. He made no distinction as to whether they wore a loop or a star on their sleeves. As far as he was concerned they were all his brothers. He spoke of his great joy that the war in Europe was over. He reminded his audience that the Japanese surrender would mean the end of their brotherhood in combat operations, but it was a "combat which might never have happened had we stuck with each other after the last war and fought together with a give-and-take for peace such as we fought to win the war." He spoke of the difficult years ahead. He thanked his British hosts for all they had done for the U.S. Navy and he thanked them for all the cheerfulness with which they imposed inconveniences and hardships on themselves for the sake of the U.S. Navy. "Truly we have been shipmates," he said. "God grant we may ever remain so, and that the goodwill, so much in evidence here tonight, may ever grow stronger among us." The formalities were concluded with speeches by the Prime Minister and the Foreign Secretary. Afterwards, naval protocol was set aside and Stark and Cunningham were surrounded by young officers, including WRENs, who asked the men for their autographs.[32]

Three days later, with the official farewells and the change of command ceremony behind him, Stark left London for Southampton and the voyage homeward. Even then, Cunningham would not let him slip quietly away. Cunningham accompanied him to Southampton, where Stark boarded the *Queen Mary* with due ceremony. There were honor guards from the three British services and a band. In the last few hours before he sailed, Stark went ashore and dined quietly with his good friends, Admiral and Lady Cunningham at the Palace House. Finally the hour of parting came. Cunningham and Stark said a final farewell on the deck of the *Queen Mary.*

The great ship slowly moved away from the pier and entered the main channel bound for New York. Stark returned to his cabin, where he found a telegram from General Eisenhower. "I have no words to express my appreciation for the great help you have given the Forces under my command over the past three years," he said. "Your assistance has been vital and the spirit in which it was rendered has been the acme of generous cooperation. Good-bye and good luck."[33]

Stark looked forward to returning home to his family, whom he had scarcely seen for more than three years. He would need their love and support. King and Forrestal had concurred in a stinging reprimand, based on the report of the Navy Court of Inquiry into the attack on Pearl Harbor, which would soon be made public. A Joint Congressional Committee was about to commence its public hearings. The next few months were going to be difficult.

15

INVESTIGATIONS

The Japanese attack on Pearl Harbor on 7 December 1941 gave rise to numerous and prolonged investigations. President Roosevelt ordered the first formal investigation in January 1942 when he asked Supreme Court Justice Owen J. Roberts to conduct an inquiry. During the war the army and the navy convened formal investigating bodies and ordered several one man investigations as well. All these proceedings were secret. After Japan surrendered in August 1945, Congress established a joint committee to investigate the matter publicly. The course of the various investigations inevitably became entangled in the morass of partisan and bureaucratic politics.

After a quick trip to Pearl Harbor and superficial interviews with a number of people, the Roberts Commission made a prompt report in 1942. Although the report may have satisfied the public demand that the facts be made available, it only touched the surface. The commission members were not even told of the navy's ability to read Japanese codes. It was not until the persons who knew the facts could take time from their war responsibilities to refresh their recollections that all of the circumstances surrounding the attack could be properly presented.

In the meantime, the navy became concerned at the possibility that some of the senior officers who had extensive knowledge of the events leading up to the attack might be killed in combat. In early 1944, Secretary of the Navy Frank Knox sent Admiral Thomas C. Hart to interview a number of these officers at their duty stations in the Pacific. In spite of the fact that some of the interviews were conducted in the midst of ongoing combat operations, the transcripts of these interviews were useful in later investigations.

259

The new Secretary of the Navy, James V. Forrestal, convened a court of inquiry on 13 July 1944. Among other things, he directed the court in the precept "to give its opinion as to whether any offenses have been committed or serious blame incurred on the part of any person or persons in the naval service" and, if so, to recommend further proceedings.[1]

Admiral Husband E. Kimmel, who commanded the Pacific Fleet at the time of the Japanese attack, had been demanding for some time a court-martial in which he would claim Washington had withheld vital information from him. He had been relieved of his command shortly after the attack and sat out the war in an inactive duty status. In the popular mind, he bore much of the blame for the success of the attack. He felt that this was unfair and he wanted an opportunity to tell his side of the story and to have all the facts developed. The court of inquiry was the first step along that road and it provided Kimmel with his first official hearing. The proceedings of the court of inquiry were held in secret, however, and the court had only the power to recommend further action. Any public airing of the facts surrounding the attack would have to come later.

The first time Stark heard of the court of inquiry was on 25 July 1944, when King surprised him by ordering him to return to Washington at once. Stark's first inclination was simply to return to Washington, testify, and hurry back to his duties in London. However, Commodore Howard A. Flanigan, his deputy chief of staff, was concerned. He knew from conversations he had had during official trips to Washington that the Navy Department was not solidly behind Stark and he was apprehensive over what the court of inquiry would conclude. His fears were well grounded. The report of the court of inquiry and the subsequent endorsements by King and Forrestal did more to besmirch Stark's reputation than any other action in his long naval career.

Flanigan urged Stark to take Lieutenant David W. Richmond, USNR, who was Flanigan's executive assistant, with him to Washington. Richmond was a young lawyer who had been with a leading Washington law firm for several years before he was commissioned. At least with Richmond along, Stark would have a lawyer by his side. It was well that he did. Stark and Richmond left London by air on the evening of 26 July and arrived in Washington the following afternoon.

There was little time to prepare for the Court of Inquiry. Stark consulted his good friend Admiral Thomas C. Hart, who had commanded the Asiatic Fleet from 1939 to 1942 and who had only recently completed a series of interviews with senior officers on duty in the Pacific with respect to their knowledge of facts bearing on the Japanese attack on Pearl Harbor. Stark was called as the first witness when the court convened and was designated an "interested party," along with Admiral Kimmel. The court adjourned for one week to allow Stark to prepare his testimony.

At Stark's request, Hart agreed to be his counsel before the court. After interviewing several inexperienced navy lawyers recommended by the office of the Judge Advocate General, Stark decided to designate Richmond to be Hart's assistant. The court understood that Stark would return to London as soon as his testimony was completed and that Hart would represent him during any further proceedings. At the outset Hart did not think the court of inquiry boded well for anyone.

The two admirals and the lieutenant got to work preparing for the next sessions. The bulk of their preparation consisted of Hart telling Stark what he had developed in the course of his interviews and of Stark refreshing his recollection of events that happened in 1941. Hart found Stark hard to handle because of his propensity to wander off the main points into unimportant collateral areas.[2] The preparation was hampered by the fact that Stark was expected to testify regarding events in 1941. It was then mid-1944, and Stark in the meantime had been concerned with his heavy duties and responsibilities in connection with the war in Europe. His memory was, understandably, not wholly reliable. There was no inclination on the part of the secretary or the CNO, Admiral King, to assist Stark in refreshing his recollection by making available to him his files during his tenure as CNO. The high command of the Navy seemed to view the Court of Inquiry as the personal problem of Kimmel and Stark; the officers who were designated by the secretary to pass on requests from Kimmel and Stark for documents and files were, at times, openly hostile.

Stark testified for five consecutive days. Hart felt that his initial testimony went "pretty well," although Stark still tended to wander off the track. Kimmel was represented by an able and distinguished civilian attorney; Hart feared that he would embarrass Stark on cross-examination by what would appear to be his lack of knowledge of the affairs of his office in 1941. When Stark was allowed to step down, Hart was not particularly pleased with the performance of his client. Still, he admitted candidly that Stark did not do "too badly." He was, however, "plenty sore" at the court's "rather brutal treatment of Stark."[3] The prospect for some kind of formal censure of Stark was a little more menacing than Hart liked.

After Stark finished testifying, King thoughtfully told him to take a week's leave. Stark left Hart and Richmond in Washington to look after his interests and went off to join Mrs. Stark at Lake Carey for an entire week of rest in marvelous August weather. While Stark rested, Hart continued to attend the sessions of the Court, which he found interminable and boring and where "the ignorance and pomposity of the honorable members is . . . past understanding."[4] When Stark returned he was called once more as a witness. Stark completed his testimony, but Hart was disappointed in him as a witness.

Stark, too, was disappointed in his performance. It was clear that his own recollection was insufficient and that he needed to review numerous documents if he were ever again to testify on this matter. He would also need to review with those who were on his staff in the Office of Chief of Naval Operations in 1941 the events during the months before the attack in order to refresh his recollection and theirs of the multitude of facts that might shed light on the circumstances surrounding the attack. Even so, he admitted to Hart that he might have done better had he foregone the limited preparation he had with Hart and just "expressed" his thoughts. He also candidly admitted, "Perhaps I was tired, perhaps part of the trouble was my fondness and loyalty to Kimmel, my actual desire to share the burden and protect him so far as I could, and trying too hard to be so one hundred percent plus honest, so that in spots I may have made more or less a mess of it. I know I was depressed."[5]

Hart's 15-minute closing argument touched on the high spots of Stark's testimony and avoided attacking anyone. Hart made the point that the defense of Pearl Harbor was an army responsibility that the army had failed to discharge. He called attention to the 1935 and 1941 agreements of the Secretaries of War and Navy, which clearly established that responsibility.[6] This important point was almost completely ignored by the court of inquiry and in King's subsequent endorsement of the court's report.

Hart's statement was in distinct contrast to the two and one-half hour argument Kimmel's attorney made. When the court finally closed, Hart felt that Stark was certain to be criticized. He had little confidence in either the competence of two members of the court or in what the final judgment of all three members would be. The president of the court was Admiral Orin G. Murfin. He and another member, Vice Admiral Adolphus Andrews, failed to impress Hart with either their knowledge of the matters under investigation or their competence to handle the knowledge they acquired. Hart distrusted Andrews because he sensed that Andrews was jealous of Stark's appointment as Chief of Naval Operations in 1939. Apparently, Andrews felt that he should have had that position.[7] The third member was Admiral Edward C. Kalbfus. Both Hart and Stark respected him and had confidence in his abilities.

Stark returned to London and left Hart and Richmond to look after his interests before the court for the month of September. At that time it was clear there would be a major congressional investigation when the war ended. Kimmel might even get the court-martial he was demanding. In such an event, Stark was certain to be called as a witness and he wanted to be prepared. Richmond remained in Washington not only to assist Hart, but also to commence the lengthy and involved process of identifying and obtaining copies of relevant documents. This process was accomplished somewhat unofficially, against a background of almost overwhelming reluctance of the Navy Department to cooperate with Stark in any respect. When Richmond returned to London on 30 October, he took with him a large pouch of material for Stark's review.

The court concluded its work on 19 October, after having travelled to Pearl Harbor to question Admiral Nimitz and certain officers who had been on Kimmel's staff at the time of the attack. In accordance with its precept, the court submitted findings of fact, opinions and recommendations to the Secretary of the Navy on 20 October. Two findings of fact particularly applied to Stark. The first (number XVIII) was that Stark's "war warning" dispatch of 27 November 1941 "standing alone, could not convey to the commanders in the field the picture as it was seen in Washington."[8] That message began with the ominous words, "This dispatch is to be considered a war warning." It warned that an "aggressive move by Japan is expected within the next few days." It ordered an "appropriate defensive deployment" pre-paratory to execution of War Plan 46.[9] Unfortunately, the court did not have before it the extensive personal and unofficial correspondence between Stark and Kimmel in 1941. In his letters, Stark kept up a drumfire of warnings about the possibility of attack and of his view of the deteriorating diplomatic relations between Japan and the United States.

The court did find, however, that even if Stark had telephoned Kimmel on the morning of 7 December to tell him that a break in diplomatic relations was imminent "there was no action open, no means available to Admiral Kimmel which would have stopped the attack, or which could have had other than negligible bearing on its outcome."[10]

The other finding of fact (number XIX) was a variation. The court felt that Stark should have transmitted the latest information available in Washington to Kimmel and that failure to do so was a military error.[11] In reaching this finding, the court ignored the telegram containing the 14-part message and the one o'clock delivery message about which Marshall and Stark conferred and which Marshall sent. Stark asked Marshall to have it delivered to Kimmel in addition to the army command. Although an unfortunate set of circumstances delayed its delivery, and it might have been sent through navy channels, the indisputable fact remains that Stark did send this information to Hawaii shortly after he received it.

Based on these findings of fact, the Court of Inquiry concluded that Stark "failed to display the sound judgment expected of him." However, the report added, "The Court is further of the opinion that, had this important information been conveyed to Admiral Kimmel, it is a matter of conjecture as to what action he would have taken." In conclusion, the court found that "no offenses have been committed nor serious blame incurred on the part of any person or persons in the naval service."[12]

Although the report was hardly an endorsement of Stark's performance in the critical period immediately preceding the Japanese attack on Pearl Harbor, Stark fared much better than did General George C. Marshall in the report of the Army Pearl Harbor Board of Investigation, the proceedings of which had been held during approximately the same period as those before the Navy Court of Inquiry.

The Army report stated flatly that Marshall "failed in his relations with the Hawaiian Department" in four instances. Three of them dealt with failure to transmit the latest and sufficient information to Hawaii. The fourth dealt with his failure "to investigate and determine the state of readiness" in the Hawaiian Department. It was a serious charge to level against the Army Chief of Staff who continued to hold that position throughout World War II.[13]

Following well-established procedure, the report of the Court of Inquiry was first reviewed by the Navy's Judge Advocate General, Rear Admiral T. L. Gatch, before it was sent to King and then to the Secretary of the Navy, James V. Forrestal. Gatch noted that the court concluded, but did not say specifically, that the evidence adduced failed to show any causal connection between Stark's failure to send certain information to Kimmel and the damage wrought by the Japanese at Pearl Harbor. It was an important point.

On 6 November 1944, King signed an endorsement written by Vice Admiral Richard S. Edwards that severely faulted Stark. He concluded that Stark should be relegated to a position not requiring the exercise of superior judgment. The gist of King's comments was that Stark had not provided Kimmel with an "adequate summary of information available in Washington." Specifically, he said Stark did not inform Kimmel of the American note of 26 November; that Kimmel was not informed of the Japanese request for information about ships in Pearl Harbor; that Stark "failed to appreciate the significance" of the 1:00 P.M. message; that Kimmel was not informed of the execution of the "Winds Message"; and finally, that there was a "certain sameness of tenor" of the information that Stark sent to Kimmel.[14] The subsequent Congressional investigation showed that the execution of the "Winds Message" (indicating where the Japanese would strike) was never received in Washington.

It was a stinging rebuke. Eventually King persuaded Forrestal to concur in his endorsement. Meanwhile, Forrestal directed Admiral H. Kent Hewitt to conduct his own inquiry into certain additional aspects. Stark knew nothing of the court's report or of what King and Forrestal were doing about it.

Only a few days after signing his endorsement, King, on 10 November 1944, sent Stark a handwritten letter, sealed in an envelope on which he wrote "To be opened only by Admiral H. R. Stark. EJK." He wrote,

I feel that I owe it to you to let you know now the probable outcome of the Pearl Harbor Inquiry. I do this without knowledge of the Secretary or of anyone else.

You have been found at fault for not keeping Kimmel more fully informed as to critical developments, in fact, a reading of your dispatches to him have a degree of sameness which was not indicative of the increasingly critical situation as seen in Washington at the time.

It looks as if you were concerned—very much about protecting the source of "Magic."

Secretary Forrestal is to exchange views with Secretary Stimson very soon. I know it to be the Secretary's intention to talk to the President within a few days. There is nothing actionable against you or Kimmel. No G.C.M. The evidence will not sustain any charges—but it may be that you will be placed on the retired list as of 30 November, ostensibly because your 64th birthday is November 12.

I know that the foregoing must be unwelcome to you—it is also unwelcome and distressing to me to have to write it—but I do not intend that you shall learn of things after the fashion of "a bolt from the blue." I have told you the "worst."

Remain Cheerful!

With best wishes, as always

King[15]

It is a remarkable letter. King implied that "the worst" originated with the court. In this respect he deliberately misled Stark. On the other hand, he was under no obligation to inform Stark of how things were going; his concern that Stark not learn of the bad news as a bolt from the blue showed some kindness and consideration.

Stark replied on 21 November in a similar handwritten letter, to be opened only by King. Like King's letter, this one illustrates the author's personality and character. He said,

Thanks for your personal note. I am glad to be warned—appreciate your telling me "the worst."

Meanwhile, I shall go ahead 4 bells as usual.

If it be felt necessary to have the blow described, I shall of course have to take it and shall try to remain cheerful.

I do hope that should you and the President feel my retirement at this time is necessary and it be coincident with, or immediately following release of the findings of the Court, it will not be construed in the public mind as admission that the blame for P.H. is laid to the Navy.

As a naval officer I am, as you well know, most reluctant to have the "rap" for P.H. fall on the Navy—more especially as the defense of P.H. was an Army responsibility.

Am so glad the "nothing actionable" vis G.C.M. against Kimmel. All good wishes

Keep Cheerful,

Sincerely,

Betty[16]

November came and went. Stark's 64th birthday was celebrated in London by his staff and by the high command of the Royal Navy, but there was no suggestion from Washington that he would be retired. Stark next heard the report of the court of inquiry mentioned when he went to Malta in January 1945, to meet President Roosevelt before the summit conference at Yalta. When Stark went to call on Roosevelt, Harry Hopkins asked him if he had seen the report of the Navy Court of Inquiry. Stark said he had not. Hopkins then said, "The President is mad as a hornet over them [the endorsements by King and Forrestal] and is going to write his own endorsement." Roosevelt looked awful and Stark wondered how long he could go on. Stark felt like saying, "Harry, don't let him wait too long." But he restrained himself.[17] The President died suddenly on 12 April 1945 without having written the endorsement.

When Stark returned home in August 1945, it was clear that he would retire at as yet some unspecified date in the near future. He had reached the statutory age for retirement the previous November, and saw clearly that his moment had passed and that the leadership of the navy was now in other hands. His return to Washington was scarcely noticed. Considering his seniority as a four star admiral with six years in grade, his previous post as Chief of Naval Operations and his most recent post in London, it is surprising that the Navy Department failed to give him at least some official greeting. He simply arrived in New York on 21 August on board the *Queen Mary* and flew to Washington, D.C., the next day.

In another sense it is not at all surprising that the Navy Department gave scant attention to his return. For one thing there were other admirals, such as Nimitz, Halsey, and Spruance, who had distinguished themselves in wartime combat commands. Stark, on the other hand, held an administrative and logistics command, which never quite captured the imagination of the naval establishment or excited much interest in it. The real reason, however, was that Stark returned from London under the cloud of the Court of Inquiry. King and Forrestal knew about it. Stark was out of favor in the Navy Department. This explains the U.S. Navy's ingratitude and failure to render him even simple military honors on arrival home.

The day after his return home, Stark reported his arrival to the Navy Department and then drove with his daughter, Mary Semans, to Lake Carey where he was reunited with Mrs. Stark at their summer home. A few days later the storm broke.

President Truman released the complete reports of the Navy Court of Inquiry and the Army Pearl Harbor Board of Investigation. A banner headline in *The New York Times* for 30 August 1945 proclaimed MacArthur's arrival in Japan and "censure" for Stark and Marshall.

Newspapers carried extensive accounts, as well as the texts of the report of the Navy Court of Inquiry and the lengthy endorsements by King and Forrestal. Stark was publicly faulted for failure to transmit information to Kimmel in the period immediately preceding the Japanese attack on Pearl Harbor. During the week before Labor Day, he carefully read the newspapers and mentally digested what had been made public.

Stark kept his feelings to himself. Nevertheless, he was surprised and shocked at the severity of King's endorsements, which Forrestal supported. In his endorsement dated 6 November 1944 on the report of the Court of Inquiry, King recommended to the Secretary of the Navy that Stark and Kimmel be relegated "to positions in which lack of superior judgment may not result in future errors." He did not recommend trial by general court-martial. In his endorsement dated 13 August 1945 on the report of Admiral Hewitt's further Pearl Harbor investigation, King expressed a similar opinion to the Secretary of the Navy. He pointed out that because Stark and Kimmel had been relegated to their present positions, no further action was necessary.[18]

It was bad enough that King said what he did, but the fact that King had deliberately misled him in his letter of 10 November 1944 hurt. From Stark's standpoint, the man he had rescued from the professional oblivion of the General Board and later recommended to succeed him as Chief of Naval Operations had smeared him.

Moreover, King's pretension to objectivity was marred. He had first-hand knowledge of the events for which he faulted Stark. He had been in Stark's office frequently in the days before the Japanese struck. He was in Stark's office the day the "war warning" message was sent. He and Stark discussed it and other dispatches and the intelligence upon which they were based. As the Atlantic Fleet commander, King had the opportunity to urge sending more information, whatever that might have been. He certainly could have protested a "sameness of tenor" if he had detected it at the time. The fact is that he did not. While Stark, and his principal assistants, Rear Admirals Royal K. Ingersoll and Richmond K. Turner, wrestled with the important question of what to tell the fleet commanders and how to phrase it to convey the gravity of the situation, King remained silent and acquiesced in what they did.

Reaction from Stark's friends was not long in coming. Turner, whose independence of mind was well known, stood squarely behind Stark and offered to do whatever he could to help. Captain Scott Umsted at the Naval War College told Stark that the general opinion on the staff there was that he had been "rottenly treated."[19]

The most outspoken statement of all came from Hart, now a United States Senator from Connecticut. He wrote to Stark, "I feel like telling Ernie that he is just a plain SKUNK."[20]

Stark's friends in the Royal Navy were astounded. They could not understand how, after Stark's "magnificent work over here," the U.S. Navy could cast a blight on him. They thought it "detestable ungentlemanly behavior" and a "deplorable lack of recognition" shown for his services.[21]

Despite what Stark's friends and supporters at home and abroad might have thought, the notion that the Japanese attack on Pearl Harbor was somehow the fault of the navy was firmly etched in the public mind. Therefore, Stark, as head of the navy at the time of the attack, must bear at least part of the responsibility and blame for it. King's censure of Stark supported this concept. The public was not informed of King's silence when the dispatches in question were sent.

Stark's case was not helped by the fact that during the war he was largely out of the public eye and that his contributions were administrative, logistical, and political. Marshall was in the public eye during the war and was regarded as a hero, despite what the Army Pearl Harbor Board reported. This is at least a partial explanation of why Marshall's reputation was not tainted as was Stark's.

By dwelling on the narrow point of what he thought were Stark's shortcomings, King missed the larger and more fundamental issue. The army was clearly responsible for the defense of Pearl Harbor and failed to defend it. In this sense, Pearl Harbor was an army disaster. By failing to point out this fundamental fact, King did the navy great harm.

For some unexplained reason, there was little if any interest in the Navy Department to explain in the ensuing Congressional investigation that the disaster at Pearl Harbor was not a naval disaster, but an army disaster. There was no question that it was the army's responsibility to defend the naval base at Pearl Harbor and the army did not do it. Instead, the prevailing attitude in the Navy Department was that this investigation—like the Navy Court of Inquiry—was primarily the concern of Admirals Kimmel and Stark.

This attitude first manifested itself in assigning Stark to a small office in an obscure part of the building. Clearly, if Stark were to give meaningful testimony on the complex events preceding the attack on Pearl Harbor, he would need staff assistance in his preparations. Instead of making the considerable navy bureaucracy available to Stark, the Navy Department assigned Yeoman Louise Wolstoncroft as his secretarial assistant. Rear Admiral (formerly Commodore) Flanigan had left London in March 1945 to become Director, Naval Transportation Service in Washington. Richmond had resumed his place on Flanigan's staff in April, although he continued to assist Stark in the collection of documents. When Stark returned to Washington in August, Flanigan relieved Richmond of his duties and sent him to Admiral Stark's office as his assistant. This was an unofficial arrangement, for which the Navy Department deserves no credit. As far as King and Forrestal were concerned, it was up to Stark and Wolstoncroft to defend the Office of the Chief of Naval Operations.

Richmond was later able to catch one of his partners, Lieutenant Malcolm Johnson, on his way to discharge and have him retained long enough to assist in the preparation for the Congressional investigation.

As they had during the proceedings of the Court of Inquiry, Stark and Richmond, in particular, experienced great difficulties in obtaining copies of navy documents and other exhibits that were necessary for the preparation of Stark's testimony. Commander John F. Baecher, USNR, a special assistant to Secretary Forrestal, was supposed to procure whatever documents Stark needed, but he continually interposed objections and excuses as to why they were not available or why copies could not be made. His lack of cooperation was unreasonable, unjustified, and extremely irritating to Stark's assistants. Richmond believed that his attitude was a result of instructions from higher authority. Yet, in a strange way, Baecher's attitude had a positive effect on Stark's preparations. It made him and his small staff work harder and search more diligently. As a result they felt they obtained more than they would have if Baecher had given them his full cooperation.

During the period of preparation, Captain Neil Deitrich, who had been on Stark's staff in London, became Flag Secretary to King in Washington. He appreciated Stark's situation and, without disturbing his close relationship with King, he was helpful to Stark and his staff in turning up some of the hard-to-find files and papers relevant to the investigation.

The navy's attitude and lack of cooperation with its former Chief of Naval Operations was almost the exact opposite of what the army was doing. Marshall was Chief of Staff at the time of the Japanese attack and he held that position in 1945. The army presented a solid phalanx to the outside world in its successful effort to protect the reputation of George C. Marshall and to obscure the army's responsibility to defend Pearl Harbor. Marshall had an extensive legal and secretarial staff working full time on the preparation of his testimony. They had complete cooperation and support from the War Department.

The Navy Court of Inquiry was a rehearsal for the Joint Congressional Committee that investigated the attack on Pearl Harbor. The resolution constituting the Joint Committee was enacted in September 1945; public hearings started in November 1945 and continued until the end of May 1946. The end of the war meant that secret intelligence could be made public, if in the wisdom of Congress and members of the Congressional Committee its publication would be in the national interest. The most sensational secret of all was that the United States cracked the Japanese codes before Pearl Harbor and was reading their most sensitive and secret diplomatic and military messages. Known as Magic, this intelligence was obviously invaluable. When the decision was made to publish these intercepts, there were those in the navy and elsewhere in the government who thought the action bordered on treason. Following their revelation, nearly every major power immediately changed its codes. The end of the war also meant that many key military and naval officers who were busy fighting the war and could not testify before the previous investigating tribunals were now available. The hearings were front page news for months.

Stark began his preparations in earnest for the forthcoming Congressional hearings when he returned to Washington in early September. He retained a leading Washington lawyer, Hugh Obear, of the firm Douglas, Obear, and Campbell, as his counsel. Obear accompanied him to hearings and sat with him at the counsel table. Richmond, who was working full time to assist Stark, was joined by a friend of the Stark family, James E. Webb, a lawyer who had recently completed his service as a major in the U.S. Marine Corps. (In later years Webb became Director, Bureau of the Budget, Under Secretary of State, and the Administrator of NASA.)

Preparations were extensive and thorough. While Richmond sought documents and other materials from the Navy Department and skirmished with Baecher, Stark corresponded with the men who had been with him in Washington in 1940 and 1941. Mrs. Frank Knox wrote to him about the late secretary's whereabouts on 7 December 1941. In mid-October, Stark and Richmond went to San Francisco to discuss at length the events leading up to the Japanese attack on Pearl Harbor with Admirals Richmond K. Turner and Royal K. Ingersoll, both of whom were in Stark's office at the time—Turner as head of the War Plans Division and Ingersoll as Assistant Chief of Naval Operations.

Stark's small legal staff was joined on occasion by his son-in-law, Edwin W. Semans, who was a lawyer in Philadelphia. These lawyers conducted numerous dry runs with Stark to prepare him as a witness before the Joint Congressional Committee. Stark made it abundantly clear that he did not want them to pull any punches just because he was an admiral. Their preparation of him as a witness was strict and even rough at times when they bluntly told him to stay on the point of the questions they posed and encouraged him to discipline his answers. Notwithstanding the assistance from counsel, Stark made decisions as to content, order, and emphasis. He would state only what he could remember or what could be documented by his staff's research.

After nearly four months of preparation, Stark was called to testify. When he took the witness stand on New Year's Eve, 1945, Stark read his prepared statement well and with great effect. He went into considerable detail regarding the discharge of his duties as Chief of Naval Operations with reference to the expansion of the entire naval establishment, its strength and efficiency; to plans for the use of the fleet in war; to assignment of forces available in accordance with war plans; and to keeping the fleet commanders informed of important political and military developments affecting them.[22]

He also put into the public record all of the relevant documents he had in his possession and his best recollection as he had refreshed it over several months. Among these documents were the personal, but semiofficial, letters he and Kimmel exchanged throughout 1941. This correspondence shows both men to their advantage: Stark frankly and candidly informed Kimmel of the latest thinking in Washington, warned him of the impending war with Japan, and honestly told him what was being done to prepare for it. Kimmel unhesitatingly told Stark what he needed, what he was doing with the forces at his disposal and asked Stark for clarifications of policy. Stark left nothing out of his testimony consciously or deliberately. If something were omitted, it was because he simply could not remember it.

After completing this thorough and lengthy statement, Stark was subjected to cross examination by counsel for the committee and then by its members. Most members of the committee had been prosecuting attorneys at one time; Richmond was apprehensive that under cross-examination Stark would bog down in a mass of detail and not get his points across. Richmond admitted later that his fears were completely unjustified; and that Stark's performance surpassed Richmond's expectations. He attributed Stark's performance not so much to the preparation he and the other lawyers gave him, but to the estimation that Flanigan made of him, "A damn good man."

Throughout his preparation and his testimony, Stark steadfastly refused to attack anyone or even to appear to point a finger at anyone. He consistently rejected advice from his lawyers that he emphasize the army's responsibility to defend Pearl Harbor, whether or not any ships had been in port. He refused to express any opinions that would reflect on Kimmel or anyone else. He felt that the only honorable and gentlemanly thing to do was to stick to the facts, rather than to give present impressions of what happened or to engage in conjecture as to what might have happened if some things had been done differently. When asked by Committee members to express an opinion as to what someone else should have done or whether someone else performed properly, he declined. He said he would present all the facts as he knew them; any opinions or conclusions were for the Committee to draw.

He felt strongly, and possibly naively, but correctly that setting the record straight in his testimony would result in the committee reaching fair and just conclusions. His character was such that he could do nothing else. He refused to attack anyone, or even to attempt to shift any blame. He and Marshall remained good friends and consulted at times about details in preparing their respective testimony. At one time Stark and Kimmel had been good friends, but Kimmel's summary relief and subsequent treatment had made him bitter. Kimmel's bitterness saddened Stark, although he understood it. He would do nothing to add to Kimmel's burden by expressing opinions or trying to second guess him.

By the end of January 1946, Stark completed the bulk of his testimony before the Joint Congressional Committee, except in one respect. There was one gap: He simply could not recall where he was on the evening of 6 December 1941. Although the fact was of questionable relevance, his inability to recall it bothered him and some members of the committee as well. Despite trying to refresh his recollection by the study of countless documents relating to a complex series of events, Stark drew a blank when it came to what he had done on that evening. In May 1946, his good friends, Captain and Mrs. Harold D. Krick, visited him in Washington. Over dinner Stark casually mentioned his inability to remember where he was that evening.

Krick spoke up and said that he and his wife dined with the Starks on the evening of 6 December 1941. Then they went to a performance of *The Student Prince* at the National Theater. When they returned to Stark's quarters on Observatory Hill, a steward told Stark that Roosevelt had called earlier on the private telephone line. Krick recalled that Stark went upstairs, presumably to return the call, and then rejoined his guests. Still, Stark did not recall talking to the President and felt he would have remembered it if he had. Nevertheless, he notified Senator Alben W. Barkley, chairman of the Joint Congressional Committee. Barkley called a special session at which Krick testified.[23]

When Stark finished testifying, there was no further reason for him to remain on active duty. He retired from active naval service on 1 April 1946, after nearly 47 years of active duty. He retired in the grade of admiral, the highest rank he held on active duty, with neither fanfare nor ceremony. After a few courtesy calls on the top navy brass, he just went home.

He found it hard to realize that he had retired. The past 47 years had been full and happy years. "Fair and square" was the way he described them. He confided to his diary, "My feelings (are) much mixed, but nothing but gratefulness for the opportunity to give what I had to my country—and always with the wish to give more."[24]

When he arrived home, he was deeply touched by a telephone call from his old friend "Tommy" Hart, "a fine bunch of fiber" he called Hart. Later Richmond and William Leckie from the COMNAVEU staff came by for dinner. That evening Secretary Forrestal telephoned and asked him to call at his office the next morning.

It was an extremely pleasant meeting in the Secretary's office. Forrestal was particularly anxious to wish Stark good luck in his retirement and to express appreciation for his testimony before the congressional committee. Stark's testimony impressed Forrestal. He wanted Stark to know that he thought it helped both Stark's reputation and the navy as a whole. Naturally, Stark was delighted to hear it.[25]

More good news came at the end of July 1946 when the majority report of the Joint Congressional Committee was published. It was an exhaustive and generally well-balanced report, covering nearly 500 pages. It vindicated Stark and successfully refuted the findings of the Navy Court of Inquiry and the censorious endorsements written by King and Forrestal. Both had censured Stark for "failure" to give Kimmel "adequate summary of information available in Washington." The Joint Congressional Committee reviewed the dispatches and correspondence sent to Kimmel and concluded "that he was fully informed concerning the progressive deterioration of relations with Japan and was amply warned of the imminence of war with that nation."[26]

In regard to the "war warning" dispatch of 27 November 1941, the Committee concluded that by ordering Kimmel to take "an appropriate defensive deployment preparatory to carrying out the tasks assigned to WPL-46," Stark indicated that Kimmel's situation was subject to possible danger requiring action under the war plan. Since Washington had informed Kimmel of its best estimate of where the major enemy effort would come, it was Kimmel's responsibility to be prepared for the worst contingency. For the fleet based at Pearl Harbor, that clearly meant an attack on Pearl Harbor.[27] Moreover, the overwhelming preponderance of testimony by both army and navy officers was that the Japanese destruction of codes in the first week of December meant that war was imminent. Stark informed Kimmel of the destruction of the codes, but Kimmel failed to grasp its significance.[28]

Specifically, where King faulted Stark for not sending Kimmel information about the American note of 26 November, the committee did not. They concluded that even if Kimmel had all the diplomatic intelligence available in Washington, it would have shown that "there was only the barest possibility that Japan would continue the negotiations; for the messages indicate throughout a conflicting and variable disposition by Japan with respect to pursuance of the negotiations and her desire for peace."[29] The committee concluded that the purpose of the "war warning" dispatch of 27 November was to make clear beyond question the seriousness of the situation. By implication, the conclusions conclusively refuted King's allegation about the "sameness of tenor" of the dispatches Stark sent to Kimmel.

King had faulted Stark for not informing Kimmel of the so-called berthing plan messages in which the Japanese consul in Hawaii was asked to report on ships in Pearl Harbor. King concluded that this dispatch indicated Japanese interest in Pearl Harbor as a possible target. The committee disagreed with King.[30] They were unable to conclude that this dispatch pointed to an attack on Pearl Harbor, because at about the same time the Japanese showed similar interest in Puget Sound, Panama, the Philippines, Singapore, and Batavia. The committee felt, however, that such dispatches "should have received careful consideration and created a serious question as to their significance."[31]

After a careful and thorough examination of all the evidence, the committee concluded that "no genuine 'winds' message in execution of the code and applying to the United States was received by the War or Navy Departments prior to the attack on December 7, 1941."[32] This conclusion flatly contradicted King's assertion that there was such a dispatch. In this particular, the evidence was simply against King.

Elsewhere in their report, the committee endorsed Stark's performance of his duty. In so doing, the committee had before it not only the entire proceedings of the Navy Court of Inquiry and the Hewitt investigation, but also the proceedings of Admiral Hart's investigation, the proceedings of the Army Pearl Harbor Board and the several supplementary army and navy investigations. This portion of the report is worth quoting at length, because it places in perspective not only what Stark did, but also the duties of the Army Chief of Staff and how both Stark and Marshall responded.

They [Stark and Marshall] had the duty of alerting our outposts in view of the critical situation in our relations with Japan in the days before December 7, and of informing them of probable enemy action. In the dispatch of November 27, sent Admiral Kimmel and Admiral Hart, the commander in chief of the Asiatic Fleet, there was outlined what at the time was regarded and appeared to be the major strategic effort of the enemy. The Japanese major effort did follow the course outlined in the dispatch. Pearl Harbor was not known to be a point of Japanese attack but it was known that such an attack was a possibility and both responsible commanders in Hawaii were accordingly ordered to take action contemplated to meet this possibility.

o   o   o

Hawaii was but one of many points of concern to General Marshall, the Chief of Staff, and Admiral Stark, the Chief of Naval Operations. . . . Theirs was the obligation of mapping the strategy of global war, of advising and counselling the President and others on military and naval matters, of following and encouraging the progress of preparation for defense in the event of war, of outlining and justifying to the Congress the manifold needs of the Army and Navy, of overall responsibility for many military and naval outposts and interests, of disposing and allocating the scanty materials of war consistent with the overwhelming demands and requirements from many quarters, and of performing the innumerable functions of the Chief of Staff and Chief of Naval Operations in a democracy that was all too slowly preparing itself aganst the inevitable day of war. Such diversity and magnitude of responsibilities is to be distinguished from that of the outpost commander with his singleness of purpose and well-defined sphere of activity. It was the duty of General Marshall and Admiral Stark to alert our military and naval garrisons which they attempted to do and felt assured they had done. To superimpose the administrative burden of supervising details would be to enmesh them in such a confusing and bewildering network of detail as to defeat the very purpose for which the positions of Chief of Staff and Chief of Naval Operations were created.[33]

It was a ringing affirmative statement for the historical record of how both Stark and Marshall perceived their duties and performed them. It remained for Stark to clear his navy record of the blemish King and Forrestal placed on it.

King's criticisms of Stark, which Forrestal endorsed, still rankled him. Not only did he feel they were unjust, but the Congressional Committee disproved them. Yet they remained. Stark was concerned about his record, because it "is about all we bring out of the navy at the end of a life of service," along with friendships. To have his record "at the very last and for the first time, given an all time smear," which so many thought was unwarranted, was galling.[34]

No matter how much this blemish irritated and vexed him, Stark studiously avoided doing anything that might appear as campaigning for some kind of redress. He let others take up his cause. One of the first was his old friend Admiral Hart, who in 1946 was a United States senator from Connecticut. Hart set out to convince Forrestal to change his endorsement on the Report of the Navy Court of Inquiry in light of the conclusions of the Joint Congressional Committee.

About a month after the Joint Congressional Committee published its report, Hart had dinner alone with Forrestal. This meeting was in response to a letter Hart sent to Forrestal. Hart pointed out that Stark was treated far more severely by navy reviewing authorities than the army treated Marshall. He suggested that Forrestal reconsider the navy's action in Stark's case to bring him "into better balance with his opposite number in the Army."[35]

Hart obtained no definite promise of action from Forrestal, but Forrestal admitted that he had made a "decided mistake" in his endorsement. Although he remained discreet, Forrestal made it very clear to Hart that he felt King had given him wrong advice. Not only did King give him wrong advice, but he did so forcefully. Forrestal sincerely regretted having succumbed to King's insistence on the statements that Stark be relegated to a position in which he would not have to exercise superior judgment.

Forrestal's regret was well founded. King's recommendation on 6 November 1944 that Stark be relegated to a position not requiring the exercise of superior judgment was ridiculous. By that time, Stark had served with distinction as Commander, United States Naval Forces, Europe and as Commander TWELFTH Fleet. It is probably true that Stark's orders to COMNAVEU were dictated by Roosevelt, but Stark's designation as TWELFTH Fleet commander on 1 October 1943 was made by King. Before the 13 August 1945 endorsement was made, Stark had been decorated by King George VI for his service. On the same day that King's 13 August 1945 endorsement was signed, Stark was being honored by the Board of Admiralty in London.[36] In August 1945, King had also recommended Stark for a third Distinguished Service Medal "for exceptionally meritorious service as Commander of United States Naval Forces in Europe from April 30, 1942 to April 15, 1945 and as Commander, TWELFTH Fleet from October 1, 1943 to August 15, 1945."[37] Eisenhower awarded Stark the U.S. Army Distinguished Service Medal in 1944. He summarized Stark's naval accomplishments by saying, "Admiral Stark was responsible for the planning, preparation and coordination of the United States naval aspects of the launching of the campaign for the liberation of Europe." He lauded Stark's "keen foresight and exceptional administrative ability."[38]

It was clear to Hart that if there were no other considerations, Forrestal would change his endorsement. However, there was considerable concern in the Navy Department in 1946 that if Forrestal wrote a more favorable endorsement for Stark, Kimmel would come out with new demands for a general court-martial. At that time none of Forrestal's advisers in the Navy Department wanted to stir up anew the question of Pearl Harbor. They had had enough. So had Forrestal.

Hart was optimistic that the wrong against Stark would eventually get some measure of correction. He hoped that there would be a full measure. He advised Stark for the immediate future that he should do nothing but be patient and wait. He felt that he had pressed that matter as far as it was safe to do.[39]

There was nothing for Stark to do except to maintain a dignified silence. The injustice of the endorsements was not all that bothered him. The Navy Department had taken no action on King's recommendation that he be awarded his third Navy Distinguished Service Medal for wartime service in London. Although King had been extremely severe in his review of the report of the Navy Court of Inquiry and concluded that Stark should not hold a position requiring the exercise of superior judgment, at the same time he recommended that Stark receive the DSM for service requiring the exercise of superior judgment. It was an inexplicable inconsistency.

Normally Stark did not "give a damn about medals," as he told a close friend.[40] But, he did not like to be singled out by the navy as being about the only naval officer of rank in Europe during World War II whom the navy ignored. Apparently the King and Forrestal endorsements stalled consideration of the award in the Navy Department Board of Decorations and Medals. This example of bureaucratic cowardice may have offended Stark, but, as Vice Admiral Sir Geoffrey Blake, formerly the Admiralty's Liaison Officer to him in London, said, it mystified and infuriated Eisenhower, Harriman, and Stark's British friends. They knew what he had done in London and they were at a loss to understand why the Navy Department refused to recognize Stark's services.

Nothing happened for two years. Then in July 1948 King recanted part of his endorsement. In a letter to Secretary of the Navy John L. Sullivan, King said he had reconsidered his endorsement. Certain portions of it "stand out as not being in accord with the realities of the situation existing when I signed it." Specifically, he referred to his conclusions that Stark failed to exercise superior judgment and that he should be relegated to a position where he would not have to exercise it. He admitted that Stark's performance of duty in London "was in all respects outstanding." For this reason, "the suggestion that he be relegated to a subordinate position in which superior judgment would not be required seems to me now to have been singularly inappropriate." Continuing, King told Sullivan that if he were writing the endorsement again or if he had expressed himself more accurately at the time, the paragraphs in question would have read differently. King provided the revised text of these paragraphs, which concluded that "assignment to other duties, then and now, represented appropriate administrative action."[41]

King noted that Stark was awarded the Distinguished Service Medal for his work as Chief of Naval Operations up to March 1942. He asked Sullivan to approve his recommendation of August 1945 that Stark receive the DSM for his work in London. Sullivan needed no urging. He formally concurred with King's letter, ordered it made an official part of Stark's service record and saw that Stark received his third DSM.

It was a welcome, but a partial, victory for Stark. King had changed his mind about his conclusions, but he refused to acknowledge that the grounds upon which he based his original conclusions had been disproved. Sullivan never knew why King changed his mind, but he took great pleasure in presenting the DSM to Stark in the presence of Fleet Admirals King and Leahy and Admirals Louis Denfeld and Arthur W. Radford. Afterwards he invited Stark and his family to have dinner aboard the *Sequoia*, the secretary's official yacht.[42]

King's change of mind was almost the last official act in this voluminous official record of the investigations of the attack on Pearl Harbor. His biographer says it was the only time he ever admitted he was wrong. At least King removed, for record purposes, the stinging endorsement he wrote in 1944. Stark's friends were optimistic that Forrestal, too, would change his endorsement, thus removing the last and only blemish on Stark's record. Unfortunately, before he acted Forrestal leapt to his death from a window at the Bethesda Naval Hospital on 22 May 1949.

It remained for Secretary Sullivan to close the record. This he did on 26 May 1949 when he officially concurred in King's statement about Stark, saying; "In view of the fact that such action (King's amendment) did not specifically amend the endorsement placed on this record by the Secretary of the Navy, this memorandum is for the purpose of confirming that concurrence."[43]

16

RETIREMENT

Retirement did not come suddenly to Stark. It crept up on him. When he returned to Washington in August 1945, it was clear that for all practical purposes his naval career was largely behind him. He remained on active duty, technically assigned to the Secretary of the Navy, for the duration of the extensive Pearl Harbor hearings. The preparation for his testimony was a heavy burden, and the time he spent testifying was a time of strain and stress. But he came through his final task with flying colors. Finally, by early spring there was no further reason for him to remain on active duty and he retired with little fanfare.

There were loose ends to be taken care of. The greatest one was to take Mrs. Stark to England. She had patiently waited at home in Washington and at Lake Carey during the war years while Stark was in London, and for years before that she had put up with the inconveniences and difficulties of a navy wife. Now it was Stark's turn to give her a well-deserved trip. Besides, Stark wanted his friends in Britain to meet her and he wanted to show her some of the places in England of which he had grown so fond.

There was another purpose, too, for this trip. Oxford University wanted to award him an honorary degree of Doctor of Civil Law. In 1945 when the news was announced in London that he would be going home, the university informed him that the honor had been awarded to him and that it would be conferred on 25 October 1945. Unfortunately, Stark could not be present at that time. Because the rules of the university required him to be present, it was arranged that he would return to England for the next Encaenia, to be held on 26 June 1946.

The Starks sailed from New York on the *Queen Mary* on the first of June.[1] From Southampton they drove to London, stopping at Romany in Virginia Water, where Stark showed his lady the gracious country house where he had enjoyed many quiet, restful weekends. Although Stark had leased it at his own expense during the war, the U.S. Navy later bought the estate for the use of Stark's successors in London.

It was a whirlwind visit to London, which made Mrs. Stark feel like a debutante. They stayed at the Connaught, one of the finest hotels in London. Admiral and Lady Cunningham were among the first of Stark's large coterie of friends to extend gracious hospitality to them. The Admiralty saw to it that the Starks were seated in the Saluting Stand near the Royal Family for the magnificent Victory Parade formally celebrating the victory of the British Commonwealth over the Axis.

A few days later they were seated on the dais at the Guildhall when the Lord Mayor of London formally presented the Freedom of the City of London to Admiral Cunningham, Field Marshal Sir Alan Brooke and Air Marshal Portal. They lunched at the House of Lords as guests of Stark's friend and intimate, Vice Admiral Sir Geoffrey Blake, who had been the Admiralty's liaison officer to him. Later they attended a debate in the House of Commons.

Though their official engagements were extensive, there was time for Stark to show his beloved Kit the sights of London. He took her to St. Paul's Cathedral, the Tower of London, and Westminster. They toured the country to Dover on an incomparably fine day. They saw the splendid cathedral at Canterbury, where little more than a year before Stark had been one of the distinguished guests at the enthronement of Geoffrey Fischer as Archbishop. From Dover they went to Stratford and then to Oxford.

At the ancient University at Oxford, the ceremony conferring the honorary DCL followed the ancient custom and was conducted entirely in Latin. Stark was duly robed in an academic gown and after suitable instruction followed the prescribed procedure. It was a splendid occasion and his British friends drew great satisfaction from the award of still another honor to him. Stark was not the only American to be so honored that day. Fleet Admiral Ernest J. King also received an honorary DCL.[2]

Their trip to England concluded with a visit to Cliveden, where at long last Mrs. Stark could meet the Astors and see where the Admiral had felt so much at home. On the last day of June they sailed for home. Sir Geoffrey Blake was on the pier to see them off.

Stark settled comfortably into retirement. He spent summers in the unpretentious and extremely liveable family house overlooking Lake Carey in the Pennsylvania mountains near Wilkes-Barre. His daughters Mary and Kewpie, along with their husbands and children, were frequent visitors at Lake Carey and at the Starks' home in Washington. He kept in touch with his many friends, many of whom were in high places. When George Marshall was Secretary of State and then Secretary of Defense, Stark offered him a few days of peace and quiet at Lake Carey. He followed Mountbatten's rise to Viceroy of India and then to First Sea Lord with interest. In 1953, when his friend Dwight Eisenhower became President, Stark sent him a four leaf clover, which the new President acknowledged with gratitude. He resumed correspondence with his old friend, Admiral Kichisaburo Nomura, whom he had last seen on a Sunday afternoon in November 1941.

Stark devoted himself to charities and causes that needed both his help and his financial acumen. He worked with the Navy Relief Society, which prospered as a result of his efforts. He took an interest in Wilkes College in Wilkes-Barre, Pennsylvania, where in 1936 he donated to the college the house he inherited from his sister. He served as chairman of the Wilkes College Board of Trustees from 1959 to 1964, during which time he helped raise substantial sums of money for this four-year liberal arts college. Later the Stark Learning Center was named for him. Completed in 1975, it is an impressive complex of classrooms, a large lecture hall, and faculty offices.

In 1955 the Trustees of Colonial Williamsburg presented the first Williamsburg Award to Winston Churchill "For his unexampled contribution in our time to the historic struggle of men to live free and self-respected in a just society." The actual presentation was in December at a dinner held at Draper's Hall in London. The guest list was a roster of every living civil and military official of importance in Great Britain during World War II. Stark took unabashed pleasure at seeing so many of his old friends once again. In deference to his wartime position, he was seated at the head table.[3]

Stark's class at the Naval Academy, 1903, was a closely knit group of men. Their fiftieth reunion in 1953 at the Army-Navy Club in Washington was a gala affair. In 1966, when Rear Admiral A. H. Van Keuren died, they decided to close the books on the Class of 1903. The balance of $121.69 in the class treasury was donated to charity. At that time Stark and six of his classmates survived, including Vice Admiral Walter S. Anderson, whom Stark succeeded as captain of the battleship *West Virginia* and who served as a rear admiral under him, and Admiral Samuel M. "Mike" Robinson, who, as Chief of the Bureau of Ships, was responsible for building the vast naval armada Stark succeeded in getting Congress to authorize and fund when he was Chief of Naval Operations.[4]

Stark's final honor came in 1965 when his friend Sir Winston Churchill died. Queen Elizabeth II invited Stark to attend the funeral as a guest of the Royal Family. Unfortunately, Stark, who had just celebrated his 84th birthday a few weeks before, was in bed with the flu and both Mrs. Stark and his doctor flatly refused to let him go to London.

A good and happy man, Stark wished to share his joy in living and his thrill at being a navy man with everyone. He cherished and cultivated old friends. Every year on 12 November he celebrated his birthday with his oldest and dearest friends. Pat Flanigan arranged some parties at "21" in New York and at the New York Yacht Club. Later parties were held in Washington.

As time passed, the Starks continued to be blessed with good health, a loving family, and a wide circle of friends. Mrs. Stark died in 1970 at the age of 90. Mary, now a widow, moved into the large house in Spring Valley to be near her father and to care for him. The next year Stark's health declined and he died peacefully on 20 August 1972 in his ninety-second year. Full military honors attended his funeral on 23 August 1972 at Arlington National Cemetery.

NOTES

The great majority of references are to documents deposited with the Naval Historical Center, Washington Navy Yard, Washington, D.C. For this reason, the depository is referred to simply as NHC. It is not to be confused with the Naval Historical Collection at the Naval War College, Newport, Rhode Island, to which only a few references are made.

There are two collections of Stark papers. One is his personal papers. Access to these papers requires permission of the Stark family. These are referred to in the notes as Stark Personal Papers. There is also a collection of official Stark papers that are open to the public, referred to in the notes as Stark Official Papers. Both collections are at the Naval Historical Center, Washington Naval Yard, Washington, D.C.

1. *Chief of Naval Operations*

1. Letter, Claude A. Swanson to Franklin D. Roosevelt, 24 January 1939; and letter, Charles A. Edison to Roosevelt, 7 March 1939, President's Secretary's File, Franklin D. Roosevelt Library, Hyde Park, New York. Hereinafter, Roosevelt Library.

2. Interview by LCDR Robert Dunny, 26 May 1948. File: Stark, Box 9, MS Collection 37, Thomas Buel/Walter Whitehill Collectors, Naval Historical Collection, Naval War College, Newport, Rhode Island.

3. Letter, Stark to Roosevelt, 17 March 1939; and letter, Roosevelt to Stark, 22 March 1939, President's Personal File, Roosevelt Library.

4. John Bartlett, *Familiar Quotations*, p. 451.

5. Letter, Stark to Claude C. Bloch, 24 August 1939, Box 2, Series I, Stark Personal Papers.

6. Letter, Stark to Bloch, 26 August 1939, Box 2, Series I, Stark Personal Papers.

287

7. Letter, Bloch to Stark, 29 August 1939, Box 2, Series I, Stark Personal Papers.

8. Letter, Stark to James O. Richardson, 18 January 1940, Box 2, Series I, Stark Personal Papers.

9. Letter, Stark to Richardson, 12 February 1940, Box 2, Series I, Stark Personal Papers.

10. Letter, Stark to Bloch, 8 September 1939; and letter, Stark to Bloch, 14 October, 1939, Box 2, Series I, Stark Personal Papers.

11. Letter, Bloch to Stark, 19 September 1939; and letter, Stark to Bloch, 22 September 1939, Box 2, Series I, Stark Personal Papers.

12. "Diary of Admiral H. R. Stark, CNO 1939–1942," Box 4, Series II, Stark Personal Papers. Hereinafter Stark Diary, 1939–1942.

13. Richard W. Leopold, *The Growth of American Foreign Policy*, p. 560; Samuel Eliot Morison, *History of United States Naval Operations in World War II: Vol. 1, The Battle of the Atlantic*, p. 14.

14. Letter, Stark to Thomas C. Hart, 30 October 1939, Box 2, Series I, Stark Personal Papers.

15. Morison, *Naval Operations, Vol. 1*, p. 14.

16. Stark Diary, 1939–1942.

17. Letter, Stark to Bloch, 24 August 1939, Box 2, Series I, Stark Personal Papers.

18. Letter, Stark to Richardson, 16 August 1940, Box 2, Series I, Stark Personal Papers.

19. Letters, Stark to Bloch, 24 August 1939 and 20 November 1939; and letter, Stark to Richardson, 16 August 1940, Box 2, Series I, Stark Personal Papers.

20. Letters, Stark to Kimmel, 13 January 1941 and 10 February 1941, Box 2, Series I, Stark Personal Papers.

21. Letter, Stark to Hart, 11 December 1939, Box 2, Series I, Stark Personal Papers.

22. Robert G. Albion and Robert H. Connery, pp. 87–88, based on an interview with Moreell.

23. Letter, Stark to Hart, 19 February 1940, Box 2, Series I, Stark Personal Papers.

24. Tracy B. Kittredge, "United States-British Cooperation, 1939–1942," Chap. 8, Appendix A, p. 135.

25. Letter, Stark to Hart, 9 February 1940, Box 2, Series I, Stark Personal Papers.

26. Ibid.

27. Ibid.

2. Dollars Cannot Buy Yesterday

1. Letter, Stark to James O. Richardson, 18 January 1940, Box 2, Series I, Stark Personal Papers.

2. U.S. Congress, House of Representatives, Committee on Naval Affairs, *Hearings to Establish the Composition of the United States Navy*, p. 1854; and U.S. Congress, Senate, Committee on Naval Affairs, *Hearings on Construction of Certain Naval Vessels*, p. 21. The best study done on naval policy is George T. Davis, *A Navy Second to None*. Unfortunately, it was written in late 1939 and thus does not cover the two 1940 naval expansion bills.

3. House Committee on Naval Affairs, *Composition of the United States Navy*, p. 1847.

4. R. S. Crenshaw, "Memorandum for the Chief of Naval Operations, Subject: Two Ocean Navy—Numbers and Types," 26 September 1939 in General Board File 420-2 (1939), Records of the General Board, NHC.

5. Letter, Stark to Claude C. Bloch, 22 September 1939, Box 2, Series I, Stark Personal Papers.

6. Crenshaw Memorandum.

7. Vincent R. Murphy, "Memorandum for Director, War Plans Division: Shipbuilding Study," 2 October 1939 in General Board File 420-2 (1939), Records of the General Board, NHC.

8. *The New York Times*, 5 November 1939, p. 1. *The New York Times* erred in reporting the proposed tonnage for auxiliaries at 125,000 tons. It was 200,000. Cf. House Committee on Naval Affairs, *Composition of the Navy*, p. 1709.

9. *The New York Times*, 5 November 1941, p. 41. The text of the draft bill is in House Committee, Naval Affairs, *Composition of the Navy*, p. 1709.

10. Harold D. Smith, Director of the Budget, "Memorandum for the President Subject: H.R. 8026, to establish the composition of the United States Navy, etc.," 30 January 1940, Official Files, Franklin D. Roosevelt Library, Hyde Park, N.Y.

11. But not the first. The new Secretary of the Navy, Charles A. Edison, who had been acting Secretary since Claude A. Swanson's death in the summer of 1939, was the first witness. Apparently, he was called to make what for all intents and purposes was a public recantation of his well-intentioned, but politically unwise proposal to give the President power to commandeer defense plants, among other extraordinary powers, in a declared national emergency short of war. This proposal received strong and intense criticism from members of Congress on the grounds that it would give the President dictatorial powers. Edison stated, "So I ask the country not to jump to the conclusion that I am so intrigued with the idea of national defense that I would sell democracy short to get it." He admitted there was no immediate emergency requiring the legislation at that time. Vinson stated no such bill had been introduced and that he did not contemplate introducing the proposed bill the Secretary had sent to the Speaker of the House. After Edison had made his statement, Vinson dismissed him. House Committee on Naval Affairs, *Composition of the Navy*, pp. 1710–1712. Edison told Stark he was grateful for the opportunity to back away gracefully from an untenable position. Stark telephone conversation with Melvin A. Mass, 9 January 1940, Stark Official Papers.

12. House Committee on Naval Affairs, *Composition of the Navy*, p. 1714.

13. Ibid., p. 1851.

14. Ibid., p. 1715.

15. Ibid., p. 1716.

16. Ibid., pp. 1717–1718. Considerable confusion arose in the course of the committee hearings over the actual size of the navy, expressed in total tonnages and in what precisely was proposed in the construction program, which would be authorized by a 25 percent increase. Even today this confusion extends to anyone attempting to get a clear picture of naval strength at that time. Part of the confusion can be attributed to the category "underage," which applied to ships within a specified number of years of their completion. Many ships, particularly destroyers and battleships, however, were kept in commission after they became overage. Compounding this confusion, the President had authority under the Vinson-Trammel Act of 1934 to replace ships when they became overage, but this replacement authority did not extend to ships authorized in the 20 percent expansion authorized by the Second Vinson Bill of 1938. Thus, it was necessary to distinguish replacement ships under

construction from expansion ships under construction. In addition, new ships could be commissioned and could be actually serving with the fleet while still being categorized as "built or building" so long as the government had not accepted them (which would not be until the contractor had corrected any outstanding deficiencies). Because of the possibility, if not certainty, of confusion, Vinson's attempts to keep the broad outlines of what was already authorized and what was proposed assumed even greater importance for the understanding of the committee and the public.

17. Ibid., pp. 1716–1717, 1719.

18. Ibid., pp. 1722–1723.

19. Stephen E. Pelz, *Race to Pearl Harbor: The Failure of the Second London Naval Conference and the Onset of World War.*

20. House Committee on Naval Affairs, *Composition of the Navy*, p. 1729.

21. Ibid., p. 1730. The battleships being replaced were *Arkansas, Texas, New York, Nevada, Oklahoma* and *Pennsylvania*.

22. Ibid., pp. 1801, 1802.

23. *The New York Times*, 1 July 1938, p. 1. U.S. State Department, *Foreign Relations of the United States: Diplomatic Papers, 1938*, Vol. 1, pp. 891–917.

24. House Committee on Naval Affairs, *Composition of the Navy*, p. 1733.

25. Ibid., pp. 1731–1733.

26. Chairman, General Board to Secretary of the Navy, Serial No. 1859, 30 June 1939, General Board File 420-6, Records of the General Board, NHC.

27. House Committee on Naval Affairs, *Composition of the Navy*, p. 1739.

28. *The New York Times*, 14 January 1940, Sec. 4, p. 6.

29. Stark telephone conversation with William D. Leahy, 10 January 1940, NHC.

30. Stark telephone conversation with Melvin Maas, 9 January 1940, NHC.

31. Stark telephone conversation with William D. Leahy, 10 January 1940., NHC.

32. Ibid. House Committee on Naval Affairs, *Composition of the Navy*, p. 1780.

33. House Committee on Naval Affairs, *Composition of the Navy*, p. 1780.

34. Ibid.

35. Ibid., p. 1782.

36. Ibid., p. 1793.

37. Ibid., p. 1785.

38. Ibid.

39. Ibid., p. 1786.

40. Ibid., p. 1787.

41. Ibid., p. 1773.

42. *The New York Times*, 24 January 1940, p. 9.

43. U.S. Congress, House of Representatives, Committee on Naval Affairs, Report No. 1593, *Establishing the Composition of the United States Navy and Authorizing the Construction of Certain Naval Vessels*, p. 5.

44. Ibid.

45. House Committee on Naval Affairs, *Composition of the Navy*, pp. 1868–1869.

46. House Committee on Naval Affairs, Report No. 1593, p. 3.

47. U.S. Congress, *Congressional Record*, 12 March 1940, pp. 2731–2733.

48. Letter, Stark to Bloch, 11 May 1940, Box 2, Series I, Stark Personal Papers.

49. Stark telephone conversations with David I. Walsh, 11 April 1940 and Carl Vinson, 11 April 1940, Stark Official Papers, NHC.

50. Senate Committee on Naval Affairs, *Hearings on Construction*, pp. 1–134 passim, p. 22.

51. *The New York Times*, 23 April 1940, p. 1; Senate Committee on Naval Affairs, *Hearings on Construction*, pp. 187–202 passim.

52. Stark telephone conversation with Cordell Hull, 22 April 1940, Stark Official Papers, NHC.

53. B. Frank Freidel, *Franklin D. Roosevelt: Vol. 2, The Ordeal*, pp. 43–45.

54. Stark telephone conversation with Franklin D. Roosevelt, 22 April 1940, Stark Official Papers, NHC.

55. Stark telephone conversation with Joseph K. Taussig, 23 April 1940, Stark Official Papers, NHC.

56. *The New York Times*, 24 April 1940, p. 22.

57. Ibid., 4 June 1940, p. 14. As late as August 1978 Taussig's widow clearly remembered this incident. She emphasized that his intentions were solely to speak his own mind honestly and candidly and not to embarrass the President.

58. Letter, Stark to Bloch, 11 May 1940, Box 2, Series I, Stark Personal Papers; *The New York Times*, 4 June 1940, p. 14.

3. Shifting, Probable Wars

1. Letter, Stark to Thomas C. Hart, 22 June 1940, Box 2, Series I, Harold R. Stark Personal Papers, NHC. See also Harold R. Stark, "Memorandum for the President," 18 June 1940, President's Secretary's Files. Roosevelt Library.

2. *The New York Times*, 2 July 1940, p. 1.

3. U.S. Congress, House of Representatives, Committee on Naval Affairs, Report No. 2640, *Establishing the Composition of the United States Navy to Authorize the Construction of Certain Vessels*, p. 1.

4. U.S. Congress, House of Representatives, Committee on Naval Affairs, *Hearing on H.R. 10100 to Establish the Composition of the United States Navy, to Authorize the Construction of Certain Vessels and for Other Purposes*, p. 3603.

5. U.S. Congress, Senate, Committee on Naval Affairs, Report No. 1946, *Construction of Certain Naval Vessels*, 76th Cong., 3d Sess., p. 8.

6. Letter, Stark to Hart, 18 January 1941, Box 2, Series I, Stark Personal Papers, NHC.

7. Stark memorandum "Rough Informal Estimate of the Foreign Situation," 1 March 1940, President's Secretary's File, Roosevelt Library.

8. Letter, Stark to Husband E. Kimmel, 13 January 1941, Box 2, Series I, Stark Personal Papers.

9. Interview, Vice Adm. Charles Wellborn, Jr., 24 April 1979.

10. "Diary of Admiral H. R. Stark, CNO, 1939–1942," Box 4, Series II, Stark Personal Papers. Hereinafter Stark Diary, 1939–1942; James R. Leutze, *Bargaining for Supremacy*, p. 78; Mark S. Watson, *Chief of Staff: Prewar Plans and Preparations*, pp. 105–106; Stetson Conn and Byron Fairchild, *The Framework of Hemisphere Defense*, p. 37.

11. Tracy B. Kittredge, "United States-British Cooperation, 1939–1942," Chap. 8, pp. 160–161; Stark Diary, 1939–1940, 28 May 1940.

12. William L. Langer and S. Everett Gleason, *The Challenge to Isolation*, Vol. 2, "United States-British Cooperations, 1939–1942," p. 550.

13. Kittredge, "United States-British Cooperation, 1939–1942," Chap. 8, p. 162; Stark Diary, 1939–1940, 25 May 1940.

14. Kittredge, "United States-British Cooperation, 1939–1942," Chap. 8, p. 162.

15. Leutze, *Bargaining for Supremacy*, p. 80; U.S. State Department, *Foreign Relations of the United States: Diplomatic Papers 1940*, Vol. 1, p. 233.

16. Stark Diary, 1939–1940, 28 May 1940.

17. Kittredge, "United States-British Cooperation, 1939–1942," Chap. 8, Note 40, p. 127.

18. Ibid., Chap. 8, Appendix A, p. 126.

19. Langer and Gleason, *Challenge to Isolation*, Vol. 2, p. 516.

20. Leutze, *Bargaining for Supremacy*, p. 81; Forrest C. Pogue, *George C. Marshall: Vol. 2, Ordeal and Hope*, p. 53.

21. U.S. State Department, *Foreign Relations of the United States: 1940*, Vol. 3, p. 347.

22. *The New York Times*, 11 June 1940, p. 21.

23. Ibid., p. 170.

24. Langer and Gleason, *Challenge to Isolation*, Vol. 2, p. 550.

25. Kittredge, "United States-British Cooperation, 1939–1942," Chap. 8, Note 53, p. 128.

26. Ibid., Chap. 8, p. 171. See also, Letter, Henry Morgenthau, Jr., to Franklin D. Roosevelt, 1 June 1940; letter, Roosevelt to Stark, 12 June 1940, Stark Personal Papers.

27. Letter, Stark to James O. Richardson, 29 June 1940, Box 2, Series I, Stark Personal Papers.

28. Arthur J. Marder, *From the Dardanelles to Oran*.

29. Mark Lincoln Chadwin, *The Hawks of World War II*; Harold J. Stuphen, "The Anglo-American Destroyers–Bases Agreement, September 1940."

30. Stark's "Memomorandum for the Secretary," 17 August 1940, File: DD/EF13, Chief of Naval Operations files, NHC. See also, Stark, "Memorandum for the President," 21 August 1940. President's Secretary's Files, Roosevelt Library. In his Memorandum of 17 August 1940, Stark referred to sovereignty over these islands, presumably meaning over the entire islands and possessions. This must have been a slip of the pen and Stark may have meant sovereignty only over enclaves in which bases would be situated.

31. Stark, "Memorandum for the Secretary," 17 August 1940.

32. Letter, Stark to Richardson, 1 May 1940, Box 2, Series I, Stark Diary, Stark Personal Papers.

33. James O. Richardson, *On the Treadmill to Pearl Harbor: The Memoirs of Admiral James O. Richardson, USN*, p. 307.

34. Letter, Stark to Richardson, 1 May 1940, Box 2, Series I, Stark Personal Papers.

35. Letter, Stark to Richardson, 7 May 1940, Stark Personal Papers.

36. Richardson, *On the Treadmill to Pearl Harbor*, pp. 308–309.

37. U.S. Congress, Joint Committee, *Hearings on the Investigation of the Pearl Harbor Attack*, Part 5, p. 2189.

38. Letter, Stark to Richardson, 27 May 1940, Box 2, Series I, Stark Personal Papers.

39. U.S. Congress, Joint Committee, *Pearl Harbor Attack*, Part 5, p. 2189.

40. Letter, Stark to Richardson, 7 May 1940, Box 2, Series I, Stark Personal Papers.

41. Letter, Stark to Richardson, 22 May 1940, Box 2, Series I, Stark Personal Papers.

42. Letters, Richardson to Stark, 13 May 1940 and Stark to Richardson, 22 May 1940, Box 2, Series I, Stark Personal Papers.

43. Letter, Richardson to Stark, 1 May 1940, Box 2, Series I, Stark Personal Papers.

44. Letter, Richardson to Stark, 22 May 1940, Box 2, Series I, Stark Personal Papers.

45. Letter, Stark to Richardson, 27 May 1940, Box 2, Series I, Stark Personal Papers. In his memoirs, Richardson quotes at length this letter from Stark, but he conveniently omits the opening sentence: "I know exactly what you are up against."

46. Letter, Richardson to Stark, 22 May 1940, Box 2, Series I, Stark Personal Papers.

47. Samuel Eliot Morison, *Naval Operations: Vol. 3, The Rising Sun in the Pacific 1931–April 1942*, p. 47.

48. Leutze, *Bargaining for Supremacy*, p. 77.

49. Interview with Vice Adm. Charles Wellborn, Jr., 15 December 1975.

50. Richardson, *On the Treadmill to Pearl Harbor*, p. 435.

51. Letter, Rear Adm. Robert E. Melling, USN (Ret.) to author, 5 September 1978.

4. Germany First

1. Winston Churchill, *The Second World War: Vol. II, The Gathering Storm*, pp. 497–498.

2. Mark S. Watson, *Chief of Staff: Prewar Plans and Preparations*, p. 117.

3. The account of this meeting comes from the testimony of James O. Richardson, in U.S. Congress, Joint Committee, *Pearl Harbor Attack*, Part 1, pp. 305 ff.

4. Letter, Stark to Roosevelt, 6 November 1940, President's Secretary's File, Roosevelt Library.

5. Letter, Commander in Chief, United States Fleet (Richardson) to Chief of Naval Operations (Stark), 22 October 1940, Stark Personal Papers.

6. Stark Diary, 1939–1942.

7. Louis Morton, "Germany First: The Basic Concept of Allied Strategy in World War II," in Kent Roberts Greenfield, ed., *Command Decisions*, p. 38.

8. Letter, Stark to Thomas C. Hart, 12 November 1940, Box 2, Series I, Stark Personal Papers.

9. All quotations from and references to Plan Dog Memorandum are taken from Stark's own copy, Box 5, Series III, Stark Personal Papers.

10. Morton, "Germany First."

11. Letter, Stark to Hart, 12 November 1940, Box 2, Series I, Stark Personal Papers.

12. Leutze, *Bargaining for Supremacy*, p. 181.

13. Stark Diary, 1939–1942; Leutze, *Bargaining for Supremacy*, pp. 186–187; Letter, Stark to Ghormley, 16 November 1940, Box 5, Series III, Stark Personal Papers.

14. Langer and Gleason say Roosevelt "shied away from immediate and formal approval of Plan Dog and its implications" (William L. Langer and S. Everett Gleason, *The Undeclared War 1940–1941*, p. 222). It is an accurate as well as an excessively charitable description.

15. Harold L. Ickes, *The Secret Diary of Harold L. Ickes: Vol. III, The Lowering Clouds*, pp. 388–389.

16. Leutze, *Bargaining for Supremacy*, p. 205.

17. U.S. Congress, Joint Committee, *Pearl Harbor Attack*, Part 5, p. 2332.

18. Kittredge, "United States-British Cooperation, 1939–1942," Chap. 13, p. 318, and OPNAV dispatches 022331 and 022334 December 1940, Chap. 13, note 35, p. 250.

19. U.S. Congress, Joint Committee, *Pearl Harbor Attack*, Part 5, p. 2332.

20. The only known record of this meeting was made by Gen. George C. Marshall in Watson, *Chief of Staff*, pp. 124–125.

21. Stark Diary, 1939–1942.

22. Kittredge, "United States-British Cooperation, 1939–1942," Chap. 14, p. 332.

23. Letter, Stark to Roosevelt, 24 January 1940, President's Personal Files, Roosevelt Papers.

24. Kittredge, "United States-British Cooperation, 1939–1942," Chap. 14, Appendix A and p. 336.

25. Leutze, *Bargaining for Supremacy*, p. 231.

26. Ibid., pp. 241–242.

27. Stark Diary, 1939–1942; Leutze, *Bargaining for Supremacy*, p. 244.

28. Stark Diary, 1939–1942; Leutze, *Bargaining for Supremacy*, pp. 247–248.

29. Robert E. Sherwood, *Roosevelt and Hopkins*, p. 273, and U.S. Congress, Joint Committee, *Pearl Harbor Attack*, Part 15, pp. 1485–1550.

30. U.S. Congress, Joint Committee, *Pearl Harbor Attack*, Part 3, p. 1052.

31. Harold J. Sutphen, "The Anglo-American Destroyers—Bases Agreement, September 1940."

32. Letter, Stark to Husband E. Kimmel, 4 April 1941, Stark Personal Papers.

33. Maurice Matloff and Edwin M. Snell, *Strategic Planning for Coalition Warfare 1941–1942*, p. 46.

34. Chief of Naval Operations letter serial 038612, 3 April 1941, Stark Personal Papers.

35. Matloff and Snell, *Strategic Planning*, p. 46.

5.   *Quasi-War in the Atlantic*

1. "Diary of Admiral H. R. Stark, CNO, 1939–1942," Box 4, Series II, Harold R. Stark Papers, NHC. Hereinafter Stark Diary, 1939–1942.

2. Letter, Stark to Husband E. Kimmel, 19 April 1941, Box 2, Series I, Stark Personal Papers.

3. Letter, Stark to Kimmel, 26 April 1941, Box 3, Series I, Stark Personal Papers.

4. Robert J. Quinlan, "The United States Fleet: Diplomacy, Strategy and the Allocation of Ships (1940–1941)," in Harold Stein, ed., *American Civil-Military Decisions*, p. 183.

5. Letter, Stark to Kimmel, 24 May 1941, Box 3, Series I, Stark Personal Papers.

6. Letter, Stark to Charles M. Cooke, 31 July 1941, Box 2, Series I, Stark Personal Papers.

7. Kittredge, "United States-British Cooperation, 1939–1942," p. 541.

8. Memorandum of Conference in Office of Chief of Naval Operations, 14 July 1941 and Memorandum of Conference in Office of Chief of Naval Operations, 22 July 1941, Chief of Naval Operations Files, NHC.

9. Kittredge, "United States-British Cooperation, 1939–1942," p. 549, n. 25.

10. Ibid., p. 550.

11. Ibid., p. 551, 548, n. 23.

12. Letter, Stark to Kimmel, 31 July 1941, Box 3, Series I, Stark Personal Papers.
13. Letter, Stark to Cooke, 31 July 1941, Box 2, Series I, Stark Personal Papers.
14. Ibid.
15. Stark Diary, 1939–1942; Ernest J. King and Walter Muir Whitehill, *Fleet Admiral King*, p. 320.
16. Stark Diary, 1941–1942.
17. Ibid. The best account of the Atlantic conference is Theodore A. Wilson, *The First Summit.* See also, King and Whitehill, *Fleet Admiral King*, pp. 331–337.
18. Kittredge, "United States-British Cooperation, 1939–1942," p. 553, n. 31.
19. Ibid., p. 588, n. 85.
20. Letter, Stark to Kimmel, 22 August 1941, Box 3, Series I, Stark Personal Papers.
21. Kittredge, "United States-British Cooperation, 1939–1942," p. 588.
22. U.S. Congress, Joint Committee, *Pearl Harbor Attack*, Part 5, p. 2295.
23. Ibid., pp. 2293–2296.
24. Kittredge, "United States-British Cooperation, 1939–1942," p. 593–594.
25. Ibid., p. 595.
26. Ibid.
27. Sherwood, *Roosevelt and Hopkins*, p. 379.
28. Stark, "Memorandum for the Secretary of State," 8 October 1941, Box 28, Series IV, Stark Personal Papers.

6. *A Very Glaring Phrase*

1. Letter, Stark to James O. Richardson, 22 November 1940, Box 2, Series I, Stark Personal Papers.
2. The Joint Board, *Joint Action of the Army and the Navy*, p. 2. See also, Tracy B. Kittredge, "The Muddle Before Pearl Harbor," in *U.S. News & World Report*, 3 December 1954, p. 58. This long article is by far the best treatment of the events leading to the attack on Pearl Harbor. See also, Roberta Wohlstetter, *Pearl Harbor Warning and Decision*, p. 19.
3. U.S. Congress, Joint Committee, *Pearl Harbor Attack*, Part 5, pp. 2127–2128.
4. Letter, Stark to Husband E. Kimmel, 10 February 1941, Box 2, Series I, Stark Personal Papers.
5. Letter, Stark to Kimmel, 13 January 1941, Box 3, Series I, Stark Personal Papers.
6. Letter, Kimmel to Stark, 18 February 1941, Box 3, Series I, Stark Personal Papers.
7. Kittredge, "The Muddle Before Pearl Harbor," p. 61–62.
8. U.S. Congress, Joint Committee, *Pearl Harbor Attack*, Part 14, p. 1397; Stark to District Commandants, 14 May 1941, Box 3, Series I, Stark Personal Papers.
9. Letter, Stark to Kimmel, 26 April 1941, Box 3, Series I, Stark Personal Papers.
10. Letter, Kimmel to Stark, 14 June 1941, Box 3, Series I, Stark Personal Papers.
11. Interview with Vice Adm. John J. McCrea, 21 March 1978; letter, Thomas C. Hart to Stark, 27 April 1940, and letters, Stark to Hart, 23 December 1940 and 24 February 1941, Box 3, Series I, Stark Personal Papers.
12. Letter, Stark to Hart, 25 February 1941, Box 3, Series I, Stark Personal Papers.
13. U.S. Congress, Joint Committee, *Pearl Harbor Attack*, Part 16, p. 2152.
14. Letter, Stark to Kimmel, 10 February 1941, Box 3, Series I, Stark Personal Papers.

15. Stark, "Memorandum for the President," 11 February 1941, Box 2, Series II, Stark Personal Papers.

16. Stark Diary, 1939–1942. See also, Robert J. Quinlan, "The United States Fleet," pp. 173–174; Samuel Eliot Morison, *Naval Operations; Vol. 3, The Rising Sun*, p. 56, n. 19; Stark Diary, 1939–1942; and Stark to Hart, 22 March 1941, Box 3, Series I, Stark Personal Papers.

17. Letter, Stark to Kimmel, 19 April 1941, Box 3, Series I, Stark Personal Papers.

18. Ibid.

19. Letter, Kimmel to Stark, 26 May 1941, Box 3, Series I, Stark Personal Papers.

20. Letter, Stark to Hart, 24 July 1941, Box 3, Series I, Stark Personal Papers.

21. Chief of Naval Operations dispatch 252023Z July 1941, in U.S. Congress, Joint Committee, *Pearl Harbor Attack*, Part 14, p. 1400.

22. U.S. Congress, Joint Committee, *Pearl Harbor Attack*, Part 14, p. 1396.

23. Letter, Stark to Kimmell, 28 August, 1941, Box 3, Series I, Stark Personal Papers.

24. Letters, Stark to Hart, 22 September 1941, and Stark to Kimmel, 23 September 1941, Box 3, Series I, Stark Personal Papers.

25. Letter, Stark to Hart, 22 September 1941, Box 3, Series I, Stark Personal Papers.

26. U.S. Congress, Joint Committee, *Pearl Harbor Attack*, Part 29, p. 4022.

27. Letter, Stark to Hart, 22 September 1941, Box 3, Series I, Stark Personal Papers.

28. U.S. Congress, Joint Committee, *Pearl Harbor Attack*, Part 14, p. 1402.

29. Ibid.

30. Letters, Kimmel to Stark, 22 October 1941, and Stark to Kimmel, 7 November 1941, Box 3, Series I, Stark Personal Papers.

31. Letter, Stark to Hart, 7 November 1941, Box 3, Series I, Stark Personal Papers.

32. Letter, Stark to Kimmel, 14 November 1941, Box 3, Series I, Stark Personal Papers.

33. U.S. Congress, Joint Committee, *Pearl Harbor Attack*, Part 20, pp. 1104–1105.

34. James H. Herzog, *Closing the Open Door*, pp. 198–204.

35. Letter, William R. Smedberg III to author, 4 June 1980; Stark Diary, 1941–1942.

36. U.S. Congress, Joint Committee, *Pearl Harbor Attack*, Part 14, p. 1405.

37. "Memorandum for the President," 27 November 1941, Box 28, Series IV, Stark Personal Papers.

38. Letter, William R. Smedberg III to author, 4 June 1980.

39. Letter, Stark to Kimmel, 25 November 1941, Box 3, Series I, Stark Personal Papers.

40. U.S. Congress, Joint Committee, *Pearl Harbor Attack*, Part 4, p. 1751.

41. Ruhl J. Bartlett, ed., *The Record of American Diplomacy*, pp. 634–636.

42. Letter, John McCrea to author, 20 May 1980.

43. U.S. Congress, Joint Committee, *Pearl Harbor Attack*, Part 4, p. 1406.

44. Stark Diary, 1941–1942.

45. U.S. Congress, Joint Committee, *Pearl Harbor Attack*, Part 15, p. 1768.

46. Ibid., Part 5, 2131.

47. Kittredge, "The Muddle Before Pearl Harbor," p. 120.

48. U.S. Congress, Joint Committee, *Pearl Harbor Attack*, Part 5, p. 2302. Wohlstetter, *Pearl Harbor Warning and Decision*, p. 42.

49. Kittredge, "The Muddle Before Pearl Harbor," p. 130.

50. Ibid., p. 133.

7. *Pearl Harbor to Arcadia*

1. Samuel Eliot Morison, *History of United States Naval Operations in World War II: Vol. 3, The Rising Sun in the Pacific*, p. 101. U.S. Congress, Joint Committee, *Pearl Harbor Attack*, Part 26, p. 135.

2. Telephone conversations, Harold R. Stark–Claude C. Bloch, 7 December 1941, and Royal E. Ingersoll–Claude C. Bloch, 8 December 1941, Stark Official Papers, NHC.

3. Letter, Rear Adm. Robert E. Melling to author, 5 September 1978.

4. Stark Diary, 1939–1942.

5. Letter, Frank Knox to Theodore Roosevelt, Jr., 18 December 1941, Frank Knox Papers, Library of Congress.

6. Vernon E. Davis, *Origin of the Joint and Combined Chiefs of Staff*, pp. 180–181.

7. Walter Muir Whitehill, memorandum of conversation with Ernest J. King, 4 July 1950. Box 4. File: EJK 1942, Thomas Buell/Walter Whitehill Collectors, Research Source Materials on FADM Ernest King. MS Collection 37. Naval Historical Collection, Naval War College. Hereinafter, Research Materials on FADM King; King and Whitehill, *Fleet Admiral King*, p. 355.

8. Winston S. Churchill, *The Second World War: Vol. 3, The Grand Alliance*, p. 608.

9. U.S. Congress, Joint Committee, *Pearl Harbor Attack*, Part 15, p. 1511. U.S. Department of State, *Foreign Relations of the United States: The Conference at Washington, 1941–1942, and Casablanca, 1943*.

10. King and Whitehill, *Fleet Admiral King*, p. 351.

11. U.S. Department of State, *Foreign Relations: Conference at Washington, 1941–1942*, pp. 69–74.

12. Ibid., p. 77.

13. Stark attended this dinner, although the list given in U.S. Department of State, *Foreign Relations: Conference at Washington, 1941–1942*, p. 80, erroneously omits his name. See Stark Diary, 1941–1942.

14. U.S. Department of State, *Foreign Relations: Conference at Washington, 1941–1942*, pp. 82–90.

15. Ibid., p. 84. The minutes of this meeting can be found in pp. 82–90.

16. Ibid., p. 93.

17. Gerow's notes of the meeting of Roosevelt, Churchill, and the chiefs of staff on 26 December 1941 describe King as being "lukewarm" to the idea (U.S. Department of State, *Foreign Relations: Conference at Washington, 1941–1942*). King and Whitehill simply recount this incident without giving King's opinion (King and Whitehill, *Fleet Admiral King*, p. 362). The concept of unified command worked well and it is unlikely that after World War II King would admit he had opposed it, if he had; and, if King had favored it, he and his biographer would most likely have said so. Thus, their failure to indicate King's opinion at this time gives rise to an inference that King did not favor it and corroborates Gerow's observation that King was "lukewarm." However, Pogue relies on Stimson's diary and claims that King spoke up for unified command, Pogue, *George C. Marshall*, p. 278. Stimson's well-known bias against the navy makes his recollection suspect.

18. Stark Diary, 1941–1942; Pogue, *George C. Marshall*, p. 278.

19. U.S. Department of State, *Foreign Relations: Conference at Washington, 1941-1942*, p. 128.

20. Ibid., pp. 153, 162–171.

21. Ibid., p. 166.

22. Sherwood, *Roosevelt and Hopkins*, p. 465; U.S. Department of State, *Foreign Relations: Conference at Washington, 1941-1942*, p. 285.

23. U.S. Department of State, *Foreign Relations: Conference at Washington, 1941-1942*, p. 282.

24. Ibid., pp. 138–139.

25. Ibid., pp. 286, 288.

26. Ibid., p. 197.

27. Ibid., pp. 230–232.

28. Davis, *Origin of the Joint and Combined Chiefs of Staff*, p. 176.

29. Walter Muir Whitehill, memorandum of conversation with Ernest J. King, 4 July 1950. Research materials on FADM King.

30. Walter Muir Whitehill undated "Memorandum: Chapter 11 #1," Folder: Cinclantflt, Box 2. Research materials on FADM King.

31. Walter Muir Whitehill memorandum of conversation with Capt. Tracy B. Kittredge, 28 August 1952, Box 9. File: Stark. Research materials on FADM King.

8. *A Meeting with the President*

1. Letter, Knox to Stark, 19 May 1942, Frank Knox Papers, NHC.

2. Letter, Stark to Roosevelt, 7 March 1942, Official Files, Roosevelt Library.

3. Letter, Knox to Stark, 21 March 1942, Stark Personal Papers.

4. "Admiral H. R. Stark Fitness Reports 1905–1945," Box 23, Series II, Stark Personal Papers.

5. Letter, Anne H. Sims to Stark, 30 April 1942, Box 2, Series I, Stark Personal Papers.

6. Stark, "Notes on President's Conference," 27 April 1942, Stark Personal Papers.

7. Letter, Stark to Knox, 2 May 1942, Knox Papers, NHC. Classified Memorandum, Stark to Secretary of the Navy, 2 May 1942, Frank Knox Papers, Library of Congress.

9. *Arrival in England*

1. J.V.B. (Babcock?), "Hasty Estimate of Situation Concerning Methods of Cooperation Between this Organization, Admiralty and Navy Department," 28 October 1917, Box 1, Stark Official Papers.

2. Memorandum, Stark to Frank Knox, 2 May 1942, Knox Papers, Library of Congress.

3. "FOLUS: British Liaison with COMNAVEU," undated. Presumably drafted by Tracy B. Kittredge, Item 54, Series II, COMNAVEU Files, NHC.

4. "Adm. Stark : Diary as COMNAVEU," Item 172, Series II, COMNAVEU Files, NHC.

5. "Adm. Stark: Diary as COMNAVEU."

6. Ibid.

7. Letter, Stark to Knox, 28 May 1942, Knox Papers, NHC.

8. Letter, Stark to Knox, 4 May 1942, Knox Papers, NHC.

9. Letter, Stark to Knox, 2 June 1942, Knox Papers, NHC; "Adm. Stark: Diary as COMNAVEU."

10. COMINCH message 091600 July 1942, "Adm. Stark: Diary as COMNAVEU."

11. COMNAVEU message 141711 July 1942, "Adm. Stark: Diary as COMNAVEU."

12. Letter, Stark to Knox, 6 October 1942, Knox Papers, NHC.

13. COMNAVEU Message 082214 October 1942 and COMNAVEU HI COM 091620 October 1942, Box 7, Series I, COMNAVEU files.

14. COMNAVEU HI COM 142000 October 1942, COMNAVEU Files.

15. Letter, Stark to Knox, 7 December 1942, Knox Papers, NHC.

16. "Adm. Stark: Diary as COMNAVEU"; Memorandum, Stark to King, 22 May 1942 and letter, Stark to King, 22 May 1942 in "Convoy and ASW Materials," Box 7, Series III, COMNAVEU Files.

17. Letter, Stark to Knox, 14 May 1942, Knox Papers, NHC.

18. Letter, Stark to Knox, 17 May 1942, Knox Papers, NHC.

19. Letter, Stark to King, 2 June 1942, Knox Papers, NHC.

20. Letter, Stark to King, 19 June 1942, Stark Official Papers.

21. Letter, Bullitt to Knox, 20 July 1942, Knox Papers, NHC.

22. Letter, Stark to Knox, 9 September 1942, Knox Papers, NHC.

23. Samuel Eliot Morison, *Naval Operations, Vol. 1, The Battle of the Atlantic,* pp. 167–168.

24. Letter, Stark to King, 2 June 1942, Knox Papers, NHC; "Adm. Stark: Diary as COMNAVEU."

25. Letter, Stark to Knox, 1 September 1942, Knox Papers, NHC.

26. "Convoy and ASW Materials" pp. 8–13.

27. Letter, Stark to King, 17 June 1942, King Papers, NHC. "Adm. Stark: Diary as COMNAVEU"; Letter, Stark to Knox 20 June 1942, Knox Papers, NHC. Letter, Stark to King, 17 June 1942, Ernest J. King Papers, NHC. This letter and its attached memoranda provide details of Stark's trip. See also, "Adm. Stark: Diary as COMNAVEU."

28. Letters, Stark to Mr. and Mrs. A. C. Howard, 14 June 1942; A. C. Howard to Stark, 22 June 1942, Box 1, Series I, Stark Personal Papers, NHC.

10. North Africa and de Gaulle

1. Dwight D. Eisenhower, *Crusade in Europe,* p. 54.

2. Commander, U.S. Naval Forces, Europe (COMNAVEU), "Administrative History, United States Naval Forces in Europe 1940-1946," pp. 170–171, COMNAVEU files, NHC.

3. Sherwood, *Roosevelt and Hopkins,* p. 607.

4. King and Whitehill, *Fleet Admiral King,* pp. 406, 407; Personal Diary, Harold R. Stark, author's possession. Hereinafter Stark Personal Diary.

5. COMINCH messages 061240 August 1942 and 181625 September 1942, Box 6, Series I, COMNAVEU files.

6. COMNAVEU, "Administrative History," p. 181.

7. ETO Draft Outline Operation Torch, File 182, Series II, COMNAVEU files.

8. Harry C. Butcher, *My Three Years With Eisenhower*, p. 49; Samuel Eliot Morison, *Naval Operations in World War II, Vol. 2, Operations in North African Waters*, p. 16; "Adm. Stark: Diary as COMNAVEU." Item 172, Series II, COMNAVEU files, NHC.

9. COMNAVEU, "Administrative History," p. 184.

10. Ibid., p. 190.

11. CO, Base Two message 122030 October 1942 and letter, Bennett to Eisenhower, 17 October 1942, File 192, Series II, COMNAVEU files; letter, Bennett to Kirk, 25 November 1942, File 183, Series II, COMNAVEU files; COMNAVEU, "Administrative History," p. 191, Morison, *Naval Operations, Vol. 2, Operations in North African Waters*, pp. 225–230.

12. Memorandum by Tracy B. Kittredge, 1 September 1942, Knox Papers, NHC.

13. Letters, Knox to Stark, 16 September 1942 and Stark to Knox, 6 October 1942; Memorandum, Roosevelt to Knox, 3 September 1942, Knox Papers, NHC.

14. Letter, Stark to Knox, 2 November 1942, Knox Papers, NHC.

15. Ibid.

16. Letter, Stark to Knox, 7 November 1942, Knox Papers, NHC, "Adm. Stark: Diary, as COMNAVEU."

17. *The New York Times*, 28 October 1942.

18. U.S. Department of State, *Foreign Relations of the United States, 1942*, Vol. 2, passim, pp. 123–673.

19. "Adm. Stark: Diary as COMNAVEU"; Letter, Stark to King, 10 May 1942, King Papers, NHC.

20. U.S. Department of State, *Foreign Relations, 1942*, Vol. 2, p. 534.

21. Kittredge Memorandum, 30 July 1942, Box 207, File: Agreement, COMNAVEU files.

22. U.S. Department of State, *Foreign Relations, 1942*, Vol. 2, p. 538.

23. Kittredge Memorandum, 3 August 1942, Box 207, File: Agreement, COMNAVEU files.

24. Commander, U.S. Naval Forces, Europe (Stark) to Commander in Chief, U.S. Fleet (King), letter serial 00796, 9 September 1942, COMNAVEU files.

25. Kittredge Memorandum, 9 November 1942, Document 1, Commander, U.S. Naval Forces, Europe (Stark) to Director, Office of Naval Intelligence attached to letter serial 01449 of 10 December 1942, COMNAVEU files. Hereinafter referred to as COMNAVEU letter, 10 December 1942.

26. *The Speeches of General de Gaulle*, p. 173.

27. Kittredge Memorandum, 12 November 1942, Document 12, COMNAVEU letter, 10 December 1942. Tracy B. Kittredge MSS Diary, COMNAVEU files, NHC.

28. Kittredge Memorandum, 17 November 1942, Document 23(a), COMNAVEU letter, 10 December 1942.

29. Ibid.

30. Kittredge Memorandum, 14 November 1942, Document 17, COMNAVEU letter, 10 December 1942.

31. Eisenhower, *Crusade in Europe*, p. 131.

32. Secretary of the Navy Frank Knox to Stark, 17 November 1942, in "Selected Documents from the Correspondence of Admiral Harold R. Stark, U.S. Navy, Commander, U.S. Naval Forces in Europe, Vol. 2," p. 33. Hereinafter, "Selected Documents." COMNAVEU files, NHC. Secretary of War Henry L. Stimson told

Knox that General Patton was alarmed at the possibility of an uprising of tribes in Morocco, which was apparently forestalled by the cooperation of Darlan and others. Had it occurred, Patton estimates that 60,000 troops would have been required to quell it.

33. Letter, Stark to de Gaulle, 14 November 1942, "Selected Documents, Vol. 2," p. 18.

34. Jacques Soustelle, *Envers et contre tout*, Vol. 2, pp. 18–19.

35. Letter, Stark to Winant, 16 November 1942, "COMNAVEU Documents, Vol. 2," p. 22.

36. Soustelle, *Envers et contre tout*, Vol. 2, p. 19.

37. Letter, Stark to de Gaulle, 23 November 1942, "Selected Documents, Vol. 2," p. 24.

38. U.S. Department of State, *Foreign Relations, 1942*, p. 445.

39. Ibid., pp. 446–447.

40. Letter, Stark to Knox, 18 November 1942, "Selected Documents, Vol. 2," p. 32.

41. Letter, Stark to Knox, 16 November 1942, "Selected Documents, Vol. 2," p. 20. Kittredge Diary, COMNAVEU files, NHC.

42. Letter, Stark to Knox, 16 November 1942, "Selected Documents, Vol. 2," p. 20.

43. Letter, Stark to de Gaulle, 18 November 1942, "Selected Documents, Vol. 2," p. 25; Stark to Pleven, 18 November 1942, "Selected Documents, Vol. 2," p. 27.

44. Kittredge Diary, "Adm. Stark Diary as COMNAVEU."

45. COMNAVEU message 181701Z November 1942, London No. 1. Top Drawer, HI COM Dispatches, COMNAVEU files.

46. Secretary of the Navy message 190115Z November 1942. Ibid.

47. Stark to Knox message, "COMNAVEU Documents, Vol. 2," p. 30.

48. Kittredge Diary.

49. U.S. Department of State, *Foreign Relations, 1942*, pp. 546–547; Kittredge Diary. An interesting sidelight to this first meeting of the President with a representative of the French National Committee is that it was the second time one was scheduled. Welles had arranged a meeting of the President with Tixier, at his request, for 7 November. This meeting was the result of a letter from de Gaulle to the President via Tixier and Welles. The letter contained a long, but eloquent and moving statement by de Gaulle of his position and that of the French National Committee. The President returned the letter to Welles and agreed to meet Tixier. The meeting never took place because, as Welles pointed out, Tixier never showed up. No other reference to this meeting has been found, not even an indication of its cancellation. There is no known explanation of why it never took place. Welles to Roosevelt, 27 October 1942, and Roosevelt to Welles, 29 October 1942. Department of State 851.01/400-3/6. Also, Welles memorandum of 6 November 1942, 851.01/400-5/6. U.S. National Archives.

In referring to de Gaulle's letter, the desk officer commented to Welles that "it is two years too late and takes ten pages of introduction to get down to the very little meat there is in it." This comment must surely rank as one of the most pedestrian ever made by a State Department officer. It is comparable to calling Cyrano de Bergerac's panache a feather. The State Department was at least consistent in its view, because it did not publish the first ten pages. For the full text see de Gaulle, *Unity-Documents*, p. 66 ff.

50. Letter, Stark to Winant, 18 November 1942, "Selected Documents, Vol. 2," p. 29.

51. Letter, Stark to Winant, 20 November 1942, "Selected Documents, Vol. 2," p. 34; letter, Stark to Knox, 16 November 1942, "Selected Documents, Vol. 2," p. 20.

52. Kittredge memorandum, 24 November 1942, Document 32(a), "Selected Documents, Vol. 2."

53. Kittredge Diary.

54. Ibid.

55. Leahy to Stark (Commander in Chief, U.S. Fleet message 252035Z, November 1942), HI COM Dispatches, COMNAVEU files.

56. Stark Diary. Kittredge memorandum of conversation, 26 November 1942, "Selected Documents, Vol. 2," p. 41.

57. Letter, Stark to Knox, 27 November 1942, "COMNAVEU Documents, Vol. 2," p. 43.

58. Winston S. Churchill, *The Second World War, Vol. 4, The Hinge of Fate*, p. 648.

59. Letter, Stark to Knox, 27 November 1942. Knox Papers, NHC.

60. Ibid.

61. Ibid.

62. Ibid.

63. Stark to Knox message 271213Z November 1942. HI C Dispatches, COMNAVEU files, NHC.

64. Stark to Knox message 281446Z November 1942.

65. Leahy to Stark message 29 November 1942 in "Selected Documents, Vol. 2," p. 51.

66. Leahy, William D., *I Was There*, p. 136.

67. Kittredge Diary.

68. Letter, Eisenhower to Marshall (Chief of Staff, U.S. Army), 21 December 1942. Box 204, File: February 1943, COMNAVEU files. See also, Letter, Eisenhower to Marshall, 21 December 1942; letter, Eisenhower to Adjutant General, War Department (AGWAR), Algiers message 2831, 23 December 1942, Box 204, File: February 1943, COMNAVEU files.

69. Letter, Stark to Eisenhower, 16 December 1942, "COMNAVEU Documents, Vol. 2," p. 63.

70. Ibid.

71. COMNAVEU message 251700Z December 1942. HI COM Dispatches, COMNAVEU files.

72. Kittredge memorandum, 28 December 1942, Box 204, File: CDR Clark, COMNAVEU files.

73. Churchill, *The Hinge of Fate*, p. 645.

74. Leahy to Stark, Chief of Naval Operations (OPNAV) message 261625Z December 1942. HI COM Dispatches, COMNAVEU files. "Selected Documents, Vol. 2."

75. Kittredge memorandum, 28 December 1942. HI COM Dispatches, COMNAVEU files. COMNAVEU message 281034Z December 1942.

76. COMNAVEU message 281034Z December 1942. HI COM Dispatches, COMNAVEU files.

77. COMNAVEU (Stark) message to Commander in Chief, U.S. Fleet (King) 011701Z April 1943, HI COM Dispatches, COMNAVEU files.

78. Memorandum, 1 March 1943 in "Selected Documents, Vol. 3," pp. 29–32.

11. The Submarine Menace

1. Stark, letter of instructions to Ghormley, 4 April 1941, in "Convoy and ASW Materials," Box 7, Series III, COMNAVEU files, NHC. Hereinafter, "Convoy and ASW Materials."

2. Samuel Eliot Morison, *Naval Operations, Vol. 1, The Battle of the Atlantic*, p. 413.

3. Robert E. Sherwood, *Roosevelt and Hopkins*, pp. 550–551; letter, King to Stark, 21 May 1942, King Papers, NHC.

4. Letters, Stark to King, 18 June 1942; Stark to Knox, 30 July 1942, "Convoy and ASW Materials."

5. Letters, Knox to Stark, 29 August 1942, Knox to Roosevelt, 19 October 1942, Knox to Stark, 20 October 1942, "Convoy and ASW Materials." See also, King and Whitehill, *Fleet Admiral King*, pp. 446–448.

6. Letter, Stark to Knox, 9 September 1942, "Convoy and ASW Materials"; Morison, *Naval Operations, Vol. 1, The Battle of the Atlantic*, p. 410.

7. Letter, Stark to Knox, 6 October 1942, "Convoy and ASW Materials."

8. Letter, Stark to King, 4 April 1943, "Convoy and ASW Materials"; Stephen W. Roskill, *The War at Sea, 1939–1945, Vol. 3, The Offensive*, p. 88; Winston S. Churchill, *The Second World War, Vol. 4, The Hinge of Fate*, p. 130.

9. Letters, Stark to King, 19 February 1943; 9 April 1943, "Convoy and ASW Materials."

10. Stark, Memorandum to War Cabinet Anti-U Boat Warfare Committee 31 March 1943 (A.U. (43) 86), File 168, Series II, COMNAVEU files; letters, Stark to King, 4 April 1943 and 9 April 1943, "Convoy and ASW Materials."

11. Minutes, War Cabinet Anti-U Boat Warfare Committee, 31 March 1943, File 168, Series II, COMNAVEU files; letter, Stark to King, 4 April 1943, "Convoy and ASW Materials."

12. Draft letter, Prime Minister to President, Box 18, Series II, COMNAVEU files.

13. Letter, King to Stark, 3 May 1943, King Papers. Samuel Eliot Morison, *Naval Operations, Vol. 10, The Atlantic Battle Won*, pp. 90–91.

14. Letters, Stark to Knox, 29 April 1943, Stark to King, 24 April 1943, "Convoy and ASW Materials."

15. Letter, Stark to Knox, 31 May 1943, Knox Papers, NHC.

16. Letter, King to Stark, 18 March 1943, "Convoy and ASW Materials."

17. Letter King to Stark, 3 May 1943, "Convoy and ASW Materials."

18. Letters, Knox to Stark, 28 May 1943; Stark to Knox, 11 June 1943, Knox Papers, NHC.

19. Notes from Admiralty Anti-U-Boat meeting and letter, Stark to King, 15 June 1943, "Convoy and ASW Materials."

20. Morison, *Naval Operations, Vol. 10, The Atlantic Battle Won*, p. 365.

21. Letters, Knox to Stark, 14 July 1943; Stark to Knox, 28 July 1943; Stark to Knox, 2 August 1943, Knox Papers, NHC.

22. Letter, Stark to King, 31 August 1943, "Convoy and ASW Materials."

23. Letters, Devers to Stark, 16 July 1943; Stark to Devers, 21 July 1943, "Convoy and ASW Materials."

24. Summary of Admiralty Appreciation of U-Boat Situation, "Convoy and ASW Materials."

25. Letter, Slessor to Stark, 20 December 1943, "Convoy and ASW Materials."

26. Letter, Stark to Knox, 15 November 1943, Knox Papers, NHC.

27. Roskill, *The War at Sea, Vol. 3, The Offensive,* pp. 38–40; Morison, *Naval Operations, Vol. 10, The Atlantic Battle Won,* pp. 139–145.

28. Letter, Stark to Howard A. Flanigan, 5 October 1943, "Convoy and ASW Materials."

29. Stark Press Conference, 10 September 1943, "Convoy and ASW Materials."

30. Morison, *Naval Operations, Vol. 10, The Atlantic Battle Won,* p. 324.

31. Stark memorandum for Capt. Kline, 28 September 1944. "Convoy and ASW Materials."

32. Letter, Cunningham to Stark, 28 September 1944, "Convoy and ASW Materials."

33. Letter, Stark to Cunningham, 2 October 1944, "Convoy and ASW Materials."

34. "Memorandum on the Trend of the Anti-U-Boat Campaign," 2 October 1944, "Convoy and ASW Materials."

35. Stark "Memorandum for Commodore Flanigan," 16 November 1944, "Convoy and ASW Materials."

36. Letter, Stark to King, 6 November 1944, "Convoy and ASW Materials."

37. Letter, Stark to King, 1 December 1944, "Convoy and ASW Materials."

38. Letters, Cunningham to Portal, 6 January 1945, and Portal to Cunningham, 10 January 1945, "Convoy and ASW Materials."

39. Letter, Stark to King, 22 October 1944, "Convoy and ASW Materials."

40. Morison, *Naval Operations, Vol. 10, The Atlantic Battle Won,* pp. 334–336.

41. Memorandum, Capt. Ingram to Stark, 11 January 1945; Admiralty dispatch to COMINCH 30 December 1944; letter, Kirk to Stark, 31 December 1944, "Convoy and ASW Materials."

42. Admiralty dispatch to CINC Mediterranean, 14 January 1944; letter, Cunningham to Stark, 20 December 1944, "Convoy and ASW Materials."

43. Letter, Stark to Cunningham, 15 January 1945, "Convoy and ASW Materials."

44. Memorandum of conversation, King and Cunningham, 9 February 1945, "Convoy and ASW Materials."

45. Memorandum to Stark, 23 January 1945, "Convoy and ASW Materials."

46. Letters, COMTENTH Fleet to COMA/S Development Detachment, 17 January 1945; Stark to King, 3 March 1945, "Convoy and ASW Materials."

47. Letter, Cunningham to Stark, 6 April 1945, "Convoy and ASW Materials."

48. Morison, *Naval Operations, Vol. 10, The Atlantic Battle Won,* pp. 358–361.

12. *Naval Preparations for Overlord*

1. Letter, Stark to Frank Knox, 20 March 1944, Knox Papers, NHC.

2. "Rattle Conference Minutes," File 149, Series II, COMNAVEU files, NHC.

3. "Brief of Largs Conference," File 150, Series II, COMNAVEU files.

4. "Rattle Conference Report," File 152, Series II, COMNAVEU files.

5. COMNAVEU, "Administrative History," NHC, pp. 198–199.

6. Ibid., p. 201.

7. Ibid., pp. 214–219.

8. Ibid., p. 234.

9. Ibid., pp. 225–226, 228.

10. Ibid., p. 266; Richmond interview 4 December 1980.
11. COMNAVEU, "Administrative History," p. 237.
12. Ibid., p. 270.
13. Richmond interview 4 December 1980.
14. Alfred R. Stanford, *Force Mulberry*.
15. Richmond interview 4 December 1980.
16. "Memorandum of Conference in Admiral Horne's office 5 January 1944," Box 2, Stark Official Papers.
17. Richmond interview 4 December 1980.
18. Letter, Stark to Rear Admiral George B. Wilson (COMNAVEU Chief of Staff), 23 December 1943, File 171, Series II, COMNAVEU Files.
19. Ibid.
20. Letter, Stark to Wilson, 29 December 1943, File 171, Series II, COMNAVEU Files.
21. Letter, Stark to Wilson, 23 December 1943, COMNAVEU Files.
22. Letter, Stark to Wilson, 1 January 1944, File 171, Series II, COMNAVEU Files.
23. Letters, Stark to Wilson, 23 December 1944, 29 December 1943, and 1 January 1944, COMNAVEU Files.
24. Stark Personal Diary, author's possession.
25. COMNAVEU, "Administrative History," p. 249.
26. Letter, Stark to Knox, 20 March 1944, Knox Papers, NHC; Stark Personal Diary.
27. Letter, Stark to Knox, 20 March 1944, Knox Papers, NHC.
28. "Report of Inspection Trip, February 22 to February 29, 1944," author's possession.
29. Letter, Knox to Stark, 10 March 1944, Knox Papers, NHC.
30. Letter, Stark to Knox, 20 March 1944, Knox Papers, NHC.
31. Stark Personal Diary.
32. Stark Personal Diary; Dietrich interview 13 October 1980; Edward Ellsberg, *The Far Shore*.

13.   The Invasion of Normandy

1. Stark Personal Diary, author's possession.
2. Samuel Eliot Morison, *Naval Operations I, Vol. 11, The Invasion of France and Germany, 1944–1945*, p. 176.
3. Letter, Stark to King, 23 June 1944, Box 4, Stark Official Papers.
4. Stark Personal Diary.
5. Letter, Stark to King, 23 June 1944, Stark Personal Diary.
6. Stark Personal Diary; Letter, Stark to Mrs. Stark, 18 June 1944, author's possession.
7. COMNAVEU, "Administrative History," in unpublished MS, NHC, p. 280.
8. Ibid., p. 281.
9. Ibid., pp. 287, 291.
10. Letter, Stark to King, undated, Box 140, Series II, COMNAVEU files, NHC.
11. Ibid.
12. Roland G. Ruppenthal, *Logistical Support of the Armies*, Vol. 1, pp. 55–57.
13. Memorandum, Stark to King, 22 October 1944, King Papers.

14. Letter, Eisenhower to Adjutant General, War Department, 15 July 1944; Service Record of Harold R. Stark, Navy Department.

15. Letter, Stark to unknown addressee, 10 October 1944, Box 44, Stark Official Papers; Stark Personal Diary.

16. Letters, Stark to King, 7 October 1944, Stark to Edwards, 7 October 1944, King Papers.

17. Letter, Stark to Hull, 6 October 1944, King Papers.

18. Frank Knox Memorandum for the President, 22 March 1944, Knox Papers, NHC; letters, Stark to King, 27 July 1944, King to Stark, 27 August 1944, Stark to Chief of Naval Personnel, 27 July 1944, King Papers. Stark Personal Diary.

19. Richmond interview 4 December 1980.

20. Stark Personal Diary. Letter, Stark to Mrs. Stark, 23 April 1944, author's possession.

21. Letter, Stark to Mrs. Stark, 16 November 1944, author's possession.

14. *The End of the War*

1. COMNAVEU, "Administrative History," p. 377.

2. Ibid., p. 376.

3. Ibid., pp. 377–383.

4. Ibid., p. 387.

5. Letter, Willis Sargent to Stark, 6 August 1958, Box 11, Series III, Stark Personal Papers NHC.

6. Ibid.; COMNAVEU, "Administrative History," pp. 383–384.

7. COMNAVEU, "Administrative History," p. 388.

8. Ibid., p. 387–403.

9. Ibid., p. 436.

10. Ibid., p. 330.

11. Ibid., pp. 332–333.

12. Samuel Eliot Morison, *Naval Operations, Vol. 11, The Invasion of France and Germany, 1944–1945*, p. 318; COMNAVEU, "Administrative History," p. 334; Memorandum, Howard A. Flanigan to Stark, 1 November 1944, Box 170, Series II, COMNAVEU Files.

13. COMNAVEU, "Administrative History," p. 341.

14. Ibid., pp. 340–345.

15. Letter, King to Kirk, 7 April 1945, King Papers.

16. Richmond interview 4 December 1980.

17. Letter, Willis Sargent to Stark, 6 August 1958, Box 11, Series III, COMNAVEU Files.

18. Memorandum, Flanigan to Stark, 1 November 1944, Box 170, Series II, COMNAVEU Files.

19. Stark Personal Diary.

20. Letters, Stark to Pound Ser. 00297, 28 July 1943, Stark to Pound Ser. 00347, 10 August 1943, Box 65, Series II, COMNAVEU Files.

21. Stark Memorandum, "Trip to the Continent," author's possession.

22. Stark Personal Diary; miscellaneous correspondence, Box 4, Stark Personal Papers.

23. Program, "A Service of Thanksgiving to Almighty God, 13 May 1945," Box 4, Stark Personal Papers.

24. COMNAVEU, "Administrative History," pp. 428-433.

25. Letter, Stark to King, 5 July 1945, Box 4, Stark Official Papers.

26. "Diary Admiral Stark's Trip to the Mediterranean," author's possession.

27. Ibid.

28. Memorandum, "From Admiral Stark's letters to Mrs. Stark on his trip to Norway and Denmark," author's possession.

29. Memorandum, Box 4, Stark Official Papers.

30. Letters, Hewitt to Stark, 8 July 1945 and Stark to Hewitt, 16 July 1945, Box 4, Stark Official Papers.

31. "Remarks of First Sea Lord," Box 25, Stark Personal Papers.

32. "Admiral H. R. Stark's Talk at Greenwich Naval College," author's possession. Viscount Cunningham of Hyndhope, *A Sailor's Odyssey*, p. 654.

33. Dispatch, Eisenhower to Stark, Box 25, Stark Personal Papers.

15. Investigations

1. U.S. Congress, Joint Committee, *Pearl Harbor Attack*, Part 32, pp. 5-6.

2. Diary of Thomas C. Hart, NHC.

3. Ibid.

4. Ibid.

5. Letter, Stark to Hart, 20 September 1944, Box 28, Series IV, Stark Personal Papers, NHC.

6. The Joint Board, *Joint Action of the Army and the Navy*, 1935. See also, U.S. Congress, Joint Committee, *Pearl Harbor Attack*, Part 5, pp. 2127-2128.

7. Hart Diary.

8. U.S. Congress, Joint Committee, *Pearl Harbor Attack*, Part 39, p. 317.

9. Ibid., part 14, p. 1406.

10. Ibid., part 39, p. 318.

11. Ibid.

12. Ibid., part 39, pp. 297-321.

13. Ibid., part 39, pp. 23-295, 176.

14. Ibid., part 39, pp. 335-345.

15. Letter King to Stark, 10 November 1944, author's possession.

16. Letter, Stark to King, 21 November 1944, author's possession.

17. Letter, Stark to William R. Smedberg, III, 26 August 1946, author's possession.

18. U.S. Congress, Joint Committee, *Pearl Harbor Attack*, Part 39, pp. 335-345.

19. Letter, Umsted to Stark, 4 September 1945, Box 28, Series IV, Stark Personal Papers.

20. Letter, Hart to Stark, 31 August 1945, author's possession.

21. Letter, Sir Geoffrey Blake to Stark, 30 August 1945, author's possession. Richmond interview.

22. U.S. Congress, Joint Committee, *Pearl Harbor Attack*, Part 5, pp. 2096-2135.

23. Ibid., Part 11, pp. 5543-5560.

24. Stark Personal Diary.

25. Ibid.

26. U.S. Congress, Senate, *Report of the Joint Committee on the Investigation of the Pearl Harbor Attack*, p. 100.

27. Ibid., p. 108.

28. Ibid., p. 206.

29. Ibid., p. 200.

30. Ibid., p. 190.

31. Ibid., p. 190.

32. Ibid., p. 192.

33. Ibid., p. 238–240.

34. Letter, Stark to Smedberg, 26 August 1946, author's possession.

35. Letter, Hart to Forrestal, 1 August 1946, author's possession.

36. Remarks by First Sea Lord, 13 August 1945, Box 25, Stark Personal Papers.

37. COMINCH (King) to Secretary of the Navy, letter Serial No. 02426, 16 August 1945, Box 23, Series III, Stark Personal Papers.

38. Letter, Eisenhower to Adjutant General, War Department, 15 July 1944, Stark Selection Board Jacket.

39. Letter, Hart to Stark, 27 August 1946, private possession.

40. Letter, Stark to Smedberg, 26 August 1946, private possession.

41. King and Whitehill, *Fleet Admiral King*, pp. 632–634.

42. Letter, Sullivan to author, 30 May 1978.

43. Stark Service Record, Navy Department.

16. *Retirement*

1. Log of trip to England 1946 and letter, Douglas Veale, Registrar, Oxford University to Stark, 12 June 1945, Box 24, Series III, Stark Personal Papers.

2. King and Whitehill, *Fleet Admiral King*, p. 5.

3. Various documents, file: Williamsburg Award, Box 30, Series III, Stark Personal Papers.

4. Various documents, file: Class of 1903, Box 30, Series III, Stark Personal Papers.

BIBLIOGRAPHY

Unpublished Sources

Naval Historical Center, Washington, D.C.
    Chief of Naval Operations Files
    Commander, U.S. Naval Forces, Europe (COMNAVEU) Files: includes "Adm.
    Stark: Diary as COMNAVEU."
    Thomas C. Hart Diary
    Ernest J. King Papers
    Frank Knox Papers
    Records of the General Board
    Harold R. Stark Official Papers
    Harold R. Stark Personal Papers: includes Stark's Diaries for 1939–1942.
Franklin D. Roosevelt Library, Hyde Park, New York
    President's Personal Files
    President's Secretary's Files
University of Southern California, Los Angeles, California
    William H. Standley Papers
Federal Records Center, Suitland, Maryland
    Bureau of Ordnance Files
National Archives, Washington, D.C.
    Department of State Files
    Navy and Old Army Branch
    Pearl Harbor Liaison Office
    Secretary of the Navy Files
Library of Congress, Washington, D.C.
    Frank Knox Papers
Naval War College, Newport, Rhode Island
    Naval Historical Collection: Thomas Buell/Walter Whitehill collectors, includes
    Research Source Materials on FADM Ernest King, Thomas Buell and Walter
    Whitehill collectors.
Interviews
Charles F. Adams
Capt. William F. Amsden
Louise Arnold
Brig. Gen. Charles Bolte

Capt. Dayton Clark
Barbara Krick Cooper
RADM Neil K. Dietrich
William R. Emerson
Katharine Stark Gillespie
Hon. W. Averell Harriman
VADM Edwin B. Hooper
VADM John L. McCrea
Edward B. Mulligan
William A. Reitzel
David W. Richmond
Robert Robbins
ADM Harold R. Stark
Mary Stark Semans
CDR Alfred R. Stanford
VADM Charles Wellborn, Jr.

Government Records

de Gaulle, Charles, *Unity-Documents*, New York: Simon & Schuster, 1959.
Documents on American Foreign Relations, Boston: World Peace Foundation, 1944, vols. 4, 5, and 6.
The Joint Board, *Joint Action of the Army and the Navy*, Washington, D.C.: U.S. Government Printing Office, 1935.
U.S. Congress, *Congressional Record*, 12 March 1940.
U.S. Congress, House of Representatives, Committee on Naval Affairs, Report No. 1593, *Establishing the Composition of the United States Navy and Authorizing the Construction of Certain Naval Vessels*, 76th Cong., 3rd Sess., 1940.
————, *Hearing on H.R. 10100 to Establish the Composition of the United States Navy, to Authorize the Construction of Certain Vessels and for other Purposes*, 76th Cong., 3rd Sess., 1940.
Report No. 2640, *Establishing the Composition of the United States Navy to Authorize Construction of Certain Vessels*, 76th Cong., 3rd Sess., 1940.
————, *Hearings to Establish the Composition of the United States Navy*, 76th Cong., 3rd Sess., 1940.
U.S. Congress, Joint Committee, *Hearing on the Investigation of the Pearl Harbor Attack*, 79th Cong., 1st Sess., 39 vols., 1946.
U.S. Congress, Senate, Committee on Naval Affairs, *Hearings on Construction of Certain Naval Vessels*, 76th Cong., 3rd Sess., 1940.
————, Report No. 1615, *Construction of Certain Naval Vessels*, 76th Cong., 3rd Sess., 1940.
————, Report No. 1677, *Construction of Certain Naval Vessels*, 76th Cong., 3rd Sess., 1940.
————, Report No. 1946, *Construction of Certain Naval Vessels*, 76th Cong., 3rd Sess., 1940.
————, *Report of the Joint Committee on the Investigation of the Pearl Harbor Attack*, 79th Cong., 2nd Sess., Document No. 244, 1946.
U.S. Department of State, *Bulletin*, vols. 7, 8, and 9.
————, *Foreign Relations of the United States: The Conference at Washington, 1941–1942, and Casablanca, 1943*, Washington, D.C.: U.S. Government Printing Office, 1968.

Bibliography

311

_____ , *Foreign Relations of the United States: Diplomatic Papers, 1938*, vol. 1, Washington, D.C.: U.S. Government Printing Office, 1955.

_____ , *Foreign Relations of the United States: Diplomatic Papers, 1940*, vol. 1, Washington, D.C.: U.S. Government Printing Office, 1955.

_____ , *Foreign Relations of the United States, 1941* (7 vols., Washington, D.C.: U.S. Government Printing Office 1959), vol. 2.

_____ , *Foreign Relations of the United States, 1942* (7 vols., Washington, D.C.: U.S. Government Printing Office 1962), vol. 2.

_____ , *Foreign Relations of the United States, 1943* (6 vols., Washington, D.C.: U.S. Government Printing Office 1964), vol. 2.

Books

Abbazia, Patrick, *Mr. Roosevelt's Navy*, Annapolis: U.S. Naval Institute Press, 1975.

Albion, Robert Greenhalgh, *Makers of Naval Policy 1798–1947*, Annapolis: Naval Institute Press, 1980.

Albion, Robert Greenhalgh, and Robert Howe Connery, *Forrestal and the Navy*, New York: Columbia University Press, 1962.

Baldwin, Hanson W., *The Crucial Years*, New York: Harper & Row, 1976.

_____ , *United We Stand*, New York: Whittlesey House, 1941.

Bartlett, John, *Familiar Quotations*, Boston: Little, Brown and Company, 1968.

Bartlett, Ruhl J., *The Record of American Diplomacy*, New York: Alfred A. Knopf, 1941.

Burns, James MacGregor, *Roosevelt: The Soldier of Freedom*, New York: Harcourt Brace Jovanovich, Inc., 1970.

Butcher, Harry C., *My Three Years With Eisenhower*, New York: Simon & Schuster, 1946.

Butler, J. R. M., Ed., *History of The Second World War, Vol. IV*, Michael Howard, *Grand Strategy August 1942–September, 1943*, London: Her Majesty's Stationery Office, 1972.

Catroux, General, *Dans la bataille de Mediterranée*, Paris: René Juillard, 1949.

Chadwin, Mark Lincoln, *The Hawks of World War II*, Chapel Hill: University of North Carolina Press, 1968.

Chalmers, W. S., *Max Horton and the Western Approaches*, London: Hodder and Stoughton, 1954.

Churchill, Winston S., *The Second World War, Vol. 2, The Gathering Storm*, Boston: Houghton Mifflin Co., 1948.

_____ , *The Second World War, Vol. 3, The Grand Alliance*, Boston: Houghton Mifflin Co., 1950.

_____ , *The Second World War, Vol. 4, The Hinge of Fate*, Boston: Houghton Mifflin Co., 1951.

Clark, Mark W., *Calculated Risk*, New York: Harper and Brothers, 1950.

Conn, Stetson and Byron Fairchild, *The Framework of Hemisphere Defense*, Washington, D.C.: Office of the Chief of Military History, Department of the Army, 1960.

Crusoe, *Vicissitudes d'une Victoire*, Paris: Les Editions de l'ame Française, 1946.

Cunningham of Hyndhope, Viscount, *A Sailor's Odyssey*, London: Hutchinson & Co. Ltd., 1951.

Davis, George T., *A Navy Second to None*, New York: Harcourt, Brace and Company, 1940.

Davis, Vernon E., *Origin of the Joint and Combined Chiefs of Staff*, Washington: Historical Division, Joint Secretariat Joint Chiefs of Staff, 1972.

de Gaulle, Charles, *Unity 1942-1944*, New York: Simon & Schuster, 1959.

Earl of Avon (Anthony Eden), *The Reckoning*, Boston: Houghton Mifflin Company, 1964.

Ehrlich, Blake, *Resistance France 1940-1945*, Boston: Little, Brown and Co., 1965.

Eisenhower, Dwight D., *Crusade in Europe*, Garden City, N.J.: Doubleday & Company, Inc., 1948.

Ellsberg, Edward, *The Far Shore*, New York: Dodd, Mead & Co., 1960.

Farago, Ladislas, *The Broken Seal*, New York: Random House, 1967.

_____ , *The Tenth Fleet*, New York: Ivan Obolensky, Inc., 1962.

Feis, Herbert, *The Road to Pearl Harbor*, Princeton: Princeton University Press, 1950.

Freidel, B. Frank, *Franklin D. Roosevelt, Vol. 2, The Ordeal*, Boston: Little, Brown and Co., 1952.

Funk, Arthur Layton, *Charles de Gaulle: The Crucial Years 1943-1944*, Norman: University of Oklahoma Press, 1959.

Giraud, General, *Un seul but, la Victoire*, Paris: René Juillard, 1949.

Goodheart, Philip, *Fifty Ships That Saved the World*, Garden City: Doubleday & Co., 1965.

Greenfield, Kent Roberts, ed., *United States Army in World War II, The European Theater of Operations*, Washington, D.C.: Office of the Chief of Military History, Department of the Army, 1959.

Hart, Robert A., *The Great White Fleet*, Boston: Little, Brown and Company, 1965.

Herzog, James H., *Closing the Open Door*, Annapolis: Naval Institute Press, 1973.

Hoehling, A. A., *The Week Before Pearl Harbor*, New York: W. W. Norton & Company, 1973.

Hull, Cordell, *The Memoirs of Cordell Hull*, 2 vols., New York: The Macmillan Company, 1948.

Ickes, Harold L., *The Secret Diary of Harold L. Ickes, Vol. III, The Lowering Clouds*, New York: Simon & Schuster, 1954.

Kimmel, Husband E., *Admiral Kimmel's Story*, Chicago: Henry Regnery Co., 1955.

King, Ernest J., and Walter Muir Whitehill, *Fleet Admiral King*, New York: Da Capo Press, 1976.

Langer, William L., *Our Vichy Gamble*, New York: Alfred A. Knopf, 1947.

Langer, William L., and S. Everett Gleason, *The Challenge to Isolation*, New York: Harper & Row, Vol. 1, 1952, Vol. 2, 1952.

_____ , *The Undeclared War 1940-1941*, New York: Harper & Row, 1953.

Leahy, William D., *I Was There*, New York: McGraw Hill, 1950.

Leopold, Richard W., *The Growth of American Foreign Policy*, New York: Knopf, 1962.

Leutze, James R., *Bargaining for Supremacy*, Chapel Hill: University of North Carolina Press, 1977.

Macmillan, Harold, *The Blast of War*, New York: Harper & Row, 1968.

Marder, Arthur J., *From the Dardanelles to Oran*, London: Oxford University Press, 1974.

Matloff, Maurice and Edwin M. Snell, *Strategic Planning for Coalition Warfare 1941-1942*, Washington, D.C.: Office of the Chief of Military History, Department of the Army, 1953.

Melosi, Martin V., *The Shadow of Pearl Harbor*, College Station: Texas A&M Press, 1977.

Morison, Samuel Eliot, *History of United States Naval Operations in World War II, Vol. 1, The Battle of the Atlantic*, Boston: Little, Brown and Co., 1960.

————, *History of United States Naval Operations in World War II, Vol. 2, Operations in North African Waters*, Boston; Little, Brown, and Co., 1947.

————, *History of United States Naval Operations in World War II, Vol. 3, The Rising Sun in the Pacific, 1931–April 1942*, Boston: Little, Brown and Co., 1961.

————, *History of United States Naval Operations in World War II, Vol. 10, The Atlantic Battle Won*, Boston: Little, Brown and Co., 1956.

————, *History of United States Naval Operations in World War II, Vol. 11, The Invasion of France and Germany, 1944–1945*, Boston: Little, Brown and Co., 1957.

Murphy, Robert, *Diplomat Among Warriors*, Garden City: Doubleday & Company, Inc., 1964.

Passy, Colonel (André Dewavrin), *Missions secrètes en France*, Paris: Librairie Plon, 1951.

————, *Souvenirs*, 2 vols., Monte Carlo: Raoul Solar, 1950.

Pelz, Stephen E., *Race to Pearl Harbor: The Failure of the Second London Naval Conference and the Onset of World War II*, Cambridge: Harvard University Press, 1974.

Pendar, Kenneth, *Adventures in Diplomacy*, New York: Dodd, Mead and Company, 1945.

Pogue, Forrest C., *George C. Marshall, Vol. 2, Ordeal & Hope*, New York: Viking Press, 1966.

Richardson, James O., *On the Treadmill to Pearl Harbor: The Memoirs of Admiral James O. Richardson, USN*, VADM Geo. C. Dyer, USN (Ret.) ed., Washington, D.C.: Naval History Division, Department of the Navy, 1973.

Roskill, W. S., *The War at Sea 1939–1945, Vol. 2., The Period of Balance*, London: Her Majesty's Stationery Office, 1956.

————, *The War at Sea 1939–1945, Vol. 3, The Offensive*, London: Her Majesty's Stationery Office, 1960.

Ruppenthal, Roland G., *Logistical Support of the Armies*, Vol. 1, Washington, D.C.: Chief of Military History, Department of the Army, 1953, pp. 55–57.

Sherwood, Robert E., *Roosevelt and Hopkins*, New York: Harper Brothers, 1948.

Slessor, Sir John, *The Central Blue*, London: Cassel and Company Limited, 1956.

Soustelle, Jacques, *Envers et contre tout*, 2 vols., Paris: Robert Laffont, 1950.

Speeches of General de Gaulle, The, New York: Oxford University Press, 1944.

Stanford, Alfred, *Force Mulberry*, New York: William Morrow and Company, 1951.

Stark, Charles R., *The Aaron Stark Family*, Boston: Wright & Potter, 1927.

Steele, Ronald, *The First Offensive 1942*, Bloomington: Indiana University Press, 1973.

Stimson, Henry L., and McGeorge Bundy, *On Active Service in Peace and War*, New York: Harper and Brothers, 1947.

Tate, Merze, *The Unites States and Armaments*, Cambridge: Harvard University Press, 1948.

Viorst, Milton, *Hostile Allies*, New York: The Macmillan Company, 1965.

Warner, Oliver, *Cunningham of Hyndhope*, London: John Murray, 1967.

Watson, Mark S., *Chief of Staff: Prewar Plans and Preparations*, Washington, D.C.: Office of the Chief of Military History, Department of the Army, 1950.

Werth, Alexander, *De Gaulle*, New York: Simon & Schuster, 1965.

White, Dorothy Shipley, *Seeds of Discord*, Syracuse: Syracuse University Press, 1964.

Wilson, Theodore A., *The First Summit*, Boston: Houghton Mifflin Co., 1969.

Wohlstetter, Roberta, *Pearl Harbor: Warning and Decision*, Stanford: Stanford University Press, 1962.

Woodward, Sir Llewellyn, *British Foreign Policy in the Second World War*, London: Her Majesty's Stationery Office, 1962.

Articles

Heinrichs, Waldo H., Jr., "The Role of the United States Navy," in Dorothy Borg and Shumpei Okamoto, eds., *Pearl Harbor as History*, New York: Columbia University Press, 1973.

Kittredge, Tracy B., "The Muddle Before Pearl Harbor," *U.S. News and World Report*, 3 December 1954.

Morton, Louis, "Germany First: The Basic Concept of Allied Strategy in World War II," in Kent Roberts Greenfield, ed., *Command Decisions*, Washington, D.C.: Office of Chief of Military History, Department of the Army, 1960.

Quinlan, Robert J., "The United States Fleet: Diplomacy, Strategy and the Allocation of Ships (1940–1941)," in Harold Stein, ed. *American Civil Military Decisions*, Birmingham: University of Alabama Press, 1963.

Ruppenthal, Roland G., "Logistical Support of the Armies," Vol. 2, in Kent Roberts Greenfield, ed., *United States Army in World War II, The European Theater of Operations*, Washington, D.C.: Office of the Chief of Military History, Department of the Army, 1959.

Dissertations and Unpublished Manuscripts

Berg, Meredith, "The United States and the Breakdown of Naval Limitation, 1934–1939," Ph.D. dissertation, Tulane University, New Orleans, Louisiana, 1966.

Commander, U.S. Naval Forces, Europe, (COMNAVEU) "Administrative History, United States Naval Forces in Europe 1940–1946," Naval Historical Center, Washington, D.C.

Enders, Calvin, "The Vinson Navy," Ph.D. dissertation, Michigan State University, East Lansing, Michigan, 1970.

Kittredge, Tracy B., "United States-British Cooperation 1939–1942," Unpublished M.S., Naval Historical Center, Washington, D.C.

Stark, Harold R., Personal Diary.

Sutphen, Harold J., "The Anglo-American Destroyers–Bases Agreement, September 1940," Ph.D. dissertation, The Fletcher School of Law and Diplomacy, Tufts University, Medford, Massachusetts, 1968.

Walter, John C., "The Navy Department and the Campaign for Expanded Appropriations 1933–1938," Ph.D. dissertation, University of Maine at Orono, 1972.

INDEX

315

Hart, Thomas C. (Admiral), 7, 13, 14, 15, 42, 72, 75, 100, 104, 105, 108, 110, 239, 259, 261, 262, 263, 269, 275, 277, 278, 279, 280

Hawaii, 7, 8, 9, 49, 54, 55, 56, 57, 58, 59, 62, 63, 77, 81, 97, 98, 100, 102, 116, 265, 276, 277

Hawaiian Department (Army), 98, 265

Hawaiian Detachment, 8

Heidelberg, 247, 248

Hemisphere Defense Plan No. 4, 89

Hemmings, Howard, 249

Hewitt, H. Kent (Vice Admiral), 160, 215, 240, 245, 255, 265, 268

Hitler, Adolf, 5, 10, 15, 23, 38, 44, 49, 51, 52, 54, 61, 68, 85, 86, 87, 88, 90, 96, 97, 128, 129, 138, 153, 155, 161, 182, 224, 236, 249

Hollywood Hotel, 200

Home Fleet (British), 148, 150, 152

Hong Kong, 111

Honolulu, 106, 111

Hood, HMS (battle cruiser), 86

Hopkins, Harry, 120, 125, 158, 245, 267

Horne, Frederick J. (Vice Admiral), 211, 212, 213

Hornet, USS (aircraft carrier), 121

Horton, Sir Max (Admiral), 195, 196, 197, 198, 216

House of Commons (U.K.), 232, 283

House of Lords (U.K.), 283

House Naval Affairs Committee, 17, 21, 22, 32, 41

House of Representatives (U.S.), 18

Houston, USS (cruiser), 1

Howard, John (Ensign USNR), 153

Hull, Cordell, 36, 37, 84, 85, 86, 95, 100, 103, 104, 107, 109, 112, 166, 230

Hull, England, 207

Hyde Park, 84

Iceland, 87, 88, 89, 190

Imperial Japanese Navy, 9, 44, 45

Indochina, 107, 108

Ingersoll, Royal K. (Captain, later Rear Admiral), 13, 94, 109, 114, 269, 272

Ingram, Jonas (Admiral), 197

Inspector of Ordnance, 6

International Court of Justice, 237

Iowa, class of battleship, 27, 28

Ireland, 195

Italian Communist Party, 251

Italy, 17, 32, 42, 45, 47, 49, 55, 82, 251

Itchen, HMS (destroyer), 193

Jackson, Robert H., 54

Japan, 6, 7, 8, 15, 17, 19, 23, 29, 32, 34, 43, 44, 49, 56, 77, 82, 83, 84, 94, 97, 100, 107, 113, 114, 121, 249, 259, 263, 264, 268, 273, 275, 276

Jessup, Phillip, 237

Johnson, Barclay G. (Lt.), 205

Johnson, Malcolm (Lt.), 271

Johnston Island, 116

Johore State, 121

Joint Army-Navy Board, 13, 15

Joint Chiefs of Staff, 125, 136, 155, 176, 188, 215, 228, 237, 238, 239

Joint Congressional Committee, 258, 271, 272, 274, 275, 276, 278

Joint Planning Committee, 13

Joint U.S. Advisor's Committee, 237

Jones, John Paul, 256

Joubert, Sir Phillip (Air Chief Marshal), 148

Judge Advocate General, 261

Juin, Alphonse (General), 178, 230

Justice Department, 54

Kalbfus, Edward C. (Admiral), 263

Kamchatka Peninsula, 102, 103

Kearney, USS (destroyer), 94, 106

Kennedy, Joseph P. (Ambassador), 47, 48

Kimmel, Husband E. (Admiral), 54, 61, 84, 85, 86, 98, 99, 100, 103, 104, 105, 106, 108, 110, 112, 114, 116, 260, 261, 262, 263, 264, 265, 266, 268, 269, 273, 274, 275, 276

King Alfred, HMS (training school), 161

King, Ernest J. (Admiral), 61, 84, 85, 89, 91, 93, 94, 104, 108, 109, 111, 117, 119, 121, 125, 128, 131, 137, 140, 141, 143, 146, 149, 156, 157, 158, 159, 163, 165, 184, 185, 186, 187, 188, 189, 190, 191, 192, 194, 196, 197, 200, 201, 202, 203, 204, 208, 209, 215, 216, 222, 225, 229, 231, 237, 238, 240, 241, 243, 245, 254, 255, 257, 260, 261, 262, 265, 266, 267, 268, 269, 270, 271, 275, 276, 277, 278, 279, 280, 281, 283

King George V, HMS (battleship), 74, 75, 76

Kirk, Alan G. (Captain, later Rear Admiral), 46, 142, 178, 179, 194, 197, 208, 209, 222, 226, 227, 239, 241, 242, 243, 244, 247

Kittredge, Tracy B. (Lt., later Commander), 136, 137, 165, 166, 169, 171, 174, 177, 178, 179, 181, 230, 237

Knox, Frank, destroyers for bases agreement, 52–54, 60, 63, 66, 73–74, 82, 84, 87, 88, 93, 98, 100, 109, 114, 116,

About the author:

While a Naval Officer student at the Fletcher School of Law and Diplomacy, B. Mitchell Simpson, III, met Admiral Stark and became deeply interested in the career of this little known Chief of Naval Operations. Later, he began work on the Stark biography while he was on the faculty of the Naval War College. Following his retirement after 20 years of active Naval service in a wide variety of ships, Simpson devoted three years to the research and writing of this biography. It is based on the public record and Admiral Stark's private papers. Simpson is now a practicing attorney in Newport, Rhode Island, where he lives with his wife and two daughters.